Preposterous Violence

PREPOSTEROUS VIOLENCE

Fables of Aggression in Modern Culture

JAMES B. TWITCHELL

New York   Oxford
OXFORD UNIVERSITY PRESS
1989

Oxford University Press

Oxford New York Toronto
Delhi Bombay Calcutta Madras Karachi
Petaling Jaya Singapore Hong Kong Tokyo
Nairobi Dar es Salaam Cape Town
Melbourne Auckland

and associated companies in
Berlin Ibadan

Library of Congress Cataloging-in-Publication Data
Twitchell, James B., 1943–
Preposterous violence: fables of aggression in modern culture
James B. Twitchell.
p. cm. Bibliography: p. Includes index.
ISBN 0-19-505887-9
1. Popular culture—History. 2. Amusements—History.
3. Violence in the mass media—History. I. Title.
CB358.T84 1989 302.2'34—dc19 88-31227 CIP

9 8 7 6 5 4 3 2 1

Printed in the United States of America
on acid-free paper

To my mother, my sisters, my wife, and my daughters

Contents

1

The Ritualization of Violence: Fables of Aggression, 3

2

The Imaging of Violence in Early Modern Popular Culture, 48

3

Preposterous Violence in Prose Fiction:
The Coronation of Stephen King, 90

4

Disorderly Conduct Illustrated:
The Rise and Fall and Rise of Comics, 129

5

"Cut to the Monster": The Motion in Motion Pictures, 181

6

Don't Touch That Dial: Violence on the Video Altar, 221

7

Conclusion: Stay Tuned, 263

Notes, 289

Works Cited, 310

Index, 325

Preposterous Violence

The Ritualization of Violence:
Fables of Aggression

"I hope you're going to have some gratuitous violence with this."
ALGERNON, the weapons expert, displaying
a pen that shoots bullets
"I certainly hope so too."
JAMES BOND, *Never Say Never Again*

We hope so too. Why? Why are we drawn, especially in our youth, to watch scenes of gratuitous violence which we would abhor in reality? And why do we in our maturity often find these selfsame scenes objectionable and worthy of censure?

The scenes I have in mind are ones of violence, specifically ones of preposterous violence. By "preposterous" I mean so exaggerated that most of the audience know full well that what they are watching is make-believe. The scenes are caricatures—often literally cartoons—of recognizable sequences. By "violence" I mean more than a force directed against an object (the literal definition: *vis* = force + *latus* = participle of *fero*, the Latin verb for "carry"). I mean a force directed against a victim, usually a specific human being. The inclusion of some direct object is implied in the verb "violate" as well as in the noun "violation," which share a common etymology with "violence." The implication of "violence" is that a force is inflicted on someone for which some violation is the result. So to rephrase my subject: I am interested in why we are entertained by watching scenes in which bad things happen to good people, or more appropriately, by watching scenes in which even worse things happen to bad people.

I am particularly interested in how such concussive scenes have been broadcast to an eager audience for the last two hundred years—from the engravings of Hogarth to the television antics of Hulk Hogan, the professional wrestler. I will concentrate on the modern world because this is the world of the repeatable image, the redundant scenario, the one endless loop endlessly transported to us via the mass media. Thanks to print and electronic transmission, a fusillade of gratuitous violence bombards us each day in a never-ending sequence, but such pantomime violence—whether painted on a cave wall, carved in the Assyrian stone reliefs, envisioned in the crucifixions of medieval and Renaissance Christs, acted out on the Jacobean stage, animated in Victorian *Punch and Judy* shows, or illustrated in *EC* comics—has always appealed to some of us. Now we have only to flip a switch or turn a page to find violent entertainment, whereas before the eighteenth century we found it only by traveling to some specified locale. Although mass media have compressed time and collapsed space, the same stories are being told.

While we have tended to blame declining social standards, foreign influences, or base human desire for such vulgarities, I believe that the vulgar results not from misuse so much as from overuse. I intend to argue that, in the more appropriate colloquial term, *junk* is what results when an adolescent, usually male, audience commandeers the attention of a medium and endlessly rehashes certain motifs. When the technologies and efficiencies of production make it economical to mass produce an "entertainment" for young men, "junk" will result. The mark of such entertainment is that it will be both avidly consumed by some and vehemently condemned as trash by others. I will examine some instances of junk in pulp fiction, illustration, movies, television drama, toys, music videos, and arcade games, and I will argue that because they are "junk," because they are produced to be mindlessly consumed, they often present an uncorrupted view of the fantasy life of adolescents. In those fantasies is the lore of the ages, the unutterable concerns of the race, the deepest commands of the species.

Such "junk" entertains at the most compromised of levels. Exploitation is approbation. It comes to us or, rather, we go to it, without pretense or affect. Ask a consumer of cultural *schlock*, be it comics, Stephen King, professional wrestling, or top-40 popular music, to explain the worth of what he is consuming and he will probably tell you, "I know it's junk, but who cares? I like it." Such commodity entertainment makes no plea; it is not moral in any self-conscious way, nor educational in the usual sense. In fact, if well-intentioned adults attempt to make it

M. Stevens, *The All-Collision Channel* (© 1985 The New Yorker Magazine, Inc.)

moral, educational, or uplifting, they will fail. As Jules Feiffer has written of comic books, "Junk, like the drunk at the wedding, can get away with doing or saying anything because, by its very appearance, it is already in disgrace. It has no one's respect to lose; no image to endanger" (p. 7).

The very senselessness and vulgarity of such exhibitions have made preposterous violence not just unattractive for many to view but unimportant for critics to study. The critic usually says, "Here, quit looking at *that*, let me show you this work of art. It will do you good." Indeed, our censorious response to violence in popular culture is ancient. The fifth-century theologian Salvianus condemned "amphitheaters, concert halls, games, parades, athletes, rope dancers, pantomimes and other monstrosities" for offering pictures which could not be assimilated by the unformed mind, thus causing "people to commit fornication mentally" (pp. 162–63). And before Salvianus was the third-century Christian convert Tertullian, who assured us that public shows consumed by the masses were "idolatry," seducing the audience into brutality and crassness (p. 243). Thus historically most critics have been strong enough, like Ulysses, to hear the music of the Sirens but have made it their business to cover the ears (or, more appropriately, the eyes) of young mariners until the danger has passed. Contemporary critics of mass media are not, in other words, the first to discover the dangers of violent spectacle. As old as the youthful desire to see violence enacted is the mature concern that such sights should be viewed only with the utmost care. The *locus classicus* is St. Augustine's example of young Alypius who, against his will, was spirited off by friends to the gladiatorial games. At first Alypius covered his eyes, but when the crowd shouted excitedly he opened them. Augustine continues his cautionary tale:

> If only he had closed his ears as well! For an incident in the fight drew a great roar from the crowd, and this thrilled him so deeply that he could not contain his curiosity. Whatever had caused the uproar, he was confident that, if he saw it, he would find it repulsive and remain master of himself. So he opened his eyes, and his soul was stabbed with a wound more deadly than any which the gladiator, whom he was so anxious to see, had received in his body. He fell, and felt more pitifully than the man whose fall had drawn that roar of excitement from the crowd.
>
> When he saw the blood, it was as though he had drunk a deep draught of savage passion. Instead of turning away, he fixed his eyes upon the scene and drank in all its frenzy, unaware of what he was doing. He revelled in the wickedness of the fighting and was drunk with the fascination of bloodshed. He was no longer the man who had come to the arena, but simply one of the crowd which he had joined, a fit companion for the friends who had brought him.
>
> Need I say more? He watched and cheered and grew hot with excitement, and when he left the arena, he carried away with him a diseased mind which would leave him no peace until he came back again, no longer simply together with friends who had dragged him there, but at their head, leading new sheep to the slaughter. (*Confessions*, book 6, part 8, pp. 122–23)

Although Augustine feels that nothing more needs to be said about the relationship between sympathetic identification and the subsequent degeneracy caused by watching savage scenes—*concupiscentia oculorum*, he called it—the history of modern Western culture has shown a manifold increase in the number of such spectacles, albeit usually in fictional form. Thanks to electronic media, the increase in the past two decades has been exponential. For those who, like Ulysses, would muffle the ears of the young and keep their hands tied to the oars, the music of these Sirens has never been noisier.

On the rare occasions that commodity entertainment has been taken seriously in the academy, the conclusions have been uniformly censorious. When was the last time an academic praised any literary work on the paperback bestseller list, or an action/adventure show broadcast in prime time, or a music video, a comic, a video game, or in fact anything that adolescents crave? The adjective I have already used in place of "preposterous" betrays our grown-up response to what we once took seriously—the violence carried by broadcast media of all sorts is "gratuitous." The not-so-subtly implied assumption is that these scenes have no proper place in our culture. They are unnecessary. Moreover, if you watch too many of them for too long, aggression will increase and antisocial behavior may result. A generation of social scientists has assured us that bulk consumers of this stuff can be affected, and they point to statistics to show that what goes in through the eyes of an impressionable teenager quite possibly will soon come out in hostile behavior.

As dangerous as their music is, the Sirens won't be silenced. Stephen King and his confrères sit atop the bestseller lists of the *New York Times,* squeezing out the deserving descendants of Emily Dickinson and Henry James. *The A-Team* and the bust-'em-ups of the commercial networks rob PBS of its future audience and force it to limp toward the money pumps of Mobil or, worse, to hold another "begathon." There are no good foreign films down at the Cinema 16 because the Hollywood schlockmeisters insist on cloning the *Rambos* or the *Friday the 13ths* into a never-dying family of sequels and prequels, each more lurid in its display of violence. Professional sports have become charades of choreographed fighting; rock 'n roll has vandalized the FM frequencies; video arcades are all over the mall; violent cartoons have captured weekday afternoon television. The quick fix of frantic action is upon us. The carnivalization of culture is upon us. In the modern Gresham's law of entertainment, junk shows force out the good. No medium is safe.

I hope to show that the barbarians have been at the gates for some time. Juvenal warned that although the masses could be temporarily placated by "bread and circuses" ("*panem et circenses*"), the fall of the state was imminent. No matter that he miscalculated by more than a few hundred years, the injunctive cry of "*panem et circenses*" has been oft repeated. Modern reformers of popular culture from Marx, Nietzsche, Freud, Ortega y Gasset, and T. S. Eliot to the current crop of gloommeisters like Newton Minow and Neil Postman have echoed the melancholy refrain. Blaming the mass media for the "Closing of the American Mind" and the decline of "Cultural Literacy" has never been more popular. It is an academic growth industry. Yet what do we get for all this concern? Not necessarily more bread, but certainly more circuses. Why?

The real question about spectacles of symbolic violence is not how to do away with them, but why they are there in the first place and in the second place why they won't go away. The real question is not whether they cause violent behavior (they may well do so) but why they are so entertaining. Preposterous violence is fun. Whatever inheres in these crude circuses is something that won't be soaped away with rating systems, revisions, or outright censorship. Whatever preposterous violence holds is something that young males will expend great energy to share vicariously. Call it escape, call it wish-fulfillment, call it exploitation, call it junk, call it what you will, scenarios of disorderly conduct have been

Well Scene, Lascaux, c. 15,000–10,000 B.C. (Institut Géographique National)

with us, are with us, and will undoubtedly stay with us. These fables of aggression were probably first told by our Magdalenian ancestors in their cave paintings of nasty brutes chasing stick men. Turn on your television set during prime time and you will see this story retold.

I intend to take a close look at this story, starting with the gothic novel and Hogarth's illustrations and ending with the pantomimes of disorder on contemporary television. Why not start instead with the cave paintings, the medieval grotesqueries, the saints' lives, the Renaissance imagery of the Crucifixion, or blood-and-thunder revenge tragedies? Because, due to the printing press, Hogarth and the novelists were able to find the first mass audience for what is now an accepted grammar of visual imagery. They were able to cartoon scenes of concussive violence which are still being replayed on the endless reruns of popular culture. Here at the apogee of the Age of Reason, in the fullest light of the Enlightenment, we see the power of contrived turbulence, the power of the irrational, the power of the ungovernable, the power of a "text" in which the oldest anxieties of ordinary people, especially young males, can find expression again and again and again.

Historically, mass-produced images of aggression have appeared as other forms of recreational violence have subsided. I do not want to argue that the slain gladiator necessarily became the crucified Christ, but only that we are willing to tolerate different levels of violence in different media, with different participants, at different times. Each technically advanced medium becomes the chief carrier of kinetic scenes, tempers the content of the previous medium, and draws down upon itself the predictable scorn of those who are no longer actively interested. The decline of popular recreational violence involving animals is usually attributed to the rebirth of evangelical Puritanism and the rise of romantic sensibilities about nature. I argue in Chapter 2, however, that in the history of preposterous violence the development of each new medium also shifts the content of all other media. Thus bear- and badger-baiting, cockfighting as well as "throwing at cocks," bull-running, and other "injustices" against what was becoming known as "our natural brethren" were largely banned just as violent scenes were appearing in mass-produced illustrations and print.[1] The end of most orchestrated and systematic violence to domestic beasts presaged the transfer of much of this entertainment to other—in this instance, artificial—displays.

Concurrent with the decline in animal violence was the rise of a new show of violence, this time directed not against domestic animals, which sustained man, but against the family, which supported man's social and reproductive stability. *Punch and Judy*, imported to England from the Italian Pulcinella shows, took on a ferocious cast in the nineteenth century as the father/husband bludgeoned his child, wife, neighbor, horse, dog, policeman, hangman, and even the devil, as he played out the choleric pantomime of modern life. We enjoy watching violence toward whatever we are dependent on, and when we began to depend more on the family than on farm animals, we made the family our scapegoat. This burlesque of family strife both found an eager audience and brought down the wrath of censors. By the end of the Victorian age, censors had so tempered violence that the outrageous reprobate, Punch, had become an avuncular candy vendor tossing goodies to the kiddies. He now survives only as a summertime, seaside resort attraction, but his violent spirit lives on in today's electronic media. A new suit of mythic colors and a new medium were all he needed to become acceptable.

In the nineteenth century, while protectors of manners were laboring to clean the streets first of animal violence, then of puppeteers, the alleys were still like those pictured in the eighteenth century by Hogarth. Violent pornography and, more important, a new violence in the gothic genre were moving into the book stalls. The dominant myths of modern horror—the Frankenstein monster, Dracula, and Dr. Jekyll and Mr. Hyde—were finding a corpus first in the novel, then on the stage, and as we know all too well, were en route to the medium they have so dominated—the cinema. The *fin de siècle* gothic novels of Bram Stoker, Robert Louis Stevenson, H. G. Wells, and Oscar Wilde showed, if it needed to be shown, that silver-fork fiction did not tell the story that part of the newly literate descendants of the bull-running and *Punch and Judy* audience wanted to hear. This cash-carrying populace wanted thrills, they wanted violence, they wanted monsters at work. The success of *Grand Guignol* productions has always been judged not by how many of the audience will scream, but by how many will *pay* to scream.

Indeed, the Hollywood cinema did capture those monsters as well as the screamers. But the novel was not safe . . . yet. Within the gothic was another genre, a genre that used the same tangled causality and tortured *mise en scène,* the same reliance on the turbulent, but attempted to overcome it with intelligence. This is the only genre that is American, at least in partial inception—the detective novel. The most literate practitioner was English, Arthur Conan Doyle, but the innovator was American, Edgar Allan Poe. It was Poe who first held the wires together and knew how much shock could be conducted through this form of stimulation. The macho detective novel, which has come and gone through various fashions, has left such varied and violent "guns for hire" as Hammett's Sam Spade, Chandler's Philip Marlowe, Macdonald's Lew Archer, Spillane's Mike Hammer, Fleming's James Bond, and now Robert Parker's Spenser and the protagonists of Elmore Leonard and Evan Hunter.

These cartoons of rough-and-tumble problem-solving are essentially yet another frame in which fables of aggression can be told protected from censorship. Like the gothic, the hardboiled detective novel and the derring-do spy story are simple variations on a theme we never grow tired of. The damsel in distress in the older genre is replaced, in the new, by a murder victim or valuable property that is misappropriated; the detective/spy enters and is empowered to set things right. However, he wants more than to balance the scales of justice; he eventually wants vengeance. To accomplish this he must fight and brutalize his way to the culprit. Women and other obstacles are pushed aside. He destroys them violently with hot sex and/or hot lead. From Sam Spade and Lew Archer to Joe Mannix and James Bond the story is the same: first a villain, then a crime, then let's have a little violence. No one has complained about violence in prose fiction for the last generation; no one has grabbed these books from pudgy fingers. Sex in fiction still rings the alarm, but violence does not.

At the end of the 1960s the Museum of Modern Art mounted a special show, *The American Action Movie 1946–1964,* in which it was clear from the *catalog raisonné* that we had isolated yet another offending medium. It was the movies and their ceaseless flicker of violent images that were responsible for the debasement of Western aspirations and the increase of juvenile delinquency since the 1950s. We might be able to blame the gothic and the monsters on the English, but the action movie belonged to us. As early as the 1940s, it was obvious that the gunshots, fisticuffs, and general hullabaloo were an American product, unfortunately being consumed in bulk at home and exported to innocents abroad. But just as the Hollywood censors at the Hays office were about to reopen for the business of protecting adolescent audiences from what they wanted to see, a still more serious threat appeared.

Like the Holy Roman Empire, which was neither holy nor Roman nor an empire, the comic book was neither comic nor a book. It was, in the words of its most persistent critic, the psychiatrist Fredric Wertham, a disease, a weed, a poison. What makes the action comic so ripe for study in the context of preposterous violence is that its rise, shine, evaporation, and fall show with gnomic concision how a modern medium transforms to carry a message; how it is simultaneously sustained and criticized for delivering some forbidden *frisson* or tremble to a youthful audience; and how rapidly it disappears, not as a result of censure but as a result of audience eagerness for novelty in a new medium. The minute the youthful audience finds thrills elsewhere, it abandons the clichéd text for the new. Rusty rides at the carnival are an eloquent testament to how quickly one roller coaster will render other shudders obsolete. The audience will wait patiently for one tummy-turning ride only so long as no new loop-the-loop is discovered nearby. Then, just when they outgrow this appetite, they can look forward to preventing their children from lining up for a still newer thrill. So the comics—the infamous *EC* (E for Educational!), *DC* (D for Detective), and all their colorful brethren—were the subject of a Senate investigation into violence and in the early 1950s had to go underground for a while. Several years later the senators could have cared less. They had a new worry— a worry they are still investigating.

Television, the gentle giant turned psychopath, is the current subject of national soul-searching and hand-wringing. Quasi-medical ailments, which were being diagnosed in the 1950s as "TV bottom," "TV tummy," "TV jaw," and "TV squint" were developing into TV addiction. TV violence proliferated. The comics were off the hook. Dr. Fredric Wertham was back in the clinic, and Dr. Thomas Radeki, head of the National Coalition on Television Violence, was front and center. The patient who had just survived an overdose of pulp fiction, radio dramas, violent movies, and comics now needed to be saved from Saturday morning television.

In the last thirty years, matters have gotten no better; in fact, they are worse. Would that Augustine could see what modern-day Alypius is now watching. The cyclopean-eyed vampire, television, threatens to suck our children dry of lifeblood and turn them into antisocial thugs. The current threats are not just music videos, heavy metal bands, video games, or the rental of *Faces of Death Parts 1, 2, 3 . . .*, but also "interactive toys" with which Junior can join Captain Power and the Soldiers of the Future in zapping with his Power Jet Pistol a host of invaders who appear on his television screen. In the 1960s crime soared; SATs plummeted. Think of what life will be like in the 1990s after these toys have had their effect. As the government insisted on placing warnings on cigarettes, so a number of concerned groups want warnings issued before each violent show. In the same spirit, the Parents' Music Resource Center has lobbied for a similar display on all record jackets, particularly of violent rock 'n roll LPs: "Caution: This Record May Be Hazardous to Your Health." And why has music become so violent and, especially, why has teenage music become so turbulent? It has been contaminated by television. Music to dance to has become music to watch. The music video has lobotomized an already subliterate form of entertainment.

Hasn't the same fate happened to sports? Because of television, "professional" wrestling, always a ludicrous parody of the real sport, has become even more bizarre. The market share on WTBS and the USA Cable Network is larger for wrestling than for recognized athletic events, even for collegiate football. Not only does mass-produced television "junk" fill the airwaves, not only has it made potent allies of rock 'n roll and music videos, but it also threatens the integrity of all performances, be they athletic or musical. The audience has, because of TV, become accustomed to seeing displays of outrageous behavior. Displays of violent temper and "spontaneous" donnybrooks are no longer reserved for managers of baseball teams. No longer do players have nicknames like "Lefty" and "Red"; now we have "Mad Dog," "The Enforcer," "The Assassin," "The Hammer," "Animal," and the like. The marked increase in violence in such sports as ice hockey, football, and even in basketball is a result of audience enthusiasm for circuses, for diversion which can be directly related to the penetration of television into all visual experiences. The vocabulary of sport now includes "late hit," "good fight," "slam-dunk," "hit men," "clear the bench," and other terms generated from the grammar of violence. Almost all technological advances in the broadcasting industry have been concerned with transporting violent images more effectively. The "isolated camera," "superslow motion," and "instant replay" allow us to consume again and again what is often only a fraction of the total action. What television has done to popular music—the music video—it promises to do to that most cherished of American teenage values: sportsmanship. We have at last isolated the chief Siren.

Such are a few of the violent "texts" I undertake to study: the illustrations of Hogarth, the organized animal entertainments of the eighteenth century, the *Punch and Judy* shows of the nineteenth, the high-gothic horrors, the novels of Stephen King, the comic book, the stalk-and-slash film, professional wrestling, and prime-time action/adventure television. I intend to take seriously this motley collection of some of the worst that has been thought and said during the last two hundred years. Any treatment of such a panoply is selective, prejudicial, and reductive. The first question has to be: Can anything conceivably important be salvaged from this flotsam of modern culture even if one could sort through it? How can this stuff—junk—which gives even popular culture a bad name, be worthy of the kind of attention usually concentrated on works of art? My answer is that I think the information carried within these fables must be important. However incomprehensible it may be, any entertainment with such a large and enduring audience is self-evidently important. If we take as a touchstone Samuel Johnson's "nothing can please many, and please long, but just representations of general nature" (*The Preface to Shakespeare*), we will see that what has pleased many and pleased long are exactly those displays which we contend are not only ephemeral but also excisable as worthless junk. Whether we like them or not, they are "just representations of general nature." I am going to argue that the very stories we criticize most vociferously are indeed some of the most important socializing rituals that this culture has developed.

To understand this conundrum, we need to realize that popular culture is not a debased form of art culture. It has a different ontology and epistemology—a different audience with different supply and demand curves. Questions of what these fables are and how we know about them have no counterparts in high culture. For instance, as contrasted with canonical art, most of the scenarios of preposterous violence exist independently of any individual artist.[2] Who knows who had a hand in creating *Robocop, The A-Team,* or *EC* comics? Or what about *Punch and Judy* or the vampire? To paraphrase Walt Whitman that great artists need good audiences, in popular culture nothing is possible without an audience and the best audience is the biggest. Perhaps the radio is a good analogy. There are a number of stations broadcasting different fantasies at different frequencies, and we "tune in" at different times of our lives to different positions on the dial. When we are young we want rock 'n roll, then as we get older maybe country music tells stories which interest us, or maybe we will develop a taste for the classical. The station succeeds by being able to target an audience and keep it listening long enough to hear the sponsor's message. Radio stations sell audiences. What they transmit is secondary. So in anatomizing how violence is *textualized* in various popular culture media, we are forced to concentrate instead on the only stable part of the process—the audience and its size.

In interpreting a "serious" work of art, we might ask what the artist uncovers, both in his own psyche and in our own, by allowing the retributive violence of a Hamlet or the self-aggrandizing violence of a Lady Macbeth to play itself out. However, in the analysis of popular culture texts—escapist entertainment—the analysis perforce shifts to who wants escape from what to where, and how many are lined up in front of the box office to take the trip. How many fingers are on the dial? Essentially this is why we have had to wait until the eighteenth century to find these stories told. For unlike Greek drama, medieval martyrologies, blood-

and-thunder Elizabethan and Jacobean revenge dramas, evangelical ser-mons, or pirate and highwayman almanacs, modern fables of preposter-ous violence depend on mass media to distribute them. And mass media depend on what is truly modern—a consuming audience with disposable income.

The questions then become: Why are these the stories to be repeated and why are they repeated so often? Wouldn't once be enough? Why have we been attracted to these particular scenes? Are we only drawn during a particular phase of maturation? How does the audience find these stories and encourage them to be told? Why have veritable indus-tries of transmission evolved whose major task is to broadcast just these concussive fables? Why do certain scenes not only exist independent of artists but also seem in many cases to depend on anonymity? We as-sume, or at least are taught, that high art memorializes what we must never forget—"short time's endless monument." Could it be, however, that in the modern world mass culture repeatedly plays out what was never in the province of high art but was in the only province of mass indoctrination—namely, religion? In no way do I suggest that meta-physics has been displaced by popular culture, only that the crucial role we have assigned to religion seems now to be performed by "mere" entertainment. I intend to show that "mere" is a synonym for ritual, that ritual is a keystone of making sense of the world, and that repeti-tion of specific scenes for a specific audience is one of the methods by which we "grow up" and adopt a culture.

Art culture and popular culture need not be seen as antithetical, need not be high and low, U and non-U, canonical and commodity, jewels and junk. They have been identified as such by those who have had to support, or in the current jargon "privilege," certain works which de-mand critical exegesis to be "appreciated." Actually, popular and art cultures are positions in a continuum, not at opposite ends but as stages of information. Cranky Dwight Macdonald may have had truth upside down when he first claimed in "A Theory of Mass Culture" that "mass-cult . . . doesn't even have the theoretical possibility of being good." Mass culture is not interested in being good; it is only interested in being consumed. The more important the scene, the less likely that an artist's name will be involved, and the more likely a dismissive adjective will be attached. For instance, where we find the words "pandering," "titillation," "mere," "sentimental," and especially "escapist" used as descriptive terms, we will probably find a rich lode of social ore. Those who now cry that Stephen King's fiction travesties the novel forget that the novel itself was not so long ago accused of subverting literature. If we want to discover what is crucial and valued in our culture, we need to study what we repeat, what we censure, what we throw away, what "lowers standards." We need to study junk. We need to look at travesties. Clichés and stereotypes become so because of overuse, not because of neglect. Repetition in popular culture is ritualization, and ritual is a key to what is truly "privileged" information.

The most obvious place to find such rituals is in the entertainments we first encounter in childhood that tide us over into adolescence. If you study the eager consumers of vulgarities, you will soon see that this audience is characterized not so much by class (as we tend to assume, due in part to Marxist interpretations of the culture industry) as by maturity. The responsive audience, the believing and hence the consuming audience of mass media productions—television, movies, even print—is clearly the teenage audience. But how does knowing the audience help us to understand the attraction of symbolic violence? Simply this: While we may not be able to locate exactly the element within rituals that attracts different audiences, we do know the needs within this specific audience that keep it interested. This audience needs information. Here anthropologists, sociologists, and psychologists all agree. The primary concern of early adolescence is the transition from individual and isolated sexuality to pairing and reproductive sexuality. It is a concern fraught with unarticulated anxiety and thus ripe for the resolutions of violence.[3]

Consider the movies, for instance. The major audience for movies is currently between the ages of twelve and twenty. If you think they are not making movies the way they used to, you are right. "They" are making movies for the only people in our society with sufficient interest and the disposable income necessary to see them. Many movies are prescreened with different endings so that the most popular resolution can be included in the final print. The audience most commonly chosen for test previews is made up of teenagers. If the bulk of media productions seems made for the mindless, or at least for the feeble-minded, remember that this is essentially the way we characterize adolescence. Life-span psychologists like Daniel Levinson and Gail Sheehy assure us that adolescence is a stage of cultural assimilation which lasts, at least in our culture, well into the twenties. Adolescent assimilation of rituals and values determines much of what is broadcast on television, provides the audience for Hollywood films, and is responsible for much of the fictional pulp which has been filling book shelves since the mid-nineteenth century.

In terms of popular entertainment, adolescence is a "taste culture." Herbert J. Gans defines such tastes as more than distinctive demarcations of consciousness, social status, or educational level. Tastes are indicative of biological stages as well. Those tastes we acquire during adolescence never leave us because they are somehow central to our survival. The texts may change; the psychological needs remain the same. Whatever it is that informs youngsters between eight and fifteen is something that is never made fully manifest, never fully understood, something that remains latent for the rest of our natural days and that links the generations, though it may seem to cause the gaps. Hence, we outgrow childhood tastes, but we all continue to be interested in the mysteries we first came across in adolescence.

Studying violent fables thus begins with adolescent taste. When the audience comes to the campfire, what does it ask to hear? As reader-response critics have suggested, whatever it is we call "meaning" is not generated by private authorial codes but by audience inception and completion. In popular culture spectacles, not only is the display generated by popular demand, but interpretation is passed around by the unconscious codes of the consumers. The audience creates, transforms, and interprets the scenarios of preposterous violence according to deep-seated, nonsequential, possibly even biological patterns. When the pattern fits, the audience stays to watch and listen. When it misses, something else results (quite possibly art) and the mass audience moves elsewhere—to another campfire.

Ancient examples of these dynamics are the lion-hunt panels that Assyrians carved at the same time that the classic urns of ancient Greece were crafted. In art history there is no doubt which of these images resides in textbooks, and which resides in popular culture. While the urns have assumed normative status in artistic judgment, the lion hunts are usually given as examples of prole spectacle.[4] Although these are isolated and incomplete panels of King Ashurbanipal's hunts, they tell us much about our enduring desire to watch certain scenes and about our almost equally enduring repression of that desire.

In one of the central wall reliefs, we see a condensation of Assyrian art of this period. The first thing we notice is the action, a destined action characterized by violence. Everything concentrates on the inevitable concussion of straight-standing king and charging beast. The narrative line is direct and unambiguous. The lion in stop-action sequence is released from confinement and runs straightaway into the waiting spear of kingly power. The king is thick-set and weighty, protected by his minions; he is a stocky matador who must stand firm in the face of danger. The lion/bull has been "picked" into fury not by a banderillero but by the servant who has opened the cage. Our socialized sympathies (at least since Romanticism) are with the lion; our gut feelings are with the king. The sense of redundancy is inherent in these images; they form an unreeling procession from right to left, almost like film unspooling on sprockets, almost like a flip-book of stationary pictures, each one a little different to give the illusion of action. The action is compressed and condensed: King of beasts meets king of men. King of beasts will die.

The motif of repeated violence and death in the other wall reliefs is almost unbearable to the sensitivities of anyone not raised on television.

Ashurbanipal Hunting Lions, c. 650 B.C. (British Museum)

Little wonder that art critics have spurned these scenes. In the battle panorama, the sky is literally filled to the horizon, in cookie-cutter repetition, with wounded and dying enemies. As in the lion hunt, these scenes make no attempt at realism: They are pantomime violence. The lion cage to the right and the king to the left are simply markers to the cartoon excitement in the middle. That excitement cannot be escaped or denied. A powerful force is carried to an object, in this case the king, who confronts it and prevails.

In other scenes from the lion-hunt panels, we look at one more aspect

Ashurbanipal II at War, c. 875 B.C. (British Museum)

Ashurbanipal Killing Lions, c. 650 B.C. (British Museum)

Ashurbanipal Killing Lions, c. 650 B.C. (British Museum)

Ashurbanipal Killing Lions, c. 650 B.C.. (British Museum)

of preposterous violence: the lack of affect in the killer's demeanor. The king delivers the *coup de grâce* to the already wounded bull/lion with the impassivity of a Mr. T, or a Rambo, or a comic-book hero. His minions stand by. Have they caught the disease of violence from watching the king too long? Or is this violence at all? Perhaps they are living out a fantasy which we could see imaged on the cave walls, or on the flickering TV. All around them lie the wounded bodies of other lions. Ironically, the only emotion is on the dead faces of the beasts.

Is this the savage, barbaric, uncivilized, and therefore best-forgotten stuff of ancient man? Or is there some deep power of aggression which still lingers in our breasts? Why can some of us not stop looking at it?

Wounded Lions, c. 650 B.C. (British Museum)

Wounded Lions, c. 650 B.C. (British Museum)

Why do others feel the need to criticize it? Western humanism has done its best to pretend that such violence is behind us, that it is the Greeks who carried the day. If you listen to academic critics, you will believe that the Assyrians are still best forgotten. But we may suspect differently. It may be that the Assyrians won the imaginations of the West.[5]

Of course, the Assyrian reliefs are, as the critics contend, savage, propagandistic, repetitive, and crude, but they are much more. They are images that people wanted to look at, wanted to stand before and watch, wanted to be shocked by. From all accounts such violent chronicles were the highlights in the royal citadels of Nimrud and Nineveh, yet the simplicity and multiplicity of such reliefs imply that little discrimination was practiced by either artist or audience. Call the reliefs propaganda, call them brutal, call them cartoons; it is just as likely one could call them something that was demanded by, and enjoyed by, an eager audience.

The major audience for such entertainments has been, is, and will continue to be adolescent males. From the broken rock near many of the cave-wall paintings of animal-man violence, archaeologists have conjectured that young men were allowed to go deep into the caves to overcome their fears by heaving their weapons at the images. There were probably other audiences as well, but this particular audience responded with active aggression. Do we still practice such homeopathic magic? Although many other audience groups may patronize *Rambo, WrestleMania, The A-Team,* stalk-and-slash films, horror comics, heavy metal music, rock videos, electronic arcade games, and the like, the audience most interested, most titillated, most informed by such events

"AAAAALLLLL RIIIGHT!"

Koren, *Aaaaalllll Riiight!* (© 1986 The New Yorker Magazine, Inc.)

are the group we feel the most anxious about and the most eager to direct and/or control—young men.

To appreciate how the entertainments of preposterous violence are audience-generated, we need first to realize that, as opposed to high art, the material of popular entertainment is constructed from back to front. As in a liturgy, the recitative nature of audience participation is central. In high art, or perhaps more accurately, in taste cultures of the mature, the assumption is made that the "reader" decodes a message left by the author. The audience negotiates with the text, bringing cultural expertise to bear. Although meaning is not something sent along a wire like a current, the model is linear, from author to medium to audience. For all the clatter in postmodern criticism, the critic may co-opt the author, but the critical work still travels the same line. In fact, it is not happenstance that modernism should have risen concurrently with the dominance of mass media entertainment. For modernism in large degree is a reaction against the successes of mass media. Rather than a revolt, however, modernism only exaggerates what was inherent in high culture. The author has meaning, the reader must petition for it, the critic intercedes. The reader must study the critic who studies the text. Just a glance at one of the great works of modernism, Eliot's *The Waste Land*, will show the extent the modern poet/critic was willing to go to remind us of the process, and just a glance at a postmodern text, Jacques Derrida's *Glas*, for instance, will show that the petitioning process remains intact.

Popular culture has no intermediaries. It is not foisted on us by some "masters-of-the-media" cabal, not contrived by artists or critics. Rather, as Leslie Fiedler has written of television executives in *What Was Literature*,

> It turns out, however (think of the astonishing number of TV shows in which large sums of money have been invested that bomb each season), that they are more often wrong than right in their guesses. Far from manipulating mass taste, its so-called masters breathlessly pursue it, cutting each other's throats, risking bankruptcy to find images which the great audience will recognize as dreams they have already dreamed, or would if they could. No wonder they think of themselves as riding a tiger. (p. 101)

The stuff of popular culture is avidly consumed not only by adolescents who crave fashion but also as part of a search for an order beneath the disposable surface. Very often this truth has to do with social forms, with patterns of reproduction, with fight or flight alternatives, with how to fit in, with how to behave, with how to make sense.

In popular culture, efficiency is everything, repetition and predictability the rule. What must be achieved is not just any of a number of responses but one primary response. Ambiguity is anathema, as is eccentricity, as is art. As any parent knows, what is important must be repeated with almost mindless dedication: "Look both ways before crossing the street," "Stay away from strangers," even "Eat your food," or "Time for bed." Much parent-child interchange seems phatic when actually it is ripe with the central meanings of life. So too is the folk wisdom, misnamed "folk*lore*," which so often seems nonsensical yet which is central to cultural stability.

The paradox of popular culture is most clearly seen in fairy tales. We start telling fairy tales to our children before they can absorb such stories, even before we are aware of what such stories may mean. We are not sure why we tell these particular stories except that they were the ones told to us. Soon the child knows several and asks that certain ones be repeated and that certain parts be exaggerated. "Tell me Little Red Riding Hood and this time really describe the wolf." What we censor, children replace. We tell these stories, unaware that their meanings are profound and socially important. We rarely realize we are playing out an ancient bardic role which human societies have established for growing children. Until some critic like Bruno Bettelheim or Robert Coles comes to explain the particular resonance and significance, we are unaware of the purpose of these tales. They are only fairy tales, we say, only stories to put children to sleep by, to dream by.

Although there are many complex models of communication, it is important to stress that television, the modern bard, also depends on the "reader" to make pivotal decisions on which tales are told. A typical television show, for instance, needs an audience of at least 25 million people just to stay on the air, and so it must show people images they want to see badly enough to endure the commercials and not change channels. The reason Nielsen ratings are so important is that network executives really don't know what to broadcast. They need to be told what stories to tell. So in this sense the audience is the initiating and consuming author of its own imagination. When one thinks of how television imagery is constructed and transmitted, one realizes that the system of signifiers, the images themselves, must be what most of us who watch *want* to watch. The idea of making an audience from scratch is absurd on the face of it. Essentially, television "freely" broadcasts these images because sponsors want to send their own images embedded within other stories. The entertainment, the fable, is simply there as the sugar coating to induce the audience to swallow the commercial pill— the *quid pro quo* of mass media. Television networks sell audience share, not programs. Television is a merchandising medium, a show business. "I'll show you this," it says, "if you'll watch that."

Preposterous violence has proven to be one of the most alluring sequences into which advertising can be embedded. We like to watch violence and we have for a long time. Because we so quickly concentrate on violence, it has been used to attract our attention by numerous institutions long before the modern world of mass media. In fact, the most enduring self-contained sign system of preposterous violence in Western popular culture is the Passion of Christ, especially the Crucifixion. The central image in Christianity has been of God becoming a man, who then suffered as a man, and after death became God again. The middle part of this transformation has historically been the most visually arresting, given the progressive increase in violence to Christ as he was reimaged from the stoic mystic in the late Middle Ages to the suffering human in the Renaissance. While it might be sacrilegious to consider the Passion of Christ as an advertisement for the institution of the Catholic Church, there may be some provocative similarities.

The question of why Christ was suddenly made a man in Renaissance imagery and then why this aspect of Christ's earthly pain was forgotten is the subject of one of the most provocative books on violence ever written, Leo Steinberg's *The Sexuality of Christ in Renaissance Art and in Modern Oblivion*. Steinberg's thesis essentially is that the medieval church realized that as long as Christ was God, the Crucifixion was only an empty sequence. How could God suffer human pain? What torture could be inflicted on God? Only mortals could suffer from violence. But how could God be made a believable man? The answer, as we see in Renaissance art, is that God became human by becoming sexual. Once sexual, he is human and once human he becomes susceptible to pain. Christ's sexuality was visually achieved in a number of ways, most obviously by picturing him nursing at his mother's breast. But this did not really show Christ as a sexual man. Hence, the development of the tradition of "ostentatio genitalium" or the exposure of Christ's penis. Deapotheosizing was done, as Steinberg illustrates with numerous examples in Renaissance art, by painting Christ's outright nudity as an infant and then as a baby boy who is going to be, or who has been, circumcised. This ithyphallic imagery, as well as the increasing concentration on celebrating the circumcision, represents a dimly conscious design on the church's part to reinforce the doctrine of incarnation while catering to the desires of the audience. Jesus is a man, a man who can withstand preposterous violence. This imagery was no more foisted on an unsuspecting audience by a conniving church than television forces action/adventure shows on unsuspecting viewers. The audience *wants* certain stories and supports a medium which produces and shows them. The church, like the network sponsor, broadcasts a sequence of images in part because it needs the audience attention. The audience will not watch what it does not want to see.

Steinberg is primarily concerned with the imagery of Christ's sexuality and the development of motifs such as the diaphanous veil, which becomes the "banner loincloth" barely covering the genitals while accentuating potency, and such as the proleptic images of nursing, circumcision, and occasionally even erection, which essentially remind us "Ecce Homo."* On the following pages, for instance, are images of Christ at the beginning and ending of his mortal life. The focus is clearly on his sexuality. Although Steinberg is not interested in the Crucifixion as the

---

* I regret that the Chancellor of Bob Jones University has seen fit to withhold publication rights to Maerten van Heemskerck's *Man of Sorrows*, c. 1525–30, which is held in the university's collection. This example of the humanity of Christ can be seen, however, on page 87 of Steinberg's *The Sexuality of Christ in Renaissance Art and in Modern Oblivion*.

Hans Baldung Grien, *Holy Family*, 1511 (Geisberg 59)

shifting of audience interest, I certainly am. For here in the heart of Christian mythography is a ritualized sequence of preposterous violence which is startling. Without arguing the logical merits or the articles of faith, the fact that God, who is omniscient and omnipotent, sacrifices his son to show compassion is a perplexing concept. Unless, that is, the audience somehow wants it that way. Unless the dominant icon, the crucified Christ, somehow plays out a mactation rite which we want to see and for which there is a stabilizing social reward.

Before the invention of movable type, the dominant mass media in Western culture were the walls and surfaces of churches. It is on these

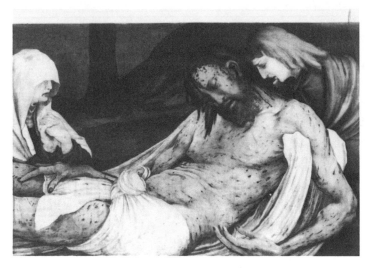

Matthias Grünewald, *The Dead Christ* (Musée d'Unterlinden, Colmar, France)

Fra Angelico, *Christ on the Cross with the Virgin and St. John* (Museo di San Marie, Florence)

Giovanni Bellini, *The Blood of the Redeemer* (National Gallery, London)

surfaces that the image of the crucified Christ was repeatedly cast in mortar, paint, wood, stone, and iron. Although many parts of the Crucifixion sequence were introduced and repeated, in the late Middle Ages the figure of the Roman legionnaire first appeared in the Crucifixion panorama. To prove to himself that Christ was both real and dead, this soldier pierced the crucified Christ's left side with a spear. Blood appeared—important blood for it showed that incarnation was complete. Christ was a man; he bled. Renaissance churchmen pointed to this as the fourth time Christ's blood had been shed: first at the circumcision; then at the Agony in the Garden—the flagellation (a scenario of preposterous violence in itself); then at the nailing to the cross; and now the post-mortem bloodletting. What is intriguing, however, is that in later reiterations, such as Van Der Goes's *The Entombment* and Louis Morales's *Pieta*, the blood trickles not down Christ's side as the laws of gravity would dictate but into the groin area. Often the blood is even expressed from the body by Christ's volition.

Clearly, blood flowing from breast to groin or into a vessel so obviously contradicts natural consequences that a symbolic reading is inescapable. Additionally, the first and last wounds of Christ's passion are etched in blood as if to establish the thematic symmetry. I don't wish to belabor this imagery but only to suggest that we are getting a ritualistic repetition of a sequence which is accepted by both artist and audience without criticism, let alone symbolic inspection. In much the same way that the diaphanous veil, or "perizonium," is gently lifted by the wind both to cover and to display Christ's genitals (often painted over during the Enlightenment), so too this blood metaphor becomes a leitmotif throughout the Renaissance, reinforcing certain violent parts of the Passion of Christ.

Why? Could it be that the imagery of the Crucifixion competed with other image sequences for audience attention? Remember, the Christian fathers did not represent the Crucifixion realistically before the Council of Chalcedon ("two natures and one person") in the fifth century. Rather, the event had been symbolized first by a lamb, then by a cross. It was only during the late Middle Ages that the crucified Christ appeared, eyes closed in mystic transcendence. The expanded version of the Crucifixion sequence in which the eyes were closed in pain appeared during the Renaissance. New characters were added, including mourners, the two thieves, the legionnaire who pierced Christ's side, and the soldiers offering vinegar or casting lots. This is the imagery we have received, and it has changed little over the last two centuries, perhaps because by the early eighteenth century the theme of the Crucifixion was supplanted by more secular concerns and because painters, poets, and audience went elsewhere to other stories to celebrate both the transcendental vision and the appetite for violence. Just as the actual violence of the gladiatorial games was supplanted by the religious violence of Christianity, so the Passion was supplanted by the secular violence of print and illustration. Our sensitivity, however, to the enfleshment of God and to violence directed against this flesh has not disappeared. It made Martin Scorsese's *The Last Temptation of Christ* a box-office success.

Still, just prior to the introduction of modern scenarios, a story coalesced that provided the template of future myths. Yes, Christ is the Incarnation. Yes, Christ is suffering. To achieve this suffering, violence, often of quite a sadistic nature, has been performed. The fact that the flagellation of Christ was a popular subject, and an important prelude to the Crucifixion (now almost unheard of and unpainted), may be a testament to our finding other image systems with other sacrificial victims to conduct the *frisson*. On the next few pages, for instance, are Christological images not often seen in modern renditions but which were common during the Renaissance.

Modern sensibilities have shifted from concentrating on Christ as the victim of preposterous violence to focusing on new scenarios in which the victim's identity is relatively incidental. In the eighteenth century, animal victims may have deflected some of this interest, but with the rise of mass media anonymous scapegoats have played a decidedly central role. In the nineteenth century, the young, sexually innocent female became the dependable victim of the de Sadean rituals. Since the gothic, we have never wanted for a steady supply. Virgins are still recruited for the horror film; Indians used to do the same for the Western; foreigners have been the whipping boys of such entertainments as the detective

Duccio, *The Flagellation* (Muso dell Opera del Duomo, Siena, Italy)

Aragon, *The Flagellation* (Collection of the Comtesse Parni, Paris)

genre, professional wrestling, and adventure tales. For a number of reasons, most importantly a change in audience composition, we no longer have much interest in *innocent* prey. Often someone becomes a victim by initially victimizing others, thereby becoming an object for the more powerful forces of social order. The modern victims of television dramas are most often economic overreachers and swindlers. They want our *things*. In this sense they *deserve* the preposterous violence they encounter. In no way are they Christlike, but the stylized violence achieves the same shock.

That we accept the victim without question is the key to understanding the formula of broadcast violence. In narrowcast communication like prose fiction or poetry, the authorial voice is important and locatable and must somehow arrange the parties. In broadcast media, from folk-

Gaspard Isenmann, *Christ at the Column* (Musée d'Unterlinden, Colmar, France; photo: O. Zimmermann)

song to television, the audience usually knows the roles, knows how to recognize and categorize the action. After all, the mass audience is the source of popular culture. Like the child preparing for bed, it demands certain stories. Television, comics, pulp novels, and splatter movies are tribal entertainments—bedtime stories. They essentially confirm, not enrich; repeat, not originate; reassure, not rearrange. They communicate information we cannot otherwise express. In fact, more like architecture or furniture, they rest on assumptions of stability. In the main, the fables of aggression play out to this mass audience an unreeling sequence of images which claim to be destabilizing but are instead vehicles of repression.

As we have seen in Assyrian art and Christian iconography, gratuitous violence needs a context, and it is the development of that modern context that *Preposterous Violence* intends to examine. Part of this context is ideological, part is theatrical, part historical, and part sociobiological. While my concern will be to set preposterous violence in historical context and to anatomize its content, I am also interested in how deeply based the production, transmission, and consumption of these images are in the socializing codes of the species. As with many exchanges involving mass audiences, we tend to blame the messenger for the message, or better yet, blame the teller and the tale instead of realizing that we, the audience, are in some manner responsible for our folklore. Although blaming the American Broadcasting Company, Cannon Films, *EC* comics, the World Wrestling Federation, (or even the Catholic Church), and a host of other industries which transport these shocks has satisfied our need for an easy explanation, it has not led to any understanding of why these institutions flourish.

Since the promulgators have proved resistant to criticism, we might do well to shift our attention to what we know of audience response. Two important facts: although females are not excluded, the primary audience for preposterous violence is male and, although other maturity levels differ in their interest, the most interested audience is adolescent. Since this is the sex, male, and the maturity level, adolescent, might there be some connection between what this audience feels most anxious about and what these programs offer in the way of behavior possibilities? Since this is an audience both capable of and aroused about reproduction, could preposterous violence have some sociobiological function?

The male is rewarded in the reproductive sweepstakes for taking risks. His genetic future, as opposed to that of the female, is increased by aggression, by "profligacy." But if he is too aggressive, if he becomes violent and antisocial, he will be removed from the game. This is not a paradox new to sociobiology, although sociobiology has made such paradoxical distinctions crucial.[6] Males are selected *both* for aggressive tendencies and for a willingness to avoid conflict. They are victims of ambivalence and are rewarded for it. They maximize their genetic chances by taking chances with a number of partners; females increase their genetic chances by doing the opposite, by choosing a stable partner. In the breeding patterns, males contend with other males in order to gain access to females, while females concentrate on creating the most beneficial environment in which to raise their children to reproductive age. From such biogenetic considerations come such human social behaviors as polygamy rather than polyandry, patriarchy rather than matriarchy, or even hypergamy, the female desire for an older, established mate in order to better protect her offspring.

Unless certain restraints are imposed, male competition will prove self-defeating. The willingness to be violent has made the species dominant, but unrestrained violence could undo eons of evolution. By a myriad of repressions, deflections, and projections, younger males have to learn to equilibrate—to exchange certain biological behaviors for cultural ones. We have done this quite unconsciously, but the results are obvious. The incest taboo is one clear example. To militate against intrafamilial strife, certain women are put off-bounds, not necessarily because they are any more or less desirable, but because sex with these women could provoke

real violence and disrupt the most efficient human social unit, the breeding family. Over thousands of generations those families who were able
to economize and repress were those who succeeded in spreading their
influence, namely their genes. Violence became ritualized, aggression
rechanneled, civilization began having its discontent.

In all human societies the adolescent years are the most aggressive.
The mating season begins. According to criminal justice experts, eighteen is the peak year for this aggression to find violent expression in our
culture. True, such behavior is exacerbated by poverty, discrimination,
and unstable family life, but as James Q. Wilson and Richard J. Herrnstein have contended in their controversial *Crime and Human Nature*,
"constitutional" factors such as body type, intelligence, and genetic heritage are more causative. We may well find that just as a certain percent
of the population cannot interpret taboos such as those against incest, so
there are others who cannot decode the restrictions on aggression. While
it may seem that the scenarios of symbolic violence, along with social
conditions like poverty, *cause* violent displays, such behavior may be
more directly connected to biological predispositions. In fact, there seems
to be a direct relationship between sensation-seeking behavior and levels
of sex hormones, particularly testosterone, as well as monoamine oxi-
dase, or MAO, an enzyme that regulates levels of such brain chemicals
as serotonin. Teenage boys with a high level of testosterone and a low
MAO level are not only likely to be more aggressive but are also probably the most enthusiastic consumers of fictionalized aggression.

Because aggression is potentially so dangerous, it is logical that ritual
increases when violence is closest to the surface. Such potentially dangerous behavior must be redirected before it can be externalized. Victor
Turner has coined and popularized the term "liminal" to describe the
unstable audience most receptive to the stabilizing force of centering
rituals. In his felicitous analogy, symbolic rituals are to action what metal
containers are to a radioactive isotope, containing without snuffing out
content. Essentially, Turner's thesis is that transitions between zones (or
"tastes"), be they temporal, spatial, or social, always increase the risk of
breaking down repressed desire. Rituals become fences around danger.
Life at the edge is always hazardous to the health of those on the edge—
the "liminaries"—as well as to those on either side. Violence can erupt
and with it the threat of retaliation. Everyone is anxious. And so to
mitigate and deflect that risk and anxiety, societies celebrate specific rites
of separation and incorporation and thus facilitate the transition of the
liminaries into the next phase. In elaborating on the dangers of transit-
ing zones, Turner is depending on Arnold Van Gennep's theory of the
rites of passage:

> The life of an individual in any society is a series of passages from
> one age to another and from one occupation to another. Whenever

there are fine distinctions among age and occupational groups, progression from one group to the next is accompanied by special acts, like those which make up apprenticeship in our trades. Among semicivilized peoples such acts are enveloped in ceremonies, since to the semicivilized mind no act is entirely free of the sacred. In such societies every change in a person's life involves actions and reactions between sacred and profane—actions and reactions to be regulated and guarded so that society as a whole will suffer no discomfort or injury. Transitions from group to group to group and from one social situation to the next are looked on as implicit in the very fact of existence, so that a man's life comes to be a succession of stages with similar ends and beginnings: birth, social puberty, marriage, fatherhood, advancement to a higher class, occupational specialization, and death. For every one of these events there are ceremonies whose essential purpose is to enable the individual to pass from one defined position to another which is equally defined. (p. 3)

What Turner has done with Van Gennep's thesis is to focus on the period inside the passage, the liminal period, in which the novice, the liminoid, has been pushed from one group into temporary exile with those of the same sex and maturity. Turner's examination of this pivotal point of transition from phase to phase, or state to state, acknowledges a profoundly paradoxical point. In the liminal period, the group in exile suffers from a lack of identity, a breakdown of self-consciousness, while at the same time there is the concomitant congealing power of the group. What provides the unease also provides the palliative. Since the individuals are at their most vulnerable, the gang protection is the most intense. The potential for violence is also the most acute and the dangers the most palpable, yet the process of maturation cannot occur without first separating the adolescents from the mooring of childhood. Once unhooked, they are dangerous to everyone including themselves. This is when fables of aggression are told.

The need for ritual is most extreme in adolescents. The novice is between boy and man, girl and woman, and is at the most dangerous point because confusion can produce violence and violence can lead to revenge. If the species is to survive, rituals must be invoked to facilitate generative sexuality while simultaneously deflecting aggression. On one hand, the "liminaries" are ground down, hazed, ridiculed, asked unanswerable riddles. On the other hand, they are reinforced, instructed, apprenticed, protected. Since the boys pose the more dangerous threat, in primitive societies they are often taken to special places and held in limbo, while the girls are allowed to remain within the tribe. Often the boys are taken to see special images. We may still provide such deflective patterns, albeit in spite of ourselves. "Joining the Scouts" is a vestige of one of our most trusted methods to remove, indoctrinate, and return males during adolescence. In much the same way that our earliest known relatives were taken deep into the caves of Lascaux and Niaux to witness the terror paintings, so our boys file into horror movies, or endure hazing, or watch videos, or listen to heavy metal music, or generally consume scenarios of seeming depravity in order to return to the tribe. In primitive fables the young man may also be instructed in the use of some weapon of aggression, a spear, a knife, or an instrument. In the modern updating of the Western movie, he is taken "out back behind the barn" and taught to use the six-shooter. In the music video, the guitar becomes a blasting weapon, an Uzi with strings. As Turner elaborates, we may not have a hard time seeing correspondences between savage and "civilized."

> Sacred objects may be shown, myths recited in conjunction with them, answers may be given to riddles earlier left unexplained. Very often masked figures invade the liminal scene—usually framed in a sacred enclosure, cave, *temenos,* or other sequestered site—these masked figures being themselves liminal in their bizarre combinations of human, animal, vegetable and mineral characteristics. Such masks and monsters are often composites of factors drawn from the culture of mundane, quotidian experience, but split off from their normal, expectable contexts and recombined in grotesque, weird, even anatomically impossible configurations, which have as at least one of their functions, that of provoking the novices or initiands, the "liminaries," into thinking hard about the elements and basic building blocks of symbolic complexes they had hitherto taken for granted as "natural" units. Actuality, in the liminal state, gives way to possibility, and aberrant possibilities reveal once more to liminaries the value of what has hitherto been regarded as the somewhat tedious daily round. A manheaded lion, leaping in firelight from the bush may make one think about the abstract nature both of human heads and of feral bodies, or of the relationship between culture which can *manufacture* monsters, and nature which generates lions, or of the symbolism of social control—a chief has lion-like powers; each culture will stress its own salient dichotomies and draw its own lessons. Thus masks and monsters may be as much pedagogical devices as instruments of coercion through terror and awe; like other liminal things they are probably both. ("Variations on the Theme of Liminality," p.38)

While it may be taxing to think that the onrush of a manheaded lion is in any way like the bluster of Mr. T or the furious villainy of cartoon nasties, or of cinematic monsters, the audience which responds to these images transforms them into metonyms of frightening anxiety and then overcomes them. The ritualizing of such anxiety is a central activity of the transitional audience as it attempts to assimilate the new codes. That sex and violence come to be linked in adolescent consciousness is a vestige of an ancient conundrum: to propagate efficiently we must be competitive to a point just short of violent. Not to be competitive is not to be efficient and not to be efficient is to risk not having a genetic future. Yet to be violent is to risk not having a genetic present.

The ritualizations of competition, be it in pecking orders, sexual taboos, territoriality, or the like, have one goal in common: efficient reproduction and stable childrearing. What separates man from animal, as Darwin first pointed out, is that much of our biological drive has been shifted to the secondary process of socialization. And as Freud elaborated, redirecting such explosive forces as the sex drive into surrogate forms has demanded a price. We may condemn our appetites for pornography or violent entertainment or, more fundamentally, for voyeurism itself, but when we look at the tribes and cultures which have squabbled themselves out of existence we may be thankful that such aggression has been sublimated. The question is not whether pornography causes sexual stimulation, or whether preposterous violence causes violent acts. That may be so. The question is instead to what degree sex and violence, if not repressed, will result in destructive forms. If a causality exists between fiction and fact, then it may be the reverse of what we expect—the real causes the pretend. Admittedly, when we look at modern mass media we may have second thoughts about how successful the deflection of violence has been, but when we look at the ravages in modern history we may well prefer the vulgar ritual.[7]

I make this point because, although I have no interest in real violence, I doubt very much if stylized and fictionalized violence "leaks" into the real world as much as logic or some social scientists argue that it does. What *is* dangerous is when humans slip free of a code system, or else confuse the systems in such a way as to believe real action is exempt from real consequences. If only television were as influential as its critics claim, we might switch from the violent *Magnum P.I.* to watch Barry Manilow in concert and become loving, tender people. Or would we? It seems doubtful, from the point of view of the species' history, that the human brain, which came of age in the Olduvai Gorge, can be returned to the jungle at such a speed simply by watching flickering pixels on a nineteen-inch screen. In the scale of time, television has existed for less than a wink, and if it is indeed undoing what oral and print cultures so laboriously built, then those traditions may be far more ephemeral than advertised.

If one looks back into our cultural history, or if one compares our current situation with others, it is probable that our levels of actual violence are not connected to our consumption of pantomime violence. Real violence probably has more to do with the percentage of eighteen-year-old males in the population and what most of them are doing with their free time than with any other variable. The production and transmission of horror myths, for instance, have more likely flourished *after* social upheaval rather than before. Hence after the French Revolution, after the uprisings in the 1840s, in the late 1920s, and in the 1970s, fictive violence found an eager audience—or still better, an audience was able to find an exciting *frisson*. During the two world wars, popular culture was almost totally free of the rituals of preposterous violence, since the "real stuff" sufficed. The boys went away. Fables of aggression are not a by-product of a permissive society, or of a collapsing frontier, or of an unruly people. Although cultural historians like David Brion Davis and Richard Slotkin have argued persuasively for the place of a particular violence in American mythology, the pubescent fantasies coded in the texts I am studying transcend national experience. Such texts seem instead to be the result of what happens when a relatively free mass media allow an adolescent audience with disposable time and money to play out aggressive fantasies.

Bruno Bettelheim contends in "Violence: A Neglected Mode of Behavior" that

> we shall not be able to deal intelligently with violence unless we are first ready to see it as part of human nature, until we have gotten so well acquainted with it, by learning to live with it, that through a slow and tenuous process we may one day domesticate it successfully. In short, we cannot say that because violence *should* not exist, we might as well proceed as if it did not. (p. 191)

Bettelheim concludes that we must learn how to dissipate our adolescent aggression in nonviolent ways, but that it will not disappear, nor should we want it to. Peter Marsh argues in *Aggro: The Illusion of Violence* that aggressive fantasies are central to the maturation of males regardless of cultural context. To ask that masculine fables be nonviolent is not just asking too much, but asking the wrong question. If we can learn anything from history, from gladiatorial games to medieval tournaments to dueling to trench warfare to modern combat, it is that we seem programmed to, and have benefited from, aggression. It is a central aspect of our social and sexual selves. Rather than attempt to exorcise it, we should make sure to ritualize it in the least disruptive and most socially advantageous ways.

The anthropologist Robin Fox has argued in "The Inherent Rules of Violence" that we do exactly that. The ritualized interplay of fictional threat and counterthreat allows us to be aggressive without doing injury. He reports on a month spent observing the barroom behavior of the Tory Islanders off the coast of Ireland. Boys exchanged insults, holding each other back from contact, threatening but not striking—all hallmarks of aggressive adolescent males at play. Fox observes:

> At first sight, it seems to be an unstructured scuffle. But this is the main point I want to make about Tory fights: they are never unstructured. This may seem strange, for it appears that fighting is

something below the level of culture and rules; that it takes men back to something primeval, to a state of nature that is red in tooth and claw. Perhaps. But equally primeval is the principle of ritualization, and I think that this is the clue to the islanders' ability to manage their aggression. The principle of ritualization can be stated in a general form: in any community of animals there usually exist forms of combat that allow antagonists to settle their differences with violent exertion and yet with a minimum of serious damage. Sometimes the exertion itself can become ritualized—as when an exchange of shots at a distance is a duel, or the drawing of blood in a fencing match satisfies the honor of the antagonists. . . .

I am reminded of ritual fights—or as the ethnologists call them, agnostic encounters—of animals. It seems that men, including Tory men, try to ritualize combat between members of the same community, much as animals do. As [Konrad] Lorenz has pointed out, many animals that are equipped to kill have powerful inhibitions against killing their own kind. Very often combats are reduced to exhausting wrestling or butting matches, or even to simple displays of threat and counter-threat. The stags who compete for harems at rutting time lock antlers and wrestle. Stallions, playing the same game, nip each other on the neck, instead of slashing each other with their hoofs. Some animals, like the fiddler crab with his great, exaggerated right claw or the marine iguana with his horny crest, have evolved special organs for this purpose. Man has not evolved special organs. Instead he has that remarkable organ, culture, to do this ritual work for him. Perhaps this is an example of culture building on nature, rather than as is usually assumed, running counter to it. (pp. 138, 145)

The playground ritual is extended to the pub ritual, or the athletic game, or even to the front lines. In fact, as Robert Axelrod reported in *The Evolution of Cooperation*, during World War I, highly articulate and formulaic conventions developed in the trenches with shots being "answered," not to injure, but to deflect real conflict. Unconsciously, human beings develop a tit-for-tat program to maximize individual and group safety. In *St. Joan*, George Bernard Shaw blames Joan for spoiling the ritual. When Joan insists that the French generals stop knocking the English off their horses and get on with the business of killing them, she is effectively doing in the protective routine and, for Shaw, changing the world forever. Just as there are rules in boys-at-war, so are there rules in fictionalized entertainments of boys-at-war. These rituals, whether conducted via illustrations, novels, movies, television, comics, et al., are male displays of aggressive behaviors. They "show the colors," parade the willingness to fight, yet protect all participants from real injury. We are tempted to think we can do away with reality if we first can do away with the strutting display of aggression. But as we found out through attempts to regulate sexual behavior by outlawing pornography, the relationship between artificial and real is more complex than logic would suppose.

Peter Marsh uses the term "aggro," a British coinage from football chants, to describe young men's peculiarly explosive displays of excitement. The bluster of English or American punk and heavy metal rockers, of German *Halbstarke*, of French *blousons noirs*, and of Swedish *raggare* exaggerates the mature male response to aggression. Here are adolescent males who crave certain prescribed excitement motifs. Here are anxious teenagers who are quick to react if routine is rearranged. Here are groups most sure of what they are most insecure about—sexuality. It is hard to believe that what they crave is reassurance, that they are involved in acting out a latency fairy tale in which "happily ever after" results from threat and counterthreat. Ironically, they are as eager to enter the sexual sweepstakes as they are frightened by it. They simply do not know how to behave. They are aggressive by nature. Culture tries to make them less so through pantomime. When matters go awry, as they do in Anthony Burgess's *Clockwork Orange* or William Golding's *Lord of the Flies*, the young males can become fierce, eager to hunt, eager to fight. Adolescence passes. After the boys have reproduced, they are usually a little stunned to realize how hard it is to control their own adolescent sons. Married men with children stay home from the hunt, from war, not so much because they need to protect their families as because they are no longer aggressive, no longer so willing to be violent.

One of the more interesting components of adolescent aggression rituals is the role of women. If sex is the reward for aggression, one would expect that women would appear as the dim reward of male concentration. And indeed this does seem to be the case in most of the rituals we are about to examine. From Hogarth's illustrations of female victims to the *Punch and Judy* shows, in which Judy plays a cameo role in introducing the action, to professional wrestling, or to television shows like *The A-Team*, the presence of desired female attention is always on the periphery. Women are rarely involved in violence except as victim or reward. They may precipitate or conclude, but they do not participate. In professional wrestling, for instance, there is man vs. man, tag teams of two-to-twenty men vs. two-to-twenty men, male midgets, as well as female vs. female; but rarely are women involved with men and never is the conflict female vs. male. Is this because no such match could be staged? Or is it because no such match could find an audience? If women are to be the prize for violence, then they must not be participants and should rarely even be onlookers.[8]

Could it also be that in a patriarchy the role of women must be maintained as stable, or else the sex roles will crumble and real violence ensue? If so, might the women's movement, which stresses cooperation rather than competition, subvert some of the more exaggerated rituals? What if Billy Jean King vs. Bobby Riggs were played out not as parody but as a normal contest? One can only speculate about the consequences of rearing competitive males in the context of competitive females. Would the attendant confusion of the young males only heighten the level of aggression if females were no longer trophies and became themselves participants in aggressive enterprise? Could there be a connection between heightened male "aggro" and women who were no longer willing to be put on a pedestal? And what if women no longer desired to bear children? Would zero population growth mean more violence as the breeding pool evaporated and left some of the young men stranded?

With the possibility that preposterous violence is ritualized aggression which ironically stabilizes and marks out the psychological territory of "aggro," while at the same time subverting direct action, is there any reason to believe we are fundamentally different from our forebears? Is there any compelling reason to view our socializing behaviors as different from those of other cultures past and present? Is there any reason to believe that we in Western Europe and America are a different species? Is there any reason to believe that political and social movements like women's liberation have changed the level of male "aggro"? While we may bemoan the forms our current "entertainment" rituals may take, could they not emanate from a central anxiety? If so, what is that ur-anxiety to which we are still responding?

The answer is clear. If what males want is sex, what they fear is exactly what these rituals play out—unmediated violence. We absolutely abhor real violence unless it is done by others to others at a distance. In adolescence we play out fears, mediated safely in the protective husk of fiction, as a kind of mastery control—counterphobia. This is, after all, the standard explanation of repetition compulsion, and if we agree on anything it is that violent rituals are repeated as are few other routines in our culture. The threat of violence, however, and its connection with sexuality may alert us to deeper possibilities. The fact that violence, or even the threat of violence, triggers such a complex transformation of our physical being—the production of adrenalin, for instance, the tightening of the neck muscles, the discharge of corticotropin, a host of other involuntary responses in the limbic system—may be a clue to a still deeper ambiguity of our being.

We are programmed to respond to threats of violence. But we are not violent as a matter of course: aggressive, yes; violent, no. We may seem violent, going by television or the daily papers, but human violence that is natural, even instinctive, is rare. It has to be, or we would long ago have paid the price of intraspecies discord which no species can afford indefinitely. As Anthony Storr has argued in *Human Aggression*, the only animal like a violent man is a violent man. But violent men are not often encountered. When one is found, he is news—literally. In fact, the "news" industry is supported by reports of violent men from all over the globe. Just as the entertainment industry is supported by fictionalizing or imagining such violent men, so too is the journalism. Yet the fact remains: Most of us most of the time are not violent. We are petrified by the very idea. Adolescent males, however, are a slightly different story.

As Fox has suggested, violence, or the threat of violence, is the price of getting into the breeding pool; hence it is particular to young men. But if the predisposition for violence is a stage of maturation, why are we obsessed with it for a lifetime? René Girard in *Violence and the Sacred* suggests an answer. It is not violence we fear so much as violence without resolution. What we really fear is *retributive* violence. When we are angered we strike, not randomly but at a victim. Once the human victim has been struck, he retaliates, making the attacker his victim, and as Kurt Vonnegut has made a career of saying, "so it goes." The human phenomenon of "second strike" or "retaliatory strike," which is a keystone of our national "defense" policy, pays tribute to the fact that human males, as opposed to most other male animals, play "tit for tat" as an unconscious second nature.

Humans desperately want to avoid retributive violence. After all, what we have by way of a culture is precisely what has resulted from repressing aggression. Since it is not first-strike violence but revenge violence which we must repress, we have maintained elaborate myths of played-out revenge. Ancient stories of rival brothers such as Cain and Abel or Jacob and Esau, of animal or child slaughter such as Ajax or Medea, of a father sacrificing a son such as Abraham and Isaac, exploit and condemn a very disruptive attribute of violence: vengeance. If unavoidable, however, violence must be done within limits. Dueling, for instance, seems a contradiction to our inhibitions and predispositions about conflict. But for all its attendant masculine puffery about honor, it is an efficient way to renounce not immediate violence, which is forced out into limited action, but prolonged strife, which can threaten indefinitely. In this elaborate male ritual, the participants follow prescribed rules such as choosing proper weapons, minding the mark, and standing ground. The most important function, however, is performed by the seconds whose job is to report that the duel was fought and the danger is now past. The feud is over. Retaliation is unnecessary. Peace is restored. With the rise of the mass media in the late eighteenth century, dueling was subsumed into the cultural mythographies of remembered revenge. The lesson is clear. While from time to time we experiment with real-life revenge, we know that if we were to go too far we would soon disappear from the globe. "Vengeance is mine, saith the Lord" for good reason.

But how did we learn to repress most of this behavior? Since myths come after, not before, the actions they mean to temporize, was there an action so traumatic that we have been reminding ourselves never to allow it to happen again? Freud certainly thought so. Extrapolating from the "primal horde" thesis posited by Darwin and others, he supposed that our actions betray that an early violent disaster really did happen. He hypothesized that at the dawn of history and language, families lived in small tribes and bred incestuously. Incest was accepted because kinship was vague and no violence resulted. In fact, while mothers knew who their sons were, fathers did not know whose daughters were whose, so hording was difficult. As in bands of chimpanzees and gibbons, and even baboons and some gorillas, a strong human male may have taken over the fecund females and refused to allow the other males sexual access to any of them. As the sociobiologists attest, humans will countenance any prohibition sooner than sexual denial. Reproduction is not a right or a duty; it is *the* categorical imperative. The strong male forbade the boy cubs to come close. These women were his; they were "taken," and the boys were driven out. Patriarchy began. Aggression began. The young males were doubtless enraged by this sexual denial and bound together to fight the oppressor, their father. Freud continues the story:

> One day the brothers who had been driven out came together, killed and devoured their father and so made an end of the patriarchal horde. United, they had the courage to do and succeed in doing what would have been impossible for them individually (some cultural advance, perhaps, command over some new weapon, had given them a sense of superior strength). Cannibal savages as they were, it goes without saying that they devoured their victim as well as killing him. The violent primal father had doubtless been the feared and envied model of the company of brothers; and in the act of devouring him they accomplished their act of identification with him, and each of them acquired a portion of his strength. The totem meal, which is perhaps mankind's earliest festival, would thus be a repetition and a commemoration of this memorable and criminal deed, which was the beginning of so many things—of social organization, of moral restrictions and of religion. (*Totem and Taboo*, pp. 141–42)

It is important to stress (as Freud really didn't, if only because he could not have realized how he would be misread) that the boys did not want to copulate *only* with their mothers or their sisters, even if they could have known who they were. They simply wanted to copulate, to act on the demands of their sexuality. But once the act was done, once they had destroyed, literally consumed, the father-oppressor and then had satisfied their sexual desire, they were intelligent enough to realize that they were now fated to assume his role and would now have to do battle among themselves as well as against a new generation of young-sters. And so over generations of inter- and intrafamilial turmoil, a so-cial contract, the first cultural bargain, was struck: Certain universally recognizable women were "put aside," made off-limits to the males of the family. They were tabooed. They were tabooed not because they were objects of stronger desire but because relationships with *these* women would rend the fabric of the only society known, the clan. Here violence would begin, violence which has retribution as its overhanging threat. If there was an original sin in human culture, here it was.

Successive generations felt the guilt of the patricide and, to a lesser degree, of the incest, and fearful for their own survival, they saw to it that their young learned the rules before it was too late for all of them. Violence must be contained at all costs. Freud's story continues:

> The tumultuous mob of brothers were filled with the same contra-dictory feelings which we can see at work in the ambivalent father-complexes of our children and of our neurotic patients. They hated their father, who presented such a formidable obstacle to their crav-ing for power and their sexual desires; but they loved and admired him too. After they had got rid of him, had satisfied their hatred and had put into effect their wish to identify themselves with him, the affection which had all this time been pushed under was bound to make itself felt. It did so in the form of remorse. A sense of guilt made its appearance, which in this instance coincided with the re-morse felt by the whole group. The dead father became stronger than the living one had been—for events took the course we so often see them follow in human affairs to this day. What had up to then been prevented by his actual existence was thence forward pro-hibited by the sons themselves, in accordance with the psychological procedure so familiar to us in psychoanalysis under the name of "deferred obedience." They revoked their deed by forbidding the killing of the totem, the substitute for their father, and they re-nounced its fruits by resigning their claim to the women who had now been set free. (*Totem and Taboo*, p. 143)

From this first communal renunciation came the sublimation of psychic energy that has, in a sense, separated us from animals and given us what they lack: religion, art, culture, taboos on incest, history, politics, neu-roses, and fables of aggression.

Freud did not really believe that the primal horde "scenario" had to take place; it did not have to, but we act as if it did. The "omnipotence of thoughts," our imaginations, our dream lives, can produce effects every bit as real as any "reality." And these "thoughts," as Freud found—and modern anthropologists and psychologists have at least concurred with him in this instance—are especially accessible in the fantasy life of neurotics, children, and "savages." Often individuals in these groups even believe the scenario to be true, while the rest of us simply act *as if* it happened. We act as if certain females really are forbidden. We act as if the fate of Oedipus would be ours if the taboo were violated. We act as if retaliatory violence would result. Adults make sure the information is not lost on the next generation, even if it means, as it often does, that they are frightened, sometimes horrified, by the mere contemplation of this forbidden act and its violent eruption of familial chaos.

The "universal horror of incest," as Freud called it, is therefore a way of deflecting the anxiety of sexual ambivalence, just as the universal fear of violent retribution causes us to temper aggression. Just as we may be curious in childhood about sex with a parent or sibling, so in adolescence we may be curious about acts of physical violence, but we unconsciously recall the hopeless tangle of patricide and cannibalism and suppress the desire. Freud had read his Victorian anthropology. We had overthrown the king and we had better make sure our fate was not his. So we "celebrate" the grisly act by repeating the scenes through totems and myths, as if to confess our own hostile desires while repressing those of our children. This celebration eventually becomes one of the central events in the rites of passage through latency, for the young must be led across the minefield of sexuality and violence not only for their own sakes, but for ours as well. They must be taught not just "when" but especially "with whom" to have sex, or they will be violent and send us all back into the bush. The town is better than the jungle; linen sheets are better than leaves. So conscience was born; so culture began.

Among the many qualifications René Girard adds to the primal horde thesis, the most important is his feeling that violence need not be directed solely against the father. Rather, this aggression can be directed against any competitor for any object of desire. Desire is only possible once it has been created by competition. Still, the human response to the trauma of the primal horde is clear. As Girard and his American colleagues, Walter Burkert and Jonathan Smith, explain in *Violent Origins: On Ritual Killing and Cultural Formation,* such profound destabilization must never happen again. We have developed rites and rituals to deflect these ultimately self-destructive impulses. We call those rites and rituals "culture." When we think they are a little vulgar, we call them "popular culture." We claim they are forgettable, yet each generation remembers them.

In the West, prior to the rise of mass media, the mechanisms to deflect or contain retributive violence were two-fold and interlinked: a judicial system and a religious system. These were not fail-safe institutions, as history proves, but they channeled retributive violence away from the immediate into the symbolic. Since they could not suppress vengeance—which is almost instinctive—they recontextualized it. The judicial system still prohibits us from literally "taking the law into our own hands," while the religious has a divine surrogate to do the job. The judicial system publicizes revenge, making it an open display rather than a private matter, and the Christian religion posits an afterlife which promises to set earthly matters right. In addition, as we have seen, in Christianity we are provided with the scapegoat of God himself as a man who suffers for our sins, suffers by self-sacrifice, and redeems us through eucharistic transformation. Girard summarizes his general thesis:

> I have regarded violence as something eminently communicable. The tendency of violence to hurl itself on a surrogate if deprived of its original object can surely be described as a contaminating process. Violence too long held in check will overflow its bounds—and woe to those who happen to be nearby. Ritual precautions are intended both to prevent this flooding and to offer protection, insofar as it is possible, to those who find themselves in the path of ritual impurity—that is, caught in the floodtide of violence.
>
> The slightest outbreak of violence can bring about a catastrophic escalation. Though we may tend to lose sight of this fact in our own daily lives, we are intellectually aware of its validity, and are often reminded that there is something infectious about the spectacle of violence. Indeed, at times it is impossible to stay immune from the infection. Where violence is concerned, intolerance can prove as fatal an attitude as tolerance, for when it breaks out it can happen that those who oppose its progress do more to assure its triumph than those who endorse it. There is no universal rule for quelling violence, no principle of guaranteed effectiveness. At times all the remedies, harsh as well as gentle, seem efficacious; at other times, every measure seems to heighten the fever it is striving to abate. (*Violence and the Sacred*, pp. 30–31)

The elaborate rituals of judicial and religious systems drain off retributive violence, trick it into spending itself on surrogate forms. However, the law *is* violence, religion *is* violence; the gun is just not pointed at our heads, at least not so that we can see it. These scapegoat systems depend both on our eagerness to avoid violence in real forms and on our eagerness not to examine too closely what violent pantomimes really do. We trick ourselves into being tricked by these systems because the reward of security is so important. Girard uses the Greek term *pharmakon* to describe the paradoxical combination of both poison and antidote. The sacrifice, the act of original violence, is redirected from immediate object to secondary object as an act of self- and societal preservation. It short-circuits the destructive process via ritual, via masque, via charade. In so doing, the ritual does what is to be avoided—it enacts violence, a pantomime violence. In Girard's metaphor, just as a booster shot inoculates against disease by introducing enough poison in amounts necessary to stimulate the immune system, so ritualized violence both plays out the trauma and protects against it.

I stress this point now, not only because it is central to Girard's thesis, but also because I will argue that the rise of entertainment violence in popular culture has co-opted much of the force of religion and jurisprudence. Mass media carry much the same ritualized content throughout culture. Perhaps ironically, as the mythic powers of religion and law have been disappearing, we have returned to one of the pre-Gutenberg purposes of popular culture—the communication of taboo.

Like *pharmakon*, "taboo" also carries mixed messages. On one hand, "taboo" refers to the sacred, and on the other hand, to the profane. To "taboo" an act is to delineate the desired and forbidden. What we will see in the rituals of preposterous violence are elaborate sequences—very often self-contained myths—which allow us to violate a taboo in fiction, most obviously the taboos on the expression of aggression, in order to experience second hand an action denied in actuality. For instance, the myths of the vampire, the Frankenstein monster, and Dr. Jekyll and Mr. Hyde allow the "monstrous double" to get loose and play out forbidden action. So too have we a ragtag population of liminal characters, from the *Grand Guignol*, professional wrestling, *Punch and Judy*, and *The A-Team*, who, by virtue of being neither inside nor entirely outside our social context, behave as projected players in an ancient script of reciprocal violence. They are literal and figurative cartoons of human adolescence. In a sense they are the cultural dream protecting us from the biological nightmare.

In arguing that popular culture does the work of the judicial system and organized religion by providing a cohesive system for mythologizing aggression, I realize I am dangerously close to arguing for its cathartic value. In no way do I wish to suggest any Aristotelian sense of catharsis in which the audience is purged of passions. Preposterous violence is not made up of tragic or purgative rituals and these rituals do not arouse pity or terror, nor do they cleanse. They excite, incite, becalm, delay, and defuse aggression. It is worth noting that prior to Aristotle, *katharma* was synonymous with *pharmakon* in signifying at once poison and remedy. Perhaps because of the influence of Aristotelian views of tragedy, one should substitute "pharmakopic" for "cathartic" in discussing preposterous violence. I stress this now because one of the more popular social science approaches to rituals of preposterous violence, carried to extremes by Dr. Fredric Wertham in his crusade against comics in the 1950s, is to argue that watching violence makes us more prone to violence. Possibly, for some consumers, this is true in the very short run, but it inhibits the desire for violence in the majority over time. As Girard states, and as I hope to demonstrate by anatomizing some specific examples, the role of violent theater, cinema, pantomime, television, musical events, and a host of such circuses is not finally escape, but return, a return to our "natural" selves, a safe return to levels of contained aggression.

Hence, these rituals are part of an "education"—in the literal sense of the word—a leading-out of adolescence, and also part of our induction into reproductive sexuality. That they should appear just before procreation rituals; that they should stress repetition; that they should seem indestructible; that they should be scorned by the mature yet avidly consumed by the young, especially young males, are matters that attest to their deep resonance, their durable attraction, and quite possibly their social necessity.

2

The Imaging of Violence
in Early Modern Popular Culture

Every people loves its own form of violence.
CLIFFORD GEERTZ quoting Balinese proverb
"Feathers, Blood, Crowds, and Money"

In the late 1730s in a printing shop outside Paris, a handful of young apprentices, for no apparent reason, slaughtered all the neighborhood cats. In fits of laughter they gleefully bashed the heads of cats, snapped the spines of cats, squashed the bodies of cats, twisted cats at the mid-section, and suffocated cats. They even improvised a gallows and hung cats by the neck. They were soon joined in their revelry by the older journeymen printers. The men and boys then gathered the dead and half-dead cats in bags and dumped them in the courtyard, improvised a mock trial, posthumously condemning them to death, and then administered last rites.

When the wife of the print-shop owner returned home to find that her favorite cat, which she had named La Grise, had had its spine crushed with an iron bar, she was hysterical. And when her husband found out what the boys had done, he was aghast. But when he confronted the boys, they pleaded innocent, especially with regard to La Grise. After the master and his wife retired, the lads again dissolved into gales of laughter.[1]

The young men—there were never female apprentices in the printing trades—continued to think that the slaughter of cats was so humorous that they pantomimed the entire event for months to come. More than twenty times they reenacted the roles of their triumph. They would pick one from their number to play the cat—the dupe—as they repeated their heroic roles as cat killers. The butt of this joke was called, in a provocative linguistic transformation, the "goat," and the game, "prendre la chèvre" (get the goat), was an unconscious reenactment of one of the most ancient rituals of our species. Find a victim, especially a victim who cannot retaliate, and vent aggression on him or her. The scapegoat, reformatted in this case into a scapecat, receives the literal brutality, which is then channeled into surrogate forms. The youthful horde is now able to recreate via "entertainment" a most serious crisis and overcome it.

Why should cats have become goats? Couldn't the apprentices have found more suitable sacrificial victims? And what was the serious crisis? Why should these boys in the eighteenth century have been so distraught as to kill house cats? Why were the reenactments so humorous that they were repeated so often? Why were the apprentices not punished? Their behavior was certainly not something *we* would imitate. Robert Darnton, the historian/anthropologist, attempts a political and economic explanation in *The Great Cat Massacre and Other Episodes in French Cultural History*. Essentially, he argues, the apprentices were caught in a frustrating dilemma to which they had no easy response. They lived in the printing house; they had no rights, no credit, no job security. They could be treated arbitrarily and thus often acted as they were treated. The bourgeois master ran the shop with the meager support and sympathies of the medieval seignior. Nascent capitalism was in many ways far more distressing than the factory system of the nineteenth century. Instead of the mellow preindustrial shop remembered by Victorian historians, this workplace was closer to a madhouse. Each man knew his job, and, although the jobs were divided, there was no sense of purpose. Young males lived together, worked together, played together. But for what? For the master and the mistress? But they were not a family. For pride? But this was piece work. For money? But there was little. For what then?

They didn't know. No one knew. There were no mythologies of work—no work ethic. What the workers did know was that from time to time they felt frustrated, and in these times they would be mischievous, even violent. These explosive potentials are obvious enough to anyone who observes boys at work when the work turns dull, when they seemingly lose concentration and they gang up on some victim. But why should cats be the object of their united attentions and then the subject of their recreative pantomimes? Clearly, eighteenth-century cats were not twentieth-century cats.

With the rise of the bourgeoisie, the domestication of animals continued out of the barnyard into the house. Animals, which had had outside jobs herding flocks or cattle or catching mice, were allowed inside to become pets. The apprentices, barely a generation away from living off the land, must have been perplexed by this new social hierarchy, this new rung in the chain of being. As the cats were rising in status, the boys were at greater risk of losing theirs. That the mistress had a favorite cat, a cat which she named and tended while the boys were nameless and untended, is important, because La Grise will be singled out for special slaughter. As Darnton points out, the boys certainly had every reason to feel jealousy, even hostility, toward animals living under the same roof who were tended and fed better than they. So when they turned their wrath on La Grise, they were doing something we can understand, perhaps even sympathize with, or at least something we can acknowledge that "other people" could do. Had they killed only this cat, a socioeconomic explanation might suffice. But they killed *all* the neighborhood cats. They captured, tortured, killed, bagged, and then piled up the surrounding cats who had not given offense.

To understand why these unoffending cats were susceptible to such treatment, we need to remember that cats have only recently come into their protected status. In the term made popular by Clifford Geertz, Darnton, and the New Historians, the "mentalité" of these French boys was based on assumptions no longer extant in Western culture. Cats are no longer goats. In fact, as any trip down the food aisle at the local supermarket or the pet store will prove, cats have become family members. The days of torturing cats by pulling their legs apart while burying a straw mannequin representive of King Carnival at the end of Lent, as was the custom in Burgundy, or of stuffing cats into an effigy of the pope and then burning it to provide sound effects, as was the custom on Guy Fawkes Day in London, are now not only over, not just forgotten, but are almost inconceivable. Morris the cat is a pet. We cannot easily imagine that whenever there was a bonfire celebration, as on the day of St. John the Baptist (June 24), Morris was especially susceptible to bagging, suspension, and incineration as a matter of course.[2]

Could the transformation from purr to squeal have been so appealing that cats could be sacrificed for shrieks only? Cats must mimic more than the sounds of human agony. Like other animals in other cultures, cats have a rather particular attraction/revulsion for young males—an experience that is similar to how we linguistically respond to female dogs. The insult is "son of a bitch" not son of a cow—the veiled insult with cat is "pussy."[3] For the French, the semiotics of the word for cat— "le chat," "la chatte," and "le minet"—yield a similar concatenation. The difficult, exasperating, contentious, frustrating, yet indomitable cat becomes an object of scornful, sexual reverence. If so, the particular treatment of the mistress's pet cat, La Grise, becomes clear. While much of the young men's aggression is no doubt economic and political, part is surely sexual. Their aggressive action concentrates on the off-limits woman, the master's wife—for the Freudian: the surrogate mother. In killing the cat, in a sense, they have cuckolded the father. Since cuckolding is exactly the kind of human action that calls forth revenge, they had better make sure there can be no retaliation. Thus they choose a victim which will not call forth vengeance. A cat will suffice; so, in fact, will all cats.

Their response now is not so difficult to understand. The cat is, to paraphrase Claude Lévi-Strauss's famous dictum, an animal not to eat, nor just an animal to profane in language like the female dog, but rather an animal to sacrifice. Remember that after the master returns and sees what the apprentices have done to the cats, he turns on his heel and leaves in a huff. The boys fall into fits of laughter. As one young eyewitness, Nicolas Contat, in retrospective third-person narration, recalls:

> Madame to Monsieur: "These wicked men can't kill the masters, so they have killed my pussy. . . . " It seems to her that all the workers' blood would not be sufficient to redeem the insult. The poor grise, a pussy without a peer!
>
> Monsieur and Madame retire, leaving the workers in liberty. The printers delight in the disorder; they are beside themselves with joy.
>
> What a splendid subject for their laughter, for a *belle copie*! They will amuse themselves with it for a long time. Léveillé will take the leading role and will stage the play at least twenty times. He will mime the master, the mistress, the whole house, heaping ridicule on them all. He will spare nothing in his satire. Among printers, those who excel in this entertainment are called *jobeurs*; they provide *joberie*. (as quoted in Darnton, p. 104)

While we may understand that their violence was "a splendid subject for laughter," the subsequent transposition into ritual is harder to comprehend. One of the original conspirators, Léveillé, now takes to ceremonializing the event. He mimics the action; in printer's jargon he "prints" a "copie." Little does he realize that what he is doing is following an ancient pattern. In much the same way that schoolboys mindlessly reenact a prank by picking on one of their own, usually a weakling, to perform the part of the victim, so these apprentices find a victim to play the part of the goat, the butt, the cat, the pussy. Léveillé is also foreshadowing the future. He contains it in a medium. Essentially, the boys do to the event what printing does to ideas: They fix it, memorialize it. Then they repeat it. During those encores the apprentices and journeymen printers beat their mallets, run the composing sticks across the tops of type cases, shake the presses, and generally make the instruments of their boredom into the instruments of their entertainment. This violent whimsy, however, has an etiology deep in human experience. Recall the Assyrian tablets. Again and again the lion is let loose and again and again the lion is killed.

The young men did not perform this travesty once or twice; they staged the play some twenty times. For workers who were in the business of creating repeatable images and sequences, they pantomimed the very process they felt anxious about. They even coded the entertainment so that it could be efficiently recalled: "Among printers, those who excel in this entertainment are called *jobeurs*; they provide *joberie*." As Darnton explains, the violent massacre became a "copie," the "copie" became a "joberie"—the path from act to re-act to ritual. The boys were creating a folklore that illustrated with unconscious concision what combusts when a group of adolescent males, sealed off from women, are forced to live closely together.

One might ask why the master, or the older printers, not only allowed the act to go unpunished but endured the disruption of the subsequent mockeries. True, they could not intercede to stop the killing, but certainly they could stop the mythic resurrections. One might as well ask why we don't make a concerted effort to censor once and for all action comics, stalk-and-slash movies, violent television, heavy metal music, and the like. The answer is as obvious as Poe's purloined letter. While we say that images of violence are distasteful, we act otherwise. While we claim to be offended, many of us are not. We are drawn to these images. While we claim they are the pandering scenarios of the smarmy culture industry, at some point we may acknowledge their attraction. And while we contend that adolescents must be controlled, in a way we wish them to run wild—at least temporarily.

The apprentices were clearly in an unstable social situation. The word "apprentice" and its social history describe our continuing perplexity. These boys were "bound by law" in order to "apprehend" a trade. But why was indentureship necessary? Wouldn't they volunteer to learn a valuable trade? The apprentices were trapped in a liminal zone of labor without reward and of social status without place. And in general, since all male adolescents represent both a danger and a reward, they are held in a social limbo. As Arnold Van Gennep first theorized, successful societies have developed special worlds in which young men can imitate, subvert, or escape the world of their elders. In the premodern age, these rituals were connected to guilds, to the Masons, to any number of paramilitary, parareligious secret organizations to serve the needs of both the cadets and their elders. We have not lost our need for temporary separation. In our modern world this period of incubation is usually connected to schools, and the most obvious ritual is that of the fraternity system. We tolerate all manner of excessive behavior, much of it unlawful, much of it violent, in the hope that our nonindentured but captive apprentices will "sow their wild oats" and be able to enter society quietly and productively. We accept, and occasionally encourage, a kind of saturnalia reminiscent of the cat massacre, complete with high jinks and pranks. Much of this behavior has been ritualized around the violent sport of football (team rivalries, bowl games, Homecoming). Still, we also have a distinct mark, a line in the sand beyond which we say "no more." After four years of exemption, in the spring we have a commencement, a matriculation out of adolescence and back into society.

Although anthropologists often travel into the farthest reaches of Africa or Australia or to a distant South Sea island to seek out such rituals of maturation, they could stay right at home and see that similar rites of passage are often still tied up, as they were in the eighteenth century, with the enactment of mimic aggression. Obviously, the interests of actors and witnesses must be served. Players and audience cannot be separated. Watching constitutes a bond; seeing becomes an oath. Predictably, such a spectacle is the most necessary when the possibilities for real trauma are the most possible. J. S. La Fontaine's *Initiation: Ritual Drama and Secret Knowledge Across the World* amplifies initiation rituals which, while seeming to promise freedom from restraint, are in truth signs of submission. Something must be given up and usually this is the sacrifice of individual aggression. As in the case of the cat massacre, authority is not overthrown, but accepted. The boys return to their machines.

Adolescent rituals of aggression are always spectacles, whether conducted by the Masons, the Hopis, the Romans, or by the football coach. They are intended to be watched many times over, be it twenty times or two hundred. Margaret Mead once complained in "Ritual and Social Crisis" that "the American attitude toward ritual differs rather sharply from the attitudes toward ritual in the rest of the world. Americans have come to think that doing anything twice has no value. I would hazard that this attitude has been influenced especially by television. The television audience expects and demands that everything be new and different" (p. 97). But she is mistaken. The opposite is true. On the other hand, Robert Bocock overstates the case in *Ritual in Industrial Society* by contending that such matters as "handshaking, teeth cleaning, taking medicines, car riding, eating, entertaining guests, drinking tea, or coffee, beer, sherry, whisky, etc., taking a dog for a walk, visiting relatives, routines at work, singing at work, children's street games, hunting . . ." are the stuff of modern rituals. At least Bocock realizes that no society can exist without a safety net of rituals. Critics may claim that repetition in mass media is not ritual but is instead mindless dreck. And for them it is. But for the young such diversions are often socializing rituals. These rituals form the road map, so to speak, by which we find our way through otherwise bewildering passageways. While we may not know where such maps come from, we do know that when we are lost we need them desperately and seek them out.

As in the case of the printer's apprentices, ritual quickly generates an implicit text which serves a deeper social purpose. In this case the killing of the cats soon developed a subtext—the control of aggression through sacrificial scapegoats.[4] The blinding of Gloucester in *King Lear*, the burning of Diaphanta in *The Changeling*, the impaled heart in *'Tis Pity She's a Whore*, the savage meal in *Titus Andronicus*, the tongue biting in *The Spanish Tragedy*, the red hot poker in *Edward II*, to say nothing of the seeming omnipresence of bloody daggers, burning body parts, and banquets of cannibalism, are all theatrical, not mythic, conventions. The author struggles for variety, not similarity. He wants to present something new. The images shock, they do not inform; they raise the neck hair, not the consciousness. They cannot be repeated very often because the author depends on the unexpected. These are stage pictures, metaphysical conceits, to be pushed aside by the plot. But in the rituals of preposterous violence, just the opposite is encountered. We can predict how the monster is going to act with the sacrificial victim. Teenagers would all agree about the habits of the vampire, the Frankenstein monster, and the werewolf. These images and texts remain redundant and stable. Only the audience changes as the young grow into and out of the ritual. To find more of this kind of violence, we need to turn from the factory to the field—literally *in* the field. For it was in the field that the ancient rituals of the cave were enacted before being transferred to the electronic caves of the movie house and livingroom. While the aristocratic males took to the field to choreograph the rituals of chivalry, the proletariat boys took to the field to enact their violent routines not against well-protected humans but against domestic animals.

The English traditionally believed that the most shocking cruelties to animals were practiced by their continental neighbors. Had they known about the French apprentices, they might have tsk-tsked knowingly. Catholicism allowed the French and Spanish to behave abominably to soulless animals. Protestantism tempered such excess to some degree. The common northern European response to Mediterranean animal/man ritual is seen in the English condemnation of the bullfight. The adventurous young Englishman on the Grand Tour of Europe usually attended one *corrida* and then became outraged at the carnival of slaughter. As the empathetic William Beckford dutifully wrote in his journal: "I was highly disgusted with the spectacle. It set my nerves on edge and I seemed to feel cuts and slashes the rest of the evening" (p. 127).

Still, although the English typically were disgusted by the pageantry of the bullfight ("a damnable sport," to poet laureate Robert Southey), they were not repelled by the spectacle of torturing a bull. The nineteenth-century English seemed more upset that the crowd was so unruly and that the ceremony was so religious than that an animal was suffering to death. Over generations the Spanish and Portuguese mythologized the combat between matador and bull into a heroic metonym of human and animal, God and man, in which destiny was determined. Here was a fixed contest complete with a panoply of lesser encounters between bull and banderilleros, bull and picador. By the eighteenth century, the bull-fight had achieved a ritualized three-act form in which the bull was introduced, tested, and finally brought face to face with death. Variations were scorned. Admittedly, the predictable conclusion was not without risk, for the *coup de grâce* could work both ways. Although the end was preordained, the combatants, like their gladiatorial predecessors, were continually in danger, albeit not as much as their victims.

Had the fastidious William Beckford stayed at home, he could have witnessed his own national brand of blood ritual. For the insular English had adapted their own celebratory violence, making do with their rather limited stock of animal victims. Young Englishmen preferred watching battles between bull and dogs, rather than between bull and man. Human beings were not involved. Such bull-baiting was a northern European transformation of an ancient spectacle of tauricide which was itself almost a cave wall come alive. Although the English thought the French notoriously cruel to animals, the French had their own opinions about the English at the end of the seventeenth century:

> They tie a Rope to the Root of the Horns of the Ox or Bull, and fasten the other End of the Cord to an Iron Ring fix'd to a stake driven into the Ground; so that this Cord, being about 15 Foot long, the Bull is confin'd to a Sphere of about 30 Foot Diameter. Several Butchers, or other Gentlemen, that are desirous to exercise their Dogs, stand round about, each holding his own by the Ears; and when the Sport begins, they let loose one of the Dogs: The Dog runs at the Bull; the Bull, immoveable, looks down upon the Dog with an Eye of Scorn, and only turns a Horn to him to hinder him from coming near: The Dog is not daunted at this, he runs round him, and tries to get beneath his Belly, in order to seize him by the Muzzle, or the Dewlap, or the pendant Glands . . . The Bull then puts himself into a Posture of Defense; he beats the Ground with his Feet, which he joins together as close as possible, and his chief Aim is not to gore the Dog with the Point of his Horn, but to slide one of them under the Dog's Belly, (who creeps close to the Ground to hinder it) and to throw him so high in the Air that he may break his neck in the Fall. This often happens: When the Dog thinks he is sure of fixing his Teeth, a turn of the Horn, which seems to be done with all the Negligence in the World, gives him a Sprawl thirty Foot high, and puts him in Danger of a damnable Squelch when he comes down. This Danger would be unavoidable, if the Dog's Friends

Bull—baiting, c. 1800 (from *Country Life*, November 14, 1941)

were not ready beneath him, some with their backs to give him a
soft Reception, and others with long Poles, which they offer him
slant-ways, to the Intent that, sliding down them, it may break the
Force of his Fall. Notwithstanding all this Care, a Toss generally
makes him sing to a very scurvy Tune, and draw his Phiz into a
pitiful Grimace: But unless his is totally stunn'd with the Fall, he is
sure to crawl again towards the Bull, with his old antipathy, come
on't what will. Sometimes a second Frisk into the Air disables him
for ever from playing his old Tricks: But sometimes too he fastens
upon his Enemy, and when once he has seiz'd him with his Eye-
teeth, he sticks to him like a Leech, and would sooner die than leave
his Hold. Then the Bull bellows, and bounds, and kicks about to
shake off the Dog; by his Leaping the Dog seems to be no Manner
of Weight to him tho' in all Appearance he puts him to great Pain.
In the End, either the Dog tears out the Piece he has laid Hold on,
and falls, or else remains fix'd to him, with an Obstinacy that would
never end, if they did not pull him off. (Misson, pp. 24–27)

Bull-baiting was not spontaneous happenstance but a well-planned
community affair. Usually the ritual was staged as a diversion after a
wake or an election or as part of a major holiday. Since the bull was a
major expense which could not be defrayed by the proceeds from paying
spectators, as at the Iberian bullfights, the baiting depended on the largess of a charitable landowner. Unlike their Teutonic counterparts who
took bull- and bear-baiting seriously enough to sink amphitheaters into

the ground in which to stage the fights for paying customers, the English relied on iron rings fixed into the roadways of a publican's yard. Since the English had no indigenous bear population, bear-baiting was almost nonexistent. Bears were imported, however, as were tigers, but the bull was the primary participant. Badger-baiting was never popular among young men for its object was not to watch the wearing away of the bull's superiority but to wager on how many times the badger could be drawn from its "box" to attack the dog.

The baiting of various types of animals was, of course, considered a test of the dog and not a spectacle of unnecessary violence. By the early nineteenth century bull-and-terrier dogfights were regularly held in the Westminster Pit where upwards of three hundred spectators paid two shillings to watch and wager. Various types of English bulldog were bred only for this combat and were often exported abroad.[5] As Ronald Paulson has noted in his essay "The English Dog," the eighteenth century marked the split in popular treatment of man's best friend. The spaniel, often a woman's lapdog, was superseded in popularity by the "man's dogs"—breeds that included the pit bull or the pug whose job was to fight and kill, and the gentleman's hunting dog or the hound whose job was to pursue or retrieve. The English trademark, the bulldog, did not look as he does now but rather as Hogarth portrayed him. That Hogarth used the pit/pug to satirize contemporary personages is a tribute to the rising reputation of this combative canine. By the nineteenth century the bulldog's position as the right-hand friend of John Bull was secure.[6]

The English adoration of the bulldog was understandable, the hostility toward the bull less so. At first glance, the bull symbolizes the opposite of the French cats. He is distant and implacable, yes, but hardly inscrutable. What they both are is sexual, and worse, sexual without humility. A bull is castrated to become an ox; a tomcat is burned or pelted. Additionally, what all these animals—the bulldog, the bull, and the cat—share is a sense of liminality. They are just on the edge of man's place and nature's world. In a sense they mimic the adolescent male's place and as such are both an apt image for the projection of anxiety and a medium for the transmission of violent ritual.

A similar pairing of adolescent audience and animal victim occurred in that other diversion in which the bull played the scapegoat: bull-running, which was a minor part of the Spanish *corrida*. In the morning before the *corrida*, the bulls were run from their overnight stockade into their stadium stalls. Young boys often ran before the bulls and showed their machismo, not by standing up to the bulls like the matador but by stampeding before them like steers. Although today this part of the Spanish ceremony has been eliminated since the bulls can be trucked into the center of town, vestiges still remain in Pamplona where adoles-

William Hogarth, *The Bruiser* Second Stage, 1763 (British Museum). The bear is a likeness of the poet and satirist Charles Churchill; the urinating dog is Hogarth himself.

cent boys (now often Americans fresh from reading Hemingway) still have a chance to act out the rites of literal passage.

Bull-running was also popular in certain English locales, but it evolved differently in keeping with English sensibilities. Adolescent boys played the part of the dogs in bull-baiting. The "running" was an all-day affair in which the object was not to kill the bull by force, which would have been a betrayal of motive, but to have the bull die of exhaustion. The most famous of these affairs was in Stamford, Lincolnshire. On the 13th of November, the town streets were closed off and a bull, ears and tail cut, nose stuffed with pepper, body smeared with soap to make it slippery, was let loose. The enraged animal then charged into the crowd of boys who slapped, baited, stoned, caped, and generally harassed the bull. These participants, called "bullards," might even tuck one of their own into a barrel and have it rolled toward the horn-tossing bull, again vaguely imitating the spectacle of bull-baiting with dogs. After a break for lunch and rest, the bull would be driven out of town to the bridge over the Welland River. He was surrounded, exhausted again by pitching and snorting, and finally thrown over the rail into the water. This was called "brigging" the bull, but it was not a foregone conclusion. Just as an occasional "brave" bull might be spared the matador's sword, so an especially brave bull who was too strong to be brigged might be returned to pasture. If he was brigged, however, and if he reached the shore, he was set upon by dogs who joined the boys. The bull was now mutilated. The dogs were called off, the limping bull led back to town where he was slaughtered. Since the bull was very often a gift from the landowner, the meat was sold cheaply to the poor, a token of aristocratic largess.

Although the bull was the largest of the domestic animals in England to participate in ritualized violence, he was by no means the most popular. That distinction went to the rooster. As in the case of the bull, the sexual symbolism was self-evident. The crudest of the rooster torments was a boy's pastime called "throwing at cocks" or "cock-scaling." A taciturn James Spershott of Chichester describes what this pastime entailed:

> On Shrove Tuesday the most unmanly and cruel exercise of "cock scaling" was in vogue everywhere, even in the High Church "lighten" and many other places in the city and in the country. Scarcely a churchyard was to be found but a number of those poor innocent birds were thus barbarously treated. Tying them by the leg with a string about 4 or 5 feet long fastened to the ground, and, when he is made to stand fair, a great ignorant merciless fellow, at a distance agreed upon and at two pence three throws, flings a "scail" [stick] at him till he is quite dead. And thus their legs are broken and their bodies bruised in a shocking manner. . . . And wonderful it was that men of character and circumstance should come to this fine sight and readily give their children a cock for this purpose. (p. 14)

Once a boy outgrew "cock-scaling," he was ready for its adult counterpart, the oldest and farthest-reaching spectator sport involving violence to animals—cockfighting. From the twelfth century to the present day, it has proved to be one of the longest-lasting rituals of violence to animals throughout the world. Where "throwing at cocks" had a foregone conclusion, the cockfight is a toss-up and therefore had become a wagering contest The wagering, done furiously around the cockpit, has more than money and blood involved. As Clifford Geertz has shown in "Feathers, Blood, Crowds, and Money," it is an almost universal projection of family and town rivalry. The betting is not on the rooster but on the integrity of the handlers and owners. Thus cockfighting does not have an adolescent male audience but a mature one. Social complexity, not furious action, is the allure. In Welsh cockfights, for instance, thirty-two cocks, sixteen on a side, battle down to the last one along the lines of, say, tennis at Wimbledon. The event is best described by an early eighteenth-century German tourist in England:

> When it is time to start, the persons appointed to do so bring in the cocks hidden in two sacks, and then everyone begins to shout and wager before the birds are in view. The people, gentle and simple (they sit with no distinction of place) act like madmen, and go on raising the odds to twenty guineas and more. As soon as one of the bidders calls "done" . . . the other is pledged to keep his bargain. Then the cocks are taken out of the sacks and fitted with silver spurs.. . . As soon as the cocks appear, the shouting grows even louder and the betting is continued. When they are released, some attack, while others run away . . . [others] are impelled by terror to jump down from the table among the people; they are then, however, driven back on to the table with great yells (in particular by those who have put their money on the lively cocks which chase the others) and are thrust at each other until they get angry. Then it is amazing to see how they peck at each other, and especially how they hack with their spurs. Their combs bleed terribly and they often slit each other's crop and abdomen with the spurs. There is nothing more diverting than when one seems quite exhausted and there are great shouts of triumph and monstrous wagers; and then the cock that appeared to be quite done for suddenly recovers and masters the other. When one of the two is dead, the conqueror invariably begins to crow and jump on the other. . . . Sometimes, when both are exhausted and neither will attack the other again, they are removed and others take their place; in this case the wagers are canceled. But if one of them wins, those who put their money on the losing cock have to pay up immediately, so that an hostler in his apron often wins several guineas from a Lord. If a man has made a bet and is unable to pay, for punishment he is made to sit in a basket fastened to the ceiling, and is drawn up in it amidst peals of laughter. (Uffenbach, pp. 48–49)

Clearly, this was proletarian entertainment, and one catches in Spershott's tone that, as he wrote about cock-scaling in 1780, the tide of sentiment was changing. By the time cockfighting was outlawed in 1840, the British had already contributed a number of variations in keeping with Protestant capitalism. Although most "mains" were aligned so that two teams fought serially, the English enjoyed the "battle royal" in which a large number of cocks were let loose at once and the victor was the last one left standing. As spectator violence, however, the cockfight was certainly not in the same category with other rituals, primarily because of audience composition and sophisticated symbolism. The importance of the transfer of money and social representation makes this more an adult than an adolescent ritual.

In a society based on agriculture, blood sports involving domestic animals, be they dogs, bulls, roosters, or cats, were predictable. But in a society based on mechanical engines, the machine is the victim. After all, we have demolition derbies in which automobiles are destroyed, and car-bashing with a sledgehammer is a staple of fraternity fund-raising. In more agrarian times, such spectator events were tied to the rhythms of farm life. Fairs were usually held between tasks—in late autumn after the crop was harvested or in early spring after planting. Occasionally, the fairs followed such unscheduled events as royal births, coronations, military victories, and the like, which occasioned shows of celebratory violence. It should be noted that together with violence to animals, there were human contests as well. Here symbolic and real violence were mixed. Cudgeling with stick and shield and single-stick combat with one hand tied behind the back were bloody sports indeed. According to a 1753 advertisement, victory was determined by the "breaking of head," which was even defined: "No Head to be deemed broke unless the Blood runs an Inch" (as quoted in Malcolmson, p. 43). This was real violence in which real pain was inflicted on real humans.

Indeed, the audience for these events is the same which excitedly watches professional wrestling, roller derby, *The A-Team*, or the most recent stalk-and-slash movie. Adolescent boys have not changed; the displays they watch have. Pit bull terriers still fight and cocks still battle around the world, but the audience for these wagering events is one which has different interests and some disposable income. These are audiences of older men, and these men do more than watch: They participate by betting. The animals are the cards or dice; they represent a different medium, albeit one still imbued with blood, honor, gore, and pride. What is not so clear is why domestic animal events of all varieties appeared in such profusion between the Restoration and the French Revolution, and then why they were so easily restricted. Perhaps they could only find an audience in times of relative tranquility, but why didn't they appear in such numbers at other quiet times after the eighteenth century?

First, the rise of industrialization changed the seasonal habits of the common worker. Holidays geared to the hiring of field hands or the reaping of crops all but disappeared in a manufacturing environment where all days and all weeks were standardized. There were no saturnalian respites in which to safely vent aggression. Last Monday in the mill is the same as next Thursday. Plough Monday, Guy Fawkes Day, May Day, sheep-shearing days, and the like were not part of the six-day work week. And Sunday was no day for revelry, even during the Enlightenment, but a day of enforced quiet in which contemplation of the preposterous violence of Christianity sufficed. Additionally, the Enclosure Acts and legislation forbidding the blocking of thoroughfares severely restricted what had been the display grounds of such celebrations as bull-baiting. While the rise of the machine age restricted both the time and place for such events, the invention of steam-driven presses and the production of cheaper paper provided a new medium for satisfying the appetite for violence.

Second, a century-old effort to restrict blood sports, which had surfaced in Oliver Cromwell's Protectorate Ordinance of 1654, was revived in the late 1700s by John Wesley and his followers. The Puritan response in 1654 had been complex, based ostensibly on the sorry state of humanity. Why make it worse, was the rationale. The historian Thomas Macaulay cynically suggested that the Puritans disallowed bear-baiting not because of the pain of the combatants but because of the pleasure it accorded the spectators. No matter, the insensitivity of linking violence and pleasure was acknowledged and censured. The resurgence of Wesley's new Puritanism, evangelical Methodism, in the late eighteenth century was far more effective than the Cromwellian reform because it was designed not by the few for the many but by the many for the masses. The consensus was that the world was wicked enough without contributing to the degradation of God's work—especially in public. A turning heavenward meant a turning-away from the pleasures of the earth. Moreover, it also meant turning back to a different medium of preposterous violence—the imagery of the suffering of Christ. Here, for instance, is an evangelical preacher exhorting his flock to turn from the carnival celebration of human wakes, which often involved violence to animals, to the metaphysical sufferings of violence to Christ:

> What spirit, then, can draw you thither to these scenes [animal violence] of frivolity and vice? Is it *there* you can contemplate the mysteries of redeeming love? Is it *there* you would think of CHRIST, His incarnation, agony, and bloody sweat, His cross and passion, His precious death and burial, His glorious resurrection and ascension? Is it *there* you would desire to live? Is it *there* you would wish to die? (As quoted in Kidd, p. 11)

Another reason that evangelical Christianity succeeded where Puritanism failed was that intellectuals were now engaged up close rather than from afar. The Romantic movement, carrying with it an eschatology quite different from that of Methodism, granted privileged status to the images of innocence—in this case the child and the animal. Thanks to Locke and the Empiricists, who informed both religious and secular movements, God's grace in the metaphysical sense now became the concept of blessedness in the human sense. The apotheosis of innocence, whether in human form (the child) or in animal (the dumb beast), was now considered to be an aspect of the divine presence. The earlier idea of the corruptibility of children and the soullessness of animals was turned topsy-turvy. In the Blakean vernacular, children were lambs and lambs were Christlike. No longer were we to have dominion over nature as we were instructed in *Genesis;* we were to harmonize with nature. No longer were we to father the child but rather to follow the child—the father of the man.

One has only to read the works of Blake, Coleridge, Shelley, Clare, or Southey to see the impact of this changing response. The most influential in spreading this new natural gospel was the young William Wordsworth. A quick look at a minor poem like *Hart-leap Well* will show how these two movements coalesced. In this poem, written at the turn of the nineteenth century, Wordsworth specifically analogizes the hunting of a stag to the crucifixion of Christ. The story tells of a duke who, unmindful of everything except his own pleasure in the pain of the hunted, chases a deer (hart) to its death. He then builds a monument on the spot to memorialize, to ritualize, his conquest over wild nature. His friends come to this spot to celebrate his triumph. However, the monument soon crumbles, leaving only a well of impure water and four aspen trees in the shape of a cross. The place becomes, at least to the peasants, cursed by nature. As if to make sure we do not miss the point that the killing of the deer/hart (dear/heart) was symbolic of the crucifixion of Christ, Wordsworth himself concludes by addressing a Christian shepherd:

> *Small difference lies between thy creed [Christianity] and mine:*
> *This Beast not unobserved by Nature fell;*
> *His death was mourned by sympathy divine.*
>
> *The Being that is in the clouds and air,*
> *That is in the green leaves among the groves,*
> *Maintains a deep and reverential care*
> *For the unoffending creatures whom he loves.*
>   . . . .
> *One lesson, Shepherd, let us two divide,*
> *Taught both by what she [nature] shows, and what conceals;*
> *Never to bend our pleasure or our pride*
> *With sorrow of the meanest thing that feels.*
>
> (ll. 161–67, 176–80)

Not all animal violence was susceptible to such an analogy. The Romantics carefully chose which "unoffending creatures" were going to be singled out for the protection of "God's holy plan." The establishment of the Royal Society for the Protection of Animals in 1824 and the Cruelty to Animals Act in 1835 effectively controlled "throwing at cocks" and other such rank displays of lower-class violence to animals. Bull-baiting was harder to control since it depended on aristocratic patronage to supply the animal. But the country squire, caught between the rising middle class, the self-conscious aristocracy, and the anxious masses, had lost his eighteenth-century Augustan independence and was in no position to risk censure. He soon acceded to social pressure. Bull-running was even harder to stifle as the argument about the need to tenderize the meat, as well as to provide for the poor, cloaked the activity in an aura of charity, if not respectability. The argument that brave bulls who refused to be "brigged" were then set free was specious; they had already been thoroughly tortured. In Stamford, the running continued well into the mid-nineteenth century and was only stopped when the RSPA threatened to send a force of special constables to put an end to it once and for all.

Meanwhile, rabbit, fox, and deer hunting continued unabated, exempt from censure and classed as aristocratic pastimes rather than as crude displays of violence against animals. Fox hunting in particular was continued because, once the stag population was depleted, the fox was the only animal left which ran in a straight line and could be pursued on horseback. Hence, the fox became known as a "predator" (rather like calling certain unwanted plants "weeds"). As the fox disappeared, vulpicide was forbidden by moral sanction but not by law. By mid-century, in a bit of aristocratic subterfuge, foxes were bred and raised on the sly in order to be hunted as a "service." E. A. Freeman's 1869 fusillade against the hunt made some difference to the plight of foxes but ultimately could not get the practice outlawed. The King's Bench in 1876 reiterated that foxhunters could not be prosecuted for trespassing—predators must be dealt with even when the predators were raised in captivity and pursued across land they were not infesting. Horse racing was never questioned: "Horses love to run."

If there really was a sea change in sensibilities about animals, as many modern critics like Dix Harwood, Dagobert De Levie, Robert W. Malcolmson, Keith Thomas, and Harriet Ritvo contend, one wonders why it did not reach further. To be sure, the Squire Allworthys no longer supplied the bulls, no longer set their dogs after ducks, no longer threw chickens into their pike-infested ponds, but other cruelties continued unchecked. Indeed, if the aristocratic appetites had not shifted much in less than a generation, why should we believe that the tastes of the common man had fundamentally changed?

To find another reason for the rise and fall of animal violence, we return for a moment to the eighteenth-century printing house in France. The apprentices were figuring importantly, not in the abatement of preposterous violence but in its change of medium. Little did the printer's apprentices know that their labor and their "joberies" were headed in the same direction. They never guessed that the twenty performances of their charade were a ritualizing of the violence to the cats, a ritualizing that was going to be memorialized by the very object and process which caused their anxiety in the first place: mechanical printing. The innovations of eighteenth-century printing would render these other pantomimes of violence into a different and exciting form. Shocks would still be visual, but instead of theatrics on the factory floor, they would be illustrations on paper. As television and the movies retribalized rituals of violence, so did machine-printed illustrations capture the excitement of popular violent entertainment. Printed pictures and printed text transferred the voyeuristic thrills from real to artificial texts. This process of transporting violent images into print, which soon supported the vast industries of the mass media, marked the beginning of the modern world.

We can see the force of shifting media in the career of a painter who became a printer more out of economic need than out of desire. William Hogarth (1697–1764) was the dour Walt Disney of his time; he transformed the illustration much as Disney did the motion picture. In the eighteenth century, relief printing—xylography—was superseded by intaglio engraving, and the efficiencies of mass production allowed a new audience to enter the marketplace with new demands. The centuries-old picture block method, which was both time and labor intensive, was made obsolete by etching an image on a plate (with a burin or with acid), then sliding the plate onto a mechanical press and printing hundreds of exact copies. This "copie" was largely responsible for the end of animal violence. The production of illustrations accelerated the transformation already occurring in the printing process itself. For just as advances in stereography had made typesetting more efficient, just as the steam-driven presses and continuous paper rolls had made printing itself simpler, and just as fast-drying inks made images longer lasting, so now did intaglio imaging make promulgating complete visual scenarios possible and especially profitable—hugely profitable.

Nothing so concentrates an artist's mind as the thought of profit. Andy Warhol was speaking for the modern world when he said wryly, "Who's art? I never heard of him," and "Profit is the finest art." Percy Bysshe Shelley's posturing notwithstanding, great artists are usually as interested in wealth as they are in being "hierophants of an unapprehended inspiration." Christianity notwithstanding, artists are usually concerned with laying up as much treasure in this world as in the next. Hogarth, one of the first modern artists, was no exception. He was the first English-born visual artist to become world-famous *and* wealthy, and he certainly knew why—because of his engravings. Although he always bemoaned his relative failure as a scenic and portrait painter, he realized that his income was assured and augmented not by the brush but by the burin.

Hogarth's genius lay not just in his excellent engravings nor in his fine satiric wit, but rather in his understanding that while individual illustrations could be provocative in themselves, they could be strung together to tell a tale with still more impact. He could draw a novel in pictures just as well as authors could draw it in chapters and an even larger audience would patronize his product. After all, visual literacy far exceeded verbal literacy in his or in any other day. While in an illustration like *Southwark Fair* Hogarth tells a story horizontally in a panorama of entertainments at an urban fair, he tells a vertical story in the eight-part *Rake's Progress*. This "novel" is a flip-card sequence, a proto-movie. Its action, like a novel's, rises to a crescendo at the end, but it travels at the speed of the eye. No words get in the way. The levels of gratification are quickly reached, yet the experience can be replayed in slow motion to deepen the effect. So popular was Hogarth's vision, and so successful his enterprise, that he soon employed studio engravers to fill in the gaps while he provided the story line. Like Disney, Hogarth made the cartoon into a mass-produced art form. His success was not without problems, however. His illustrations were forged and bootlegged to such a degree that Hogarth lobbied for the first antipirating legislation to protect his unique illustrations. In fact, the "Hogarth Act," which grants certain rights to the original artist, is still in effect and is the generating legislation of modern copyright law.

Hogarth knew very well what his fellow city dwellers wanted to see. They wanted those scenes of exaggerated violence. They wanted to see things move and collide. That we still appreciate Hogarth's images, even if they don't move at twenty-four frames a second, is a tribute both to his vision and to the fact that these desires run deep in the human psyche. *Gin Lane*, for instance, ostensibly protests the evils of gin, but its focus is on the unrestrained and unmitigated violence. The man and dog fighting for the bone, the collapsing house, the gin being forced into the mouths of innocents, the fighting beggars, the man in background center carrying an impaled child, the burial of the naked woman, the hanged man in the upper right—these images are as literally shocking today as they were in the late eighteenth century. They stimulate the movement of the eye and force us to seek order. We see concussions we can't ignore, although we may claim we want to look elsewhere. This is a new vision of city life, a modern view, a violent view. The scene has moved from the countryside into the city. It is a vision we will see again

William Hogarth, *Gin Lane*, 1751 (British Museum)

from Goya's Madrid to Crane's New York, from Dickens's London to Hugo's Paris. But most of all, of course, we cannot move our eyes past the look on that toppling baby's face—the look of complete helplessness. Yet we cannot look too long. We could have seen that on the cave wall. That wide-eyed, open-mouthed look is on the face of every sacrificial victim in every gothic novel and every horror film.

A far more arresting and certainly less explicable sequence of preposterous violence can be seen in Hogarth's *The Four Stages of Cruelty* (1751). The images here "read" almost like a storyboard for an action film: low on narrative complexity and high on iconic manipulation. Hogarth certainly intended them to shock, and in a manuscript gloss (#49 in the British Museum) he mentions his radical "in Terrorem" technique that he claims will affect "even the most strong heart."

This is the visual story: It is the ur-text of preposterous violence, the pre-electronic cartoon, the *EC* comic as art. In *The First Stage of Cru-*

FIRST STAGE OF CRUELTY.

William Hogarth, *The First Stage of Cruelty*, 1751 (British Museum)

elty, we are introduced to Tom Nero, a nascent street molester who will develop from urchinry to the psycho-killer we can still see in such stalk-and-slash movies as *Friday the 13th, Last House on the Left, When a Stranger Calls, Don't Go in the House, He Knows You're Alone, Silent Scream*, and so on into the night. Before Tom has the opportunity to brutalize women, he has a chance to practice pastoral techniques in the city streets.

Tom starts in eighteenth-century fashion by inflicting pain on animals for the sake of entertainment. In *The First Stage*, he is assisted by childhood chums in his attempts to stick an arrow into a dog's anus. Some of his cohorts are poking out the eyes of a bird, or throwing a winged cat out of a window, or hanging cats à la their French counterparts, or playing "throwing at cocks." One especially nasty act is occurring in the lower right as a chum is tying a bone to a dog's tail, a tail soon to be torn off by other street dogs. Ironically, the dog is licking the hand of his tormentor. Meanwhile, Tom is doing nothing to repress his own

William Hogarth, *The Second Stage of Cruelty*, 1751 (British Museum)

bestiality—or is it his "humanness"? Not only is he being abominable, he is also spurning the bribe proffered by the young gentleman in the frock coat. As we learn in the caption below the picture, Tom is being offered a candy, a tart, if he will just stop.

> *Behold! a Youth of gentler Heart,*
>   *To spare the Creature's pain*
> *O take, he cries—take all my Tart,*
>   *But Tears and Tart are vain.*

Tom won't stop, of course, and the young artist at Tom's left knows what the future holds in store.

Before that future hanging is realized, however, Tom has an apprenticeship to serve which would make his French colleagues blanch. In *The Second Stage of Cruelty*, the second reel, so to speak, we see Tom beating an animal, this time a collapsed horse, and this act is duplicated by a peasant bludgeoning a sheep. The caption queries,

Inhuman Wretch! say whence proceeds
   This coward Cruelty?
What Int'rest springs from barb'rous deeds?
   What Joy from Misery?

And as in the artificial violence to follow in the nineteenth century, we
are not going to be given an answer—at least not within the work. To
do so would give the acts an explanation and resolve our anxieties. This
is gothic violence, entertainment violence, gratuitous violence. One might
as well ask why we so delight in watching action/adventure movies.
Such acts of sadism simply *are*, and this is what makes them so sym-
bolically uncontrollable. Sooner ask why Christ was crucified, or why
we should have concentrated on the macabre iconography of this act.
Tom's story provides additional clues.

In *The Second Stage*, it becomes clear that Tom and the peasant are
not alone. The pompous barristers who have overloaded the coach are
implicated as much as the drowsing drayman who is just now running
over a child holding a hoop. Once again we encounter the requisite "good
man" (noting the acts in his account book; presumably he will report
them) who is as impotent as the frock-coated young gentleman we saw
earlier with the candy. The good man is important in rituals of gothic
violence for, like us, he is the helpless observer. He is the audience. This
supernumerary on the stage does what we imagine we would do: He
tries to stop the violence, he tries to control the maniac, the psycho, by
reporting him to the authorities. But in a sense he, too, is trying to
remove himself from the scene, to buy off violence with words, to gain
distance, yet to continue *looking*. In a sense, we see both the social
drama and the psychodrama of violence here played out in front of us.
How can the superego (the note taker) succeed when the ego (the law,
those barristers) refuses to confront the id-infested monster (Tom) that
surrounds them. There is simply no resolution, at least not yet.

The Third Stage of Cruelty exhibits still more of the images resonant
in ritualized violence today. In this scene, for the first time, it is dark,
and now for the first time the victim is no longer animal but human,
and a very specific human—a young woman. This is the first female to
appear in the masculine world of urban cruelty, and she is neither the
passive colluder in violence as is, say, the corpulent mother in *Gin Lane*,
nor the totally helpless victim, like the toppling baby. No, this poor
innocent is the Jamie Lee Curtis of the eighteenth century, the school-
girl victim of male aggression. The violence here is all-encompassing,
and the plate is called *Cruelty in Perfection* for a reason. Sex has entered
the picture. For not only has the woman been butchered at the neck (the
very cut seems to cry out), she has also been sexually abused, or at least
that is hinted at by her pregnant condition. Tom has used her first as

William Hogarth, *Cruelty in Perfection*, 1751 (British Museum)

sexual object and then as an accomplice in crime. The letter addressed
"To Tho. Nero at P . . ." reads:

> Dr Tommy
>
> My Mistress has been the best of Women to me, and my Conscience
> flies in my face as often as I think of wrongdoing her, yet I am
> resolv'd to venture Body & Soul to do as you would have me so
> don't fail to meet me as you said you would. For I shall bring along
> with me all the things I can lay my hands on. So no more at present
> but I remain yours till Death.
>
> Ann Gill

Ann Gill has served her purpose as a vehicle for Tom's bestial and material lusts, and he has dispatched her. In doing so he has been caught
by forces beyond human control rather than by social design. The gloss
reads:

> *To lawless Love when once betray'd,*
>   *Soon Crime to Crime succeeds:*
> *At length beguil'd to Theft, the Maid*
>   *By her Beguiler bleeds.*
>
> *Yet learn, seducing Man! nor Night;*
>   *With all its sable Cloud,*
> *Can screen the guilty Deed from Sight;*
>   *Foul Murder cries aloud.*
>
> *The gaping Wounds, and bloodstain'd Steel,*
>   *Now shock his trembling Soul:*
> *But Oh! what Pangs his Breast must feel,*
>   *When Death his Knell shall toll.*

This penultimate scene is filled with archetypes of graveyard macabre still alive and well in Hollywood: the tombstone inscribed "Here lieth the body," the bat "on leathern wing," the hooting owl, the startled watchman complete with lantern ("who goes there?"), the clock at the bewitching hour, the skull and crossbones, the crescent moon and skyful of swaggy clouds, the haunted house with escaping figure, the knife, pitchforks, the heavenly gaze of the man behind Tom ("Can such things really happen in our town?"), and especially the mouthlike wound on the maiden's neck. We know this scene well because for the last two hundred years this has been the context, be it on a movie lot of American International Pictures, in the descriptive prose of Stephen King, or on the pulp page of an *EC* comic, through which preposterous violence will pass.

In the last plate, we find one freshly killed monster being dissected by other monsters, who are made all the more frightening by virtue of their social and ethical position. Tom is being coolly opened up by a team of worthy surgeons, his eyes gouged out, his feet slit, and his guts drawn out like a hose, to be fed—with poetic justice—to the very beast on whom Tom had himself worked such unspeakable acts back in *The First Stage*. This is indeed *The Reward of Cruelty* and the gloss makes note:

> *Behold the Villain's dire disgrace!*
>   *Not Death itself can end.*
> *He finds no peaceful Burial-Place;*
>   *His breathless Corpse, no friend.*
>
> *Torn from the Root, that Wicked Tongue,*
>   *Which daily swore and curst!*
> *Those Eyeballs, from their Sockets wrung,*
>   *That glow'd with lawless Lust!*

William Hogarth, *The Reward of Cruelty*, 1751 (British Museum)

> *His Heart, expos'd to prying Eyes,*
>   *To Pity has no Claim:*
> *But, dreadful! from his Bones shall rise,*
>   *His Monument of Shame.*

The curtain has fallen on Tom, but the show was such a success that the "Son of Tom" and "Tom Returns" were to be the order of the nineteenth-century print reconstructions. Although Hogarth made desultory attempts to return to painting, his poor sales in the 1745 and 1751 auctions encouraged him to return to the audience he knew best. This lower-middle-class, predominantly young male audience wanted him to memorialize the scenes which they themselves recognized as being on the edge of decorum and they were willing to pay handsomely. The *frisson* of the forbidden has always held the matinee audience.

In *The Cockpit* (1759), Hogarth obliged and once again provided animal violence as the literal and figurative center. In what seems a gleeful

William Hogarth, *The Cockpit*, 1759 (British Museum)

transvaluation of *The Last Supper*, Hogarth casts Lord Albermarle Bertie in the role of Christ presiding over his modern disciples. Visual literacy is being played off against verbal—a scene of boisterous bonhomie is superimposed on a scene of mythic resonance. It is a scene well worth close inspection, for Hogarth is playing off two contrary movements: a satiric critique of animal violence and an indulgence in the thrills of preposterous violence. As do modern practitioners of television criticism, Hogarth is having it both ways. He is enjoying looking at what he is criticizing looking at.

What was obvious to the contemporary viewer but not to us is that the Christographic personage, Lord Bertie, is blind. He is being fleeced by his disciples. Clustered around him is a nest of human roosters stealing him blind. The rogue off to his left is actually commandeering Bertie's wager while the others are set to pounce. On either side, symmetrical clusters of riff-raff seem less interested in the battle of cocks than in laying their own wagers. Equidistant from Bertie are two churchmen, heads tilted back—one catching snuff dropped from the Frenchman's snuffbox above and the other inhaling pieties with hands clasped prayerfully. The churchmen are, or should be, upset at the proceedings under their noses, but they are powerless/unwilling to intervene. Like the barristers in *The Second Stage of Cruelty*, these churchmen wear the robes, not the commitment, of their "faith." This is, after all, a *modern* Lord's Supper.

Although the cocks occupy the middle range of the illustration and are "cut out for battle," they are clearly secondary to the observers both inside and outside the frame. Hogarth knew where the real action was, and it was certainly not with these indistinct birds. As with other animal violence, however, the birds (bulls, badgers, foxes . . .) are the focus. In the foreground, we see pickpockets, a hangman (the gibbet chalked on his back), two jockeys, and men with cudgels. Over them hang, suspended from the roof, a man locked in a basket. True, we see only his shadow, but we are told in a gloss that this was the public penalty for those who could not, or would not, pay their betting debts. In the clutter surrounding the cockpit, we see examples of Hogarth's genius for moving our eyes across the stage. Each vignette intersects with the next, and all conspire to give us the excitement of popular recreation in male eighteenth-century life—an entertainment we still crave.

For all the obvious butts of Hogarth's satire, what is assumed is also noteworthy. For instance, there are no women in this picture, even though the name of Nan Rawlings, who was a well-known trainer and feeder, appears under the illustration at two o'clock. She is involved only by allusion because women have no place in the cockpit. This is a male ritual. Second, this entertainment gathers a male crowd from all social classes. Bertie is the dupe, to be sure, but he is also the facilitator, the locus. His money is the lure attracting the crowd. As his ancestors doubtless had provided the bull for baiting or running, his aristocratic presence presides here, however ironically. Finally, there is the sense that these diversions also will not last; the presence of those churchmen, as well as of the pipe-smoking barrister, foretells that change is on its way. Hogarth knows, with a wistful sense, that the days of the cockpit are numbered. They were. The Royal Cockpit, built by Charles II, was finally closed in 1810 when the trustees of Christ's Hospital refused to renew the lease. No matter, the male appetites pictured here will find satisfaction elsewhere.

Hogarth's keen eye spotted yet another ritual of viewed violence which would reappear throughout the next century. This observance would also undergo considerable censorship and would jump the tracks to enter more rapidly moving media; first print, then electronic transmission. Like cockfighting, this other ritual came to England as a common entertainment, gathered a primarily male audience, and played out a surrogate social combat. Here, however, the combat was not between the extrafamilial tensions of different groups but between the intrafamilial tensions of the nuclear family. Often staged at fairs, the ritual was *The Tragical Comedy or Comical Tragedy of Punch and Judy*, and it proved to be one of the most enduring pantomimes of violence in Victorian England.

What television is to us, the fair was to the eighteenth century. It was the medium through which the current excitements of the day were circulated. The transformation of the country fair from crop-cycle celebration to carnival entertainment helped to end animal violence and to begin new staged diversions. Animal violence seems far too "real" to us to be countenanced as sport or pastime because animals have been transformed from dumb beasts to fellow creatures. At the same time, partly because of Darwin, humans have been changed from fallen children of God to just another evolving species. The Great Chain of Being still holds our worldview together; the rungs however have been rearranged. Nowhere can we better see this readjustment occurring than at the fair.

Hogarth's *Southwark Fair* (1733) shows not a country fair but one in the city (near the old church of St. George the Martyr), and so celebratory violence toward animals would have been difficult to enact. But violence is still very much a part of this scene. In fact, violence, both real and pretend, was such a part of the actual event that this fair was abolished in 1762 by an order of the Court of Common Council. Until then, however, Southwark Fair, together with the more famous Bartholomew Fair, was a major medium of artificial uproar.

As with such modern displays, the fair called forth high-brow condemnation. Probably the most famous indictment appears in William Wordsworth's *The Prelude.*

> *From these sights [of modern London]*
> *Take one,—that ancient festival the Fair,*
> *Holden where martyrs suffered in past time,*
> *And named of St. Bartholomew; there, see*
> *A work completed to our hands, that lays,*
> *If any spectacle on earth can do,*
> *The whole creative powers of man asleep!—*
> *For once, the Muse's help will we implore,*
> *And she shall lodge us, wafted on her wings,*
> *Above the press and danger of the crowd,*
> *Upon some showman's platform. What a shock*
> *For eyes and ears! what anarchy and din,*
> *Barbarian and infernal,—a phantasma,*
> *Monstrous in colour, motion, shape, sight, sound!*
> *Below, the open space, through every nook*
> *Of the wide area, twinkles, is alive*
> *With heads; the midway region, and above,*
> *Is thronged with staring pictures and huge scrolls,*
> *Dumb proclamations of the Prodigies;*
> *With chattering monkeys dangling from their poles,*
> *And children whirling in their roundabouts;*
> *With those that stretch the neck and strain the eyes,*

William Hogarth, *Southwark Fair*, 1733 (British Museum)

> *And crack the voice in rivalship, the crowd*
> *Inviting; with buffoons against buffoons*
> *Grimacing, writhing, screaming,—him who grinds*
> *The hurdy-gurdy, at the fiddle weaves*
> *Rattles the salt-box, thumps the kettle-drum,*
> *And him who at the trumpet puffs his cheeks,*
> *The silver-collared Negro with his timbrel,*
> *Equestrians, tumblers, women, girls, and boys,*
> *Blue-breeched, pink-vested, with high-towering plumes.*
> *All moveables of wonder, from all parts,*
> *Are here—Albinos, painted Indians, Dwarfs,*
> *The Horse of knowledge, and the learned Pig,*
> *The Stone-eater, the man that swallows fire,*
> *Giants, Ventriloquists, the Invisible Girl,*
> *The Bust that speaks and moves its goggling eyes,*
> *The Wax-work, Clock-work, all the marvelous craft*
> *Of modern Merlins, Wild Beasts, Puppet-shows,*
> *All out-o'-the-way, far-fetched, perverted things,*
> *All freaks of nature, all Promethean thoughts*
> *Of man, is dullness, madness, and their feats*
> *All jumbled up together, to compose*
> *A Parliament of Monsters. . . .*
>
> (Book 8, ll. 675–718)

While the fair is for Wordsworth a "vast mill vomiting" forth degradation, this is not quite the sentiment in Hogarth's *Southwark Fair*.
Clearly, Hogarth is satirizing the "parliament of monsters," but he is
also drawn in by the kinetic excitement of the thrill seekers. What
Wordsworth found numbing were exactly those thrills which Hogarth
knew his audience wanted.

In the corners of both of their visions is a raucously violent puppet
show—Wordsworth's line 712 and Hogarth's far right-hand side. That
puppet show more often than not was a production of the indomitable
Punch and Judy. Of the many events at the fair, it may seem startling
that *Punch and Judy* was so prominent, given that we now think of it
as so ephemeral. We see only a part of Punch's story in *Southwark Fair*.
While Hogarth's audience knew exactly what was happening when they
saw Punch astride the horse, we do not. We know more about Punch's

William Hogarth, *Southwark Fair* enlargement (British
Museum)

George Cruikshank, illustrator, "Piccini's Punch," in John
Payne Collier, *The Tragical Comedy or Comical Tragedy
of Punch and Judy*, 1828

descendants like Ralph Kramden of *The Honeymooners* or Archie Bunker
or even the Road Runner. Since we have only the dimmest memory of
this once-popular pantomime of preposterous violence left, it might be
instructive to reconstruct it in its past glory.

Punch and Judy starts abruptly with Punch beating a dog. The cartoon scenario continues with equal abruptness, moving rapidly from scene
to scene without ligatures. Punch beats up a neighbor, throws his baby
out, bludgeons his wife to death, kicks and kills a doctor, thrashes a
beggar, knocks a policeman down, hangs a hangman, and successfully
wards off the devil. As in the story of Tom Nero, it is not happenstance
that Punch's career starts with violence to animals and ends with a con-
frontation with death. What separates the characters is that Punch is
able to out-Rambo even the devil himself.

While "Punch" was entering the English cultural scene, "Guignol," the French marionette, was also coming into fashion. In the French story, a street-smart rogue moves through urban episodes which end with his bashing the fortunately thick-headed policeman. By strange twists of nomenclature, "Guignol" grafted itself onto the cabarets which catered to producing shows of the macabre. The *Théâtre du Grand Guignol* in Montmartre specialized in short plays of horror and violence evaluated in terms of how many in the audience fainted. *Guignol* is for early teenagers, *Grand Guignol* for their older brothers and sisters. In spite of desultory attempts in the nineteenth century to find an audience in England, *Grand Guignol* has remained a Paris fashion. Punch was more than able to handle the English by himself.

The best source we have for Punch is from a reconstruction of an 1827 performance.[7] While the character of Punch is ancient, a Dionysian Puck who passed through the Middle Ages as a vice character before becoming the Pulcinella of the Italian Commedia dell'Arte, the *Punch* play itself is relatively recent. The misanthrope with the hooked nose entered English culture during late Elizabethan times but did not gather an audience until he found the proper medium. If ever there was an example of how important a medium is in delivering specific rituals to a locatable audience, this was it. In the seventeenth century, Punch was variously performed by both marionette and hand-puppet. He was "won" by the hand-puppets, and to a considerable extent this fixed his actions and character, for the marionette, derisively called by the English the "French puppet," is a string-hung puppet whose actions are carefully articulated from above. These actions can be very sophisticated—the whole frame, head, hands, feet, and even the mouth can be operated. The hand-puppet, however, essentially can perform only large and crude movements, and those movements, as contrasted to the marionette, can be excitingly furious. Hand-puppets can pummel each other; marionettes can only get tangled up. Just as movies so quickly captured the violence of the novel, so the hand-puppet laid claim to the action of the marionette. By the eighteenth century, *Punch and Judy* was a hand-puppet show and a very violent one.

The man who ran the show was called the Punchman. He traveled around the countryside performing the routine, changing it slightly to suit the circumstances and his audience. The central core of violence, however, remained in place. As the puppets elbowed aside the marionettes, the show gradually became children's entertainment. And, as children, many of the most important personages of Augustan England were part of this audience, much as later generations would pass through pulp novels, horror comics, Saturday matinees, or now video arcades. Samuel Pepys praised *Punch and Judy*, as did Dryden, Shadwell, Wycherly, Otway, and even the great chum, Dr. Johnson. Steele, Swift, and

Fielding also made Punch part of their reminiscences. Yet what all these Neoclassicists saw as children was something that doubtless concerned their parents. They saw an extremely violent charade which subverted all the ideals of decorum, all the aspirations of a polite society. It was a plunge into adolescent male wish-fulfillment, a fable of aggression.

The performance usually opened with a prologue spoken by Punch, whose distinctive high-pitched voice was created by the manipulation of the "swazzle" in the Punchman's mouth.

> *Ladies and Gentlemen, pray how you do?*
> *If you all happy, me all happy too.*
> *Stop and hear my merry littel play;*
> *If me make you laugh, me need not make you pay.*

The "happy" state of affairs begins as Punch calls for his wife Judy but instead gets Toby, the neighbor's dog. Toby snaps at Punch; Punch strikes back. Toby catches hold of Punch's nose; Punch bats Toby away into the audience. As the play developed in the nineteenth century, the Punchman often used a real dog and mimicked the violence, much to the young crowd's delight. Punch then calls for Toby's master, Scaramouch, who arrives with a fiddle under his arm, and after some puerile word play which borders on the scatological, Punch knocks Scaramouch's head clean off his shoulders. (Punchmen take great pride in certain aspects of the production, one of which is the ability to get Scaramouch's head to fly straight upward when struck.) Again, Punch summons his wife Judy, and when she blearily arrives, Punch demands a kiss. He gets a slap for his effrontery. Punch then asks to kiss his child. When the child proceeds to dirty himself, Punch throws the child to the floor and beats the baby's head on the stage. Then Punch throws the child over the stage into the audience. Judy is distraught. Punch promises he will provide her with another child right then and there if she is willing. She is not—just the opposite. She wants nothing to do with him. Judy beats Punch with his own stick. They struggle; Punch gets the stick back and, Freudians take note, he pummels her to death. He sings,

> *Who'd be plagued with a wife*
> > *That could set himself free*
> *With a rope or a knife*
> > *Or a good stick, like me?*

Here enters Pretty Polly, a captivating young miss who stirs up Punch's perpetually o'er-brimming libido. After some small talk she must be off. Punch follows in priapic pursuit. He calls for Hector, his horse, who soon tosses him off; Punch breaks his leg in the fall and so calls for the doctor who arrives to inspect the broken bone. The doctor checks Punch's head, then shoulders, torso, and groin. As he is inspecting Punch's privates, Punch is affronted and pokes him in the eye, kicks him down, and when the doctor goes for the omnipresent stick, Punch grabs it away. Yet another battle ensues, this time concluding with a dead doctor.

Totally unregenerate and unremorseful, Punch celebrates by clanging on a large sheep bell. A black servant, who has been sent by his master to request that Punch be quiet, gets first the expected racial slurs and then the expected clobbering. Now passes a blind beggar who makes the mistake of asking Punch for a donation while slobbering on him. "Here's charity for you," says Punch, filling the blind man's face full of fists. In this interlude, the audience was encouraged to suggest other confrontations and the Punchman would oblige, and it is these interactive scenes that exemplify the essential nature of popular culture. Whether it is reflected in weekly receipts, box-office grosses, Nielsen ratings, or the number of quarters in the video game, the audience drives the entertainment. When an audience is displeased, it votes with its feet, and every Punchman, Hollywood mogul, network executive, and publisher learns this first or changes occupation.

So far Punch has had his way with everyone—dog, wife, child, servant, beggar—but the tide is turning. The policeman enters. "You've killed your wife and child," says the officer, "and I've come to take you up." "I've come to take you *down*," counters Punch, knocking the constable over. Next comes Jack Ketch, so notorious a hangman that, long after his time, his proper name was used in pulp novels and early comics. "You must come to prison: my name's Ketch." "Ketch this," says Punch in one of his expected fisticuff responses. The officer and Ketch regain their feet, knock Punch off his, and it's off to prison.

Once in prison the jig seems finally up. Punch will finally get his just deserts. All is readied for the celebration of retributive violence so popular in eighteenth-century urban societies—the hanging.[8] The gibbet is erected outside Punch's cell, the coffin is prepared, and Ketch asks if Punch has any remorse for all his killings. "Not me, but *you* should for hanging is immoral," replies a thoroughly modern Punch. Retributive violence is every bit as noxious as capricious violence. The argument does not succeed, and Punch is readied for the noose. At the last minute he feigns confusion and asks Ketch to demonstrate the proper threading of the neck through the noose. Ketch obliges, and straightaway Punch pulls the rope; Jack Ketch, famous hangman, is hung. Punch puts the body in the coffin and gloats.

> They're out! They're out! I've done the trick!
>   Jack Ketch is dead—I'm free;
> I do not care, now, if Old Nick
>   Himself should come for me.

Old Nick, the devil, does indeed come, and for the first time Punch is nervous. He has at last found a talent equal to his own. Punch and the

George Cruikshank, Punch's Final Triumph, "Piccini's Punch," in John Payne Collier, *The Tragical Comedy or Comical Tragedy of Punch and Judy*, 1828

devil trade punches, and lo and behold it is our Punch who carries the day. The devil is skewered on his own trident and Punch triumphantly lifts him above his head and the curtain falls.

Although the *Punch* show is rich in political, social, and religious overtones, the one overwhelming characteristic is its dedication, its ceaseless dedication, to preposterous violence. The victims of Punch's violence are thoroughly modern, and so is he. No mistreated prince, no betrayed king, no wronged noble, Punch is Everyman. He strikes out against family (wife, child), state (the constable and the hangman), and church (the devil). There are no smooth edges here. Against each he exerts his independence with blows, kicks, and punches. However much we may wish to claim Rambo, the A-team, He-man, G.I. Joe, *DC* comic heroes, and the like as unique to our degraded modern culture, all of them have Punch and his stick hovering behind the arras, waiting to show them how it is *really* done.

Punch and Judy is clearly broadcast entertainment like the popular ballad or the fairy tale sung by a lyricist responding to the demands of an audience. What is unique is that the itinerant troubadour, the Punch-man, had so much equipment. The Punch stall was carried on the back and was one of the parts of the show which was varied depending on how much territory was covered. While the Punchmen made changes in the stall and the show to establish their "signatures" or to accommodate a local audience, they were loath to reorganize the "text" because the audience might scoff and withhold approval; that is, the donation. Rather like television programming, the audience knows the tale and will wander off if the variations are too pronounced. They tune in not to be shocked by the new but rather to be comforted by the well known.

As the concern about the unruliness of public fairs increased, culminating in the Metropolitan Police Act of 1839, which restricted both the times and extent of the fairs, *Punch and Judy* was displaced. The Punchman's stall was set up either in the Victorian parlor or on the street corner. Denied the protection of the carnival and forced into the family or into public, *Punch* suffered the same pressures that children's programming does when it extends out of the Saturday morning ghetto into prime time. In other words, *Punch and Judy* came under the watchful and censorious eye of critics and reformers. Soon Toby, the dog, was no longer brutalized, the baby was no longer beaten and thrown into the audience, Judy was no longer abused, and more important, the devil was no longer skewered. In fact, by mid-century Old Nick was replaced either by an anonymous bogeyman or by a crocodile—both vague euphemisms for the devil. The sacrilegious overtones of Punch's ultimate

G. Rymer, "The Hanging Scene," 1834 (Guildhall Library, London)

Punch and Judy, "Played before Royalty"

battles were removed. Once Punch had been denied his victims, he was also denied his aggression. Once Punch had become sanitized, he lost his audience. However, while Punch was being reformed, other *fin de siècle* monsters of a more ferocious cast were being let loose. Dracula, Dr. Moreau, and Mr. Hyde were finding flesh and blood in print, and the *Théâtre du Grand Guignol* was playing to standing-room-only crowds.

From nineteenth-century drawings and twentieth-century photographs of the *Punch* show, we see how much of this encounter between audience and show still endures. In these pictures, two characteristics are instantly striking. One is that the audience is mostly eager young males. Look at their faces. The other interesting feature, less obvious but indicative of things to come, is that the display resembles the standard livingroom scene of today. Here are children, especially boys, huddled up in front of the tiny screen and held in rapt attention.

These two matters—the young audience and its intense level of concentration—alert modern critics to the dangers of television: "How can

Punch by night, 1898

we let *them* watch *that?*" In the early eighteenth century when John Dryden was attempting to update and make relevant the Tenth Satire of Juvenal, the best he could do with *panem et circenses* was this:

> But we who give our Native Rights away,
> And our Inslav'd Posterity betray,
> And now reduc'd to beg an Alms, and go
> On Holidays to see a Puppet Show
>
> (ll. 723–24)

Now listen to our great-grandparents in the nineteenth century. The novelist George Meredith, in *An Essay on Comedy*, opines that "the puppet-show of 'Punch and Judy' inspires our street-urchins to have instant recourse to their fists in a dispute, after the fashion of every one of the actors in that public entertainment who gets possession of the cudgel" (p. 18). In *Harper's Weekly* in 1872, another critic also questioned the violence, "Why children *should* be fond of such an *un*domestic

Punch and Judy pitched outside His Majesty's Theatre, Haymarket, 1910 (The BBC Hulton Picture Library)

Tom Kemp's show, Brighton, c. 1935

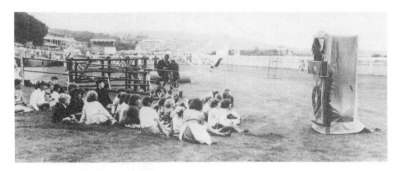

Punch and Judy at Goodwood Races, 1965 (Keystone Press Agency)

drama as portrayed in the representation of Mr. Punch's adventures can only be accounted for by that love of the horrible so innate even in infantile human nature" ("Punch and Judy Reviewed," p. 5). And seven years later in 1879, a Professor Hoffman chimed in: "It is a curious illustration of the depravity of human nature, that this eccentric drama, in which vice is throughout triumphant, and law and order goes to the wall, has maintained its popularity for so many generations" (*Drawing Room Amusements*, p. 190). Indeed, the question seems as well put by our Victorian critics as it is today. A better question might be: How can such rituals of aggression be examples of depravity when they are the norm?

Critics of the common taste have always supposed that human nature is right now being debased as it has never been debased before. So if *Punch* had to be rewritten and revised to accommodate higher ideals, then so be it. And it was, again and again and again. By century's end, in J. M. Barrie's *Sentimental Tommy*, we can even observe in an art text the cleansing of a vulgar text. Young Miss Ailie considers *Punch and Judy* too common to perform at her wedding. The show is too vulgar, too indecorous—"an encouragement to every form of vice and crime." So young Tommy suggests a few minor changes and, *voilà*, the result of his handiwork is a great success.

> Punch did chuck his baby out of the window (roars of laughter) in his jovial, time-honored way, *but* immediately thereafter up popped the showman to say, "Ah, my dear boys and girls, let this be a lesson to you never to destroy your offsprings. Oh, shame on Punch, for to do the wicked deed; he will be catched in the end, and serve him right." Then when Mr Punch had walloped his wife with the stick, amid thunders of applause, up again bobbed the showman: "Ah, my dear boys and girls, what a lesson is this we sees . . . Oh, be warned by his sad igsample, and do not bash the head of your loving wife." And there was a great deal more of the same. (p. 92)

With such revisions, poor Punch could not last long. After the closing of the fairs and the intrusion of well-meaning reformers, he was exiled to where he now resides—as seaside resort entertainment. There are still Punchmen who travel about performing the show, but it has become a curiosity viewed not so much by eager adolescents as by their nostalgic parents. After all, why should the kids watch this when they have more exciting cartoons on the "telly" at home.

The spirit of Punch, of course, lives on. The medieval vice, the Elizabethan clown, and Punch have their comedic descendants in the Marx Brothers, Jackie Gleason, Archie Bunker, the Three Stooges, and the Road Runner. His more violent descendants are elsewhere, playing out roles in action/adventure fables. Punch plays to the child, and no reformers can repress the enthusiasm for watching his particular brand of interfamilial aggression. Such violence portrays our own deep-seated wish-fulfillment. Many of these wishes are sexual. Punch's hooked nose, the use of his cudgel, the fact that Punch wants a kiss from Judy and receives instead the baby, and even the noose into which Punch refuses to be coaxed replay the excitements and anxieties of an audience on the edge of reproduction. Approaching this edge, as we have seen, inspires and invokes ritual. Nothing can stop that audience or stand in the way of its inching closer. The liminal audience watches Punch, a liminal character nonpareil, as he maneuvers past one obstacle after another en route to his final independence, his triumph against the bogey.

Although Punch was a match for death and the devil, he was no match for paper and ink. Had he only expended his prodigious energies against the stereotype, celluloid, and the cathode-ray tube, he might have survived in body rather than only in spirit. To witness his spiritual legacy, however, we need to turn to the newly dominant medium of shudders, print, and to the newly unfolding genre, the gothic.

3

Preposterous Violence in Prose Fiction: The Coronation of Stephen King

If I say it and they laugh, then it's part of the act. When I say it and they don't laugh, I take it out.

PHYLLIS DILLER, when asked how she knew what should be in her act

Phyllis Diller makes a telling point, in fact, the central point, about mass culture. The creator of an entertainment, whether it be a nightclub routine, a popular novel, a movie, or a television program, usually has no precise idea about exactly what it is he or she is doing right. The creators only know when they are told that "it works." What "works" is determined in terms of audience composition, size, and response. In the pseudoscientific jargon of popular culture, this quality is called "chemistry." Tell it again, says the audience to a Stephen King, or a Brandon Tartikoff, or a Stephen Spielberg, or a Jackie Collins. We'll still be here if you can do it right. You have "chemistry." So a Mr. King, who really doesn't know precisely what he's doing right any more than do his colleagues in other mass media, any more than Phyllis Diller knows what is funny, just does it again and again. He only knows what has sold, what has made him rich, what works, what has "chemistry." In the entertainment business, the words "derivative" and "imitative" are not terms of opprobrium but of the highest praise. Students may be taught in school that the artist is the one among us who takes the chances, but it is the popular culture entertainer who, as Leslie Fiedler has contended, really "rides the tiger." For as much as King wants to shock his audience and as much as Ms. Diller wants to make hers laugh, they really don't know *how* they do it.

Did Horace Walpole, effeminate dilettante and inveterate gossip, have any idea that his concoction of moody themes, atmosphere, plot, and characters would all stay in place long enough for an audience to gather? Did he have any idea while writing *Castle of Otranto* that young Protestant virgins, older Catholic villains, trap doors, weeping portraits, creaking caskets, and even huge tumbling helmets would startle readers into avidly purchasing his prose? Although this may seem a foolish iteration of a profound epistemological question, it has a place in the study of popular entertainment, if only because such entertainment has the express design of finding an audience and not of unfolding a truth. It may be, however, that only truth can find an audience and only truth can hold its attention. But what does the author know? Sooner ask if Samuel Richardson knew that his avuncular reprimand, "From an Uncle to a Nephew on his keeping bad Company, bad Hours etc., in his Apprenticeship," would cause a stampede to the booksellers for fiction on the etiquette of courtship. Who could have guessed that after Richardson worked for three months in attempting to find that same audience again, his *Pamela, or Virtue Rewarded* would go forth to capture an audience so large that the novel did indeed, as Richardson himself claimed, introduce a "new species of writing." What he certainly could not have known was that he was well on the way to establishing the largest and longest-lasting readership of any fiction—the audience of the romance. While the modern artist, in the wash of Romantic sentimentality, may pretend that failure is an intrinsic part of his search for truth, the popular entertainer knows differently. Truth does not exist unless perceived, and audiences, if left alone, will seek out particular truths at particular times to resolve particular problems.

The sentimental romance and the gothic novel were largely eighteenth-century inventions. They represent the two most profound transformations wrought on print media by a mass audience. These genres contain what most people wanted to read most of the time. Such books were read, as they are now, by an unsophisticated audience. With the rise of literacy in the nineteenth century, these texts were "captured" by adolescents in forms we still recognize all too easily. Although such reading material is usually characterized as "escapist" by those older and/or more sophisticated, I will argue that the opposite is true. The reading of such texts is more likely to be educational; they are rituals more of induction than of escape. I intend to demonstrate this by locating the core of both genres in the excitements of sex and violence, in the anxieties of courtship and reproduction.

Anxiety is self-evident in the sentimental novel. All one has to do is to look first at the novel's inception, and then at the spate of current examples, to extrapolate what has evolved over the last two centuries. While Samuel Richardson's *Pamela* may have grown out of the famous Letter Number 138, "A Father to a Daughter in Service on hearing of her Master's attempting her virtue," the novel itself is nothing if not an intense, almost clinical, anatomizing of sexual induction. Retelling *Pamela* grew into an industry which now produces fully one-half of all the mass-market paperbacks of today. Whatever the audience found in this book, it is something they wanted again and again and again. Harlequin Romances, one of the industry's most productive "profit centers," has accounted for fully one-third of this market by transcribing the same story. Because the formulaic patterns and covert agenda of the sentimental romance tradition have so much in common with the gothic thriller, one may be able to analogize and extrapolate between the two. The stories that they tell are really variations of one ur-story that goes like this: Boy meets girl, complications arise. If all the social forms are in place and their familial identities not too close, they can overcome obstacles, fall in love, marry, and successfully reproduce. If, however, their family roles are too close, the male will turn violent and must somehow be removed. The first story is the romance; the second is the gothic. While they both may have moments of sex and violence, the romance is able to express concussions by sentiment alone, while the gothic seems obliged to express them as action.

These fables of seduction and aggression appeared in the eighteenth century as a result of new efficiencies in production and distribution of print. The hamburger did not make McDonald's; the mass production and distribution of buns, condiments, drinks, and containers did. So did the increased availability of seating and parking. Similarly, efficiencies in production turned the print medium inside out, changing an elitist medium into one that catered to a mass audience, and in so doing changed forever the role of the story teller. A seventeenth-century novelist, usually with church or state subvention or grants from a cumbersome patronage system, had to pay a publishing charge—usually a flat fee for typesetting and a royalty for each copy sold. The more copies the printer sold, the more it cost to produce the copy. To offset the increased expenses, late Renaissance authors often tried first to find an audience to determine what was desired as reading material, and then to sell subscriptions to their productions. Only then did they write the book. The idea of a book as a *salable* commodity in the modern sense essentially followed the new twists in the curves of supply and demand wrought by technology.

Although we tend to date the rise of literacy by England's passage of the Education Act in the late nineteenth century, in the last half of the eighteenth century literacy increased almost tenfold. Simultaneously, machine-made paper and mechanical typesetting (first flat-bed and then the Napier-and-Hoe cylinder presses) caused production costs to plummet. The railroad and steamboat made distribution costs do likewise, as did the circulating libraries. By mid-nineteenth century, subscription selling was rarely needed to get a novel to market. Ironically, the new hybrids of print media—the daily newspaper, the magazine, and the monthly—soon threatened the stability of book publishing. Presses had become so efficient that both magazines and books were necessary to keep the expensive machinery operating. By the 1830s repetitive consumption was not just possible—it was necessary. Once the Stamp Act of 1712, the infamous "tax on knowledge," was finally repealed in 1855, the last economic restriction was removed. As we will see in the next chapter, this need to utilize capacity led to the publication of illustrated throwaways or comics which found a still younger audience. For the first time books could be thrown away rather than preserved. A half-century later they would be made that way on purpose. While we may think only of the waste of disposable commodities and complain that books today literally fall apart in our hands, increases in both supply and demand made it almost inevitable and even desirable that books last only for one reading.

Advances in production and distribution have accelerated this process in our century. Mercury Publishers and Pocket Books were able to introduce the paperback book in the late 1930s because of a new format, again made possible by technical changes—this time in binding. Machine-sewn signatures held in place by animal glues were costly, time-consuming, and worse, could not be used in small books. But the "perfect binding," in which cut sheets were literally stuck to the spine with synthetic glue, made the "pocket book" at last a real possibility. Once you could stick a book in your pocket, the act of reading was not just vastly extended but also declassed. As television is to the movies, the paperback was to hardcover books. Looking whenever you wanted at whatever you wanted meant that many more viewers would and could demand to be shown what they had not been able to see before. Was it any wonder that the first paperbacks were more magazines than books, that literary guild selections were elbowed aside by innovations such as the Western and the detective story? Just as confession magazines like *True Confessions* inflamed the sentimental novel of romance, so too did men's magazines like *Argosy* ignite the gothic. In the process of expanding the audience downward in age and sophistication, new tastes had to be satisfied. Violence became pronounced, and, once pronounced, soon became part of the grammar of the genre.

The same forces operate today. While both gothic and sentimental novels languished in the 1950s, they were revitalized in the following decade as they found new markets. The romance recovered, thanks to Gerald Gross at Ace Books, who realized the enduring appeal of Daphne du Maurier's *Rebecca* (first published in 1938) and who wanted to start a series to capitalize on that appeal. The market, he was sure, was there. All he needed to do was to find it.[1] What was *Rebecca* but *Pamela* filtered through *Jane Eyre?* A handsome older man and a younger, vulnerable woman confront obstacles. There was implied violence and mystery as well. Gross's success was not lost on W. Lawrence Heisey, a former Procter and Gamble soap salesman with a Harvard MBA, who in the 1970s did Gerald Gross one better. At the fledgling Harlequin Enterprises, Heisey soon mass-produced the gothic romance on a scale never seen before. He created a "product" of words in which each version was an interchangeable copy of its predecessor. Once the chassis was in place, the consumers could have whatever accessories they wanted. Harlequin in its heyday was printing at the rate of ten titles per month—the Model T of drugstore novels.[2]

The current good health of the gothic and sentimental genres shows that the mass audience which had gathered in the mid-eighteenth century to be shocked and mollified is still in place, still eager for a "good read," an emotional "trip." Harlequin's recently established Gold Eagle Books division is now making a fortune with male action/adventure books like *The Avenger* or *Cutthroat Cannibals.* In 1987 Gold Eagle shipped nearly 500 million copies of titles in its five leading men's adventure series alone. While critics shudder in disgust, readers read on. However, the intermediaries, the booksellers, have had to change their ways to survive. Just as movie theaters moved together, dropped their individual identities to become part of the Cinema 6 in the shopping mall, so B. Dalton and Waldenbooks moved into suburban shopping centers and sold books like groceries. By the mid-1970s the managers of these outlets and display centers could tell you what was selling, who was writing it, who was reading it, and what category it was in. Their computers could tell so much that retailers were soon telling the publishers what they would carry and in essence were controlling what was printed. After all, the chain stores accounted for almost twenty percent of all trade and paperback books and so could do what movie theaters did in the 1930s and what the church did in the Renaissance: They delivered a paying audience.

This is the milieu into which Stephen King must be fitted. For he is no passing fad but emblematic of new marketing and new delivery techniques. He is not the enigma portrayed by the newsweeklies, nor the vulgarizing schlockmeister that academics often deplore.[3] Instead, he is squarely in the middle of the dominant trend of print media as it has evolved for the last one hundred and fifty years. King's genius is that, as a major portion of the sentimental/gothic tradition moved to the romance, he was able to corner what remained of that market—the part that had read not for the warm tingles of courtship but for the cold shivers of violence. In fact, in *Misery*, King even attempted to get it both ways. In the midst of a tale of violent torture, a King protagonist is forced to write a sentimental romance to save himself from an over-avid reader.

Violence had always been part of the gothic. Straightforward killing, which is the most common fictional form of violence, was present from the outset. And since the unbalanced family is often the locus of gothic concentration, interfamilial murder is the norm. As opposed to the romance, which seeks to build a stable, and therefore reproductive, family, the gothic shows how unstable the family can be. In evaluating the most popular two hundred novels between 1790 and 1830, Ann Tracy counts eleven acts of filicide, twenty-four of fratricide, seven of infanticide, five of matricide, three of husband-killing, sixteen of parricide, four of sororicide, and thirteen of uxoricide. Admittedly, these acts may be accidental, often the result of schemes and often occasions for contrition, but the fact remains: The gothic draws its power from showing the nuclear family in meltdown.

As the gothic developed, family violence, which had previously been exploited in the service of plot and character development, progressively took on a life of its own. Or to be more precise, the audience which had earlier been thrilled by a lowering Montoni or Schedoni, who tried to scare the petticoats off the young victim, soon came to prefer an Ambrosio or Wolfenbach, who could, and would, translate sexual innuendo into action. What would seem to the literary historian to be the degeneration of the gothic into the "penny dreadfuls" and "bloody pulps" of mid-Victorian times was instead an expansion of the gothic's audience to include a greater percentage of newly literate adolescents. This audience did not want ambiguity; it wanted outlines, cartoon action. It is tempting to argue that the original gothic audience had become inured to violence and therefore craved new thrills and that consequently the genre grew more violent. But it is more accurate to attribute this change to a shift in audience, which in turn resulted from the precipitous drop in book prices and the equally sharp increase in literacy. Prices of entertainment pulp fell some eighty percent throughout the century, while the reading audience expanded tenfold and dropped in age. One can witness the same process in television programming. The "golden age," complete with "literate" shows like the Hallmark Hall of Fame, Voice of Firestone, Texaco Star Theater, and the General Electric Theater, among others, was not a product of a finer culture but of a different audience. Those who watched television were those who could first afford one. As the price of television sets fell and broadcast technology improved, the audience changed (grew younger, more working class), and programming had to be regeared to these new tastes in order to maximize the effectiveness of advertising.

A quick look at nineteenth-century England reveals the "coarsening" of print as it fell into younger hands. When gothic novels cost six shillings per volume and were published in three-volume editions, the only way that adolescents could get to these thrills was by renting them from the circulating libraries. In 1740 there were three such libraries in London, sixty years later almost a hundred. Much of the gothic "ratsbane" and "rubbish," issued from small presses like the scandalous Minerva Press, was not widely consumed, however, and hence elicited only scattered outrage. Still, as the following 1808 letter to the *Gentleman's Magazine* indicates, watchdogs were already raising an early howl about mass media:

> How few persons are likely to be contaminated by the performance of an immoral play, compared to those who may be rendered vicious by the publication of an immoral book, which may be circulated throughout the entire kingdom, and may enter every house . . . not a vile contemptible novel, or romance, but what will find its way to a circulating library. (Quoted in Taylor, pp. 4–5)

Soon, these three-volume works were condensed to "bluebacks" or shilling shockers where, in thirty to seventy pages, the thrills could be found between two lurid covers. Like the eighteenth-century expurgations of classic texts in which the forbidden passages were tucked into "Notes" at the back so that they could be read, as Byron said, at "one fell swoop," these early *Reader's Digests* did all the excising and published just the exciting dreck. Sure enough, more outrage erupted as Hannah Moore and "The Proclamation Society for the Suppression of Vice" once again sounded the alarm; again, too late. Between 1792 and 1841, James Catnach published reams of condensed shockers, but he in turn was elbowed aside by cheap newspapers like *Rambler's* and *Ranger's Magazine*. Catnach and others returned with a new product and recaptured the market with penny broadsides. These broadsides became the infamous "penny dreadfuls" which, when bound, were sold as novels. The most notorious of these were the Newgate novels, fictionalized biographies of such criminals as Claude Duval, Dick Turpin, and Jack Sheppard. The headwaters of modern detective fiction, these books were a major source of early elite indignation with mass media. The audience was growing larger and younger. Hannah Moore, now joined by evangelical reformers, lobbied for state censorship. By 1857 Lord Campbell's Obscene Publications Act promised to stop the flow that was by now a flood. In America, Anthony Comstock and "The New York Society for the Suppression of Vice" attempted to fight the battle against pulp contamination, but as with the English, the effort was too little too late.

Newgate novels were just too popular and, like prime-time action television, too much in demand. By mid-century, Newgates were competing with imitations like the Salisbury Square serials, which were spewed forth from the maws of massive steam-driven presses. The publishing houses of G. W. M. Reynolds and Edward Lloyd were so successful that, in the parlance of modern mass media, they "spun off" illustrated throwaways. Like Hugh Hefner hunched over color transparencies, Edward Lloyd pored over the illustrations of *People's Police Gazette*, reportedly demanding, "The eyes must be larger and there must be more blood—much more blood" (quoted in Dalziel, p. 75). Ironically, as we will see in the next chapter, it was just these illustrations, bound together as comics, which did what Hannah Moore and her followers initially desired. Print pulp decreased. Illustrated pulp more than took its place. Violence increased.

As J. H. S. Tompkins notes in *The Popular Novel in England 1770–1800*:

> The Sensational has always been present in popular literature . . . there is a universal taste for strong scenes . . . the desire to shock and be shocked is endemic in human nature and only the sophisticated feel it needs apology. Novel readers at the end of the 18th century relished an emotional orgy. . . . Critics complain through the whole period of the abuse of the marvelous in motive and incident. . . . Rape, jealous frenzy and murder are the staple ingredients of these novels and the general method is cumulative. . . . Duels and abductions appeared most frequently and have their parallels in modern magazines and newspapers. . . . The slaughterous innkeepers, corpse robbers, dungeons and ghosts are not new . . . terror is perennially fascinating to the human mind, we accumulate stock themes on which every generation draws to some extent. . . . (pp. 59, 60, 61)

What Tompkins and others who have focused only on print do not acknowledge is that as ancient as the drive for sensation may be, violence will increase in any medium which maximizes profit by maximizing production and audience. Once the adolescent male audience is allowed into the coliseum, the tenor and subject matter of entertainment become more sensational and concussive. Historically, the mass production of words lowered the marginal cost of printing, curtailed the expansion of circulating libraries, introduced first "bluebacks," then "yellowbacks," then illustrated pulp, and led to such profound innovations as serialization—all in order to capture a larger and larger, and younger and younger, audience.

Indeed, serialization transformed mass media. What serialized publication was to print, soap operas are to modern television. The serial novel was essentially a throwaway book, chapters of which appeared in monthly installments over a period of a year to eighteen months. Each installment covered three or four chapters and sold for a shilling. If one ever wonders how much the audience controls authorial design in mass media, the serializations are the ideal place to look for an answer. Sales figures for each installment were quickly generated, and the author, or better yet, teams of authors, knew which twists, which characters, which settings, were being avidly followed. Serial stories became "bloody pulps" because violence was not just salable but especially profitable. Was this not exactly the same process followed with the matinee movies of the 1930s? The studios often waited to see which adventures attracted the Saturday afternoon audience before continuing to shoot the future episodes.

The reason so many of the great English authors—Dickens, Thackeray, George Eliot, Trollope—all started their careers by writing serially is the same reason many of today's best writers produce screenplays: money first, glory second; food before fame. The image of the solitary artist toiling in the garret, careless of fortune, and interested only in art is a Romantic myth. According to Boswell, Dr. Johnson was not winking when he claimed, "No man but a blockhead ever wrote except for money." The act of writing is not done in a vacuum. Can there be a better example, albeit exaggerated, of the artist's condition than that of Dickens, pen in hand, cocking an ear to his audience? He hears their mournful wail over Little Nell, and so he extends her demise for an extra chapter in *The Old Curiosity Shop.* More chapters equal more money. The same consideration prompted his reversal of Pip's fortunes at the end of *Great Expectations,* almost as if he knew his readers, lined up along the docks of Boston Harbor and stacked ten deep in front of Trafalgar bookdealers, needed to finish one tale before he could hook them on the next. Why should artists be exempt from economic aspirations? We don't fault George Lucas for sending Darth Vader off into deep space at the end of *Star Wars* so that Lucas can see if the box-office receipts warrant Mr. Vader's sequelized return. We expect it.

To see how important the audience and the media are in determining the level of violence, we need only look at three fables of aggression that sprang loose from their print moorings and floated into other media to be consumed by other audiences. Three central myths have made their way out of the nineteenth century: Dracula, Frankenstein, and Dr. Jekyll and Mr. Hyde. Each had a stable text in prose, each broke loose because something in the story attracted an eager audience which wanted certain parts retold, and each became progressively more violent in subsequent retellings in different media.[4]

These three novels center on monsters whose names have *become* eponyms of violence, shorthand notations for action, cartoons of concussion. In their print homes, however, they are much better behaved;

their violence is tempered compared to its later appearance in other media. Dracula is a perfect gentleman, lord of the castle, who, when he travels, is outfitted with bowler and walking stick. He keeps his hideous habits well out of sight; he is the most violent in print when he is exasperated with the pesky Van Helsing. The fact that the folkloric *nosferatu*, which is feral and barbaric, was displaced first by the gentleman vampire in John Polidori's Regency fiction, *The Vampyre*, then by the unctuous Varney of Thomas Pecket Prest's pulpy *Varney the Vampyre*, and eventually by the courtly Dracula in Bram Stoker's high Victorian novel, tells much about what print demands. The more intelligently the monster talks, the more successful he will be, at least in the novel. The Frankenstein monster in print is tame, almost timid. In Mary Shelley's novel, the creature is a little large, a little petulant, a little babyfaced, but he always tries to be articulate and polite. He is even a decent-enough guest in the months when he lives cooped-up behind the DeLacy house. He is a lover of natural beauty, a reader of Plutarch, Goethe, and Milton, a self-educated bootstrap puller. If only he could have had a little mothering, he assures us, he would not have turned monstrous. He wants only a little companionship—perhaps a female friend. In fact, Victor Frankenstein could have quieted his composite creature by creating a companion for him as he had promised. (And surely if Victor was concerned about populating the world with kind and sensitive monsters, he could have made the female companion without reproductive capacities.) When you examine Dracula and Frankenstein in print, you clearly see the father figure and the adolescent self, the lord of the castle and the bumbling teenager. You are also seeing nonviolent characters whose occasional fury is condensed and/or only alluded to in passing.

When you look at Dr. Jekyll and Mr. Hyde in print, however, you see something less complex. Dracula and the Frankenstein monster are polite, misunderstood, and unhappy creatures. Mr. Hyde is a boor. He is utterly mindless, absolutely inarticulate. He is called, and is, a troglodyte. In Stevenson's novella, Hyde is not really a character at all but rather the object of a mystery. His actions are all seen second-hand and, to an extent, are distanced by the chinabox narrative. He is never directly confronted. Still, in print, Hyde's only aggressive acts are running over a little matchgirl, writing nasty commentary in Jekyll's books, messing up the laboratory, and, unfortunately, beating the old man, Sir Danvers Carew, about the head with Jekyll's walking stick.

To be explained more fully in Chapter 5, the transformation of these three monsters from art prose to popular culture has involved the barbarizing of the first two and the humanizing of the third. To make them more into vehicles of violence, they must be anthropomorphized—the scapegoat monster must be capable of suffering. As Christ must be made human if his role is to be understood, so must the antichrist. Hogarth's

Tom Nero is the ideal of subversion. Monsters in popular culture must be violent enough to mandate still more violence against themselves and yet they must be able to feel the revengers' wrath. To draw forth and legitimize that wrath, they must be provided with predictable victims to molest. Since the revengers are often adolescent males, the monsters' victims must be the objects of youthful male ardor. When the speed of transmission is fast, as with television cartoons or movies, recognition of motifs is essential. Victims of monsters in electronic media are more pronounced in their sexuality than their cousins in Victorian prose and must know exactly how to act. There is no counterpart in electronic renditions for Mrs. Mina Harker, wife of Jonathan the vampire pursuer and Dracula's second female victim in the book. There is no counterpart for Victor Frankenstein's brother William, or cousin Justine, or best friend Henry, all of whom the monster attacks en route to do vengeance on his creator. Such secondary victims clog the story which must be viewed at one sitting. However, since *The Strange Case of Dr. Jekyll and Mr. Hyde* provided us with few appropriate victims (the matchgirl and Carew), the theatrical and filmic versions added Hyde's prostitute. They added Jekyll's fiancée as well, but she is untouched; on the other hand, her *Doppelgänger*, the prostitute, is brutalized.

Without a victim there can be no violation, and without violation there can be no violence, and without violence there can be no retributive vengeance, and without vengeance there can be no preposterous violence. The victim for preposterous violence in the gothic, especially when the gothic switches its medium from print to film and spreads to a broader audience, is the about-to-reproduce female. She is the virgin on the edge of induction into sexuality, or in the nineteenth-century context, she is about to be married. In *Dracula* films the victim is Lucy; in *Frankenstein* she is Elizabeth; and because she doesn't exist in *Dr. Jekyll and Mr. Hyde*, she had to be created later, first on stage and then in the movie versions. She is a barely deflected double of Dr. Jekyll's forbidden fiancée, the seductive woman of the streets. From a sociobiological point of view, this is the female for whom males must battle. She controls their genetic future. Her unclaimed reproductive capacity, her virginity, is exactly what activates the monster. He promises to make her his "bride," and we all know what that means. In each case, violence first erupts when the young woman is withheld from the humanized monster's advances and then explodes when the young male(s) must take revenge. The Lucy character is protected by her suitors—there are four of them! Elizabeth is half-heartedly guarded by her husband-to-be, Victor. And Mr. Hyde emanates from beneath Dr. Jekyll (this in the cinematic version; there is no love interest in the printed text) when the future father-in-law character thinks Dr. Jekyll should wait before rushing into marriage and so takes his daughter away to Europe.

Initially, the act of denied sexual activity releases the monster. He is not very far below the surface anyway. To be sure, Dracula is a gentleman, the Frankenstein monster polite to a fault, and Dr. Jekyll an altruistic physician. But once partnership (sex) is denied, all hell literally breaks loose. Nothing will now restore the facade of normalcy. The unforgivable sin has been committed. The id, if you will, is loose, and although it may desire sex, it will now settle for violence. The only resolution is death. So Dracula must be brutally staked and the Frankenstein monster burned. Since Mr. Hyde can only be ejected by Dr. Jekyll, the good doctor (who is really not so good) must reassert goodness by doing evil. He must commit suicide in print while on celluloid the police finish him off.

Let's have some violence, these myths seem to say, and then let's really kill off the monster. Snarly Dracula, the glum Frankenstein monster, and confused Jekyll play out a script in which victims are frightened and often hurt and in which the victimizers themselves must finally be horribly killed. Like the detective story, the gothic contains two stories of violence, one natural and the other preposterous. The first is committed by the monster on his victims, a violence usually cloaked in the guise of sating some hunger (blood, power, sex). The second is the scenario of revenge. Here the violence is done to "it" by us. We follow the vampire hunters/detectives as they track the creature down and destroy him. We are part of the mob chasing the Frankenstein monster and hunting for Mr. Hyde. If the monster commits "x" violence, our vengeance can be "2x." The monster is willing enough. He almost always cooperates. Dracula is happy to be staked: "To die . . . to *really* die . . . that must be wonderful." In the novel, the Frankenstein creature, having wreaked havoc, peacefully wanders off among the ice floes to immolate himself. (Where he gets the firewood is anyone's guess. Perhaps from the same place where he finds all the oversized clothing that fits his nine-foot-tall frame.) In the movies, however, we like to be the ones to fan the flames. And at the end of the cinematic Dr. Jekyll/ Mr. Hyde movies, the dying Hyde's face transforms into the much-relieved visage of Jekyll. All is finally well. Violence by him on us, and by us on him, is quelled. These fables of aggression end with the reproductive future assured. Mina Harker does indeed give birth to her husband's baby; Victor Frankenstein has learned his lesson and now can get married, and presumably Dr. Jekyll's fiancée can find a mate.

The gothic genre is not sex *and* violence. The gothic is repressed sex and therefore violence. Had sex been possible, the gothic conventions would have been shoved aside and the romance tradition would have carried the story. But in the gothic, sex is never possible. Violence is. The question then becomes why sex is not possible. Or, more precisely, why to the audience of these myths is the kind of sex posited in the stories not able to reach completion? In the romance tradition, sex is possible, even inevitable, after some relevant link has been snapped into the chain of causality. But there is no such link in the gothic; quite the opposite. The victim learns that this character, the monster, cannot be countenanced, even though in each case what he wants seems so trifling—just a kiss on the neck, just companionship, just a chance to blow off steam.

In *Dreadful Pleasures: An Anatomy of Modern Horror,* I argued that the monsters in these myths were displaced family members and that the horror generated was often that of inappropriate seduction—the horror of incest. In *Forbidden Partners: The Incest Taboo in Modern Culture,* I tried to show how important reproductive codes were embedded elsewhere in our other fables. But what I could not explain was why these print stories should have become so much more violent in other media. Was it because when they changed the medium from gothic novel to penny dreadful to stage production to celluloid to comic book to television they became "hyped up" to attract the audience? Could electrons and photons so hyperbolize the stories of print and pulp? Surely the medium played an important part, but was it the message that somehow had changed? Was it because the myths met a younger and younger audience as they traveled out of the nineteenth century? Each younger audience had different anxieties that exaggerated different aspects of the myths. These anxieties were always sexual, but once the myths met the adolescent audience, sex was linked not with procreation or love but with confusion, and confusion with violence.

These stories have *become* progressively more violent. They are, perhaps, the most violent in our culture. Dracula, although sometimes played for a mature audience as was the 1978 version starring Frank Langella, is more usually a snarling menace. Observe the difference between the controlled Dracula as played by the melancholy Bela Lugosi and the modern hyperactive one played by Christopher Lee (of Hammer Studios' wildly successful series from *Horror of Dracula* in the late 1950s to *Dracula A.D. 1972*) and you will see how violent the movie version has become as audience age level has dropped. Frankenstein's monster, largely because of Boris Karloff's acting and Kenneth Strickfaden's make-up, is now the inarticulate, lumbering juggernaut with plenty of muscle but without a speck of brain power. He was the exact opposite in print. Mr. Hyde has broken loose from his overly idealistic host and is terrorizing local theaters as the stalk-and-slash, slice-and-dice psycho-killer of the *He Knows You're Alone, Don't Go in the Attic, Friday the 13th* genre. Violence, which had always inhered in the gothic myths, has come loose from the text and is played out independent of the original story line. What has remained is the two-part structure: monsters attack our virgins and we retaliate with an attack on him. Of late, however, our counterattacks have often proved feckless, thereby necessitating a sequel.

We may be tempted to claim that violence begets violence, that audiences habituated to a certain degree of excitement will crave more and more thrills in order to be shocked. Instead, it may be true that younger audiences are claiming the stories and electronic media are responding. In fact, the audience age for the gothic has steadily decreased as violence has increased. The print audience of the Victorian penny dreadfuls and bloody pulps had shoved aside the novel audience by the turn of the century. In our century, the movie audience, whose average age was in the thirties when Universal Studios was producing their horror sequence from 1932 to 1948 (from Lugosi's Dracula to Karloff's Frankenstein to Chaney Jr.'s Wolfman), has been replaced by the current pubescent (twelve to nineteen) audience of *Aliens, The Fly, Halloween 4*. The reason that "they're not making movies the way they used to" is rather simple. The only audience with enough time and disposable income to see films is primarily made up of adolescents.

What is this audience reading? Or has this audience deserted print for the movies and television? Has violence become so visual and kinetic that it has forsaken ink forever to be conveyed in unending reels of film and the short-hand sequences of action/adventure television? What has happened to the print cartoons, the *EC* comics of prose? This entertainment violence is currently carried in the prose of the most popular and successful and rich writer alive—Stephen King. His genius for transforming sequences of preposterous violence into print promises not only to resurrect the moribund print gothic from intellectuals on the one hand and schlock romance on the other, but also to blur still more the distinctions between media. His monsters, grafted onto the Victorian archetypes, have revived the violence/vengeance paradigm with such success that "Stephen King" has become an adjective. He has endowed these monsters with an immediate imagery and startling violence never before seen in print. His "postliterate prose," as *Time* disparages it, is the logical and inevitable result of advances in publishing, increasing literacy, shifting demographics, advertising culture, and electronic media.

Although Stephen King's audience is vast, the prime audience (and by that I mean the audience that he writes for that awaits his next book or movie) is primarily adolescent.[5] Let us remember that in our culture adolescence extends into the mid-twenties and beyond. I do not disparage this audience; we have all been part of it, and all great artists—Voltaire, Twain, Swift, Dickens—have known how to find it, but King's genius is that he has been able to rivet that audience in place. We meet the works of Stephen King after Maurice Sendak and before Ruth Westheimer. For many of us, Stephen King is all we will ever read. It surely is a sign of his "reach" that New American Library, King's paperback publisher, has commissioned a *Teacher's Manual: The Novels of Stephen King* in which the manual's author includes a helpful "Note to the Teacher." If you are having trouble teaching "good" books, the fellow teacher explains, realize that the student of today will probably read only horror stories:

> Students should naturally be encouraged in this effort, and the horror genre should not be shunned if that is the area of a student's particular interest. Given a chance, student fans of horror are likely to select a novel by Stephen King for their outside reading assignment. The teacher, therefore, should be aware that the works of Stephen King are not for the squeamish or easily offended reader. His characters are realistically portrayed and possess the habits, frailties and attributes of people we know and meet every day; they smoke cigarettes, drink to excess, use profane language, and engage in sexual liaisons, just as many real people do. Similarly, King's depictions of violence are graphic, created in order to achieve a total and realistic effect. (Zagorski, pp. 17–18)

For those who grew up before reading a King novel became a stage of maturation, some background may be in order. Stephen King is an industry which is essentially in the business of providing violent shock, or in Mr. King's words: "What I owe my readers is a good ride on the roller coaster, and that's all" (quoted by Janeczko, p. 10). In this carnival Mr. King is the barker, or as he says, a "brand name." Like a brand name, he is literally all over the place, in every nook and cranny an adolescent can find. His novels are omnipresent in bookstores and grocery stores in large "terror-tory" displays—the Stephen King boutique. Adaptations of his novels and short stories, as well as his own screenplays, appear almost monthly on television or at the movies. He has also now taken to directing his own work *(Maximum Overdrive)* to give the film what his audience claims is lacking—the "Stephen King touch." That "touch" is really a shove, for what Stephen King does best is to create a cinematic world in which violence erupts with startling, explosive power.

To create believable sequences of unbelievable violence, King translates popular culture into prose seamlessly. The technique is not peculiar to King—consider the works of Thomas Pynchon or Donald Barthelme—but King does it with no intellectual filter, with no self-conscious art. His worlds are echo chambers of popular culture. The incantative method is a variation of stream of nonconsciousness, an endless litany of brand names, song lyrics, road signs, route numbers, TV listings, *People* magazine tidbits—you name it. If it passes through the average day, it will pass as well through the novels. This stuff is the matrix that holds sequences together, like the recognizable objects inside scenes that make us believe movie sequences. They are more "real" than real life because we recognize them sooner. The camera "sees" to that. Traditional gothic novels were grounded in fantasy—after all, the authors felt it necessary to create make-believe worlds or else ship their protagonists off to some Mediterranean country in order to achieve the proper *mise en scène*—but Stephen King does just the opposite. He opens up shop next door at the 7–11. He is so resolutely inelegant, so gleefully common, so vulgar, so able to extract the lowest common denominator from whatever he is describing that we forget we are reading words instead of looking at pictures. Stephen King's narrative voice is the same voice we hear at the movies doing the "voice over," and the scenes are the ones we see at the Cineplex 16. It is almost like dreaming to read his novels. It is like reading a horror movie. And, naturally enough, that is their power. As his colleague and one-time collaborator Peter Straub (*The Talisman*) has said, this style is the opposite of literary style—it is no style at all ("Meeting Stevie," p. 10). You can't really "read" a King novel in any traditional sense. If you slow down, you'll lose traction. You *have* to skim. With some insight King himself calls it the "literary equivalent of a Big Mac and large fries." His prose is best digested as it is ingested . . . or, better yet, predigested. Critics who regularly lambaste King's prose as unreadable miss the point. It can't be read; it must be looked at.

The skyrocketing of Stephen King's career is an example of what happens when hybrid techniques are introduced into mass culture. Just as the comic strip was able to link print and illustration in the nineteenth century to find a large audience, so King has combined film and prose to produce what is essentially a verbal kinescope and an even larger audience.[6] King's "agreement" with the movies has been reciprocal. Not only does his prose take the small step from page to screen, but many of his books derive from movies: *Carrie*, for instance, traces its ancestry to *The Brain from Planet Arous*, and *'Salem's Lot* derives from the Hammer Studios' *Dracula* series. More importantly, King's narrative technique is full of filmic devices: flashbacks, shock cuts, intercutting, pans, and especially camera pullbacks. Even his persona, the Stephen King who tells the tales, is the slightly wry narrator of the 1950s' outerspace horrors like *Plan 9 from Outer Space*. King is a superb arranger of scenes and whole sequences. Ironically, one of the problems encountered in putting a Stephen King novel onto film is that his sequences are better than most film directors can reproduce.[7]

By building the cinematic roller coaster in prose, Stephen King not only is the most popular writer today (some 50 million copies of six novels written in less than a decade) but also one of the wealthiest. His vision has earned him more than 30 million dollars. When *Forbes* ran a special issue on "entertainment's biggest earners" for 1986, King was up near the top with the actors, pop singers, cartoonists, and producers, just above Paul McCartney and Tom Selleck and below Kenny Rogers and Prince. King was the only author on the list and probably the most financially successful living author. When the weekly newsmagazines account for his success, they betray their bourgeois bias and his talent. *Time* considers him under the rubric Show Business, while the more straightforward *Newsweek* settles for Business. In fact, the business of delivering preposterous violence has transformed publishers' row. Because of King, much of what used to be accepted wisdom has now been called into question. For instance, it was once accepted wisdom that a novelist should never publish more than one book at a time, for doing so would rob him of his full (i.e., paying) audience. Hardcover buyers have to be given enough time to read the book before the paperback hordes gain access. Then after the first-run paperback appears, the publisher should wait awhile before releasing the rights to the often more profitable productions of television and movies. Finally, if the movie is a hit, the paperback should be reissued for those who saw the movie and now want the book.

Stephen King changed all that. He is the only writer ever to have three books simultaneously on the *New York Times* hard- and softcover bestseller lists. To some degree bowing to conventional wisdom, he did publish five books under the pseudonym Richard Bachman so as not to dilute his audience. Yet once the Bachman books were known to be by King, the only change was that they too became bestsellers. For three weeks (November 17–31, 1985 and January 12–18, 1986), King had five simultaneous entries on the bestseller list: hardcover—*Skeleton Crew* and *The Bachman Books;* mass market—*The Talisman* and *Thinner;* and trade paperback—*The Bachman Books.* In 1986–87 Stephen King published five hardcover novels with the expectation that his audience, instead of having exhausted itself, would only want more. He was right. After all, the nature of popular entertainment is repetitive consumption. The adolescent does not say, "I saw *Star Wars*," but, "I saw *Star Wars* twenty times." The secret of the carnival loop-the-loop is not that it is ridden once but that it is ridden again and again. Repetition, however, implies that whatever inheres in the experience does not so much wear out as become mastered.

What did Mr. King do in the ten years from *Carrie* in 1974 to *Pet Sematary* in 1984 that he should have become such a force in all the popular media? When you look at the novels a second time (something difficult to do because of the hazard of rereading what was not meant to be carefully read the first time), you will see that the attraction lies more in the preliterate anxieties than in the "postliterate" prose. Mr. King is able to exploit these anxieties, most of which have to do with violence, not with real violence but with the *EC* comic-book, special-effects violence of horror movies. This is violence contrived not to be taken seriously, not to be believed, but to shock and to be endured. It is violence drawn not from life but from fairy tales filtered through gothic conventions.

As in fairy tales, the usual trigger for violence is outside the natural world. The shock is generated when some force disrupts the habitual world of ordinary predictability. In *Carrie* the protagonist's telekinesis is preternatural; it just is, that's all. In *The Shining, Christine*, and *It*, the hotel, car, and town are all haunted; no explanation is necessary or forthcoming. In *The Dead Zone* a physical trauma has rearranged a chemical part of John Smith's brain so that he knows a lot of things he has no business knowing, but neither he nor we know how. In *Fire-starter*, the pyrokinesis is the accidental result of mind-altering drugs taken a generation earlier in a LSD-type of experiment. When the violence is not inexplicably preternatural, it is inexplicably demonic as in the vampires of *'Salem's Lot*, the resurrecting burial grounds of *Pet Sematary*, or the devil himself as Randall Flagg of *The Stand*. The closest that Stephen King ever comes in his novels to natural violence, that is, violence in which causality can be traced through the real world, is in *Cujo*, in which a Saint Bernard dog is made rabid by a bat's bite. A key to understanding the attraction of Stephen King's violence is that it is *never* the result of human will. It follows the naturalistic tradition of nineteenth-century novels like those of Hardy, Crane, Norris, and Dreiser, in which there is no free will at all. Motivation is straight out of *EC* comics.[8]

Perhaps a look at these novels by King will show what the largest audience for prose fiction currently wants to see. I will confine myself to commenting only on the novels from *Carrie* to *Pet Sematary*, which were directly written by King in a ten-year period, and to those sequences of preposterous violence around which the stories galvanize attention. In other words, I am going to examine only the steepest drops in the roller coaster without taking the whole ride.

Carrie is Cinderella in sneakers. All the fairy tale characters are present and accounted for. There is the wicked stepmother, the nasty sisters (the school girls), the fairy godmother (the gym teacher), the costume ball (the prom), and even the lost slipper (Carrie's humiliation at the prom). But, whereas in celluloid folklore à la Disney the handsome prince arrives the next day to put matters on a proper footing, in this telling à la King, there is no next day—literally. Carrie's coming of age ends not with an "I do" but with a boom. She blows up the castle. King is true to the real spirit of the folk tale, for often variations tell how Cinderella revenges herself on her oppressive family by cutting their hands and noses off. Carrie's coming of age (her telekinetic powers are tied to the onset of menarche) is also her coming into violence. She doesn't like this; she is not happy to have these powers, but what will be must be.

To set the stage literally for these telekinetic powers to be invoked, King's *Carrie* is publicly humiliated in a locale we all too easily remember—the shower of the high-school gym. By a series of cruel pranks, Carrie, an ugly duckling, becomes queen of the prom. At the moment when she accepts the throne some high-school nasties release a bucket of pig blood which pours down on her from the rafters. Now that vengeance is mandated, King is able to display his wares. Here in King's first piece of extended fiction, one can see how close he is to writing not the novel but the film. I quote it at length to show the almost storyboard nature of the prose.

When the buckets fell, she was at first only aware of a loud, metallic clang cutting through the music, and then she was deluged in warmth and wetness. She closed her eyes instinctively. There was a grunt from beside her, and in the part of her mind that had come so recently awake, she sensed brief pain. . . .

Suddenly, as if a videotape machine had been turned on in her mind, she saw [a teacher] running toward her, and saw her thrown out of her way like a rag doll as she used her mind on her without even consciously thinking of it.

She rolled over on her back, eyes staring wildly at the stars from her painted face. She was forgetting
(!!THE POWER!!)

It was time to teach them a lesson. Time to show them a thing or two. She giggled hysterically. It was one of Momma's pet phrases.

(momma coming home putting her purse down eyeglasses flashing well i guess i showed that elt a thing or two at the shop today)

There was the sprinkler system. She could turn it on, turn it on easily. She giggled again and got up, began to walk barefoot back toward the lobby doors. Turn on the sprinkler system and close all the doors. Look in and let them *see* her looking in, watching and laughing while the shower ruined their dresses and their hairdos and took the shine off their shoes. Her only regret was that it couldn't be blood.

The lobby was empty. She paused halfway up the stairs and FLEX, the doors all slammed shut under the concentrated force she directed at them, the pneumatic door-closers snapping off. She heard some of them scream and it was music, sweet soul music.

For a moment nothing changed and then she could feel them pushing against the doors, wanting them to open. The pressure was negligible. They were trapped.

(*trapped*)

and the word echoed intoxicatingly in her mind. They were under her thumb, in her power. *Power!* What a word that was!

She went the rest of the way up and looked in and George Dawson was smashed up against the glass, struggling, pushing, his face distorted with effort. There were others behind him, and they all looked like fish in an aquarium.

She glanced up and yes, there were the sprinkler pipes, with their tiny nozzles like metal daisies. The pipes went through small holes in the green cinderblock wall. There were a great many inside, she remembered. Fire laws or something.

Fire laws. In a flash her mind recalled

(black thick cords like snakes)

the power cords strung all over the stage. They were out of the audience's sight, hidden by the footlights, but she had had to step carefully over them to get to the throne. Tommy had been holding her arm.

(fire and water)

She reached up with her mind, felt the pipes, traced them. Cold, full of water. She tasted iron in her mouth, cold wet metal, the taste of water drunk from the nozzle of a garden hose.

Flex

For a moment nothing happened. Then they began to back away from the doors, looking around. She walked to the small oblong of glass in the middle door and looked inside.

It was raining in the gym.

Carrie began to smile.

She hadn't gotten all of them, only some. But she found that by looking up at the sprinkler system with her eyes, she could trace its course more easily with her mind. She began to turn on more of the nozzles, and more. Yet it wasn't enough. They weren't crying yet, so it wasn't enough.

(hurt them then hurt them)

There was a boy on stage by Tommy, gesturing wildly and shouting something. As she watched, he climbed down and ran toward the rock band's equipment. He caught hold of one of the microphone stands and was transfixed. Carrie watched, amazed, as his body went through a nearly motionless dance of electricity. His feet shuffled in the water, his hair stood up in spikes, and his mouth jerked open, like the mouth of a fish. He looked funny. She began to laugh.

(by christ then let them all look funny)

And in a sudden, blind thrust, she yanked at all the power she could feel.

Some of the lights puffed out. There was a dazzling flash somewhere as a live power cord hit a puddle of water. There were dull thumps in her mind as circuit breakers went into hopeless operation. The boy who had been holding the mike stand fell over on one of his amps and there was an explosion of purple sparks and then the crepe bunting that faces the stage was burning.

Just below the thrones, a live 220-volt electricity cable was crackling on the floor and beside it Rhonda Simard was doing a crazed puppet dance in her green tulle formal. Its full skirt suddenly blazed into flame and she fell forward, still jerking.

It might have been at that moment that Carrie went over the edge. She leaned against the doors, her heart pumping wildly, yet her body as cold as ice cubes. Her face was livid, but dull red fever spots stood on each cheek. Her head throbbed thickly, and conscious thought was lost.

She reeled away from the doors, still holding them shut, doing it without thought or plan. Inside the fire was brightening and she realized dimly that the mural must have caught on fire.

She collapsed on the top step and put her head down on her knees, trying to slow her breathing. They were trying to get out the doors again, but she held them shut easily—that alone was no strain. Some obscure sense told her that a few were getting out the fire doors, but let them. She would get them later. She would get all of them. Every last one. (pp. 181, 185–89)

Carrie does get every last one. Before she is drained of telekinetic energy, she destroys the entire town. That destruction, of course, is every adolescent's dream of violent getting-even: not just in school but in the entire town. This is the wish-fulfillment we all daydream of—the violence of not just getting even but of getting total dominance. "Now they'll pay attention to me."

A similar, although less pyrotechnic, kind of violence erupts in *'Salem's Lot*. Instead of destruction from without, a plague unfolds from within. In King's retelling of Bram Stoker's *Dracula*, a small Maine town is under siege not from caped and fanged monsters from Transylvania but from New Yorkers—Straker, the vampire king, and his Renfield lackey, Barstow. As the English fear the intrusion of the Slavic East, so the New Englander fears the permanent intrusion of the summer people from the city. Also coming into this sealed-off culture is Ben Mears, a mystery writer. The sides are soon drawn. Mears, the Van Helsing of the piece, gathers his troops: Matthew Burke, an English teacher; Jimmy Cody, a doctor; Father Callahan, a doubting priest; and Mark Petrie, a sixth grader who, naturally, knows all about vampires. Mark is King's ideal reader—a bulk consumer of comics, television, and, no doubt, of Stephen King novels.

Vampire stories always come in two parts. In the first part, the vampire attacks the young man and the about-to-be-wed girl. In *Dracula*, this is Lucy Westenra; in *'Salem's Lot*, this is Susan Norton. The attack is heinous, not because of the physical damage the monster does, but because he ruins the young girl as a love (read "sex") object for her suitor(s). The deflowered virgin becomes more alluring, more sexy, at the same time that she becomes sexual (read "reproductive") poison. Therefore, in the second part of the story, revenge must be played out. The young men, under the guidance of an older man, a Van Helsing figure, must destroy and dispose of the vampire. The boys can be as violent as they want; the more the better. Dracula's act has both sanctioned violent revenge and demanded it.

"You can't catch me," mocks Dracula as he promises to remove still more females from the breeding pool. He is now the young man's perfect victim. He is asking for justified wrath. The vampire also provides some perfect practice victims along the way, for he repopulates the world with lesser vampires which the band of young men can dispose of in a crescendo of violence. King does not disappoint. In the last third of *'Salem's Lot*, almost every other page has a vampire-bashing scene in gruesome detail. This vampire-bashing is made all the more enjoyable because Straker's victims are all people for whom we never cared anyway in their prevampiric roles. They get their just deserts. Like George Romero's zombies (*Night of the Living Dead, Dawn of the Dead, Day of the Dead*), these second-generation vampires move slowly and are irredeemably dumb. Killing them becomes a carnival.

But not always. One of the most interesting of these stable motif killings is the ritual sacrifice of a virgin tainted by Dracula's attack. Lucy Westenra/Susan Norton becomes a vampire, the "Bloofer Lady," and must be put out of her torment by her husband-to-be. In Stoker's *Dracula*, Arthur Holmwood must drive a phallic stake through the heart of his corrupted fiancée, Lucy. Here is that scene from Jonathan Harker's point of view:

> Arthur took the stake and the hammer, and when once his mind was set on action his hands never trembled nor even quivered. Arthur placed the point over the heart, and as I looked I could see its dint in the white flesh. Then he struck with all his might.
>
> The Thing [Lucy Westenra] in the coffin writhed; and a hideous, blood-curdling screech came from the opened red lips. The body shook and quivered and twisted in wild contortions; the sharp white teeth champed together till the lips were cut, and the mouth was smeared with a crimson foam. But Arthur never faltered. He looked like a figure of Thor as his untrembling arm rose and fell, driving deeper and deeper the mercy-bearing stake, whilst the blood from the pierced heart welled and spurted up around it. His face was set, and high duty seemed to shine through it; the sight of it gave us courage so that our voices seemed to ring through the little vault.
>
> And then the writhing and quivering of the body became less, and the teeth seemed to champ, and the face to quiver. Finally it lay still. The terrible task was over. (p. 222)

That nineteenth-century scene becomes deliriously violent eighty years later as King rewrites it:

> And suddenly a line came to him [Ben Mears] from *Dracula*, that amusing bit of fiction that no longer amused him in the slightest. It

was Van Helsing's speech to Arthur Holmwood when Arthur had been faced with the same dreadful task: *We must go through bitter waters before we reach the sweet.*

Could there be sweetness for any of them, ever again?

"Take it away!" he groaned. "Don't make me do this—"

No answer.

He felt a cold, sick sweat spring out on his brow, his cheeks, his forearms. The stake that had been a simple baseball bat four hours before seemed infused with eerie heaviness, as if invisible yet titanic lines of force had converged on it.

He lifted the stake and pressed it against her [Susan Norton's] left breast just above the last fastened button of her blouse. The point made a dimple in her flesh, and he felt the side of his mouth begin to twitch in an uncontrollable tic.

"She's not dead," he said. His voice was hoarse and thick. It was his last line of defense.

"No," Jimmy said implacably. "She's Undead, Ben." He had shown them; had wrapped the blood-pressure cuff around her still arm and pumped it. The reading had been 00/00. He had put his stethoscope on her chest, and each of them had listened to the silence inside her.

Something was put into Ben's other hand—years later he still did not remember which of them had put it there. The hammer. The Craftsman hammer with the rubber perforated grip. The head glimmered in the flashlight's glow.

"Do it quickly," Callahan said, "and go out into the daylight. We'll do the rest."

We must go through bitter waters before we reach the sweet.

"God forgive me," Ben whispered.

He raised the hammer and brought it down.

The hammer struck the top of the stake squarely and the gelatinous tremor that vibrated up the length of ash would haunt him forever in his dreams. Her eyes flew open, wide and blue, as if from the very force of the blow. Blood gushed upward from the stake's point of entry in a bright and astonishing flood, splashing his hands, his shirt, his cheeks. In an instant the cellar was filled with its hot, coppery odor.

She writhed on the table. Her hands came up and beat madly at the air like birds. Her feet thumped an aimless, rattling tattoo on the wood of the platform. Her mouth yawned open, revealing shocking, wolflike fangs, and she began to peal forth shriek after shriek, like hell's clarion. Blood gushed from the corners of her mouth in freshets.

The hammer rose and fell: again . . . again . . . again.

Ben's brain was filled with the shrieks of large black crows. It whirled with awful, unremembered images. His hands were scarlet, the stake was scarlet, the remorselessly rising and falling hammer was scarlet. In Jimmy's trembling hands the flashlight became stroboscopic, illuminating Susan's crazed, lashing face in spurts and

flashes. Her teeth sheared through the flesh of her lips, tearing them
to ribbons. Blood splattered across the fresh linen sheet which Jimmy
had so neatly turned back, making patterns like Chinese ideograms.

And then, suddenly, her back arched like a bow, and her mouth
stretched open until it seemed her jaws must break. A huge explosion of darker blood issued forth from the wound the stake had
made—almost black in this chancy lunatic light: heart's blood. The
scream that welled from the sounding chamber of that gaping mouth
came from all the subcellars of deepest race memory and beyond
that, to the moist darknesses of the human soul. Blood suddenly
boiled from her mouth and nose in a tide . . . and something else.
In the faint light it was only a suggestion, a shadow, of something
leaping up and out, cheated and ruined. It merged with the darkness
and was gone.

She settled back, her mouth relaxing, closing. The mangled lips
parted in a last susurrating pulse of air. For a moment the eyelids
fluttered and Ben saw, or fancied he saw, the Susan he had met in
the park, reading his book. It was done.

He backed away, dropping the hammer, holding his hands out
before him, a terrified conductor whose symphony has run riot. (pp.
338–40)

This is vintage Stephen King: the Craftsman hammer with the perforated rubber grip, the focus on Ben's revulsion as well as on Susan's
pain, the acute specificity of the dimple of flesh, the blood pressure, the
splattering of hammer blows, all those fluids, the cinematic effects of the
strobe light illuminating the upgushing blood, and the catalog similes—
beating like birds, like hell's clarion, like crows' shrieks, like Chinese
ideograms, like a bow, like a conductor. Most striking, however, is King's
ability to evoke and sustain a high degree of frantic, cartoonic violence
while maintaining almost bemused detachment. The reader feels like a
child at a scary movie, attempting to dive under the seat while his jovial
neighbor is telling him not to worry; it'll be over soon. So we close our
eyes, put our hands over our heads, and duck down while the film continues to flicker and our friendly seatmate tells us it's all right. Roller
coasters always end right where they started.

The scene with Susan is not the most violent (either the bludgeoning
of Straker or the slicing of Jimmy takes that honor), but it does provide
an example of how King holds his narrative together. Although plot is
in abundance, plot is always secondary to the gathering and exploding
of violence. And that violence is not mediated through past time, not
diffused through complex narrative patterns, not diluted through symbols. The archetypal forms are included only to provide the context for
frantic action. This violence is never supposed to "mean" anything; it
is simply exciting and going to grow more so with each turning page.

If *'Salem's Lot* is King's retelling of the vampire story, Stoker's *Dra-*

cula, then *The Shining* is his haunted house tale, specifically Shirley Jackson's *Haunting of Hill House*. Again, the deliberately outrageous plot allows King to produce some of his most startling *frissons*. Little Danny Torrance is taken by his violent father (the unstable duke) and docile mother (the fragile gothic heroine) to spend the winter cooped up in an ancient Colorado hotel (the gothic castle deep in the woods). On the surface the family seems hopelessly normal: battered car, diet of junk food, history of child abuse, marital stresses, alcoholism—all normal except Danny. The boy has a "shine," an ability to see the future. The hotel is supersentient as well. It has all the accouterments of the gothic castle made modern: elevators which run on their own, fire hoses which become snakes, wasps which swarm over the innocent, an exploding boiler, and even a topiary garden of large beasts which come alive.

Once again, we don't read so much for plot or character as we do for those passages of exaggerated activity. The violence of Danny's father, Jack, is the violence of the "normal"—all parents have wanted to lash out at a child or a spouse—which sets up the bizarre violence of the abnormal—the hotel's literal outburst. The Overlook Hotel carries within it scenes, again cinematic scenes, of such charge that we almost cringe while watching them. King's internal narrator always comforts us forward, leading us by the reassuring hand over what we think is familiar territory. Like the narrator in the horror film or, better still, like the narrator in Poe's "The Cask of the Amontillado," he always tells us we can go back, that we can sit in the "coward's corner," if we don't have the courage to continue. And so, of course, we continue until too late. The shackles are on our hands and we see the bricks rise up and explode in front of us. Take, for instance, what Danny sees in one of the rooms that he has been forbidden to enter. Once again, the scene unspools like celluloid on sprockets, never giving us a chance to pause, much less to contemplate. In this genre, to hesitate is to be lost. Danny sees

> a long room, old-fashioned, like a Pullman car. Tiny white hexagonal tiles on the floor. At the far end, a toilet with the lid up. At the right, a washbasin and another mirror above it, the kind that hides a medicine cabinet. To the left, a huge white tub on claw feet, the shower curtain pulled closed. Danny stepped into the bathroom and walked toward the tub dreamily, as if propelled from outside himself, as if this whole thing were one of the dreams . . . that he would perhaps see something nice when he pulled the shower curtain back, something Daddy had forgotten or Mommy had lost, something that would make them both happy—
> So he pulled the shower curtain back.
> The woman in the tub had been dead for a long time. She was bloated and purple, her gas-filled belly rising out of the cold, ice rimmed water like some fleshy island. Her eyes were fixed on Dan-

ny's, glassy and huge, like marbles. She was grinning, her purple lips pulled back in a grimace. Her breasts lolled. Her pubic hair floated. Her hands were frozen on the knurled porcelain sides of the tub like crab claws.

Danny shrieked. But the sound never escaped his lips; turning inward and inward, it fell down in his darkness like a stone in a well. He took a single blundering step backward, hearing his heels clack on the white hexagonal tiles, and at the same moment his urine broke, spilling effortlessly out of him.

The woman was sitting up.

Still grinning, her huge marble eyes fixed on him, she was sitting up. Her dead palms made squittering noises on the porcelain. Her breasts swayed like ancient cracked punching bags. There was the minute sound of breaking ice shards. She was not breathing. She was a corpse, and dead long years.

Danny turned and ran. Bolting through the bathroom door, his eyes starting from their sockets, his hair on end like the hair of a hedgehog about to be turned into a sacrificial

(croquet? or roque?)

ball, his mouth open and soundless. He ran full-tilt into the outside door of 217, which was now closed. He began hammering on it, far beyond realizing that it was unlocked, and he had only to turn the knob to let himself out. His mouth pealed forth deafening screams that were beyond human auditory range. He could only hammer on the door and hear the dead woman coming for him, bloated belly, dry hair, out-stretched hands—something that had lain slain in that tub for perhaps years, embalmed there in magic.

The door would not open, would not, would not, would not. (pp. 217–18)

All the hallmarks of King's prose are here: the specificity, the brand names, the gallop of similes, the catalog of details, the first dispassionate and then passionate tone. But what is more telling is that this sequence of stills is a throwaway scene. The woman in Room 217 is simply a light socket into which our finger is placed while King turns up the voltage. It prepares us for the later charge in which the entire hotel, like Poe's House of Usher, comes alive and explodes into smithereens. The difference is that in Poe's story we are witnesses from the outside and asked to make sense of what we have seen; in King's we are trapped within and never given pause to consider.

The only artistically pretentious movie ever made from a Stephen King novel was Stanley Kubrick's *The Shining* (1980). Kubrick attempted to fill in the blanks, plug the holes, provide causality, and develop character, explanation, and coherence. To accomplish this, the demonic Overlook had to fade while Jack, played by a hebephrenic Jack Nicholson, had to be brought front and center. Kubrick's *Shining* is a stunningly filmed and choreographed *danse macabre*, but it is not the

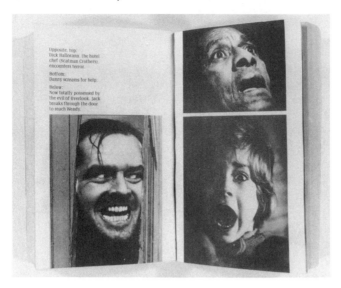

Film stills from Stanley Kubrick's adaptation of Stephen
King's *The Shining*, 1980, included in the paperback edition
of the novel (Warner Brothers/New American Library)

violent saturnalia of the novel. King himself reported disappointment
over this refining of his vision:

> Kubrick just couldn't grasp the sheer inhuman evil of the Overlook
> Hotel. So he looked, instead, for evil in the characters and made the
> film into a domestic tragedy with only vaguely supernatural over-
> tones. That was the basic flaw. Because [Kubrick] couldn't believe
> [in the supernatural] he couldn't make the film believable to others.
> The book is about Jack Torrance's gradual *descent* into madness
> through the malign influence of the Overlook, which is like a huge
> storage battery charged with an evil powerful enough to corrupt all
> those who come into contact with it. If the guy is nuts to begin with
> then the entire tragedy of his downfall is wasted. For that reason,
> the film has no center and no heart, despite its brilliantly unnerving
> camera angles and dazzling use of the Steadicam. What's basically
> wrong with Kubrick's version of *The Shining* is that it's a film by a
> man who thinks too much and feels too little; and that's why, for
> all its virtuoso effects, it never gets you by the throat and hangs on
> the way real horror should. ("Playboy Interview," pp. 74–75)

While the movie ends in an ice labyrinth, the book ends in a glorious
fireball as the ancient boiler lets loose a final burst of power. This image
of conflagration is drawn not from nature but from Hollywood. In fact,
flames end the novels *Carrie, Firestarter, The Stand,* and *'Salem's Lot*
as well. King's talent is that he is able to get inside the smoke, able to
describe the burst of violence and slow it down as do films shot in slow

motion. It is not coincidental that since *Bonnie and Clyde* and *The Wild Bunch*, in which slow motion or stop-action filming accentuated frantic activity, the same special effects have leaked into prose fiction. In *The Shining*, the process "reads" in the following way:

> The Overlook's windows shattered. In the ballroom, the dome over the mantelpiece clock cracked, split in two pieces, and fell to the floor. The clock stopped ticking: cogs and gears and balance wheel all became motionless. There was a whispered, sighing noise, and a great billow of dust. In 217 the bathtub suddenly split in two, letting out a small flood of greenish, noxious-smelling water. In the Presidential Suite the wallpaper suddenly burst into flames. The batwing doors of the Colorado Lounge suddenly snapped their hinges and fell to the dining room floor. Beyond the basement arch, the great piles and stacks of old papers caught fire and went up with a blowtorch hiss. Boiling water rolled over the flames but did not quench them. Like burning autumn leaves below a wasp's nest, they whirled and blackened. The furnace exploded, shattering the basement's roof beams, sending them crashing down like the bones of a dinosaur. The gasjet which had fed the furnace, unstoppered now, rose up in a billowing pylon of flame through the riven floor of the lobby. The carpeting on the stair risers caught, racing up to the first-floor level as if to tell dreadful news. A fusillade of explosions ripped the place. The chandelier in the dining room, a two-hundred-pound crystal bomb, fell with a splintering crash, knocking tables every which way. Flame belched out of the Overlook's five chimneys at the breaking clouds. (p. 434)

This ability to anatomize explosive violence from the inside out is central to Stephen King's *The Stand* and *Firestarter*. In *The Stand*, a tedious geopolitical fable in which an influenza virus causes the end of almost all human life, violence is the matrix which holds the disparate characters and subsidiary plots together. Naturally, it is indeed almost the end of the world when a huge nuclear bomb incinerates Las Vegas. En route to this Armageddon, King provides short incendiary previews of impending annihilation by having his own munitions' expert on board. Donald Merwin Elbert, nicknamed Trashcan Man, wanders about the subplots, blowing things up. Trashcan's primary purpose in the story is to provide the match whenever gunpowder or gasoline is around. He has a glorious time doing what a major part of King's audience also enjoys—playing with matches. Imagine all those gas stations waiting to explode, all those oil depots, those airplanes, those chemical factories, those trucks marked "Danger Flammable." In this scene he blows up Gary, Indiana:

> There was another coughing roar as rising air pressure caused the Cheery Oil Company office building to implode. Scimitars of glass whickered through the air. Chunks of concrete and cinderblock rained

out of the sky and hailed on the road. A whizzing piece of steel about the size of a quarter and the thickness of a Mars Bar sliced through Trashcan's shirt-sleeve and made a thin scrape on his skin. A piece big enough to have turned his head to guava jelly struck in front of his feet and then bounded away, leaving a good-sized crater behind. Then he was beyond the fallout zone, still running, the blood beating in his head as if his very brain had been sprayed with #2 heating oil and then set ablaze.

KA-WHAMM!

That was another one of the tanks, and the air resistance in front of him seemed to disappear and a large warm hand pushed him firmly from behind, a hand that fitted every contour of his body from heels to head; it *shoved* him forward with his toes barely touching the road, and now his face bore the terrified, pants-wetting grin of someone who had been attached to the world's biggest kite in a high cap of wind and let loose to fly, fly, baby, up into the sky until the wind goes somewhere else, leaving him to scream all the way down in a helpless power-dive. (p. 188)

The thrills of such explosions are not produced only for modern cinematic appetites. Think also of the nineteenth-century volcano paintings done by English artists who traveled to Italy just to capture the eruptions of Pompeii on canvas. Or what about the American luminists who traveled to Central America to catch sight of volcanic cones spewing magma? Or what of the sublime waterfalls and avalanches that thunder through Romantic art? Still better, what of the mid-century rage for quasi-biblical scenes detailing plague, flood, destruction, and general mayhem?

The taste for such *frisson* is old. It derives in part from the profound shifting of artistic sensibilities expressed by Edmund Burke in the mid-eighteenth century. The sublime, and all that it implied about jarring sensibilities, characterized first Romanticism and then much of popular culture. King is simply one of the more recent prose crafters of sublimities and the one most influenced by film. King's nineteenth-century counterpart would probably not be a novelist but a painter like John Martin. Martin's huge and violent visions delighted the great-grandparents of King's current audience. His apocalyptic illustrations became the standards of Victorian violence. Messotint, celluloid, and pulp did not create the appetite for visual concussion; nor have they sated it. Such imagery is the continuation of a tradition of titillation which began in earnest in the late eighteenth century and has yet to play itself out.

In *Firestarter*, King does his audience one better. Instead of having Trashcan Man perform combustible acts of legerdemain, he has a fourteen-year-old girl light the match—shades of Carrie! Here we have yet another fairy's child, this one little "Charlie" McGee, daughter of parents who were part of an LSD experiment which left them strangely

Samuel Colman, *The Delivery of Israel out of Egypt*, c. 1830 (Birmingham Museum and Art Gallery, England)

George Miller, *The End of the World*, 1830 (Sabin Galleries, Ltd.)

John Martin, *The Deluge*, 1828 (British Museum)

supernatural. Charlie's father has the ability to "push" people into doing his bidding simply by wishing them to, and Charlie has the power to burn things up just by looking at them. She looks, thinks, and . . . poof!—wish-fulfillment realized. Again, we have a child whose singular aberration makes her a social misfit while also giving her power over those who exile her. This is the adolescent audience's view of itself: ungainly, out of control, exiled, cast off. Mixed in with it is the day-dream of vengeance—retaliation on demand or, better yet, by desire. Clearly, vengeance by wish represents an immature, but powerful, problem resolution. In King, the hero(ine) is not powerful by confidence or intelligence but by fiat, by a visitation from some preternatural force. His characters derive strength not from the confidence of achievement but by gift.

Charlie's ability to ignite objects makes her the prize quest of the prize nasties, the CIA. They pursue father and daughter across upstate New York, *forcing* them to resort to violence. Along the way Charlie has the opportunity to blow up and explode an entire farm. Before our eyes, chickens, tractors, ducks, and geese all blow up in slow motion on the screen of flickering prose. To capture Charlie and her father alive, the CIA imports a real nasty, a villainous bounty hunter, John Rainbird. Rainbird wounds Charlie's father and insinuates himself into his place by seeming to protect Charlie from the CIA. The induction of the bad father is the necessary invocation for this fable of aggression, in much

John Martin, *The Fall of Babylon*, 1831 (British Museum)

the same way that Dracula is paired against Van Helsing to allow stronger retaliation. Charlie, now given carte blanche, can be a distaff Trashcan Man.

> Charlie turned toward the car and let the power loose in that direction. The power was still growing; it was turning into something that was lithe yet ponderous, an invisible something that now seemed to be feeding itself in a spiraling chain reaction of exponential force. The limo's gas tank exploded, enveloping the rear of the car and shooting the tailpipe into the sky like a javelin. But even before that happened the head and torso of the shooter were incinerated, the car's windshield had blown in, and the limousine's special self-sealing tires had begun to run like tallow.
>
> The car continued on through its own ring of fire, plowing out of control, losing its original shape, melting into something that looked like a torpedo. It rolled over twice and a second explosion shook it.
>
> She sent the force out, all of it. For a moment it seemed that nothing at all was happening; there was a faint shimmer in the air, like the shimmer above a barbecue pit where the coals have been banked . . . and then the entire house exploded.
>
> The only clear image she was left with (and later, the testimony of the survivors repeated it several times) was that of the chimney of the house rising into the sky like a brick rocketship, seemingly intact, while beneath it the twenty-five-room house disintegrated like a little girl's cardboard playhouse in the flame of a blowtorch. Stone, lengths of board, planks, rose into the air and flew away on

the hot dragon breath of Charlie's force. An IBM typewriter, melted and twisted into something that looked like a green steel dishrag tied in a knot, whirled up into the sky and crashed down between the two fences, digging a crater. A secretary's chair, the swivel seat whirling madly, was flung out of sight with the speed of a bolt shot from a crossbow. (pp. 373–74)

Unless these instances of violence are now worked into a properly unbelievable plot, a King novel can flounder. The key for the reader is to realize that while the context is recognizable, the action is *not*. One can see what happens when a King novel is rooted too firmly in the real world. In *The Dead Zone*, written roughly at the same time as *Firestarter*, John Smith has the power to see the past and future of anyone with whom he is in contact. He can find things, help in solving crimes, tell people what to do to avoid problems—he is an omniscient Ann Landers. Often, however, he cannot locate exactly when or where something will occur—hence the "dead zone." Again, his talent is a gift (resulting from a concussion), and he "pays" for it by having terrible migraines. There is little violence in *The Dead Zone* because, after the murderous Frank Dodd is done away with early in the book, there is no truly threatening villain who can sanction violence. James Bond cannot be 007 unless he has a Goldfinger, Dr. No, Emilio Largo, Blowfeld, or some other nefarious near-equal. John Smith has only Greg Stillson, a corrupt politician running for high office. John puts an end to Greg's career by showing him to be an egotistical coward, but this is hardly the stuff of shivers. Stillson is just a Watergate politician, not the devil, or a vampire, or a haunted house, or the CIA. Where are the mythic resonances in politicians? As contrasted with King's other books, *The Dead Zone* is a melancholy book and his worst bestseller. The hero has knowledge without power, is himself racked with pain, never gets the girl, and perhaps more importantly, never provides King with the fuses and TNT necessary to concoct a little explosion or two.

The next novels, *Cujo* and *Christine*, returned King to the tales he tells best—fairy tales. *Cujo* even starts, "Once upon a time," which is printed alone on a page separated from the rest of the text and is continued on page one, " . . . not so long ago, a monster came to the small town of Castle Rock, Maine." Although this "monster" is not the monster of *Cujo* but a reference to Frank Dodd, the psycho-killer of *The Dead Zone*, King is setting up the necessary context in which we can first understand and then sympathize with a two-hundred-pound, bat-bitten, and therefore rabid Saint Bernard. More importantly, in *Cujo* we are going inside the dog. This would be a narrative *tour de force* even if the dog were not rabid. *Cujo* is no send-up of the Richard Adams intricate *Watership Down* genre; *Cujo* is instead *Jaws on Paws*, a television movie for the kiddies. Once again, King's inspiration is not literary but cinematic. He recalls how the idea of the book came to him, a combination of an actual encounter with a large farm dog,

> mixed with those old "Movies of the Week," the made-for-television movies that they used to have on ABC. I thought to myself, what if you could have a situation that was an extension of one scene. It would be the ultimate TV movie. There would be one set, there would be one room. You'd never even have to change the camera angle. So there was one very small place, and it became Donna's Pinto—and everything just flowed from that situation . . . the big dog and the Pinto. (Quoted by Douglas Winter, *Stephen King*, pp. 96–97)

In no time at all, *Cujo* is up and snarling and biting and killing en route to the "movie of the week" finale: A mother, Donna, and her child, Tad, are trapped in a car, a Pinto, while the monster, Cujo, is foaming about outside trying to get in. Get the picture? Cut! Print. We are even supplied with some helpful Calvinism to get us over a few of the rough spots. Because Cujo has attacked and killed deserving victims thus far—a drunk and a wife beater—we are not entirely shocked that his victim should finally be Donna. For Donna has had a dalliance with a ne'er-do-well, tennis-playing poetaster. But what about Tad, the big-eyed, sweet-faced boychild of beatific innocence? Is this very image of Walter Keane sentimentality going to be killed? Yes, and it is one of the few genuine shocks in the King oeuvre. In the movie, Tad is spared, a concession to Hollywood's belief that only happily-ever-after conclusions succeed at the box office. But in the novel Tad's death allows Donna to unloose some vintage vengeance. The outraged mother is a potent source of preposterous violence for the same reason that youthful male violence is sanctioned. Young males battle monsters to make sure fecund females bear their children; females with children battle monsters to protect those children. Donna faces her monster, man's best friend, with the displaced instrument of manhood. This time it is not the Craftsman hammer with the perforated rubber handle but the good old American baseball bat.

> Donna cried out in a high, breaking voice and brought the bat down on Cujo's hindquarters. Something else broke. She heard it. The dog bellowed and tried to scramble away but she was on it again, swinging, pounding, screaming. Her head was high wine and deep iron. The world danced. She was the harpies, the Weird Sisters, she was all vengeance—not for herself, but for what had been done to her boy. The splintered handle of the bat bulged and pumped like a racing heart beneath her hands and beneath its binding of friction tape.
>
> The bat was bloody now. Cujo was still trying to get away, but his movements had slowed. He ducked one blow—the head of the

bat skittered through the gravel—but the next one struck him midway on his back, driving him to his rear legs.

She thought he was done; she even backed off a step or two, her breath screaming in and out of her lungs like some hot liquid. Then he uttered a deep snarl of rage and leaped at her again. She swung the bat and heard that heavy, whacking thud again . . . but as Cujo went rolling in the gravel, the old bat finally split in two. The fat part flew away and struck the right front hubcap of the Pinto with a musical *boing!* She was left with a splintered eighteen-inch wand in her hand.

Cujo was getting to his feet again . . . *dragging* himself to his feet. Blood poured down his sides. His eyes flickered like lights on a defective pinball machine.

And still it seemed to her that he was grinning.

"*Come on, then!*" she shrieked.

For the last time the dying ruin that had been good dog Cujo leaped at THE WOMAN that had caused all his misery. Donna lunged forward with the remains of the baseball bat, and a long sharp hickory splinter plunged deep into Cujo's right eye and then into his brain. There was a small and unimportant popping sound—the sound a grape might make when squeezed suddenly between the fingers. Cujo's forward motion carried him into her and knocked her sprawling. His teeth now snapped and snarled bare inches from her neck. She put her arm up as Cujo crawled farther on top of her. His eye was now oozing down the side of his face. His breath was hideous. She tried to push his muzzle up, and his jaws clamped on her forearm.

"*Stop!*" she screamed. "*Oh stop. Won't you ever stop? Please! Please! Please!*"

Blood was flowing down onto her face in a sticky drizzle—her blood, the dog's blood. The pain in her arm was a sheeting flare that seemed to fill the whole world . . . and little by little he was forcing it down. The splintered handle of the bat wavered and jiggled grotesquely, seeming to grow from his head where his eye had been.

He went for her neck.

Donna felt his teeth there and with a final wavering cry she pistoned her arms out and pushed him aside. Cujo thudded heavily to the ground.

His rear legs scratched at the gravel. He slowed . . . slowed . . . stopped. His remaining eye glared up at the hot summer sky. His tail lay across her shins, as heavy as a Turkish rug runner. He pulled in a breath and let it out. He took another. He made a thick snorting sound, and suddenly a rill of blood ran from his mouth. Then he died.

Donna Trenton howled her triumph. She got halfway to her feet, fell down, and managed to get up again. She took two shuffling steps and stumbled over the dog's body, scoring her knees with scrapes. She crawled to where the heavy end of the baseball bat lay, its far end streaked with gore. She picked it up and gained her feet again by holding on to the hood of the Pinto. She tottered back to where Cujo lay. She began to pound him with the baseball bat. Each downward swing ended with a heavy meat thud. Black strips of friction tape danced and flew in the hot air. Splinters gouged into the soft pads of her palms, and blood ran down her wrists and forearms. She was still screaming, but sounded as Cujo himself had near the end. The bat rose and fell. She bludgeoned the dead dog. (pp.287–89)

This prose has the flip-card effect of images flashed before our eyes. If it could be stabilized, the imagery would resemble a comic strip: whack-WHACK-whack-WHACK, with each whack a little more insistent. This primitiveness is one reason why King can be so ridiculed when quoted out of context and in small snippets. The colloquialisms, juxtapositions, brand names, burlesques, and all that make up his strange mélange depend on the same pulsating force of modern music. It is not happenstance that rock 'n roll lyrics almost punctuate his prose. For this is prose aspiring to be rock 'n roll. Like popular music, it is potent. Repetition with small variations and increasing crescendo has a fundamental, organic pulse to it, a pulse understood best by those who are themselves now dimly aware of an indistinct throbbing.

King's novels read like fairy tales because such incremental repetition is the core of orally transmitted lore. *Christine* is yet another *Bildungsroman*, this one telling of the coming of age of Arnie Cunningham (the confusion with Richie Cunningham of TV's *Happy Days* is purposeful; the local drive-in was called "Arnold's"). Here is the plot in brief: To get the girl, the boy must give up the car. The car, appropriately a 1958 Plymouth Fury, is haunted, like the Overlook Hotel. Christine has already suffocated a mother and child prior to being bought by, or rather prior to seducing, Arnie. In addition, the Fury has such peculiarities as an odometer which runs backwards, the ability to repair itself, and a radio which spontaneously plays tunes from the 1950s. Sentient machines are one of King's favorite subjects; in fact, his movie directing debut, *Maximum Overdrive*, details the terrors of a truck stop gone amok when the engines of the modern world conspire to overthrow their operators. With poetic justice, Christine is herself destroyed by Petunia, a septic tank truck, thereby allowing Arnie to make it safely through the traffic jam of adolescence and Stephen King readers to make it safely through yet another bulky 75,000-word novel.

Christine was written with a heavy hand. Projecting teenage libido onto a four-wheeled Fury is preposterous but predictable enough. The problem is that no violence can be first contained and then let loose. Without villains there can be no victims; without specific victims there can be no vengeance, and without vengeance violence can only be dissipated, and dissipated violence cannot be built upon. Christine is a were-wolf on treads, and she does indeed come alive, as do teenage boys, under the full moon. But every wolf needs a virgin to distress, and Leigh Cabot, the girlfriend, has no interest in either the car or the boy. So Christine spends most of her time bumping into walls at high speed, running over high-school bullies, laying rubber, and generally acting like a Tonka toy in the hands of a five-year-old.

The best of King's works from the early 1980s is *Pet Sematary*, in part because it is a retelling not of a television movie but of a literary text: W. W. Jacobs's short story "The Monkey's Paw." In effortless, colloquial prose, King gets us to accept what the Victorian readers of Jacobs knew was hokum: that resurrective powers exist and can, under certain circumstances, let the dead come back not as the living but as the living dead.

Louis Creed, an infirmary doctor at the University of Maine, is led by his neighbor Jud Candall, an old Maine guide, deep into the woods behind Creed's house to an ancient burial ground of the Wendigo Indians. We come to learn that this is a place for the dead to rest, to prepare themselves to return to the living—albeit living like a zombie. King, who is usually content to draw his fingernails across the blackboard as he runs out of class, here addresses a perplexing conundrum. If after your loved ones died you could have them by your side as slightly disturbed presences, would you want them around? Is life after death worth it for those still alive?

First to be carried by Creed into the ancient cemetery is Church the cat, who returns as a mildly loathsome and fetid beast. She is still a cat all right but by no means a pet. Then Creed's young son, Gage, is hit and killed by a truck. Now what is Creed to do? Again, King implies that free will is not a factor. The father will do anything rather than lose a child. So he is off to the Wendigo cemetery, the "pet sematary," with Gage.

Like the cat, Gage comes back. But unlike the cat, Gage contains a repressed demonic presence struggling to get out. In all King's works so far, children are portrayed as almost divine presences, as eidolons of innocence. Now we are introduced to a demonic child possessed by a fierce and as yet undeveloped resentment toward his parents.[9] In retrospect, the father should not have committed his Faustian deed. He should not have been so presumptuous. But in terms of the tale, this resurrection makes sense. This father did not sacrifice his only begotten son but rather revived him. To be sure, he carried the boy to the world beyond rather then let him molder in this one, but is that so evil? Perhaps King, almost beside himself, is showing that the apotheosizing of the child is often indulged in by those who are also the most resentful of children.

In any case, Gage returns from the dead, berserk, a cannibalistic demon. Indeed, he comes back from the dead and goes right to work on the living. Gage mutilates his mother, Rachel, and savages the neighbor, Jud. Here is what Louis Creed finds when he returns home a few days after burying Gage in the pet sematary. Again, one almost senses the Panoflex camera traveling through the scene.

Louis turned and was greeted by the sight of his wife, to whom he had once carried a rose in his teeth, lying halfway down the hall, dead. Her legs were splayed out as Jud's had been. Her back and head were cocked at an angle against the wall. She looked like a woman who had gone to sleep while reading in bed.

He walked down toward her.

Hello, darling, he thought, *you came home.*

Blood had splashed the wallpaper in idiot shapes. She had been stabbed a dozen times, two dozen, who knew? His scalpel had done this work.

Suddenly he saw her, really *saw* her, and Louis Creed began to scream.

His screams echoed and racketed shrilly through this house where now only dead lived and walked. Eyes bulging, face livid, hair standing on end, he screamed; the sounds came from his swollen throat like the bells of hell, terrible shrieks that signaled the end not of love but sanity; in his mind all the hideous images were suddenly unloosed at once. Church coming back with bits of green plastic in his whiskers, Gage's baseball cap lying in the road, full of blood, but most of all that thing he had seen near Little God Swamp, the thing that had pushed the tree over, the thing with the yellow eyes, the Wendigo creature of the north country, the dead thing whose touch awakens unspeakable appetites.

Rachel had not just been killed.

Something had been . . . something had been at her.

(!CLICK!)

That *click* was in his head. it was the sound of some relay fusing and burning out forever, the sound of lightning stroking down in a direct hit, the sound of a door opening.

He looked up numbly, the scream still shivering in his throat and here was Gage at last, his mouth smeared with blood, his chin dripping, his lip pulled back in a hellish grin. In one hand he held Louis's scalpel.

As he brought it down, Louis pulled back with no real thought at all. The scalpel wickered past his face, and Gage overbalanced. *He is as clumsy as Church,* Louis thought. Louis kicked his feet from under him. Gage fell awkwardly, and Louis was on him before he could get up, straddling him, one knee pinning the hand which held the scalpel.

"No," the thing under him panted. Its face twisted and writhed. Its eyes were baleful, insectile in their stupid hate. "No, no, no—"

Louis clawed for one of the hypos, got it out. He would have to be quick. The thing under him was like a greased fish and it would not let go of the scalpel no matter how hard he bore down on its wrist. And its face seemed to ripple and change even as he looked at it. It was Jud's face, dead and staring; it was the dented, eyes rolling mindlessly; it was, mirrorlike, Louis's own, so dreadfully pale and lunatic. Then it changed again and became the face of that creature in the woods—the low brow, the dead yellow eyes, the tongue long and pointed and bifurcated, grinning and hissing.

"No, no, no-no-no—"

It bucked beneath him. The hypo flew out of Louis's hand and rolled a short way down the hall. He groped for another, brought it out, and jammed it straight down into the small of Gage's back.

It screamed beneath him, body straining and sunfishing, nearly throwing him off. Grunting, Louis got the third syringe and jammed this one home in Gage's arm, depressing the plunger all the way. He got off then and began to back slowly down the hallway. Gage got slowly to his feet and began to stagger toward him. Five steps and the scalpel fell from his hand. It struck the floor blade first and stuck itself in the wood, quivering. Ten steps and that strange yellow light in its eyes began to fade. A dozen and it fell to its knees.

Now Gage looked up at him and for a moment Louis saw his son—his real son—his face unhappy and filled with pain.

"Daddy!" he cried, and then fell forward on his face. (pp. 400–402)

In *Danse Macabre*, Stephen King explains his technique: "I recognize terror as the finest emotion, and so I will try to terrorize the reader. But if I find I cannot terrify him/her, I will try to horrify; and if I find I cannot horrify, I'll go for the gross-out. I'm not proud" (p. 37). In so describing his craft, he also explains the technique of popular writers since the rise of mass-consumed fiction two hundred years ago. Not only would writers rather be rich than proud, but they also realize that to be rich they need to know what readers want to experience. Certain audiences want to be shocked, and since the most visceral shock is visual, they want images, scenes, and scenarios which turn their stomachs and make their eyes roll. They want violent turns and rapid descents. They want to lurch. They want to be "grossed out." They want cartoon action. And so it is to that history, the history of literal, not figurative, cartoons of preposterous violence, that we now turn.

4
=

Disorderly Conduct Illustrated:
The Rise and Fall and Rise of Comics

If cowboy films were the rage, we produced a lot of westerns. If
cops and robbers were in vogue, we'd grind out a profusion of crime
titles. We simply gave the public what it wanted—or so we thought.
STAN LEE of Marvel Comics, as quoted by
Ron Goulart, *Great History of Comic Books*

In 1982 Stephen King's *Creepshow* debuted to predictably mediocre reviews and enthusiastic fans. This forgettable movie is worth remember-
ing for a number of reasons. First, of course, the screenplay was written
by King, and the film was touted as *"Stephen King's"* Creepshow. Had
it not been written by King and aggressively advertised as such, there is
every reason to believe that *Creepshow* would have failed. The anthol-
ogy movie, which peaked in the 1960s with the English productions of
Milton Subotsky and Hammer Studios, had lost that audience to television. Second, the director was George Romero, who had directed the
classic *Night of the Living Dead*, which had gathered a huge cult following. (Romero went on to drain the genre with *Day of the Dead* and
Dawn of the Dead.) In tow was Tom Savini whose head-bursting and
body-popping special effects had made horror films in the 1970s more
visually violent. And third, *Creepshow* was an affectionate tribute to a
genre buried by film, television, and criticism—the *EC* comic book. The
violent comic book, overlooked too long, deserves study for it shows

with gnomic concision the lifespan of the industries that transport scenarios of preposterous violence.

Creepshow opens with a framing story in which a suburban father catches his adolescent son, Billy, reading a typically lurid *EC* comic titled *Creepshow*. The father holds it up like a dead fish and exclaims, "This is crap. You want to know where this is going? In the garbage. Right in the frigging garbage." Billy, like countless boys in the late 1940s, watches helplessly as his father stuffs his favorite comic in the trash. As Billy trudges up to bed, a gust of wind ripples the pages of the comic, and we are taken, thanks to the animation of one of *EC*'s artists, Jack Kamen, into the forbidden world presided over by the ghoulish maître d's of the morbid: "the Crypt Keeper," "the Old Witch," and "the Vault Keeper."

As the five internal stories unfold, the animation is gradually replaced with "real life," and real life is predictable. From here on animation is only used on the segues between stories. The stories are, of course, cartoon exaggerations, hyperbolic variations on human behavior so common to the modern comic book and its descendant, the television cartoon. For instance, in the first episode, a vintage *EC* piece, a wealthy dowager, Bedelia, is entertaining her family on Father's Day. We learn that seven years earlier she had murdered her elderly father when he had petulantly demanded his Father's Day cake for the umpteenth time. The father was no paragon of virtue, having made a fortune from bootlegging. Out of jealousy and spite, he had kept Bedelia nearby to nurse him, even killing her husband to keep her dependent. In true *EC* fashion, the first part of the story sets up the victimizer as reprehensible to the nth degree and hence entitled to a similar degree of punishment. The father has been a criminal; he has killed his son-in-law; he badgers his daughter: What's a daughter to do? Bedelia murders him.

Now a heavy-drinking Bedelia stumbles to her father's grave and, having taken a few swigs from the bottle, sees the skinless claws of her father's hands rising up from beneath his headstone. Soon, like the zombie exploding up in slow motion through the earth (a trademark of Savini/Romero films), the cadaverous father is up and throttling Bedelia, all the time cussing, "Where is my Father's Day cake? I want my cake and !*%*#x% I'm going to have it!" Father soon pulls daughter down into the grave, buries her, and heads for the family gathering, muttering, "Where's my cake?" When he arrives at the manor house, he runs into the gossipy Aunt Sylvia, corkscrews off her head, and then decorates the head like a confection. At last Father is having his cake and eating it too. The tale now abruptly returns to animation, introducing a character made famous as the narrator of *EC* horrors—the Vault Keeper—who makes a few gleefully tasteless puns before leading us on to the next tale.

What seems tame on film was lurid in comics. Even though visual

The last scene of *Father's Day*, in *Stephen King's Creepshow*, art by Berni Wrightson, New American Library, 1982 (Laurel-Show, Inc.)

shocks are the standard fare of Romero, even though Tom Savini is a virtuoso of special effects, and even though they are working from a screenplay by a master of the convulsive scene, the degree of distortion pales in comparison with the same scenes in the pulp comic. Concurrently with the movie release, New American Library issued *Creepshow* as an oversized paperback drawn in *EC* style. In an interesting twist on the "you've seen the movie, now read the book," this was a "you've seen the movie, now see what the comic would have looked like if only you had been growing up thirty years earlier."

The reason you could not have seen the comic version in the 1960s and 1970s is because in the early 1950s *EC* ("Educational Comics"— publishers of such titles as *Tales from the Crypt, Vault of Horror,* and *The Haunt of Fear*) had been hounded out of business. The last time a dime bought such lurid stories was in the fall of 1954. Then a young and destitute Stephen King could have ponied-up a dime to buy a comic. He certainly must have, for King understood their particular *mise en scène* and patois, as we see in the next four *Creepshow* episodes. A bumpkin is turned into a vegetable and commits suicide. A corrupt executive, who has buried a subordinate up to his neck in sand and has forced him to watch the death of his girlfriend who has also been buried, is himself buried by their revenant spirits. An English professor feeds his shrewish wife to a Tasmanian devil, and a Howard Hughes type, who is petrified of cockroaches, is himself made into roach food. When one does a body count on the five stories in *Creepshow*, the tally is in keeping with *EC* standards: one patricide, one suicide, three homicides, one uxoricide, and one death by cockroach.

The degree of distortion renders these deaths comic rather than terrifying. Ironically, they are far more shocking *in* comics, in large part because the illustrations can be more preposterous than Savini's special effects, and the pacing can be far more frantic. The movie, even with all its abrupt cutting, is predetermined. We know how real people behave. We know what the camera can do. In comics there is no predictability. With the comic we turn the page when we want to. The movie has its own speed; it has to move. The comic scene can linger. In fact, if you ask someone now in his forties about the comics he read as a child, you will find that some scenes can linger for a lifetime. King places this violence in its cultural context:

> The *EC* comics were like the last gasp of a more gentle romanticism. It was as though these people came out of World War Two saying, "We know now that all this bullshit we used to believe about knights in shining armor and the good guy always winning is not true." All it took was a look at those bodies. And yet at the same time, they still wanted to believe it. So you get stories where the corpse comes back from the grave and murders the people who killed him. The first half of the story, where the murder happened and the people got away with it, was an admission that the world is a terrible place— that horrible things happen, that good people are hurt and that the bad people who hurt them are not punished. And then, when the corpse came back, it was as though they were saying, "We know all this is true, but we don't really believe it is true. We think that

there is a just God who administers rough justice and puts every-thing to right in the end." Horror fiction has always been, in that sense, very romantic fiction. (Quoted by Douglas Winter, *Stephen King*, p.117)

King is clearly aware that the *EC* method of exposition informs his narrative technique. It is, after all, the *modus operandi* of preposterous violence: Violent acts call forth even more violent retribution. In an offhand comment relegated to a footnote in *Danse Macabre*, King ob-serves,

> The scene in *'Salem's Lot* which works best in the *EC* tradition—at least, as far as I'm concerned—is when the bus driver, Charlie Rhodes (who is a typical EC-type rotter in the best Herbie Satten tradition), awakes at midnight and hears someone blowing the horn of his bus. He discovers, after the bus doors have swung shut for-ever behind him, that his bus is loaded with children, as if for a school run . . . but they're all vampires. Charlie begins to scream, and perhaps the reader wonders why; after all, they only stopped by for a drink. (p. 38)

What was in these comics that was so disturbing to adults, and why were they so effectively censored? To understand this, as well as to focus on the criticism of adolescent fables of aggression in general, we need to return to an area of contemporary history that is only now being sorted out—the postwar era of Eisenhower, Dulles, and McCarthy. The early 1950s were not an aberration of modern culture but rather a time when certain forces, forces still extant, were more than usually potent and, because of television, more than usually visible.

While Joseph McCarthy was threatening many well-meaning bureau-crats with his tattered briefcase full of the "documentary evidence," Senator Estes Kefauver was threatening one of the most lucrative pub-lishing industries of all time with his cardboard boxes full of equally incendiary material. The television cameras never peeked into Mc-Carthy's briefcase—he made sure of that—and they never had to pho-tograph the stuff in Kefauver's boxes—everyone knew what was there. While McCarthy orchestrated the hysteria and the press coverage of the monster waiting at our borders, Kefauver was almost as proficient in describing the monster in the display rack down at the corner drugstore. Perhaps because it was so easy to locate and annihilate his version of the monster, Kefauver was easily overshadowed by his colleague from Wis-consin. After all, if the only person who is going to stand up to you in public is the rotund and playful publisher of magazines called *Vault of Horror*, *The Haunt of Fear*, *Tales from the Crypt* and, later, *Mad* mag-azine, it is hard to generate much friction.

Crime and communism were the twin evils of the early postwar period. Both were infecting our youngsters. Communism came from the Bolsheviks, and criminal behavior was coming from the mass media. In every poll that George Gallup took between 1946 and 1956, juvenile delinquency was feared, if not like the plague which it so resembled, then like atomic fallout. In fact, in 1959, long after the major crest of fear had passed, juvenile delinquency was still viewed with more anxiety than atomic testing. Kefauver's Senate hearings on comics were part of a broad investigation into crime, especially into adolescent crime. Juvenile delinquency was a cause célèbre because there was every indication that we were poised on the edge of a brutal uprising—an uprising of the promise of tomorrow; our youth had been infected. If it made sense to build a reinforced cement shelter for your family in the backyard, surely it made sense to check under Junior's bed.[1]

But why the panic? Was the center coming loose? Would the blood-dimmed tide, or more likely the Brylcreamed tide, of anarchy soon be let loose? Would the kids slip into their leathers, slide onto their Harleys, unwrap their chains, unpocket their switchblades, and send all their freedom-loving elders to their rooms? If you listened to J. Edgar Hoover citing the *Uniform Crime Statistics* in 1958, you might well have thought so. Our children consume, he claimed, productions which "flout indecency and applaud lawlessness" as never before. Never before have we "witnessed such a brazen affront to our national conscience." Hoover's refrain of "never before" had the ring of a Churchillian exhortation to the troops. The enemy had been spotted; we must mount the charge now. The extrapolations of crime statistics, especially those in the growth of "status crimes" (drinking, joyriding, curfew violations, delinquency), were like the stop-action photography of a fungus in the jungle. The Children's Bureau was reporting to the Senate a forty-five percent increase in postwar delinquency up to 1953, and when it published its *Facts about Juvenile Delinquency*, the conclusions were clear. Behavior was now bad, destined to get worse. The exponential growth of juvenile crime promised that drag racing, drive-ins, ducktails, blue jeans, rock 'n roll, and surly backtalk would soon be the norm. Fred Astaire and Ginger Rogers would be elbowed aside by Fabian and Annette.[2]

When in 1953 Kefauver's Senate subcommittee opened what was to be a decade of examination into delinquency, it never questioned the assumption that things were bad, getting worse. Nor did it examine how Hoover and the FBI generated those statistics. Nor did it analyze the habits of the young before the war. All that needed to be known was known. Communism was knocking on the door from without; housewives were beginning to unlatch the door from within in order to enter the marketplace; and the kids were not acting as if Father Knew Best. The mass media, which had been the purveyor of bad news, was itself the bad news. Movies, dime novels, radio, magazines, television, and comics were suspect.

As it developed, this was not a case of the messenger punished for the message; rather, it was one of certain messengers claiming that one of their own was delivering all the bad news. The movies had already paid the price; the Hays office had seen to that. In 1949 the National Association for Better Radio and Television was formed to create and enforce higher production codes, which really meant "appease the critics," since the audience was hardly disturbed. The NABRT boasted of having a prestigious board that included James Bennett of the Justice Department, the critic Gilbert Seldes, cartoonist Al Capp, Richard Clendenen of the Children's Bureau, and a gentleman we are to meet again—Fredric Wertham. The board deflected most criticism with vague promises. Television was exempt from harsh censure because of the demographics of who owned TV sets (upper middle class), where people lived (near urban centers), and what they could see (only early evening broadcasts). Radio was more carefully studied and radio crime dramas analyzed, but it seemed clear that radio was not dangerous if consumed by the small earful.[3]

The large media were protected from criticism in two ways. They were parts of American industry, important conduits for the flow not so much of information as of advertising. The sponsors of radio crime shows—cigarettes, toiletries, automobiles—were loath to give up their audiences. The movie industry could always claim its audience was self-selective, and in fact, the industry surveys of the audience of 1950 showed that the only people with sufficient disposable income and time to go to the movies were those between twenty-two and forty. Television was no menace—yet. Kids could not watch what was not there. Saturday morning did not carve out an audience until the late 1950s, and even *it* aired such innocent attractions as *Captain Kangaroo*, *Howdy Doody*, *The Gumby Show*, and *The Jimmy Dean Show*. The other protection for mass media was that audiences were as unwilling to give up their entertainment as advertisers were to give up their audiences. The democratizing effect of electronic media meant that programming was done for the largest possible audience, and that audience, by its very nature, was too big to budge.

Almost by the process of elimination, the comics were left standing alone, like the cheese in "The Farmer in the Dell." Unlike the cheese, however, they were never able to align themselves with any interested parties, having no untainted supporters—no ministers, no government officials, no intellectuals—who could vouch for them. A few social scientists came to the defense but they were a mixed blessing. It was clear that the comics were making the stink in this farmyard, not cleaning it up. Most of the comics in the late 1940s *were* hard to defend. Through their pages passed some of the most extraordinary tales of aggression since the penny dreadful. As compared to even the worst of the bloody pulps, distortion in comics was the norm. But the real reason comic books proved such a huge target was that the hands turning the pages were so young, so male, and so easy to discipline—at least initially. Here was where the juvenile delinquency virus must be entering the body politic, and here is where it must be eradicated.

By the 1950s comic books had developed into a stable commodity— neither humorous nor comic, but very profitable. Thin, thirty-two-page pamphlets trimmed to 7½ × 10½ inches, selling for a dime, they were usually wholesaled as part of a package of other print products and retailed on wire racks away from other magazines. They were easy to spot by both consumer and critic. A dime bought three to five stories told in pictures with balloon captions. These stories were colorful line drawings enfolded within often lurid and glossy covers. Often on the inside covers were advertisements for muscle-building equipment, throwing knives, bull whips, weight-gain supplements, and other such equipment with which an adolescent male could master an alien environment. To say the comics were popular is an understatement; they were one of the most lucrative products ever produced by the publishing industry. By the spring of 1954, 150 million comics were being published each month, of which more than 30 million were essentially devoted to conveying scenarios of outlandish violence. If only fifty percent of the crime and horror comics produced were sold by retailers, the annual gross would be in excess of $18 million.

The industry that provided this pulp was a direct descendant of the industry which a century earlier had provided Johnny's great-grandparents with their dollop of concussive thrills. Like the penny dreadful, the comic book was published by a few closely held corporations, which also published other magazines, usually detective, adventure, and sentimental romances under different colophons. For the most part, these publishers were located in New York City and followed similar production patterns. A publisher and editor conceived of a story line, a writer prepared a synopsis, a penciler outlined the panels, providing the dialogue balloons to be filled in later with text, and then the colorist did the final illustrative work. Just as the Newgate-novel houses such as Amalgamated Press, Aldine, Edwin J. Brett, Harkaway House, Newsagents, and Hogarth House produced penny novels of all types by mass-producing the individual parts, so the comic industry separated and distributed tasks. In fact, it is rare to find a "blood" written by a single author. Even the actual printing was divided: Newsprint was used for the inside pages, covers were done at different plants on heavier glossy paper, and collating was often completed by a third company.

The print runs were massive; they had to be. The entire run had to

"Boy reading *Menace*," Associated Press, September 30, 1954 (Wide World Photos)

be more than 300,000 copies to provide each local dealer with only three copies of a particular issue. New issues of any popular series appeared monthly or bimonthly. To maximize profit for the publisher and the middlemen, the local dealer had no control over what he carried. The comics came wrapped in a shipment from a local wholesaler who in turn got them from a national distributor. There were some thirteen national distributors who routed materials across the country and advised the wholesaler of what was selling and what should be "mixed into the bundle." The bundle might contain girlie magazines as well as scientific publications. It might contain *Bugs Bunny, Scientific American,* and *Suppressed.* While the wholesaler knew what sold well in specific locales, the distributor kept tabs on what was selling around the country. At the point of sale, the newsdealer was powerless. He was charged for the entire bundle. He could refuse to sell certain comics, keep them under the counter for a specified time, and return them for credit. The comics would then have their covers removed; their text would be combined with other comics, repackaged under a new title, and put back on sale for a quarter.

As with pulp novels, the modern transmission of fables of aggression usually follows a path of nonaccountability. Responsibility is not diffused for subterfuge but to avoid financial risk. In television, for instance, the network buys a package of shows from an independent producer based on a small sample—usually about three completed shows.

The large "packagers," say a public company like Lorimar or a private one like Stephen J. Cannell Productions, has subcontracted with the sub-producers of the "show," be it *Dallas* or *The A-Team*, to manage the production run. Meanwhile, the network has to find advertisers to sponsor this show as well as to keep the affiliated stations from shelving it or, in the newsdealer's parlance, putting it "under the counter." While the production and distribution of such entertainments may spread the financial risk, the comic industry was one of the first to see an additional strength. No one has to, or is even able to, exercise control of what is inside the product. The only information that all parties share is the knowledge of what sells and therefore what the public wants.

On April 21, 1954, Kefauver's Senate subcommittee found out some of what that public wanted. They were presented with the story lines from a few of the most popular comics. Here are snippets of the summaries they read:

Bottoms Up

One story has to do with a confirmed alcoholic who spends all his wife can earn on alcohol. As a result their small son is severely neglected. On the day the son is to start in the first grade in school the mother asks the father to escort him to the school building. Instead, the father goes to his favorite bootlegger and the son goes to school by himself. En route the child is struck and killed by an automobile. Informed of the accident, the mother returns home to find her husband gloating over his new supply of liquor. The last four panels show the mother as she proceeds to kill and hack her spouse to pieces with an ax. The first panel shows her swinging the ax, burying the blade in her husband's skull. Blood spurts from the open wound and the husband is shown with an expression of agony. The next panel has a montage effect: the husband is lying on the floor bloody, ax raised for more blows. The background shows an enlargement of the fear-filled eyes of the husband, as well as an enlargement of the bloody ax. To describe this scene of horror the text states that—"And now the silence of the Hendrick's apartment is broken only by the soft humming of Nora as she busies herself with her 'work'." She then cuts his body into smaller pieces and disposes of it by placing the various pieces in the bottles of liquor her husband had purchased. She then returns the liquor to the bootlegger and obtains a refund. As she leaves, the bootlegger says: "HMMN, *funny!* I figured that *rye* would be *inside* Lou by now!" The story ends with the artist admonishing the child readers in a macabre vein with the following paragraph, "*But* if Westlake were to examine the remainder of the case more closely he'd see that it is Lou who is inside the liquor! *Heh, heh!* Sleep well kiddies!" We then see three of the bottles—one contains an eye, one an ear, and one a finger.

Stick in the Mud

An extremely sadistic schoolteacher gives special attention to one of her pupils in order to curry favor with the boy's rich, widowed father. In a year she succeeds in marrying the man, but he turns out to be a miser. She stabs him to death with a butcher knife approximately a foot and a half in length and 3 inches wide. The picture shows the body of the old man, limbs askew, falling to the floor, emitting a gurgle. There is a large hole in his back and blood is squirting in all directions. The wife is behind him clutching the bloody butcher knife. She says: "You stupid old fool! I've stood for your miserly penny-pinching ways long enough! From now on it'll be my money . . . and I'll spend it my way! Die, Ezra . . . die!" She then covers up her crime by throwing him into a pen with a wild bull that gores his body to pieces. She now has the money, but also the stepson whom she hates. The boy suspects that she killed his father and makes her chase him around the farm by calling her names. He leads her to some quicksand and she falls in. Several pictures show her as she begs the boy to get help. He promises to do so if she confesses to him that she killed his father. She does so, and he then lets her sink to her death. A closeup is shown of the terrified woman, sunk into the quicksand which is flowing into her open mouth. The boy is quite satisfied with himself and walks about the farm humming a tune while others search for his "lost" stepmother. ("Comic Books and Juvenile Delinquency," pp. 8, 9–10)

The most famous of all the *EC* horrors, however, was a tale which is still vividly remembered by those who read it as children. As Stephen King reminisces:

"Foul Play" is the story of Herbie Satten, pitcher for Bayville's minor league baseball team. Herbie is the apotheosis of the *EC* villain. He's a totally black character, with absolutely no redeeming qualities, the Compleat Monster. He's murderous, conceited, egocentric, willing to go to any lengths to win. He brings out the Mob Man or Mob Woman in each of us; we would gladly see Herbie lynched from the nearest apple tree, and never mind the Civil Liberties Union.

With his team leading by a single run in the top of the ninth, Herbie gets to first base by deliberately allowing himself to be hit by an inside pitch. Although he is big and lumbering, he takes off for second on the very next pitch. Covering second is Central City's saintly slugger, Jerry Deegan. Deegan, we are told, is "sure to win the game for the home team in the bottom of the ninth." The evil Herbie Satten slides into second with his spikes up, but saintly Jerry hangs in there and tags Satten out.

Jerry is spiked, but his wounds are minor . . . or so they appear. In fact, Herbie has painted his spikes with a deadly, fast-acting poison. In Central City's half of the ninth, Jerry comes to the plate with two out and a man in scoring position. It looks pretty good for the home team guys; unfortunately, Jerry drops dead at home plate even as the umpire calls strike three. Exit the malefic Herbie Satten, smirking.

The Central City team doctor discovers that Jerry has been poisoned. One of the Central City players says grimly: "This is a job for the police!" Another responds ominously, "No! Wait! Let's take care of him ourselves . . . our way."

The team sends Herbie a letter, inviting him to the ballpark one night to be presented with a plaque honoring his achievements in baseball. Herbie, apparently as stupid as he is evil, falls for it and in the next scene we see the Central City nine on the field. (*Danse Macabre*, p. 36)

Even Mr. King cannot do justice to this next scene (p. 141). Words fail.

The subcommittee was especially concerned about violence which occurred out of the frame. The comics, as if paying obeisance to decorum while at the same time keeping the censor from the door, rarely showed brutality in action. We don't see Herbie literally being pulled apart. Instead, we see the result. So if a man is hacking his wife to bits with an ax, the frame will show the descending ax while the caption will read, "Bertha squealed as Norman brought the ax down. The swinging of steel and the thud of the razor-sharp metal against flesh cut the squeal short." The next frame will show him holding the ax poised again while we are told: "He brought the ax down again and again, hacking, severing, dismembering." The final frame will be just the red rivulet of blood dripping off the page. Wasn't this the way Sophocles tortured Oedipus, the way Shakespeare blinded Lear? Well, yes and no. It is actually much closer to the way Hitchcock photographed and cut the shower scene in *Psycho*. First, the shot of Janet Leigh getting into the shower, then the shower head gushing water, then the knife, then the curtain popping, then knife plunging, blood running and then slowly whorling down the drain. This is a scene in every way worthy of an *EC* issue.

Hitchcock would be praised for the sophisticated jump-cutting of this scene. But when such scenes appeared in lurid colors on cheap newsprint, the results were condemned. Adults could absorb the experience on celluloid; children would be warped by it on paper. As is often the case in popular culture, real life seemed to mimic fantasy as if some secret causality was activated. Several years before the Senate subcommittee began its hearings, *Time* magazine on October 4, 1948, after referring to comic books as the "bastard offspring of newspaper comics," reported:

The Los Angeles County sheriff had in custody a 14–year-old boy who had poisoned a 50–year-old woman. He got the idea, and the poison recipe, he said, from a comic book. There were other alarm-

"Foul Play," *The Crypt of Terror*, art by Jack Davis (William M. Gaines)

ing cases too. A 10–year-old boy's parents came home from the movies to find his body hanging in the garage. At his feet was a crime comic depicting a hanging body. Two boys, 14 and 15, were caught committing a burglary. The crime comics they had with them had inspired the crime and shown them how to do it. ("Not So Funny," p. 46)

After all, hadn't the rise of juvenile delinquency paralleled the rise of violent comics?[4] Somehow behavior was leaking from the world of make-believe into the "real" world. Ask your local juvenile delinquent what he had read recently and he was sure to tell you. As the penny dreadful had been, and as television was to be, the comics were ripe for examination and censure.

As countless astronomers have shown, it is not who first sees the new planet who makes it known; it is who first coins the label. The causal nexus between lurid scene on pulp and violent act on the street was proposed by a postwar evangelist of a fledgling social astronomy—forensic psychiatry. In the late 1940s Dr. Fredric Wertham had fired up a crusade based on the simplest principle of human behavior: Children learn by imitation; "monkey see, monkey do." What made Wertham's articulation of this equation so powerful is that he was no maiden aunt clicking her knitting needles but a practicing psychiatrist actually working with juvenile delinquents in the mysterious incubating grounds of gang violence—Harlem and Queens.[5]

By the 1950s Wertham's crusade was up and running. His explanation for delinquency was simple. Commercial culture and family culture were now at odds. Our youth had been brainwashed by a steady stream of violent imagery. An epidemic of violence would soon be at hand. Responding to questions posed by the Senate subcommittee on April 22, 1954, he stated:

> Mr. Chairman, as long as the crime comic books industry exists in its present forms there are no secure homes. You cannot resist infantile paralysis in your own home alone. Must you not take into account the neighbor's children? . . .
>
> In other words, I think that comic books primarily, and that is the greatest harm they do, cause a great deal of ethical confusion.
>
> I would like to give you a very brief example. There is a school in a town in New York State where there has been a great deal of stealing. Some time ago some boys attacked another boy and they twisted his arm so viciously that it broke in two places, and, just like in a comic book, the bone came through the skin.
>
> In the same school about 10 days later 7 boys pounced on another boy and pushed his head against the concrete so that the boy was unconscious and had to be taken to the hospital. He had a concussion of the brain.
>
> In this same high school in 1 year 26 girls became pregnant. The score this year, I think, is eight. Maybe it is nine by now.
>
> Now, Mr. Chairman, this is what I call ethical and moral confusion. I don't think that any of these boys or girls individually vary very much. It cannot be explained individually, alone.
>
> Here is a general moral confusion and I think that these girls were seduced mentally long before they were seduced physically, and, of

Fredric Wertham helping client (Library of Congress)

course, all those people there are very, very great—not all of them, but most of them, are very great comic book readers, have been and are. . . .

If it were my task, Mr. Chairman, to teach children delinquency, to tell them how to rape and seduce girls, how to hurt people, how to break into stores, how to cheat, how to forge, how to do any known crime, if it were my task to teach that, I would have to enlist the crime comic book industry.

Formerly to impair the morals of a minor was a punishable offense. It has now become a mass industry. I will say that every crime of delinquency is described in detail and that if you teach somebody the technique of something you, of course, seduce him into it.

Nobody would believe that you teach a boy homosexuality without introducing him to it. The same thing with crime. . . .

I have been for 12 years in Queens. I know these kids. I have seen quite a number of them who threw rocks. I can't see why we have to invoke highfalutin' psychological theories and why we say these people have to have a mother who doesn't give them enough affection.

> If they read this stuff all the time, some of them 2 and 3 hours a day reading, I don't think it is such an extraordinary event if they throw a stone somewhere where it may do some harm.
>
> I want to add to this that my theory of temptation and seduction, as I told you, is very, very vague. ("Comic Books and Juvenile Delinquency," pp. 85, 87, 89)

This is vintage Wertham. Ironically, the very unscientific nature of his proof gave him much credibility. His impressions had a special forcefulness because they were so commonly shared and so "logically" derived: "Things are getting worse. Why, only yesterday, I saw some young thugs fighting in the churchyard." Has a middle-aged generation ever thought it was getting the respect it deserved, or thought that law and order were as rigorously maintained as in the past? And if things are getting worse, what is a more powerful explanation of it than the existence of some new constellation of images which is now being seen?

Almost two months after Wertham's testimony, the forces marshaled against the comics could not have picked a better ally than the comics' major apologist. William Gaines was a man whose childish enthusiasm was a gun pointed at his own foot. Gaines had prepared for a career as a secondary schoolteacher, but when his father died, he inherited a publishing group known as "Entertaining Comics." The senior Gaines had published rather innocuous fare, including the famous *Picture Stories from the Bible*, which young Gaines repeatedly pointed to as an example of an educational comic. One cover of this "Christian comic book," though, shows David cutting off Goliath's head with a bloody sword. Inside are eight pages of Jesus being flagellated, Jesus on the cross, Jesus dripping blood. Young Gaines vastly expanded the business by adding a profitable run of action, crime, and horror comics.

In fact, by the early 1950s all manner of violent imagery was emanating from Gaines's various corporate entities, all headquartered at 225 Lafayette Street in Manhattan. Gaines assured the Senators that, in the creation of all these entities, there was no intent to deceive—things just happened to be set up that way. But the myth of the sleaze merchant hiding in the dark corners of the law was powerful. Indeed, Gaines's voluntary appearance before the Senate subcommittee was an effort to counter this image, but he did himself unexpected damage. He was joyfully unrepentant. He clearly did not fear the Communists, did not think censorship did any good, didn't think books did any harm, and was almost impertinent in expressing these opinions. Here he is with Senator Kefauver.

> *Senator Kefauver:* Here is your May 22 issue. This seems to be a man with a bloody ax holding a woman's head up which has been severed from her body. Do you think that is in good taste?
>
> *Mr. Gaines:* Yes, sir; I do, for the cover of a horror comic. A cover

in bad taste, for example, might be defined as holding the head a little higher so that the neck could be seen dripping blood from it and moving the body over a little further so that the neck of the body could be seen to be bloody.

Senator Kefauver: You have blood coming out of her mouth.

Mr. Gaines: A little.

Senator Kefauver: Here is blood on the ax. I think most adults are shocked by that. . . . This is the July one. It seems to be a man with a woman in a boat and he is choking her to death here with a crowbar. Is that in good taste?

Mr. Gaines: I think so.

("Comic Books and Juvenile Delinquency," p. 103)

Worse still, Gaines had recently taken to running an "editorial" on the inside covers of some of his comics. Entitled "ARE YOU A RED DUPE?," the editorial was entered as Exhibit 8b in the Senate documents; it was ripe with what postmodernist critics call polysemic readings. In a virtuoso display of critical jujitsu, Gaines has turned his critics into the very characters they are criticizing. Comics will not weaken the American fiber so that the Communist menace can prevail; the suppression of free speech will do that. The censors need censoring. Irony of ironies, buying a comic now becomes an act of red-blooded Americanism—a necessary expression of free speech. The joke of the duper duped, the anti-Communist made Communist, the investigating committee needing investigation, was lost on the Senators. They asked no further questions.

Gaines had lodged the bullet squarely in his own foot. The battle was now carried from the Senate floor onto the editorial pages of countless newspapers as well as into book-length polemics. Although in the text of "ARE YOU A RED DUPE?" Mr. Gaines had singled out Wertham and the writer Gershorn Legman as the butts of his parody, he seriously misunderstood the power of their charge. Neither man needed a ghostwriter, and both of them were able to turn their anticomic articles, which appeared in *Neurotica* and the *Ladies Home Journal*, into bestselling books, *Love & Death: A Study in Censorship* and *The Seduction of the Innocent*. And both of these books helped to put the violent comic into a deep, decade-long sleep.

The Seduction of the Innocent proved to be one of the most influential books of the 1950s, largely because of Wertham's Calvinist bearing, his evangelical enthusiasm, and his American gusto. In 1948 he volunteered to testify for a nudist magazine, *Sunshine and Health*, which had been charged with obscenity. Wertham exclaimed on the stand that this magazine was not obscene, but if the court wanted to see something really deserving of censorship, he would oblige. He pulled out of his briefcase some lurid crime comics. He waved them about. The *New York Herald*

ARE YOU A RED DUPE?

IN THE TOWN OF GAZOOSKY IN THE HEART OF SOVIET RUSSIA, YOUNG MELVIN BLIZUNKEN-SKOVITCHSKY PUBLISHED A *COMIC MAGAZINE*...

 ...SO THEY CAME AND *SMASHED* HIS FOUR-COLOR PRESS...

 ...AND *HUNG* POOR MELVIN THE NEXT MORNING!

- HERE IN AMERICA, WE CAN *STILL* PUBLISH COMIC MAGAZINES, NEWSPAPERS, SLICKS, BOOKS AND THE BIBLE. WE DON'T *HAVE* TO SEND THEM TO A CENSOR FIRST. NOT *YET*...
- FOR THERE ARE SOME PEOPLE IN AMERICA WHO WOULD *LIKE* TO CENSOR... WHO WOULD *LIKE* TO SUPPRESS COMICS. IT ISN'T THAT THEY DON'T LIKE COMICS FOR *THEM!* THEY DON'T LIKE THEM FOR *YOU!*
- THESE PEOPLE SAY THAT *COMIC BOOKS* AREN'T AS GOOD FOR CHILDREN AS *NO* COMIC BOOKS, OR SOMETHING LIKE THAT. SOME OF THESE PEOPLE ARE NO-GOODS. SOME ARE DO-GOODERS. SOME ARE WELL-MEANING. AND SOME ARE JUST PLAIN MEAN.
- BUT WE ARE CONCERNED WITH AN AMAZING REVELATION. AFTER MUCH SEARCHING OF NEWSPAPER FILES, WE'VE MADE AN ASTOUNDING DISCOVERY:

THE GROUP MOST ANXIOUS TO DESTROY COMICS ARE THE COMMUNISTS!

- WE'RE SERIOUS! NO KIDDIN'! HERE! READ THIS:

THE (COMMUNIST) "DAILY WORKER" OF JULY 13, 1953 SAID THAT COMICS PLAY THE CONSCIOUS ROLE OF:

"...BRUTALIZING AMERICAN YOUTH, THE BETTER TO PREPARE THEM FOR MILITARY SERVICE IN IMPLEMENTING OUR GOVERNMENT'S AIMS OF WORLD DOMINATION, AND TO ACCEPT THE ATROCITIES NOW BEING PERPETRATED BY AMERICAN SOLDIERS AND AIRMEN IN KOREA UNDER THE FLAG OF THE UNITED NATIONS."

THIS ARTICLE ALSO QUOTES GERSHON LEGMAN (WHO CLAIMS TO BE A GHOST WRITER FOR DR. FREDERICK WERTHAM, THE AUTHOR OF A RECENT BLAST AGAINST COMICS PUBLISHED IN "THE LADIES HOME JOURNAL"). THIS SAME G. LEGMAN, IN ISSUE #3 OF "NEUROTICA," PUBLISHED IN AUTUMN 1948, SAID:

"THE CHILD'S NATURAL CHARACTER... MUST BE DISTORTED TO FIT CIVILIZATION... FANTASY VIOLENCE WILL PARALYZE HIS RESISTANCE, DIVERT HIS AGGRESSION TO UNREAL ENEMIES AND FRUSTRATIONS, AND IN THIS WAY PREVENT HIM FROM REBELLING AGAINST PARENTS AND TEACHERS... THIS WILL SIPHON OFF HIS RESISTANCE AGAINST SOCIETY, AND PREVENT REVOLUTION."

- SO THE *NEXT* TIME SOME JOKER GETS UP AT A P.T.A. MEETING, OR STARTS JABBERING ABOUT THE "NAUGHTY COMIC BOOKS" AT YOUR LOCAL CANDY STORE, GIVE HIM THE *ONCE-OVER*. WE'RE NOT SAYING HE *IS* A COMMUNIST! HE MAY BE INNOCENT OF THE WHOLE THING! HE MAY BE A *DUPE!* HE MAY NOT EVEN *READ* THE "DAILY WORKER"! IT'S JUST THAT HE'S *SWALLOWED* THE *RED BAIT*... *HOOK, LINE*, AND *SINKER!*

"ARE YOU A RED DUPE?," *EC* comics editorial (William M. Gaines)

Tribune carried the story. Norman Cousins read it and recruited Wertham to express his views. On May 29, 1948, the *Saturday Review of Literature* published "The Comics . . . Very Funny" with the subtitle—"Marijuana of the Nursery." The article opens in what was to become a standard Wertham invocation—the litany of wrongdoing.

An anxious mother consulted me some time ago. Her four-year-old daughter is the only little girl in the apartment house where they live. The boys in the building, from about three to nine years old, hit her, beat her with guns, tie her up with rope whenever they get a chance. They hit her with whips which they buy at the circus. They push her off her bicycle and take her toys away. They handcuff her with handcuffs bought with coupons from comic books. They take her to a vacant lot and use her as a target for bow and arrow. They make a spearhead and scare her. Once, surrounding her in this way, they pulled off her panties to torture her (as they put it). Now her mother has fastened the child's panties with a string around her neck so the boys can't pull them down.

What is the common denominator of all this? Is this the "natural aggression" of little boys? Is it the manifestation of the sex instinct? Is it the release of natural tendencies or the imitation of unnatural ones? The common denominator is comic books.

It was only within a matter of months—three months to be exact—that the *vade mecum* of the American middle class, *Reader's Digest*, reprinted the article, and by fall the mothers of America were removing reams of the offending comics from under Junior's bed.

The very fragmented nature of the comics industry made any concerted defense impossible. Individual publishers had no public relation firms standing by and no lobbying agencies. Although the National Comics Publications Inc., made a number of desultory attempts to counter criticism, even running a full-page ad in the *Saturday Evening Post*, it was to no avail. This loose consortium of publishers then made a crucial mistake. They underwrote the work of academics who might be sympathetic. By the use of objective, rather than Dr. Wertham's subjective techniques, they planned to get "hard data." But when empirical information was submitted, as it was in an entire issue of *The Journal of Educational Sociology* (December 1949), it was like a drizzle on a forest fire. Who cared about academics, especially those "on the take" from the very industry under examination? Not only were comic-book purveyors hiding behind dummy corporations, but they were now also hiding behind academic puppets. By the time of Wertham's Senate appearance in 1954, many Americans were frightened, disillusioned, and angry. They were prepared not for a defense of comics but for an indictment, especially if it was in easy-to-understand language—no academic gobbledygook.

They got it. Shortly after the Senate investigation began, *The Seduction of the Innocent* appeared. The book assumes some of the same seductively innocent premises of Wertham's other statements. Stated baldly: You become what you see. Although mimetic epistemologies are surely ancient, the most enthusiastic modern articulations date from the En-

"Johnny! . . . where IS that boy?" *Saturday Evening Post*,
November 20, 1948

glish Enlightenment. If consciousness was a *tabula rasa*, then what went
on that slate could be controlled. Throughout the nineteenth century,
associationist psychologists had argued, following Locke, that since the
mind is first a taker and then a giver of sense impressions, what is initially "taken" is of paramount importance. If what we know is what we
experience, selecting experience is controlling future knowledge. Well
then, couldn't we produce a happier populace if we deleted painful experiences, especially artificial ones? Why not fill the *tabula rasa* with
attractive images? Why not, indeed? *In loco parentis* does not have to
mean mindless censorship or brainwashing; it can mean just as well a
positive and compassionate selection of rewarding occasions.[6]

The argument in Wertham's book is not that images of violence or pornography called for censorship, but that the mass consumption of certain images could lead to confused behavior, especially in the immature. *We* should be allowed to see these images; the young should not. The essence of Wertham's argument is also based on the infectious nature of certain images. Hence, inoculation and separation are the treatment. Removal of the offending virus is the goal.[7] Soon vegetable analogies get mixed in with infectious ones, take root, and a garden of bacteria results.

> Gardening consists largely in protecting plants from blight and weeds, and the same is true of attending to the growth of children. If a plant fails to grow properly because attacked by a pest, only a poor gardener would look for the cause in that plant alone. The good gardener will think immediately in terms of general precaution and spray the whole field. But with children we act like the bad gardener. We often fail to carry out elementary preventive measures, and we look for the causes in the individual child. . . . The question is, Can we help the plant without attending to the garden? (p. 2)
>
> Children are like flowers. If the soil is good and the weather is not too catastrophic, they will grow up well enough. You do not have to threaten them, you do not have to psychoanalyze them, and you do not have to punish them any more than wind and storm punish flowers. But there are some things you have to bring to them, to reach them, patiently and expertly. The most important of these is reading. A readiness to learn to read is developed by healthy children spontaneously. But for the reading process, and especially for the habit of reading, comprehending, assimilating and utilizing the printed word, the child requires the help of elders. (p. 121)
>
> Take a tree. Its health and growth depend on many factors; its age, the soil, the water, the weather, the pruning, the nearness of other trees and vegetation, absence of injury from animals such as deer and mice and pests. All these factors combined make up the health of a tree. But when you study the health and life of trees concretely you find that one single factor, *Endothia parasitica*, regardless of all the other factors, beginning in 1904 wiped out all the native chestnut trees in the United States. The agricultural experts know that. But the comics experts would call it an "oversimplification." (p. 243)
>
> We could learn from the specialists in agriculture. They teach you to let all plants and trees grow to their optimal development. They do not compromise with anything that might conceivably harm crops and they try to prevent harm by spraying trees early. They do not try to find something good in anything that interferes with growth; they do not say there must have been something wrong beforehand; they teach you how to cultivate the soil scientifically. They would know how to deal with the comic-book pest. (p. 248)
>
> If a rosebush should produce twelve buds and only one blossoms,

the bush is not healthy and it is up to us to find out what is inter-
fering with its growth. The chief content of a child's life is growth
and learning. No positive science of mental health is possible if it
permits such interference as the mass onslaught of comic books. (p.
249)

Crime comic books are showered upon us in abundance. What is
the tree on which this fruit grows? After the most careful study for
many years I have come to the conclusion that it is not a tree which
only occasionally bears poisonous fruit, but one whose very sap is
poisonous. (p. 252)

The whole question of "good" comic books can be summed up in
this way: Crime comic books are poisonous plants. The "good" comic
books are at best weeds. (p. 313)

While Wertham's analogy of comic illustrations with invading kudzu
seems felicitous, it is fraught with inconsistencies, not the least of which
is misplaced ecology.[8] But no matter. One could still argue that dangerous toxins can enter the young plants if the gardener is incautious or
careless. All Wertham need do is show that plants in garden A which
have ingested the toxin are in worse shape than those in garden B which
have not. He tries. Citing the proliferation of action comics, as well as
his first-hand contact with the troubled youth of what he terms the
"hooky club," he draws the obvious inference.

Whenever I see a book like this [the violent comic] in the hands of
a little seven-year-old boy, his eyes glued to the printed page, I feel
like a fool to have to prove that this kind of thing is not good mental
nourishment for children! What is wrong with the prevailing ethics
of educators and psychologists that they have silently permitted this
kind of thing year after year, and that after I had drawn attention
to it some of them still continued to defend it as helping children to
learn about life and "get rid of their pent-up aggressions"? However
obvious it might seem, when I saw children getting into trouble and
getting sent wholesale to reformatories, I felt that I had to go on
with this tedious work. (p.31)

Sounding like "Professor" Harold Hill of *The Music Man*, Wertham
details exactly what can happen to children in River City.

To advise a child not to read a comic book works only if you can
explain to him your reasons. For example, a ten-year-old girl from
a cultivated and literate home asked me why I thought it was harmful to read *Wonder Woman* (a crime comic which we have found to
be one of the most harmful). She saw in her home many good books
and I took that as a starting point, explaining to her what good
stories and novels are. "Supposing," I told her, "you get used to
eating sandwiches made with very strong seasonings, with onions
and peppers and highly spiced mustard. You will lose your taste for
simple bread and butter and for finer food. The same is true of

reading strong comic books. If later on you want to read a good novel it may describe how a young boy and girl sit together and watch the rain falling. They talk about themselves and the pages of the book describe what their innermost little thoughts are. This is what is called literature. But you will never be able to appreciate that if in comic-book fashion you expect that at any minute someone will appear and pitch both of them out of the window." In this case the girl understood, and the advice worked. (pp. 64–65)

If consuming fantasy does not translate into tangible action, at least it blunts the "finer feelings of conscience" (p. 91). Worse still, such fantasy can retard learning.

> Comic books harm the development of the reading process from the lowest level of the most elementary hygiene of vision to the highest level of learning to appreciate how to read a good literary book. Print is easy to read when the paper background is light and the printing a good contrasting black. Yet most comics are smudgingly printed on pulp paper. The printing is crowded in balloons with irregular lines. Any adult can check on the eyestrain involved by reading a few comic books himself. We *can* produce the most beautifully printed books and pamphlets; every morning my mail has advertising matter expertly designed and handsomely printed on expensive paper. Yet to our children we give the crudest and most ill-designed products. (p. 139)

Although Wertham argues that the fables of aggression will leak into real life, he only vaguely emphasizes his argument that links sex with violence. Violence is more susceptible to reductive causality. Teenage boys look at pulp illustrations of action; teenage boys are violent. They are not, however, sexual—not yet. Their sexuality is latent, Wertham contends, in the process of being formed.

> The short circuit which connects violence with sex is a primitive pattern slumbering in all people. It can easily be released in children if it is drilled into them early enough and long enough. It is to these primitive layers of the undeveloped mind, to this weak spot, that comic books appeal. The stories and pictures arouse vague yearning and suggest ways in which sadism can be practiced or daydreamed about. (p. 179)

Titillation is feared not because it encourages masturbation but because of something more pernicious.[9]

> Many adolescents go through periods of vague fears that they might be homosexual. Such fears may become a source of great mental anguish and these boys usually have no one in whom they feel they can confide. In a number of cases I have found this sequence of events: At an early age these boys become addicted to the homo-erotically tinged type of comic book. During and after comic-book

reading they indulged in fantasies which became severely repressed. Life experiences, either those drawing their attention to the great taboo on homosexuality or just the opposite—experiences providing any kind of temptation—raise feelings of doubt, guilt, shame and sexual malorientation.

The term *pederasty* does not mean—as is often erroneously believed—a crude physical relationship between men. Pederasty means the erotic relationship between a mature man and a young boy. (p. 189)

And where could such pederastic encounters be found? Encounters which, if seen by impressionable eyes, could be locked forever in the mind and find their way into action? The answer is everywhere: Pederasty is all over the comics. Take *Batman*, for instance:

In the Batman type of comic book such a relationship is depicted to children before they can even read. Batman and Robin, the "dynamic duo," also known as the "daring duo," go into action in their special uniforms. They constantly rescue each other from violent attacks by an unending number of enemies. The feeling is conveyed that we men must stick together because there are so many villainous creatures who have to be exterminated. They lurk not only under every bed but also behind every star in the sky. Either Batman or his young boy friend or both are captured, threatened with every imaginable weapon, almost blown to bits, almost crushed to death, almost annihilated. Sometimes Batman ends up in bed injured and young Robin is shown sitting next to him. At home they lead an idyllic life. They are Bruce Wayne and "Dick" Grayson. Bruce Wayne is described as a "socialite" and the official relationship is that Dick is Bruce's ward. They live in sumptuous quarters, with beautiful flowers in large vases, and have a butler, Alfred. Batman is sometimes shown in a dressing gown. As they sit by the fireplace the young boy sometimes worries about his partner: "Something's wrong with Bruce. He hasn't been himself these past few days." It is like a wish dream of two homosexuals living together. Sometimes they are shown on a couch, Bruce reclining and Dick sitting next to him, jacket off, collar open, and his hand on his friend's arm. Like the girls in other stories, Robin is sometimes held captive by the villains and Batman has to give in or "Robin gets killed."

Robin is a handsome ephebic boy, usually shown in his uniform with bare legs. He is buoyant with energy and devoted to nothing on earth or in interplanetary space as much as to Bruce Wayne. He often stands with his legs spread, the genital region discreetly evident. (p. 191)

If action fantasies instill the desire for or, at least, the possibility of violent action, does it not follow that homosexual fantasy should lead to homosexual encounters? Wertham need not have stopped with Batman and Robin. What about the Sandman and Sandy, the Shield and Rusty, the Human Torch and Toro, the Green Arrow and Speedy . . . ? Addressing Wertham's overly efficient use of Occam's razor, the satiric cartoonist Jules Feiffer writes in *The Great Comic Book Heroes:*

> Batman and Robin were no more or less queer than were their youngish readers, many of whom palled around together, didn't trust girls, played games that had lots of bodily contact, and from similar surface evidence were more or less queer. But this sort of case-building is much too restrictive. In our society it is not only homosexuals who don't like women. Almost no one does. Batman and Robin are merely a legitimate continuation of that misanthropic maleness that run, unvaryingly, through every branch of American entertainment, high or low: literature, movies, comic books, or party jokes. The broad tone of our mass media has always been inbred, narcissistic, reactionary. Mocking Jews because most writers weren't; mocking Negroes because all of the writers weren't; denigrating women because all of the writers were either married or had mothers. Mass entertainment being engineered by men, it was natural that a primary target be women: who were fighting harder for their rights, evening the score, unsettling the traditional balance between the sexes. In a depression they were often able to find work where their men could not. They were clearly the enemy.
>
> Wertham cites testimony taken from homosexuals to prove the secret kicks received from the knowledge that Batman and Robin were living together, going out together, adventuring together. But so were the Green Hornet and Kato (hmmm—an oriental . . .) and the Lone Ranger and Tonto (Christ! An Indian!)—and so, for that matter, did Fred Astaire and Ginger Rogers hang around together an awful lot, but, God knows, I saw every one of their movies and it never occurred to me they were sleeping with each other. If homosexual fads were certain proof of that which will turn our young queer, then we should long ago have burned not just Batman books, but all Bette Davis, Joan Crawford, and Judy Garland movies. (pp. 43–44)

Following Wertham: If Batman threatens to tip the balance toward pederasty, wouldn't the judicious application of Superman set things right? After all, doesn't Lois Lane love Superman and Superman as Clark Kent love Lois Lane? Or is this also heterosexuality run amok? Wertham on Superman:

> Actually, Superman (with the big S on his uniform—we should, I suppose, be thankful that it is not an S.S.) needs an endless stream of ever new submen, criminals and "foreign-looking" people not only to justify his existence but even to make it possible. It is this feature that engenders in children either one or the other of two attitudes: either they fantasy themselves as supermen, with the attendant prejudices against the submen, or it makes them submissive

and receptive to the blandishments of strong men who will solve all their social problems for them—by force.

Superman not only defies the laws of gravity, which his great strength makes conceivable; in addition he gives children a completely wrong idea of other basic physical laws. Not even Superman, for example, should be able to lift up a building while not standing on the ground, or to stop an airplane in mid-air while flying himself.

There are also super-children, like Superboy. Superboy can slice a tree like a cake, can melt glass by looking at it ("with his amazing X-ray eyes, Superboy proves the scientific law that focused concentrated X-rays can melt glass"!), defeats "a certain gang chief and his hirelings." Superboy rewrites American history, too. In one story he helps George Washington's campaign and saves his life by hitting a Hessian with a snowball. George Washington reports to the Continental Congress: "And Sirs, this remarkable boy, a Superboy, helped our boys win a great victory."

One third of a page of this book is a picture of Washington crossing the Delaware—with Superboy guiding the boat through the ice floes. It is really Superboy who is crossing the Delaware, with George Washington in the boat. All this travesty is endorsed by the impressive board of experts in psychiatry, education and English literature. (pp. 34, 35–36)[10]

Regardless of the reductive causality, accidental misreading (Superboy is not Superman's sidekick but Superman as a boy), and purposeful misreadings, Wertham's influence was profound and long-lasting. To say that Wertham destroyed the comic-book Goliath single-handedly would be an overstatement. He had the biggest stone, beginner's luck, and an entire Senate subcommittee to help him load the sling. The anticomic movement really had begun much earlier, on May 8, 1940, when Sterling North, book editor of the *Chicago Daily News*, lofted this pebble:

Virtually every child in America is reading color "comics" magazines—a poisonous mushroom growth of the last two years.

Save for a scattering of more or less innocuous "gag" comics and some reprints of newspaper strips, we found that the bulk of these lurid publications depend for their appeal upon mayhem, murder, torture, and abduction—often with a child as the victim. Superman heroics, voluptuous females in scanty attire, blazing machine guns, hooded "justice" and cheap political propaganda were to be found on almost every page.

The old dime novels in which an occasional redskin bit the dust were classic literature compared to the sadistic drivel pouring from the presses today.

Badly drawn, badly written and badly printed—a strain on young eyes and young nervous systems—the effect of these pulp-paper nightmares is that of a violent stimulant. Their crude blacks and reds spoil the child's natural sense of color; their hypodermic injection of sex and murder make the child impatient with better, though quieter, stories. Unless we want a coming generation even more ferocious than the present one, parents and teachers throughout America must band together to break the "comic" magazine. (p. 21)

The call did not go unheeded. Stones were picked up and thrown by almost all the cultural illuminati.[11] Certainly the most articulate, and hence the least effective Wertham ally, was Gershorn Legman. Although Legman was to make his reputation as an authority on the dirty joke, the dirty limerick, and erotic folklore, in *Love & Death: A Study in Censorship*, he inveighs against violence in popular culture—in the detective story, in advertising, in sports, in the movies, and most especially in the comics. In his chapter on comics, "Not for Children," he charges that the entire pictorial medium has become dedicated to transporting violence.

> Then came the comic-books, the secret of their unprecedented success—if anything can be called a secret that appears in sixty million copies monthly—being, of course, their violence. All comic-books without exception are principally, if not wholly, devoted to violence. And just as the murder-stories for the use of frustrated adults are politely euphemized as "mysteries," just so the yearly half-billion violence-leaflets for children are camouflaged as "funnies," as "comics," as "jokes," though there is never anything comical in them.
>
> Garishly presented in clashing colors, and cheaply printed in forty-eight pages of paper-bound pulp with even more garish covers, what recourse there is in comic-books to the printed word is, totally, language violence: full capitals throughout, bold-face accents liberally besprinkled, and exclamation points galore; with illiterate little cartouches, where no conversation is thought necessary, saying Pow, Zow, and Whammo! to indicate the administration of violence, while the victims respond with Awrrk, Aagh, Aieee, Ooof, and Uggh. (p. 31)

Legman estimated an "absolute minimum of 18,000 pictorial acts of violence for every child in America who was six years old in 1938." Surely such bulk consumption must be influencing a generation of future deviates. Thomas Radeki, president and founder of the National Coalition on Television Violence, wonders how seeing an average of twenty acts of televised violence per hour, four hours a day, three hundred days of the year cannot be producing a generation of addled Rambos. But what can be done? St. Augustine and Hannah Moore counseled Christianity; we will see Radeki's prescription in Chapter 6; here is Legman's:

> People want to know what can be done. Nothing can be done. Not for children. Comic-books do not exist in a vacuum. American parents see nothing wrong with the fictional violence of comic-books because they are themselves addicted to precisely the same violence in reality, from the daily accident or atrocity smeared over the front page of their breakfast newspaper to the nightly prize-fight or murder-play in movies, radio, and television coast-to-coast. (p. 50)

Such angst is nowhere to be found in Wertham. He exudes a boyish enthusiasm for the task at hand. Legman, however, knows too much history. His melancholy is typical of that of intellectuals jaded by the realization that they are in the minority and that no one wants what they have. If you look at the intellectuals on the other side, those who were leary about attributing too much influence to comic culture, you will see their conclusions are also melancholy. In December 1949, after the first wave of anticomic sentiment, *The Journal of Educational Sociology*, a reputable academic periodical published under the auspices of the Payne Educational Sociology Foundation, attempted a half-hearted defense in a special issue. As compared to attacks from the PTA, the pulpit, and the popular press, the academics from higher education were primarily concerned with fitting the comics into the cultural matrix of adolescent myth. To most of them, it was clear the youthful audience was moving from picture book to comic book, from one form of illustrated fairy tale to another. We all knew how violent the stories of the Brothers Grimm and Mother Goose could be, and we all knew how Mrs. Grundy had tempered their excesses. Folk tales have been censored from Charles Perrault to the confections of Walt Disney. Hence the fantasy adventures of Superman, Flash Gordon, Batman, et al.,

> seem to parallel the traditional interests of children. The myths and legends of ancient Greece, the folk legends of America's Paul Bunyan and Pecos Bill, and the classic fairy tales themselves attest to the human need for escape and wish fulfillment. Stories which push back the boundaries of reality have long served civilized man for the release of feelings of aggression and frustration. Identifying with "Superman," one can overcome all obstacles, do battle for the weak and against the wicked, triumph over one's enemies, and generally transcend the hampering restrictions of a hard world. (Frank, pp. 216–17)

The gist of most of the other articles in the special issue of *The Journal of Educational Sociology* is that the comic could become a powerful "visual aid" if it were properly adapted to classroom use. The armed services had used comics to indoctrinate troops during the war. Why not use them to educate school children? Almost without exception, the educators avoided comment on comic content and concentrated on how useful the form might be. This rather haphazard defense of the comics was seriously undercut when the Kefauver committee was informed that many of the educators were also consultants to the comic-book industry. Ironically, the most spirited defenses, hardly more than acknowledgments that comics were modern myths, were written by Dr. Jean Thompson, acting director, Bureau of Child Guidance, Board of Education, N.Y.C.; Harvey Zorbaugh, professor of education, New York University; Dr. Lauretta Bender, child psychiatrist at Bellevue Hospital; and Josette Frank, consultant on reading for the Child Study Association of America, all of whom were being paid as much as $300 a month by various publishers. So much for expert testimony. So much for the integrity of academics.

In all the brouhaha, no one, with the possible exception of Legman, attempted to fit the action/adventure comic into a history of disorderly conduct in mass media. The eruption of comics in the 1940s was no spontaneous growth which bloomed after the war but was instead only the most recent blossoming of pictographs. What was unique was their mass production, not their content. Violent ideograms are as old as man's earliest attempts to decorate the cave walls. Drawing and looking at things moving at us has been one of the most enduring preoccupations of all races. After all, what was found on the cave walls of Lascaux, on the walls of Pompeii's buildings, and on the subway walls of modern cities are the outline drawings of men in violent action.

The claim that cartooning started with the real Flintstones who drew the fictional antics of the ur-Flintstones on rock walls might be stretching the truth too far. Still, one might argue that if you unrolled the scroll work of Trajan's Column or unfurled the Bayeux tapestry, you might have an early view of the modern "strip" cartoon. One might also argue that the Parthenon friezes, Egyptian hieroglyphics (in which the cartouche, or conversation balloon, first appeared), Giotto's frescoes, the crowded canvasses of Pieter Breughel and Hieronymus Bosch, or the Jewish phylacteries are examples of our ancient voyeuristic urge to see frozen action in narrative sequence. Or what of Japanese scrolls, Mayan codices, or Grecian urns? The Assyrian stone carvings, which we saw in Chapter 1, were sufficiently violent and even organized horizontally in panels. To stretch the ancestry back so far, however, essentially removes the spine of any definition.

The modern strip cartoon developed simultaneously with print technology. Print transformed cartoon signs in two obvious ways. First, images were infinitely repeatable, and second, access to these images was simple. No one had to go deep into the cave or far into the temple or museum; a trip to the corner newsstand would usually suffice. To make that newsstand profitable, the economies of mass production refined the definition one step further. The most profitable sequences were those which were most often produced. In other words, the images and stories which were presented most often were the ones most in demand. This is an obvious but crucial distinction, for—as contrasted with art culture—in popular culture the audience rather than the artist decides what is produced.[12]

In the archaeology of language one finds the bones of forgotten culture. The modern American "comic strip" was preceded by the English "strip cartoon." While we understand the meaning of "strip" and all it implies about the sequentiality and narrative flow of print, "comic" hardly seems appropriate. "Cartoon" is still more questionable. How "cartoon," which is an art term meaning a full-scale colored drawing, got mixed up with popular "cartoon," a satiric drawing, is not clear. Probably the shared medium of pasteboard unites them (carta = leaf of paper). The confusion becomes even humorous, especially in America where "cartoon" has only one meaning.[13] Other languages have circumvented this problem by defining the medium. The French say *lande dessinée* (drawn strip), the Germans *Bilderstreifen* or *Bildergeschichte* (picture strip/story), while the Italians focus on the speech balloon and call it *fumetto* (puff of smoke).

Our linguistic confusion results from the fact that Anglo-American culture was late in acquiring and developing this medium.[14] Until Hogarth, the pictograph with trailing text was usually exploited in the service of political concerns, as it often still is. However, as early as the fifteenth century, quite another story was being told, even in England. This story was in many ways similar to that told in *EC* horror comics of the 1950s—a story of violent action: the Crucifixion. As we have seen, the Passion of Christ was one of the richest repositories of preposterous violence in high art. But it was also dominant in popular iconography.[15] For instance, in an early English woodcut, the boxes at the circumference refer to stages of the Passion—from the crowing cock at the upper left to the mortar and pestle used to grind the ointments at the lower right. The text reads, "Who in sin devoutly beholdeth these arms of Christ's Passion hath [illegible—number?] years of pardon." These easy-to-illustrate objects, originally tangential to the story, have become independent stories enjoyed for themselves.

While Christography was circumscribed by the dictates and dogmas of established ritual, saints' lives were matters of common speculation. They belonged to the folk not to the church, and hence were to become a vast storehouse of premodern gratuitous violence. One of the most famous sequences is a fifteenth-century woodcut of St. Erasmus who is said to have been persecuted under Emperor Diocletian in the third century. In the panels shown on page 160, the saint is judged worthy of a little torture. From top left to bottom right, he endures a club over the head, a spike down the throat, arrows under the fingernails, pincers on the arms, a metal scraper (a carder) on the skin, a gouger in the eye,

Lamentation over the body of Christ, c. 1500 (Bodleian
Library, Oxford, MS Rawl. D. 403 f.1v s. 976)

immersion in a bubbling pot of oil, a red-hot cuirass applied to the skin,
a winding-out of entrails, and, graciously, a severing at the neck.

These pictographs were not isolated images. Over a third of the books
printed before 1500 were illustrated, and many of the illustrations at
least implied violence. With the advent of the printing press, implication
was no longer necessary; the real stuff could suffice. Instead of showing
the tortures inflicted on the innocent, as in the case of Christ and the
saints, the new economies allowed more democratic vistas—views of torture inflicted on the less meritorious. When the heroic victim was put
aside and the deserving tyrant came front and center, the age of modern
illustrated violence could begin. Tom Nero appears. The tortures inflicted on a St. Erasmus are a preliminary to the retaliation to be inflicted on the torturers. Just deserts are sweetest because they are more
than just; they are richly deserved.

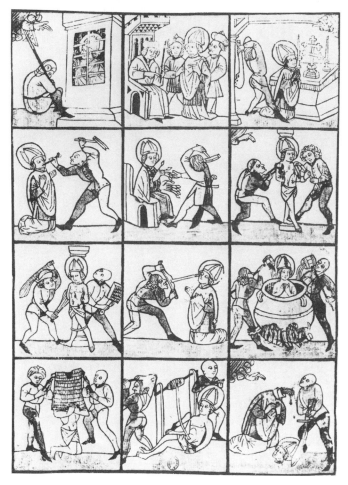

Swabian, *The Tortures of St. Erasmus*, c. 1455–65 (Cabinet
des Estampes, Bibliothèque Nationale, Paris S. 1409)

Who got these "just deserts" in the Middle Ages? Usually the Jews
did. The Jews essentially performed the scapegoat roles necessary to the
sequences of modern preposterous violence. In early Renaissance art, the
subject was the suffering of Christ and the saints; in late Renaissance
popular culture, the subject was frequently the torture of Jews. Ironically, the Jews became inverted Christs—*deserving* victims of communal
male aggression. Anti-Semitism evolved from the picturing of villain-
ous-looking mockers of Christ's agony to the picturing of deserving victims of righteous retribution. And what did they do to deserve this?
Rarely was the proffered sin the betrayal of Christ or the sin of perfi-
dious capitalism; instead the crime was usually a displaced thievery, a
sublimated betrayal.

On the next page is an inflammatory anti-Semitic broadside which

A Horrible Deed Committed by the Jews in Passau, 1477,
Nürnberg, 1490s (Münich, Staatsbibl. Nr. 118, 307)

alleges that there was a Jewish conspiracy to steal and deface the sacraments. The story line runs thus: (1) A Christian steals eight pieces of the sacrament from the church, (2) sells them to some Jews, (3) who carry them into the synagogue where (4) they are defaced. Then (5) the Jews divide up the sacrament and bury parts of it to test its efficacy and, as they do so, (6) the image of Christ and his angels show it to be real and holy. (7) The Jews are caught, (8) brought to judgment and beheaded, (9) torn with pincers, and (10) burned. The erring Christian is whipped and pinched (11) while he is transported in a cart to presumable incarceration. The last panel shows that the Christians have built a new church on the site of the razed synagogue.

Jews made the ideal villains since they provided a progressively more secular and divided Europe with a common victim. In the morality plays of ritualized violence, they proved to be the perfect devils, having both secular and religious histories of transgressions. They were not, however, alone. The other butt of illustrated violence remains to this day the most enduring Western image of violator/victim—women, especially wives. Although the comics of the 1950s rarely directed a sexual attack toward a woman, women were often the cause of violence, egging on the unfortunate male to acts he would otherwise not have performed. As in male rape fantasies, women would then "get theirs." Just as the Jews had "asked for it" by torturing the Savior, so women should be punished for making males anxious. The sexual hostility of unrequited male ardor is never far from the surface of popular culture. This was also true of the early comics, as *Peasant Dance* (1537) attests. The dance starts out as a model of restraint and good taste, but soon wine and revelry wear out the dancing husbands. One has to be led home while vomiting, another is threatened by his wife as he is in the arms of a young wench, and a third is glared at censoriously by an old biddy. In the last panel, a friend comments, "You are really too vulgar," while his cohort vomits. Boys just want to have fun; women just want to criticize.

The last panel makes clear that the males are fully culpable. The woman is set up, to be sure, by her husband's reckless behavior. Still, she is a spoil sport, and most marriage strips in the sixteenth century were far more misogynistic. In an early seventeenth-century strip (p. 164), we are provided *A precious, good, hallowed Recipe for Men who have shrewish Wives*. In this tale a man has taken a shrewish wife and explains à la Petruchio how he tames her. After she berates him in the first panel, he goes to the woods for some "herbs" to quiet her. We soon find these herbs are not nostrums of love but sticks with which to whip her. The text adds, "Listen to me, woman, since you have constantly maltreated me and taken me for a fool. I shall not spare your skin, but lick and paste your backside, and leave a memento on you to serve as an example to other shrewish wives." She takes to her bed repentant, soon dies, and is buried. In the last panel, the husband, free at last, repairs to his chums and says, "Strike up, musicians, in godly fashion, be merry, for all my sorrow is gone now that I am released from Purgatory." A demurrer is appended at the bottom of the text to the effect that these verses refer only to shrewish wives. "So I beg that no female reader should imagine that she is intended." However, the fun has been had, and this exculpation is rather like the *EC* horror/crime narrator, the Vault Keeper or the Crypt Keeper, who at the end of the story assures the "kiddies" that what they have just seen is not to be taken seriously . . . it's all in fun. Heh-heh!

While the shrewish wife and the blaspheming Jew hardly deserved their pictographic fates, a third victim appeared who was to become a

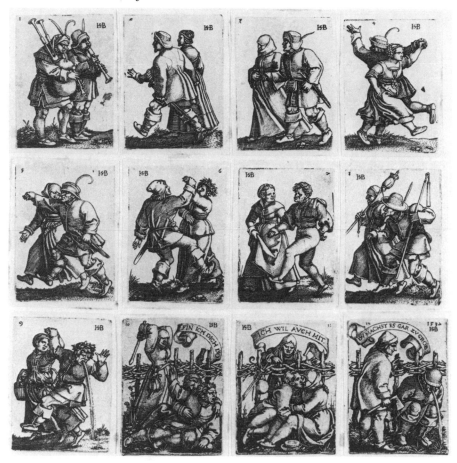

Hans Sebald Beham, *Peasant Dance*, 1537 (David Kunzle, Fig. 1–22)

mainstay of modern mythography. The rise of institutional bureaucracies eventually provided a victim upon whom countless fables of aggression could be safely imposed—the antisocial criminal. The focus is rarely on the crime alone but rather on the punishment. A male, caught, tried, sentenced, and then executed in full public view, provided one of the most popular subjects of mass-produced illustration. Illustrated punishment as popular entertainment moved from the church to the city square, from innocent victim (Jesus) to "deserving" ones (Jews and women), from fiction based on myth to fiction based on reality. The ritualistic carnivalization of suffering was now given its most stable context. Vengeance became the ultimate act in the drama of the judicial ritual.[16]

The three principal forms of capital punishment were fashioned from objects of the mundane world—the ax, the rope, and the wheel. Beheading was standard; hanging was more shameful since the body was left to rot in public view. Worst of all was the wheel, a torture until death.

A precious, good, hallowed Recipe for Men who have shrewish Wives,
1620 (Nürnberg H.B. 24, 843)

Being beaten on the wheel was such an egregious display of real violence
that it had lost much of its attentive audience by the sixteenth century.
Yet as David Kunzle contends in *The Early Comic Strip*, the wheel remained the most popular form to illustrate. As is often the case, the

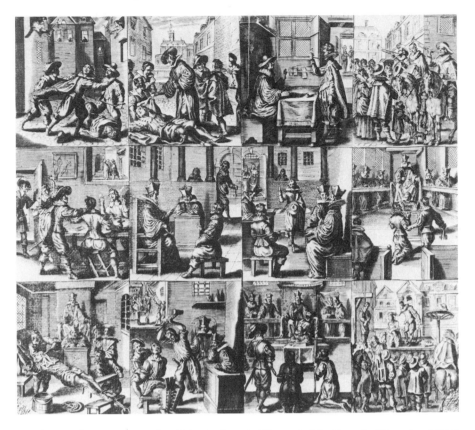

Legal Procedure against the Criminal, c. 1600, probably French (Hennin, 1876) (Cabinet des Estampes, Bibliothèque Nationale, Paris)

attraction of hyperbole draws us into fictional recreations, yet we cannot stand such exaggerations if they are made real. Even the Spanish Inquisition passed the wheel by for less outrageous forms of torture.

In the early seventeenth-century French strip shown above, we see an almost textbook picture (it may have been just that—an illustration for aspiring judges) of the judicial process as it focused on the crime in order to get to the punishment. In the first eight boxes we have the crime, discovery, complaint, proclamation, arrest, interrogation, witness's testimony, and pleading. From the ninth panel on, the excitement recommences as water torture, then the Spanish boot, and the "Amende Honorable" make the last scenes almost anticlimactic. The formulaic exposition of the first scenes, which detail the legal process, essentially sanctions our viewing of the last scenes, which detail awful punishment. On page 166 is a contemporaneous German version, which has adumbrated the central panels to concentrate only on crime and punishment.

One might dismiss these illustrations as the excesses of a barbaric era

The Horrible Murder committed in famous Halle, Saxony, by Christoph Windt from Zangen (Salzburg) (Wickiana, p. 4v)

were it not for the fact that they form one of the staples of modern mass culture. As Stephen King has said of his own peculiar trade: "The brutal fact of the matter is that we're still in the business of selling public executions" ("Playboy Interview," p. 238). Still, we don't see the imagery of distress in English iconography until the late eighteenth century, in part because the English legal process was adversarial, not inquisitional, and in part because the English were able to satisfy this desire elsewhere, as in the blood-and-thunder Jacobean revenge tragedies or in the violent stories carried in folklore and ballads.[17] Since the pre-Romantic English had no history of institutionalized torture to illustrate, they illustrated what violence they did have with a reserve which betrays suppressed enthusiasm. The exploits of famous criminals like Jonathan Wild, Elizabeth Canning, Claude Duval, Colonel Blood, and especially of Jack Sheppard (whose execution in November 1724 attracted 200,000 spectators and whose life story was celebrated by Daniel Defoe) prepared the way for their fictional counterparts of the next century. Their stories would become folklore and with incremental addition and repetition would reappear in the Victorian penny dreadfuls.

Along the way, of course, Hogarth appeared with his "strong prints for stony hearts." Whether Hogarth vulgarized art or glorified vulgarity depends on one's frame of reference. What is clear is that Hogarth was able to attract a vast audience willing to part with a shilling or two to see what he advertised as being good for them: "As the Subjects are calculated to reform some reigning Vices peculiar to the lower Class of People in hopes to render them of more extensive Use, the Author has publish'd them in the cheapest Manner possible" (*Public Advertiser*, February 13, 1751). While his artistry would never be equaled, the levels of his gleeful distortion would reappear as a hallmark of illustration, first in penny dreadfuls and later in action comics.

As Goya would later do in *Los Caprichos*, Hogarth straddled the two traditions in illustrating preposterous violence. On the one hand, he perpetuated the art tradition which began with the medieval mockeries and continued through Holbein, Dürer, Brueghel the Elder, and Bosch, to be revived in the nineteenth century by Blake, Fuseli, and Munch and in the twentieth by Kubin, Grosz, and Bacon. On the other hand, Hogarth dignified the popular culture tradition that had started with woodcuts and continued in the broadsheet cartooning of George Townshend, Thomas Rowlandson, and James Gillray, eventuating in the illustrations of the penny dreadfuls. This second tradition leads to the comic strip and from there arrives at the comic book. Beforehand, however, the strip illustration was inserted into print text to help the reader better imagine a scene.

The coupling of text and illustration had been a staple of British working-class fiction almost from the start of the eighteenth century. Once methods for reproducing pictures on paper were integrated with the printing of text, as with intaglio, the two became inseparable. As literacy increased and the economies of scale allowed larger and larger press runs, the audience increased enormously. The median age of readership dropped, adolescents became consumers, and the level of action and violence increased. Not surprisingly, so did the criticism. William Wordsworth, erstwhile radical and democrat, now poet laureate, wrote at mid-century in "Illustrated Books and Newspapers" (1850):

> *Discourse was deemed Man's noblest attribute,*
> *And written words the glory of his hand:*
> *Then followed Printing with enlarged command*
> *For thought—dominion vast and absolute*
> *For spreading truth, making love expand.*
> *Now prose and verse sunk into disrepute*
> *Must lacquey a dumb Art that best can suit*
> *The taste of this once-intellectual Land.*
> *A backward movement surely have we here*
> *From manhood—back to childhood; for the age—*
> *Back towards caverned life's first rude career.*
> *Avaunt this vile abuse of pictured page!*
> *Must eyes be all in all, the tongue and ear*
> *Nothing? Heaven keep us from a lower stage!*

Neither heaven nor the good, gray poet could stop the flow of what was becoming "popular literature" and was soon to become "boys' literature."

Penny dreadfuls were essentially a mix of the biographies of criminals commonly collected in the "Newgate Calendar" (which detailed the records of the most notorious inmates at the Tower of London), the gothic novel, and the illustrated broadside. While the penny dreadfuls initially featured such bizarre middle-aged characters as Varney the Vampire or Sweeney Todd, they eventually developed traits more in keeping with their adolescent audience. By the 1880s youthful protagonists like Jack Sheppard, Claude Duval, and Dick Turpin had their lives told repeatedly. A generation earlier, these boy heroes had been adult outlaws, and their tales were carried to an adult audience via the broadsheet. Their adventures were cautionary tales. In the late nineteenth century, however, they had become rags-to-riches success stories. Adolescent fantasies had pushed aside conservative caveats. As Patrick A. Dunae observes,

> Tucked between the illustrated covers of the dreadfuls were also boisterous tales of contemporary, though fictitious, young heroes— heroes who, having quarreled violently with their employers or schoolmasters, ran off to become pirates or highwaymen. Tales of this description, critics argued, were psychologically harmful in that they provided readers with excessive stimulation and a distorted view of the world. The tales were also considered to be a threat to society, not only because they glorified physical aggression, but because they seemed to encourage disrespect for authority. (p. 134)

Adult anxieties only increased after the passage of Forster's Education Act (1870), which promised that millions of new eyes would discover new paths to degeneration. The explosion in mass-market publishing and serialization caused an explosion in juvenile reading, which predictably called forth the William Gaineses to the market. Men like George and William Emmett, Charles Perry Brown, Samuel Dacre Clark, Charles Fox, John W. Allingham, Edwin J. Brett, and numerous others published riotous tales beneath such innocuous titles as the *Boy's Standard*, *Boy's World*, or *Our Boy's Paper*. The massive steam-driven presses printed fired-up tales of revenge, passion, and cruelty never seen before—at least never by adolescent boys. Surely, as Wordsworth had predicted, the illustrated broadside was corrupting the magazine and the magazine was corrupting the book. We were well on the way to, in Wordsworth's barely pre-Darwinian terms, the "lower stage."

Victorian Kefauvers were shocked by these "rumbustious" publications.[18] And Victorian Werthams like Edward G. Salmon published such authoritative articles as "What Boys Read" in the *Fortnightly Review* in which he cataloged both the texts and their effects. Salmon contended that boys who read this pulp and looked at these illustrations would commonly keep guns, would sneak out at night, and generally be impertinent to elders. Typical of what followed from overconsumption was a lad who "was so maddened by reading one of the tales provided for his entertainment that he shot dead his father and brother." Even staid *Punch* was forced to conclude in 1886, "It is scarcely possible to exaggerate the nauseous quality of the trash that is prepared in the shape of penny numbers" ("Editorial on Popular Literature"). The battle was soon joined by the reforming seventh Earl of Shaftsbury, the Pure Literature Society, and later by the Religious Tract Society. Common to all reformers was an abiding belief in the corruption of inherited forms and a fear of infectious disease loosed on the young. In March 1879 a spokesman for the Religious Tract Society was able to claim, based on overwhelming "evidence," that "these illustrated papers are eminently fitted to train up a race of reckless, daredevil, lying, cruel, and generally contemptible characters" (quoted in Dunae, p. 4). Excoriating the penny press in 1881, Francis Hitchman pointed to irrefutable evidence:

> An errand boy or an office lad is caught in the act of robbing his master—"frisking the till," embezzlement, or forgery. In his desk are found sundry numbers of these romances of the road, a cheap revolver, a small stock of cartridges, and a black mask. A little pressure brings out the confession that those "properties" have been bought by the youthful culprit with the intention of emulating the "knights of the road" the tale of whose exploits has fascinated him. (p. 154)

Hitchman even consulted his own "hooky club"—Newgate and Holloway Prisons—where he reported that a high proportion of the population had indeed been consuming such "rubbish" (p. 398). And who would know better than Sir Thomas Chambers, recorder of the City of London, who was able to state in *The Boy's Own Paper*: "There isn't a boy or a young lad tried at our Courts of Justice whose position there is not more or less due to the effect of unwholesome literature upon his mind." Clearly, to all these Victorians, a causality existed between fictional act and real act, and that connection must be broken for the good of society.

The most notorious of the illustrated serials was published by Newsagents Publishing Company. Starting in 1866 with the adventures of the Wild Boys—*The Wild Boys of London; or the Children of the Night, The Wild Boys of Paris; or The Vaults of Death, The Poor Boys of London; or, A Life Story for the People, The Wild Boys of London and New York*—Newsagents continued until it had gathered not only one of the largest audiences but also a goodly number of competitors. The law was not far behind. The Wild Boys were too violent and too wild.[19] In

1871 Newsagents was temporarily closed under Lord Campbell's Obscene Publication Act, and six years later, the Society for Prevention of Vice raided eleven news agents and confiscated all the *Wild Boys*. Such actions were only temporary palliatives, for obscenity was then, as now, a notoriously ambiguous term. Still, the Wild Boys had been corralled only to reappear later in different guises.

While the legal system was making perodic attempts to restrict the flow of pulp, the free market was doing its best to increase it. Good pulp, called "penny healthfuls," was even introduced in an attempt to inoculate the young against the diseases caused by the bloods. The Religious Tract Society tried its hand with the 1879 publication of *The Boy's Own Paper*, a toothless blood. But too late; time had run out. The price of wood pulp was so much lower than that of cotton-based fiber that the largest profits now lay in saturating the audience with disposable reading material good and bad. The economic reward was not in producing a lasting text which could be read repeatedly but in printing throwaway texts which could be viewed once and then repurchased in a slightly different form. The audience for exciting stories had been located; it was enthusiastic; and it wanted the same "new" stories year after year.

What had started with woodcut strip images in the early Renaissance, what had been transformed by Gutenberg technologies into printed sequences, and what had then been accompanied by textual explanations returned at the end of the nineteenth century to what were essentially woodcuts. The young, now predominantly male, audience did not want more text but less. In the 1880s Alfred Harmsworth, founder of the Amalgamated Press, realized that if he lowered the price to a halfpenny and increased the illustrations by fifty percent, he could reach an even larger audience. By the turn of the century, he had made Amalgamated into one of the most powerful houses, and foretelling the rise of the modern publishing industry, it became a corporate umbrella under which myriad publications could be produced, each trading stories, illustrations, and staff with the others. In doing this, Harmsworth also made himself into one of the first press lords—literally into Lord Northcliffe.

The penny dreadful almost disappeared in the 1890s, apparently a casualty of its own innovations. The genre was subsumed into a text form—the dime novel—and an illustrated form—the halfpenny comic. Although the original medium for the "strip cuts" (named for the wood blocks or wood "cuts") had been magazines like the *London Illustrated News* and *Punch*, Alfred Harmsworth had shown that additional money was to be made by cutting and binding the strips and selling them independently. He could then merchandise them to the same audience which was buying his halfpenny serials. Like the readers of such modern satiric strips as *Peanuts*, *Doonesbury*, or *Bloom County*, Harmsworth's

"Teaching the Young Idea," *Punch*, January 26, 1889

audience would pay to see his strips twice, once in the newspaper and again in book form. The Victorian six-frame strips usually told a story, a joke, or presented an amusing scene, and there were several strips in each issue, often mixed in with prose stories, advice, and games. Under such titles as *Puck, Merry and Bright, Funny Wonder, Larks,* and *Jolly Bits,* the strips were aimed primarily at children, but they also attracted a working-class adult audience. These "miscellanies" proved so popular that there were more than twenty lasting titles—so lasting in fact that it took the paper shortage of World War I to close them down. As the price went from one-half pence to three and one-half pence, the audience turned elsewhere for cheaper thrills.[20]

As the audience expanded downward in age, new techniques were quickly consumed. By the end of the century, comic cartoonists had already learned much of what was to characterize the modern strip. The semiotics of cartooning, thanks in large part to the German Wilhelm

Busch and the Swiss Rodolphe Töpffer, included such features as speed lines ("hites"), images of excitement like up-jumping and arms akimbo, maledicta shorthand (!#*%&*%*), and much more precise inking such as changes in lettering and letter-sizing. These innovations made action possible and, once freed from the confines of six panels, the narrative could build toward more and more violent scenes. Soon the cartoonist's lexicon contained a private vocabulary to express just such movements. Along with onomatopoeic words like *Wham! Pow! Zap!*, sleep notes (Z-Z-Z-Z-Z), and exclamation points enclosed in starbursts, which are late eighteenth-century innovations, there were "briffits," or impact clouds used to show punches, "blurgits" or repeated shade lines to show speed, "spurls" to indicate dizziness, and "agitrons" to show anxiety so intense that perspiration flies around the face of the quivering character.

In the twentieth-century movement toward greater action, naughty children and animals became bad and good adults and then evolved into supervillains and superheroes. This gradual transformation from children's jokes to adolescent adventures, especially to violent confrontations, reflected a shifting upward of audience age, and a shifting westward of the center of cartoon gravity from Northern Europe to America. The transformation quickened when comics were introduced into American newspapers.[21] The other medium that was to influence the comics was the movies. The two media continually traded stories, so that movie stars of the 1920s, especially comedians like Charlie Chaplin, Harold Lloyd, Ben Turpin, and Laurel and Hardy, had their likenesses, and very often their jokes, told in the film strip, then in the comic strip, and then in the comic book. The Universal movies of the 1930s soon were told as comics, as were the cowboy adventures of the 1940s. By the 1950s television had joined this synergism as the networks became an outlet for film cartoons as well as originators of their own animated shows. Violent cartoons like *The Road Runner* could be consumed on static pulp, in theaters, or on the small screen—all that changed was the speed of delivery and the level of audience concentration. The process is still evolving, as we will see in the last chapter, with toy companies now creating violent cartoons like *He-Man and the Masters of the Universe* in order to sell a continually expanding set of toys.

The Americanization of the comic strip, first as a gimmick exploited in intense newspaper marketing competition and then as a proto-fanzine by which the Hollywood studios broadened the audience for their cartoon characters, opened the way for new innovations. The most important development was one which looked back to the illustrated broadside and ahead to the action comics of the late 1940s—the continuous action/adventure strip. Starting with *Tarzan* in 1929 and continuing through *Dickie Dare* (1932), *Terry and the Pirates* (1934), and *Flash Gordon* (1936), these strips made no attempt to be true to the nineteenth-century cartoon but rather paid allegiance to a new standard of verisimilitude—the hyper-reality of the movies. These comics were, after all, just frames, superslow-motion movies. With the exception of a strip like *Dick Tracy* (1931), which exploited the fashion for hard-nosed realism made popular by the burgeoning detective novel, strips had to choose. Were they comic cuts or cinematic sequences? Although fables of aggression were told in both, the adventure strip was to evolve into the new hybrid carrier of turbulence.

This new carrier was the comic "book." The audience was the same audience that had been bulk consumers of the penny dreadful—the marginally literate and culturally unsophisticated: the teenager, more precisely, the teenage boy. This audience, however, was not immediately located. At first, comic books were collected strips, bound and distributed as throwaway come-ons for grocery products. The pamphlets were so popular that they were soon being sold. By the early 1930s the "book" had already assumed the $7\frac{1}{2} \times 10\frac{1}{4}$–inch format that was to become standard the world over. Publishers who had started by simply reproducing newspaper sequences under such titles as *Famous Funnies, Tiptop Comics*, or *King Comics* now had to supply an eager audience with more elaborate adventures of specific heroes.

By the late 1930s *Detective Comics* (DC) and *Action Comics* (AC) were taking a new tack to satisfy demand. They were publishing original material that had never had to pass the inspection of newspaper editors or syndicators. They published sequences expressly for people who wanted to keep these images and were willing to pay to see them. With the advent of World War II and the dislocation of the large number of late adolescent males who were cooped up on both sides of the Atlantic, these specialty publishers at last found their métier: short bursts of exploding violence in lurid color on cheap newsprint. They also found their audience—young men in uniform.

To transport these shocks, new narrative frames had to be constructed. While many of the humorous comic sequences came from the movies, the action stories often came from the pulps via the radio. Variations on the Shadow, Doc Savage, Zorro, or Jimmie Dale, in which the avenger usually adopted some form of disguise in order to reset the balance of social justice, were initially popular. The Western provided the ideal American context for this ancient ritual as the myth of the frontier demonstrated the necessity for social order. The fact that the heroes used violence was condoned, since the violence was in the service of a higher good—the survival of the family. Crime stories beyond the Western variety in which vigilante justice is achieved, provided yet another context in which two-step violence could be portrayed. The wrongdoer initiates the violent act; the law (usually a variant on J. Edgar Hoover's G-men) "comes on like gangbusters" and escalates the violence to the preposterous.[22] Social necessity mandated antisocial violence. There was big money to be made in telling these stories, as *Inside Crime, Crime and Justice, Authentic Police Cases, Crime Must Pay the Penalty, All-Famous Crimes, The Perfect Crime,* and *Crime-Fighting Detective,* showed. But the lack of product differentiation meant that profits would be continually diluted by imitators.

The problem for the producers of crime comics was that the G-men could not properly respond to the challenge because of the strictures of their law-abiding status. Whereas the Western hero, or the Masked Avenger, could finally save the day with his fists or six-shooter, the hordes of "Hoover's heroes" could not resort to the bizarre. These stories were supposed to be based in fact. So the villains could be irredeemably nasty and violent, while the men from Justice could only knock at the door and politely make arrests. The only hope was if the hoodlums resisted. When Wertham and his colleagues put this genre out of business in the 1950s, the charge was that criminal violence was glamorized in all but the last frames, thus subconsciously encouraging the audience to conclude that crime might really pay.

Enter the costumed superman. What aficionados call the "Golden Age of Comics" is the age of the caped hero, of men with colored external underwear, of men with bulging pectorals and python-thick biceps. After the eponymic Superman made his debut in 1938, the species reproduced itself like guppies on steroids: Aquaman, Batman, Captains Action/America/Future/Marvel/Victory, Spiderman, the Flash, Green Lantern, Hawkman, the Human Torch, Iron Man, Plastic Man, Power Man, Space Ranger, Sub-Mariner, the X-Men. . . . The superhero in spandex resolved the problems of the comics and enlarged the audience. Here was a pulp hero who could be a superpotent avenger of crimes every bit as nasty as the ones illustrated in the "crime does not pay" genre. Two other characters also joined the comic cast. The superman had a dual personality à la Zorro, Doc Savage, and the Shadow. He also had a young sidekick, a hero in the bud, the projected self-image of the ephebic audience: Batman's Robin, Sandman's Sandy, Shield's Rusty, Green Arrow's Speedy, to name a few. These superheroes and their various *Doppelgänger* transformations at last set the comics apart. Now radio and television would have to borrow from them.

Batman provides an example of how the various comic traditions and innovations merge in the mid-twentieth century. Batman, originally "the Batman," was straight from the pulp factories; in fact, he was a self-conscious clone of the Shadow and the Spider and a less self-conscious descendant of the Scarlet Pimpernel and the Victorian men of genteel, eleventh-hour heroism. By day, Bruce Wayne, "a bored young socialite," lives a pointless life of privilege. By night, however, he becomes "powerful and awesome," prowling the city streets (first of New York, later of "Gotham") and ridding them of urban pests. The Batman is a vigilante not an armchair detective. His forte are his fists. He does not figure things out. He fights them out. To be sure, he has his various bells, whistles, hooks, and ladders in his "utility belt," but mostly he relies on his ability to drop, pounce, and swoop into the criminal world. Although he is not averse to using fire power—in the early days he packed a .45 automatic—he prefers what the audience also has: coiled up hands. "Pow!" is his signature signed on a villain's face.

Only after the producers of *DC* comics realized that the Batman had found an audience (he was to become second only to Superman) did they divulge the "who he is and how he came to be." We learn in *DC #27* (November 1939) that fifteen years earlier Bruce Wayne's parents had been "gunned down" by street criminals, and to avenge their deaths the lad then dedicated his life to "warring on all criminals." What more heroic call to vengeance? Unlike his superhuman caped colleagues, Bruce must first perfect his own body as a weapon. We have been told earlier that if you can "take punishment" you are certified to "dish it out." After building up his body so that he will be able to "dish it out," Bruce needs only a disguise to be in business. A bat appears at the window. Bruce decides that he will be—the Batman.

By 1940 the Batman has picked up the Boy Wonder, a miniature Watson to his Holmes, a pint-sized robber of the rich, provider to the poor, a lilliputian Robin Hood right down to his Sherwood Forest costume. But Batman was really blessed by his enemies, not by his sidekick. With enemies like his, Batman needed no friends. The usual blackguards who roamed the comic pulp were a never-ending series of inflatable Joe Palooka dolls, easy to knock over and quick to get back on their feet. Superman was blessed with Lex Luther, and Captain Marvel had his Sivana, but by and large the great villains were over in Dick Tracy's strip. However, Batman's enemies were a glorious lot: The Joker, the Clay-Face, Dr. Death, Hugo Strange, the Riddler, the Penguin, and Catwoman were so exuberant that even the dour Batman could not help being enlivened.

Unfortunately, by the 1950s Batman's villains had been elbowed aside, not by the Dynamic Duo, but by the mania for outerspace invaders. Responding both to the antiviolence mood of the Eisenhower years and to the increasing anxiety over what was coming in from outerspace, aliens pestered Batman as they had been pestering his caped cousin Superman. Plot twists that made for aliens did not make for exciting revenge. Aliens were poor victimizers and even poorer victims. Superman's connection with outerspace made sense in terms of his lineage, but this was not the case with Batman. He was one of us. Coherence and tension disappeared as Batman turned Batclone and copied not only Superman's villains but his entire entourage. If Superman had a super-

Batman, Detective Comics #27 (National Periodical Publications, Inc.)

dog, Krypto, Batman would soon have superdog Ace the Bat-Hound, complete with cowl and cape. Superman had Superwoman. The pajama'd avenger then had his Batwoman and later his Batgirl whose major job was to kiss Robin, to make him blush, and to resolve whatever sexual ambivalence Wertham might have implied. The height of this supercrosspollination was that once Superman had his interdimensional imp Mr. Mxyzptlk, Batman got his Bat-Mite. "Holy copycat," as Robin might say.

The 1960s returned Batman to his senses—no more aliens, weird weapons, time travel, or weird transformations. It was business as usual, as shown on page 178. And it was this business that William Dozier and ABC were able to broadcast on Wednesday, January 12, 1966, to a startled television audience. "Wow! Holy Nielsen ratings!" as Robin might have exclaimed. Only six months earlier Dozier had glanced at a *Batman* comic on a transcontinental flight. By the time he arrived in California, he realized that here was an ideal nonanimated cartoon for television. Although Batman had twice made it to the movie screen, the television screen had so far only been the province of Superman. Dozier's inspiration was to keep the show as close to its cartoonic roots as possible. Superman had been played straight; Batman would be all curves and distortions. In fact, "Pow!," "Aargh!," and "Zowie" actually appeared on screen in speech bubbles to make sure we got the point.

The television parody was something the comic world never would have tolerated—all-out, high-camp irreverence from first scene to last. In Wayne Manor, the batmobile and the bat(motor)cycle were housed in the batcave, which was accessible only by sliding down the batpole. Alfred the butler was supercilious to a fault, and Police Commissioner Gordon was gruff to a tee. Again, the real attraction was in the nasty characters who had instigated the outrageous violence in the first place. While the Dynamic Duo had the predictable staleness of last month's bread, the Penguin, played by Burgess Meredith, the Joker by Cesar Romero, the Riddler by Frank Gorshin, and the Catwoman by Julie Newmar were as animated as the enthusiastic Nelson Riddle theme music. Little wonder so many Hollywood stars were willing to appear on a show ostensibly made for the kiddies. The televised Batman was a ham's heaven.

When in the 1970s Batman returned to the comics with his original name—the Batman—he left behind most of his pizzazz. Now he is an existential Batman, an almost diabolical Batman filled with angst and a touch of sadism. He has a more powerful torso, more pointed ears, and less-talented writers. The old villains have been supplanted by characters like Ras' Al-Ghäul, an exotic crime lord whose daughter, Talia, is in love with, and is loved by, Batman. There is also Man-Bat, a scientist whose botched experiments have transformed him into a paranoid creature of the night—an unwilling Batman. These villains are not a happy lot, as were their jovial predecessors. The hero isn't happy either, and neither are the readers. These stories are not for kids who are watching TV, but for college students curious about what they missed.[23]

Batman (National Periodical Publications, Inc.)

In the modern world, the sure sign that a mass medium is passé is when artists treat it with curiosity and academic critics hail its treatments as major new shifts in vision. In the mid-1950s, as the horror and action/adventure comics were in their death throes, art historian Lawrence Alloway coined the term ''pop art'' to categorize what seemed to be the growing trend of artists to ''ironize'' objects worn bare by

Roy Lichtenstein, *Whaam!* (Tate Gallery, London)

overexposure. There is no critical task quite as joyous as sanctifying the banal, and after all, what could follow Abstract Expressionism but concrete clichéism? Alloway was blessed with virtuoso performances: Jasper Johns's beer cans, Claes Oldenburg's stuffed sculpture, George Segal's plaster people, Robert Indiana's official seals, and most famous of all, Andy Warhol's Brillo boxes. The pop artist became rich and famous by mass-producing the very objects of mass production which had made the mass-producers rich and famous.

None of these pop artists was more influential than Roy Lichtenstein, whose "new vision" memorialized and monumentalized the comic strip. His affectionate send-up of the medium was in truth an enormous blow-up. Lichtenstein took the standard scenes of the various comic genres and magnified them so they appeared both shocking and banal. He even made the Benday tints, those dotted scenes which often form the background shades, into the size of golf balls. His *Whaam!* gave pop art a respectable name when it was purchased by the Tate Gallery in the early 1960s. Although in *Whaam! Takka Takka, Varoom, O.K. Hot-Shot*, and *As I Opened Fire* Lichtenstein's inspiration is clearly war comics, his colleagues were often more sentimental. On page 180, Mel Ramos recalls the magical objects of the Batman.

Preposterous violence is still an illustratable commodity, and from time to time a comic publisher will find a suitable subject. Conan the Barbarian, lifted from the pulps of Robert E. Howard, battles the standard Sword and Sorcery stable of greedy proto-capitalists. The X-Men and the "new" X-Men, a team of superhumans who would just as soon not be super, have a go at righting wrongs. Old Tarzan, who has been around since Edgar Rice Burroughs's moldy pulps, is occasionally resuscitated. The horror genre is profitably plundered from such noncopywritten tales as Dracula, Dr. Frankenstein, Jekyll/Hyde (from whom the Incredible

Mel Ramos, *Photo Ring*, 1962 (Louis K. Meisel Gallery,
New York; photo: Steve Lopez)

Hulk derives), and the Wolfman. Universal Studios owns the Lugosi/
Karloff/Chaney images but can't control the public-domain stories. No
violent-based fashion like Kung-Fu ("Fists of Fury"), Warlord, Transformers, G.I. Joe, Rambo, and whatever new Titan Avenger appears can
long exist before being packaged between shiny, glossy covers. The comic
industry has even taken to exploiting its own troubled past. With a note
of gleeful irony, *Eclipse Comics* reprinted in 1985 three issues of particularly gruesome pre-Wertham comics, all with the same series title—
Seduction of the Innocent!

5

"Cut to the Monster":
The Motion in Motion Pictures

We're in the business to make money, not to win Oscars. If the public were to decide tomorrow that it wanted Strauss waltzes, we'd be in the Strauss waltz business.

SIR JAMES CARRERAS, Founder and President,
Hammer Film Productions, Ltd., 1946–72

If you think, "They're not making movies like they used to," you're right. If you wish to be grammatically correct and think, "They're not making movies as they used to," you're doubly right. Motion pictures today are neither like those of fifty years ago, nor are they literally made as they used to be. We still go into the dark to see moving pictures, and they still move at twenty-four frames a second, but the pictures themselves—the way they are constructed, distributed, and consumed—are as different from the pictures of the 1930s as are "illuminated" books from "comic" books. The changes that have been wrought in movie making have resulted not so much from the changing role of the director, studio system, or shifting semantic codes. Instead, the changes have followed advances in taking pictures and then projecting them before a different audience. The much-vaunted Hollywood genius is more likely to be found tinkering with what is inside the camera or in the editing room than behind the viewfinder or in the front office. As James Agee argued years ago in *The Nation* and as Joan Didion has more recently recounted in the *New York Review of Books*, the changes academic critics like to attribute to "shifting grammar" or "evolving consciousness" are more likely the result of a new electrical cable, a new theater design, a new air-conditioning system, a new lens, a new computer program for the optical printer, a new legal clause, a new "tax break," or especially, a new shift in disposable income. For however much film scholars want to call motion pictures "cinema," to call directors "auteurs," to use words like "syntagmatic," "diachronic," and "gestalt," and to compile anthologies on "The Film as Art" or "The Art of Film," the fact remains: Movies are made to make money. The production of images on film is first and foremost a business, and only secondarily and only perhaps an art. As Charlie Chaplin said after accepting an honorary Academy Award in 1972, "I went into the business for money and the art grew out of it. If people are disillusioned by that remark, I can't help it. It's the truth." The Supreme Court has always believed it. In 1915 they held in the famous *Mutual Film Corporation v. Ohio* case that "the exhibition of moving pictures is a business pure and simple, originated and conducted for profit. . . ."

Once we accept that movies are made to make money, we will realize how important they are in cultural interpretations. As opposed to art creations, they respond efficiently to changing patterns of demand. Whereas printing changed what was written, and changed it relatively slowly, filming has changed what is seen, and changed it very rapidly. At last glance, here are the top five all-time money-making movies: *E. T. The ExtraTerrestrial, Star Wars, Return of the Jedi, The Empire Strikes Back*, and *Jaws*. In the next fifteen of the most popular films are such standards as *Grease* (#10), *The Sound of Music* (#18), and *Gone With The Wind* (#21), as well as such recent features as *The Exorcist* (#13), *The Godfather* (#14), *Superman* (#15), *Rambo* (#17), and *Gremlins* (#19). If one had to abstract the qualities that have produced the most popular moving pictures, i. e., those with the largest box-office receipts, one would have to mention that some kind of adventure is what most moviegoers want to see or, better yet, will pay to see.

The viscera have replaced intelligence in films primarily because of who wants to watch and who can pay. The median age of the theater viewer in 1950 was between thirty and fifty years old; now it is between twelve and twenty and stabilizing. About twenty-five percent of the population—adolescents—comprise almost eighty percent of the film audience. Not only are teenagers frequent consumers, they are also repeat consumers. From the age of forty on, moviegoing becomes much less frequent, and repeat viewing almost never occurs.[1] It is not uncommon for a ten-year-old to see the same film four or five times. When *Pee-Wee's Big Adventure* makes $20 million, you know that a large part of the audience is knee-high. And when kids boast that they have seen a movie ten or twenty times (as was the case with *Star Wars* and is still the case with such "cult films" as *The Rocky Horror Picture Show*), the activity of attending is assuming ritualistic importance. Their experience in the theater is certainly more complex than it is for a more mature audience. The impact of this primary audience has transformed the industry. Not only have there been such innovations as "midnight movies," which are shown to specific audiences when everyone else is asleep, but now there are "summer movies"—a distinct genre—produced for the July and August vacation audience. Clearly, a considerable part of the audience no longer goes to the movies as a privileged experience, but instead attends as a matter of course, a matter of routine.[2]

Movie theaters themselves have been transformed to accommodate the new pressures. They are no longer palaces; they are peep shows. As theaters have contracted into multiplexes, seating space has contracted. In the 1950s the average theater had more than five hundred seats, in the 1980s just over two hundred. These shopping-mall theaters, really movie dens, have been able to exploit the economies of mass production by targeting specific audiences. Should they not find an audience, the theaters are easily converted into retail space. If you notice, you will see that most of the interior walls of mall theaters are simply "hung," not fixed permanently, and if you listen to the amount of ambient noise, you will hear how temporary these walls are.[3]

With the average movie now costing almost $17 million, producers are not only looking for a big audience, they are also looking for an audience they can bank on. If they target the fifteen-year-old, they know that at least they're guaranteed the theater space, and if the film is successful, they can easily expand the audience by releasing more prints. In fact, it is not uncommon for the same film to play in more than two theaters at the same time and then to return to a cut-rate theater before making its way to videotape and from there to television. As with all mass-marketed fantasies, profits are maximized by saturating each audience with the most expensive version before shifting to the next medium and the next audience. First the hardcover, then the quality paperback, then the mass-market paperback. . . . Theater chains, like the Waldenbooks or B. Dalton book franchises, now use central data systems where all sales data are compiled daily and uploaded each night to a central office. A film "makes it" or not in a week or two. There are too many films and too few screens to "nurture a picture." As Tom Sherak, president of distribution and marketing at Twentieth-Century Fox, says:

> Since there is so much film for exhibitors to choose from, you have to open strong or exhibitors will pull your movie. A year ago a movie used to have a minimum shelf life of two weeks. Now it's

only one week, and then the movie is double-billed. In and out. (Quoted by Harmetz, "New Movies are Battling for Space in Theaters")

Even vegetables last longer than most movies.

Although both audience and producers enjoy the illusion that movies are made by creative people, such is rarely the case. We maintain the illusion in the face of all we know because, after all, doesn't it make us all feel better about guilty pleasures to think that they are somehow "artistic"? Instead of saying that movies are made by artists taking chances, however, it would be more accurate to say that most movies are, and have been, made by cost accountants trying to reduce chances. Look at who is "Hollywood." At last glance, the lineup was this: Columbia Pictures is owned by Coca-Cola; MGM and United Artists by MGM/UA Communications, of which the Texas oilman Kirk Kerkorian controls seventy-nine percent; Twentieth-Century Fox by Rupert Murdoch's News Corporation, Ltd.; Paramount by Gulf + Western; Universal by MCA; Warner Bros. by Warner Communication, Inc.; and Walt Disney by Walt Disney Co. All but one of these studios are owned by companies listed on the New York Stock Exchange. The mini-majors like Cannon, DeLaurentiis, Lorimar, New World Pictures, and Orion are also publicly traded companies. And if you were to look at the second tier of distribution—the "pay" television channels—you would find that HBO is jointly controlled by Time Inc., CBS, and Columbia Pictures, itself part of Coca-Cola; the Movie Channel is owned by Paramount (Gulf + Western), Universal (MCA), Warner Communications, and American Express, and Showtime is part of Viacom, Twentieth-Century Fox, and ABC (itself a subsidiary of Capital Cities Broadcasting). If you think that these conglomerates are more concerned about the quality of what appears on the screen than the quantity appearing below the bottom line, you are probably wrong. The Hollywood saw that "you are only as good as your last picture" refers not to critical reception but to box-office receipts.

Acknowledging this financial structure is crucial to the study of mass culture. For, Marxist critical theory aside, if ideology is important, it is a far distant contender to profit and loss. No one cares what you say or what you show. The concern is with what makes money. The question is not what is seen so much as who will pay to see it.[4] When we look at what has happened to the movie industry in the last two decades, we see a shifting of stories to capture a new paying audience, an affluent audience—the adolescents. Ideology has not shifted; semantic codes have not been subverted; rather, a new mass market has been located. The same audience which consumed horror comics, dime novels, penny dreadfuls, and other popular entertainments, whether *Punch and Judy* shows or carnival roller coasters, is making its way to the box office. What is being projected onto the screen are the same scenarios which have excited generations of adolescents: cartoon rituals of induction, fables of aggression, scenarios of violence.

As Hollywood has shifted audiences, the movies have refocused with increasing intensity on what they have always done best: the picturing of action. Moving pictures show movement; they are "motion pictures" first and only secondarily "cinema." From Eadweard Muybridge's nineteenth-century experiments in filming the movement of a running horse, to the Western gunfight of the early twentieth century, to the current *sine qua non* of movies, the high-speed car chase, the one constant is that our joy in watching movement has found the ideal medium. Yet imaging violence strikes at the center of any society's implicit promise: to restrict violence. Every censoring code—from the Production Code of 1908, to the Hays office and its publication of "Don'ts and Be Carefuls" in the 1930s, to the Catholic Legion of Decency and the Production Code Administration of the early postwar era, to the current self-registered G, PG, PG-13, R, and X rating system—has attempted to prescribe patterns not of only sex but also of violence. And every code has failed.

The current ratings system continues the industry's history of attempting to gain the largest possible audience without offending critics. What separates the present code from earlier attempts is that it is so blatantly self-serving. Instead of scaling down violence, the industry scales up the ratings. Six months after the Supreme Court's 1968 decision in *Interstate Circuit v. Dallas*, which allowed local option censorship, the industry announced its new "self-regulation." Essentially this code said, "Make any picture you want, just put it into one of these categories: G (all ages admitted), M (mature audiences suggested), R (those over sixteen or with a parent admitted), and X (no one under sixteen)." No sooner said than hedged. The age limits of R and X moved to seventeen, then M became GP (general public), then GP was changed to PG (parental guidance), and finally a new category, PG-13, was added. PG-13 is an especially interesting rating as it says specific parental guidance is suggested for those under thirteen but establishes no prohibitions. PG-13 is supposedly invoked by a single "gratuitous" drug scene (i. e., without bad consequences) or a single "sexually derived word." But what it usually means, as critic Gene Shalit and others have been quick to point out, is that the "soft R" summer slaughter movie will blend in with the PG-13. Thus PG-13 films will have *more* violence, less sex and drugs.

The gist of all these shifts is to make obvious what was clear all along to the movie makers. Since the adolescent audience is between the R and PG ratings, these are the ratings to acquire for the largest box-office receipts. Movies are made for the ratings; ratings are not made to categorize the movie. This upside-down system has produced some telling ironies. For instance, in *Student Bodies,* an otherwise forgettable send-up of the stalk-and-slash genre, a genial narrator intrudes with some foul language to say that this outburst ought to be enough to assure an R. He was correct. Sometimes the system has been grossly inappropriate.[5] The X rating, which was once used for violence—*Midnight Cowboy* and *Clockwork Orange* both had Xs—is now synonymous only with pornography. Regardless of the Motion Picture Production Code's statements about the depiction of murder on screen—"The basic dignity and value of human life shall be respected and upheld. Restraint shall be exercised in portraying the taking of life"—Brian De Palma's *Scarface* showed what they really meant. De Palma's ballet of gore worked its way up from X to R. Violence is acceptable as R; only sex is prohibited as X.

Just as the penny dreadful appeared when the economies of mass production made print accessible to the newly literate masses, so did movies become violent once the studios found an eager and affluent audience. In one of the earliest Edison Company Kinetoscopes, *The Execution of Mary Queen of Scots,* we see Mary on the block, then the swinging ax, and finally her head rolling in the dirt. Much of the early American cinema was an extension of the Buffalo Bill sideshow, complete with innumerable Indian massacres, such as in *Bronco Billy* and *Seminole Massacre.* From *The Great Train Robbery* (1903) to D. W. Griffith's *The Massacre* (1910), the American public was treated to a string of uncensored stagings of what a few years later would have been branded as unwholesome. Up until July 1, 1934, the day that a new, strict Production Code was implemented in place of the 1908 Code, the movies were filled with action. American cinema certainly was not alone. In one of the most celebrated scenes of all cinema history, the choreographed carnage on the Odessa Steps in Sergei Eisenstein's *Battleship Potemkin* (1925), we see a scene which could have come through the viewfinder of Brian De Palma, Sam Peckinpah, Walter Hill, or Martin Scorsese. Eisenstein even deliberately prolonged the sequence far beyond real-time considerations, giving the scene an almost slow-motion quality while he held the focus resolutely on the effects of violence. As with modern film, much of the *frisson* in *Potemkin* was added in the cutting room. No one can forget the rhythmic editing of the Steps sequence in which a shot of the boots of soldiers marching toward the top steps is juxtaposed with the shot of a woman protesting the soldiers' butchery, which itself is interlinked with the inevitable—the "collision" of the two images in carnage.

Still, thanks to various codes, one could hardly have characterized the bulk of Anglo-American or continental films prior to the 1970s as violent, even though certain scenes certainly demonstrated an intent to shock and a talent to horrify. In 1969 the Museum of Modern Art sponsored

Sergei Eisenstein, *Battleship Potemkin*, 1925 (Contemporary Films)

a retrospective show, *The American Action Movie 1946–1964*, which showed not only that films were perceived as too violent but that this perception was becoming institutionalized. The descriptive catalog, *Violent America: The Movies 1946–1964*, written by art historian Lawrence Alloway, was in no way censorious. Yet the show and catalog had different titles, a result of the fact that many studios would not lend their films if "violence" appeared in the show's descriptive title. Alloway accepted the premise that motion pictures demand movement and that violent and stylized movement will prevail even in the face of supposedly strict censorship. He correctly asserted that

> there is a sense in which the audience is strongly present in a movie, not only during the screening but also in its formative stages. To get financial backing for a film the producer needs to be able to define the interests of an audience not less than a year in the future; to make the film usually requires several months work at the least. As the producer's time sense is being applied to the future tastes of a statistically defined audience, he needs evidence that his theme has durability through production time. Since a good many feature films are planned to make most of their money at the time of their first release, film-makers are confronted with a difficult problem. Like car stylists, film-makers have to work for the satisfaction of a half-known future audience. The position of both Detroit and Hollywood resembles that of the speculative builders who erected the majority of New York townhouses; they were built for hypothetical clients on the gamble that changes in demand and taste would occur more slowly than the completion of the products. This is one source of the extraordinary quality that films have of being topical while being at

the same time conservative and folkloric. A successful film representing a mutation of current convention will be imitated because it introduces vital information about previously unknown audience interests. (p. 15)

Film producers, Detroit automakers, and New York speculative builders are not the only ones who work this way. Mass production has been like this since the printing press. Find an audience, fulfill its wishes, and get rich.

The three film genres which the Museum of Modern Art chose as being the most violence-prone were the Western, the detective, and the juvenile-gone-delinquent. They are all, in varying degrees, American revenge dramas in which anxieties shift from stranger on the frontier as outlaw, to stranger in the home as outlaw. Men are victimizers, and victims seek violent revenge, often through scapegoats. The narrative is fixed, characters stereotyped, vengeance mandated, and all that really changes is the speed of action and the depth of intrigue. But if you examine the films chosen to typify violence in America in the early postwar decades, your immediate reaction is that they seem tame by modern standards. This is *violent* America? These are fables for the middle aged, not for the teenagers. The hero is vulnerable, the villain flawed, the action protracted, even predictable, and sentimentality perpetually invoked. The stories are not preposterous, not cartoonic. Violence is almost always a means to an end, and the end is usually to reestablish the previolent norm, albeit with a sense of melancholy and loss. Think only of *The Killers* (1946), *Desert Fury* (1947), *I Walk Alone* (1947), *The Lady from Shanghai* (1948), *D.O.A.* (1949), *White Heat* (1949), *In a Lonely Place* (1950), *The Big Heat* (1953), *Hondo* (1955), *Backlash* (1956), *Written on the Wind* (1956), *Man in the Shadow* (1957), or *Johnny Cool* (1963), and you soon realize that nowhere in these movies do you see the intensity of violence present in such films from the late 1960s and 1970s as *Bonnie and Clyde*, *The Wild Bunch*, *Straw Dogs*, *Clockwork Orange*, the *Godfather* movies, or *Taxi Driver*. And these films are gentle compared to *Nightmare on Elm Street*, *Dawn of the Dead*, *Blood Feast*, *Basket Case*, and the current crop of gore. Violence was not so much isolated and celebrated in these films of the 1940s to the early 1960s as it was endured. Violence was harsh, ambiguous, and more often than not, used in the service of some higher social good.

By the late 1960s, however, violence had become entertainment. Why? For two reasons. First, just as the penny dreadful had robbed the mainline novel of its audience, so had television emptied the "dream palaces" of their habitués. New dreams were being provided for free—or for what seemed to be for free—right in one's livingroom. Message films, which had carried violence almost as an afterthought, could not find an audience. Even the self-consciously important films of the 1950s like *On the*

Waterfront (1954), which focused on union corruption, *Rebel Without a Cause* (1955), which dealt with juvenile delinquency, *The Man with the Golden Arm* (1955), which explored drug addiction, and *The Defiant Ones* (1958), which examined interracial relationships, were not box-office successes (and were *not* included in the MOMA show). "If you want to leave a message," the Hollywood saying went, "call Western Union." Second, the percentage of affluent adolescents, especially adolescent males, increased; they were able to bid for their own entertainment. Films could be profitable by showing what could not be seen on the livingroom screen. Russ Meyer found a niche with *The Immoral Mr. Teas*, which had too much sex, and Herschell Gordon Lewis was able to do the same with *Blood Feast*, which had too much violence. Essentially, the movies had to tell stories which were too big, too sexy, or too violent for television.

Since Hollywood had to adapt or die, adapt it did. Screen violence increased in all genres—Western, detective, combat, gangster, even domestic romance—but nowhere so much as in the genre which must generate excessive violence: the horror film. As noted in Chapter 3, when we look at the perpetrators of horror—first of monsters and then of those who must slay them—we see that while they were relatively raw in folklore, they were quickly domesticated and given better manners when transformed by print. Film or, better yet, the film audience has done the most to reverse the process. Monsters have been rebarbarized. Violence has not only been restored but magnified. We can follow this by tracking the horror monsters who have traveled from lore to print and now back to lore: (1) the vampire, (2) the man-made monster, and (3) the transformation monster.

In folklore, where the consuming audience is liminal and the tellers are mature, the vampire is the feral *nosferatu*—literally the undead—whose habits are cannibalistic. If you look at the folkloric beast, as did the celebrated Jesuit, Montague Summers, you will find a fascinorous, flesh-ripping demon who literally feeds on the flesh and blood of victims. Only later did the *Doppelgänger* transformation of victim-becoming-monster become attached to this cannibalistic narrative, and only later in print did he become the gentleman in top hat and tails. Summers, whose research almost cost him his clerical collar (he took these beasts literally), was one of the first to realize that this monster owed his livelihood to the institution which also sponsored other scenarios of preposterous violence—the Catholic Church. In the vampire, the church found an apt mythologem for the work of the devil. He was violent, yes, but he also presented himself as a victim for the priest and other true believers. Whatever else the vampire might be associated with, his attack was secondary to the violence of the revenge. The priest, with the holy iconography of wafer, holy water, cross, and stake, engaged the monster in one-sided combat. God will always defeat the devil, although the devil will always rise up again to be defeated. Scapegoats must be defeated but never destroyed.

When the feral vampire entered the polite world of adult prose fiction, he changed audiences and was transformed from demonic animal to gentleman. He developed sexual desire and his helter-skelter violence was redirected toward a specific victim. In such early prose treatments as John Polidori's *The Vampyre* and Lord Byron's "The Vampire (a fragment)," both written in 1816, the midnight marauder became a Regency gentleman.[6] As contrasted with the folk tradition, these two works were written to be read carefully, and both are notable for their total lack of violence. No matter, the vampire was up on his feet and would remain hard to keep buried for the next century and a half.

After his initial entry into polite literature, the demon reverted to violent ways as he was subsumed by popular literature. The stage plays of *The Vampyre* were full of snarls, tooth-baring, and bloody syrup. On the early Victorian stage, the themes of pursuit and vengeance were fixed into the tale by the audience's enthusiasm for melodrama. In these blood-and-thunder theatricals, the vampire's mysterious comings and goings were facilitated by a stage trapdoor, called a "vampire trap," which allowed the midnight mountebank easy ingress and exit. No records exist of these dramas other than those which indicate that the vampire was such a popular success that even the dour Scots enjoyed a version of a kilted bloodsucker, and that Goethe, seeing one of these playlets on the Continent and believing it to be by Byron, declared it was the English poet's finest work. The penny dreadful soon appropriated the vampire, giving him room to play out his violent attacks with characteristic gusto. Thomas Pecket Prest's *Varney the Vampire: or, The Feast of Blood*, published by the prolific House of Lloyd in Salisbury Square, proved to be one of the most popular renditions. *Varney* unfolds an endless scenario of attack, pursuit, annihilation, and revival with unending enthusiasm. *Varney* on a thumbnail: Varney enters a town, espies his about-to-be-married victim, beats up the boys who are his rivals, approaches the virgin, and is about to put the bite on her when one of the young swains proves heroic by protecting the girl. Then the boys are off in pursuit of Varney; they catch him, brutally beat him, and leave him for dead. The light of the moon revives Varney, and it's off again to the next town for more virgins. Varney travels through hundreds of similar episodes in almost a thousand pages of tiny type until he finally gives up the ghost and commits suicide by flinging himself into the fiery crater of Mount Vesuvius.

Varney is pure schlock melodrama and was read with such avidity that, in spite of massive print runs, individual segments were read almost to tatters. When modern collectors of Victoriana at the British

Henry Anelay, illustrator, *Varney the Vampire*, 1847

Museum attempted to piece together all the episodes, they found that
Varney had certain chapters which had presumably been handled into
dust. Just as certain of the most popular *EC* comics had literally been
read until they fell apart, so too had parts of *Varney*. The adolescent
male audience of this ageless roué had proved far more dangerous to
Varney than any of the virgins' boyfriends.

   In a mythic sense, Varney has proved indestructible. Bram Stoker
knew of *Varney*'s popularity—he had read the penny issues as a boy—
but he had more sophisticated designs on the myth. Stoker intended to
resuscitate a folkloric tale consumed by adolescents into a tale of Victorian adventure to be read by adults. His vampire would not appear in
weekly throwaways for street readers but in one self-contained novel for
adults. Stoker's novel would be no endless episodic reiteration of vam-
piric violence directed at a never-ending string of ingenues, but a mythic
panorama of demon vs. civilization, barbarian vs. science, new technology vs. old folklore, Western Europe vs. Middle Europe. Stoker maintains the pursuit and revenge, attack and retribution, but the forces are

mythic, the battle metaphoric, and the tone more common to silver-fork fiction than to the bloody pulp.

The eponymic Dracula becomes one of the central antagonists in cinematic violence. This villain far outstrips his competitors in the popularity of his violent behavior. Yet, as mentioned in Chapter 3, when we look at him in print, what is most shocking is that he is not shocking at all. In *Dracula*, the fiend rarely appears, and when he does he is usually the deferential English gentleman in bowler and pin stripes. In his conversations with Jonathan Harker about schedules, in his social niceties and interchanges with his London brokers and lawyers, Dracula always behaves as if about to take tea with the queen. When angered, it is true, he can be snarly, but his usual demeanor is accommodating almost to a fault—at least in print to a literate audience.

When Dracula migrated from print to stage, however, he, like his literary grandfather in the stage adaptations of Polidori's *Vampyre*, became far more active. In the *fin de siècle* novel, the monster gathers momentum by staying out of sight, preferring to be described by others, but in the Hamilton Deane and John Balderston stage play, he comes out front and center. Elaborate narrative turns and multiple points of view cannot support theatrical dramas. Like the shark he resembles, Dracula must move around or die. When the stage play was adapted by Garrett Ford for Tod Browning's 1931 film *Dracula*, the vampire became still more active. He became a churlish bully, a Warner Brothers gangster. Even so, with the exception of a few on-screen shoving matches with Van Helsing, one could hardly have predicted that Dracula would become such an energetic eidolon of violence. Why should he resort to physical force when all he has to do is look that look, snarl that snarl, and say, "I vant to make you my queen"?

Arguably the most immediate factor in the energizing of the vampire was the casting of Bela Lugosi as Dracula. The Browning *Dracula* was essentially a theatrical film. There was no music, except for *Swan Lake* during the credit run, and few sets or effects except for a bat flying on piano wire. Karl Freund's expressionistic angles were kept to a minimum, and the only visual risks had to do with the slit-lighting of Lugosi's eyes. Still, Lugosi, who had played the role on stage with middling success (Browning's first choice had been Lon Chaney), became a landmine waiting to explode on the screen. He made the vampire into a thug. In the novel, Dracula is tall and thin and speaks with a cultured accent; in the movie, he is squat and smelly and speaks like a pipefitter, albeit politely. Beneath the cowl and cape lurks an unpredictable immigrant from across the sea who could dismantle everything we have struggled for. He could more than assault our women. He could wreck the place.

When you look at the Universal films which followed the 1931 *Dra-*

Bela Lugosi as Count Dracula, 1931
(Universal Studios)

cula, you can see what happened when the stage play was removed as the generating text and was replaced by screenwriters fresh from other genres like Westerns and gangster films. Once the audience was located and the money counted, the sequelization began. Dracula's actions became more sadistically violent. Then as Dracula moved closer to the Saturday matinee audience, he built up still more speed and his encounters became even more concussive. The Dracula of *House of Dracula* and *House of Frankenstein*—two potboilers of the mid 1940s—almost needed Ritalin to slow down. In fact, Dracula even jumped genres to play the swaggering heavy in such oateaters as *Curse of the Undead* (1959) and *Billy the Kid vs. Dracula* (1965). Dracula was devolving; he was becoming Varney.

When the vampire king found himself in the presence of Abbott and

Costello, as he did by the 1940s, his days in the social register of monsters were clearly numbered. Dracula had become a parodic exaggeration of the beast from beyond the forest as he moved from Victorian novel to stage melodrama to screen adaptation to popular culture exploitation. Once he had moved from mature to adolescent audience, his actions became more the mimic of fairy tale giants until he had worn out his welcome and could only be sent up. Even in parody, however, Dracula was still able to shock the unwary teenager, as people who saw *Abbott and Costello Meet Frankenstein* when they were too young can attest.

After a several-year intermission in the 1950s, Dracula returned with a vengeance to terrify a new audience. This time he came not from the Balkans and the Victorian novel, not from Hollywood and Universal Studios, but from England and Hammer Studios. In an attempt to return to the "original story," as well as to avoid any copyright infringements of Universal, Hammer cast their monster along the lines of the frock-coated Victorian vampire. They found the cinematic template in Christopher Lee, a lanky, almost gaunt Englishman with needle-sharp incisors and a sexually sinister leer. From *Horror of Dracula* (1958) to *The Satanic Rites of Dracula* (1973), Lee was able to endow the role with spitting ferocity. He was obviously after more than blood. He wanted all kinds of forbidden excitement.[7] To make doubly sure the audience would stay in their seats, Hammer also added some of the most well-endowed virgins to play out the role of Dracula's bourgeois victims. Once the sexual marauder, the concupiscent victim, and the hard-as-nails avenger were assembled, the rites of violence and retaliation could recommence.

The vampire myth is now being played out as a revenge drama in which the forces of retribution became every bit as violent as the forces of disruption, if not more so. Essentially, the myth has begun to play out the primal horde scenario. In current versions, Dracula comes across the seas, chooses a full-bodied, middle-class, about-to-be-married victim, pushes her boyfriend aside, and plans to make this girl his "queen." The boys, under the tutelage of a wise older man, Van Helsing, band together to track down the absconding monster as he heads back to his homeland with the young lady tucked under his cape. They catch him at sunrise and brutally drive their phallic stake into his heart. Blood spurts skyward. The vampire is strangely relieved. The girl is returned to the boys and will be able to join the reproductive sweepstakes freed from the threat of a paternal interloper. The king is dead; long live the boys.

The vampire is now almost totally a creature of adolescents, fulfilling his eternal destiny on boxes of breakfast cereals (Count Choculas), on Halloween masks, teaching numbers on *Sesame Street* (Count Count), and as an occasional villain on Saturday morning cartoons. In over a

Frankenstein/Dracula double bill, 1939 (Forrest J. Ackerman Collection)

century he has traveled far: from folklore to theater to penny dreadful to theater again to novel to adult cinema to matinee and now back to folklore. He has been violent, then polite, and now violent. Although he is now more often a stuffed animal than a sinister menace, when he gets near the moving pictures and the adolescent audience, as he is sure to do again, the odds are that he will once again become a carrier of preposterous violence.

The Frankenstein monster has been Dracula's constant companion in popular culture, often literally filling out the double bill of our modern fantasies. Unlike the vampire, however, there was no early history of man-created monsters. The myth of the Golem—the remote-controlled protector of the Jewish ghetto—was at most only a minor influence on seventeen-year-old Mary Godwin (later to be Mary Shelley) when she set out to write a scary story. *Frankenstein*, written during the same 1816 summer that Polidori and Byron composed their vampire tales following their famous wager to write a "shocker," is the result of a young mother's attempt to deal with the grief of stillbirth. In fact, Mary Shelley even speaks of the novel as if it were that baby. In her introduction, she calls it "my hideous progeny" and bids it "go forth and prosper." She continues, "I have affection for it, for it was the offspring of happy days, when death and grief were but words which found no true echo in my heart."

It is particularly noteworthy that in the literary text the "monster" is not at all what we now recognize him to be and the revenge drama is quite the opposite of what is now played out. In the novel, Victor Frankenstein fabricates a slightly larger-than-life creature which he spurns, ostensibly because the creature is so "unaesthetic." The "creature" (nowhere does he call it "monster") looks like a big, ugly baby. But while the creature may be unattractive, he is certainly not unintelligent. Quite the contrary; he is a precocious reader who polishes off Plutarch, Milton, and Goethe in a matter of months and is nothing if not polite and deferential—at least initially. The plot essentially centers on the creature's attempt to get some attention from Victor, to be cared for, to be mothered. But Victor, ever the reluctant parent, spurns his issue. The novel is, on one level at least, a hide-and-seek played first by the creature who tries to get Victor and succeeds and then by Victor who pursues the creature. The creature has the upper hand, or rather the upper foot, because he is the fastest walker in all creation. He crosses Western Europe in only a few days! Indefatigable Victor finally pursues his alter ego to the Arctic, where the *Doppelgängers* expire of exhaustion: Victor literally and the creature figuratively.

As was the case with the vampire myth, this tale was eventually played out as a Victorian stage melodrama in R. B. Peake's *Presumption, Or the Fate of Frankenstein*. In turn, Peggy Webling adapted Peake's play for her *Frankenstein* play, which itself was adapted for the screen. While the creature moves rapidly in print, he can only trudge when on the stage. Once on the screen, he barely moves. Since the Universal director, James Whale, could not speed this monster up, he decided to slow him down. Boris Karloff's movements are painfully slow and clumsy, almost those of a teenager with oversized feet. The outfit and make-up depended on more than neck pins, overhanging forehead, and huge scars; they also included eight-pound insulated boots, which forced Karloff to move as if he could barely lift his feet. The result is Karloff's famous shuffle—"my little walk," he called it. This shuffle would find its way into other scenarios of preposterous violence, becoming by turns the lumbering of the mummy and, more recently, the rolling gait of countless zombies.

Whatever the creature lost in speed, though, he more than made up for in motivation. In Mary Shelley's novel, he is made monstrous first by lack of parental nurturing and then by Victor's broken promise to provide a female companion. In the film, neither wrong—no mothering and no one to make a mother—seemed sufficient cause for violent action. The problem was resolved in the way gangster movies resolved such motivational dilemmas: The brain of a criminal was mistakenly

Boris Karloff as the monster in *Frankenstein*, 1931 (Universal Studios)

inserted in the creature's cranium. Furthermore, new figures were introduced to exonerate young Victor—an evil scientist, Dr. Pretorius, and a hunchback, Ivor. The former performs the transplant, the latter provides the defective organ. In the Universal Frankensteins, from the original in 1931 to *House of Dracula* in 1945 (in which the Frankenstein monster plays a cameo role, as does everyone else on the Universal payroll— Dracula, hunchback, mad doctor, Wolfman, et al.), the creature's violence is explained by a twist on the Golem myth, a remote-control monster run amok. The mad scientist is the guilty party. Such motivation is nowhere in the novel and nowhere in the stage productions, so it was necessary to establish the creature as actor in the rituals of retributive violence. What better scapegoat for this audience than a monster who is, like them, first of all a misunderstood adolescent?

By the time Hammer Studios got around to remaking this myth in

Hammer Studios' Frankenstein monster in *Frankenstein and the Monster From Hell*, 1973 (Hammer Studios)

the late 1950s, they had already learned from Dracula the importance of the revenge motif. The creation scene was still central, with the evil scientist and often with the demented hunchback, but "Victor" was removed to the role of passive observer. The evil doctor was no longer Dr. Pretorius but Dr. or Baron Frankenstein, which only aggravated the mixed-up nomenclature. Who is Frankenstein? Is he the monster? The ephebic scientist? The mad scientist? In Mary Shelley's novel, Frankenstein is Victor. For Universal Studios, however, the confusion between Victor and the monster is deliberate: Who, for instance, is the "Bride" of Frankenstein—Victor's or the monster's? For Hammer Studios, Frankenstein is none other than the evil doctor.

Hammer recast Peter Cushing, their morally fierce Van Helsing from the Dracula movies, as the Faustian Dr. Frankenstein. In order to wring every last drop of violence out of the creature without activating Universal's ready corps of copyright lawyers, Hammer made the creature blatantly monstrous and often cast Christopher Lee in the role. It was a stroke of casting genius which showed how well they understood their adolescent audience. The audience didn't care about preserving the unities; it was paying for action, for violence.

The Hammer myth goes like this. The evil "Dr." or "Baron" *Von* Frankenstein has been slighted by someone or some organization. With the help of a young assistant (here the callow youth of the book and of the Universal series is reinstated), the older scientist tampers with the "secrets of nature" by transplanting, thawing, or electrifying the creature back to life. "My God!" says the youngster to his mentor, "You're creating life." "Stand aside," says the master surgeon. Once living, the monster is commanded to brutalize those who have slighted the doctor/baron. The monster does his master's bidding. Along the way, however, the young man realizes that this creature is not the monster; the creator is. The moral of this version of Frankenstein is that science should not delve too deeply and should not use its advances for personal aggrandizement, which is not at all the moral of the book, or of the Universal films. Hammer's story often concludes with the young man, aided by the monster, redressing the mad scientist's overreaching wrong. The youngster is occasionally even helped by the good townspeople, who in Universal's version had been his antagonists. In a violent climax, the monster is "destroyed" and Dr./Baron Frankenstein is driven into exile. With both creature and creator removed, this fable ends with the young man able to find a girl, the same full-figured damsel of the vampire stories, and to "create life" properly.

As the sequels were produced, plot ligatures were used to tie the individual movies together. Just as Dracula is revived by having the stake in his heart foolishly removed, or by having some dolt spill blood on his mouth or chant some voodoo nonsense, the Frankenstein sequels open with the evil doctor escaping from prison, or reappearing in some disguise, or taking some life-suspending medicine and then seeking out and reanimating the poor creature for the umpteenth time. The whole ritual, complete with its prescribed violence, begins once again. As long as the audience was coming back to the campfire, clutching its dimes and quarters, Hammer was more than willing to spin out yet another yarn.

Like the vampire, the Frankenstein creature is alive and well and still playing to a steadily younger audience. The monster also has returned to folklore in the form of a breakfast cereal ("Frankenberries") or in an image of awkward adolescence (big body, big feet, wrong brain) on such television shows as *The Munsters* and on countless cartoons. And like the vampire, he is now on screen primarily as a parody of his earlier self. Whereas Dracula has recently been sent up in such films as *Love at First Bite* and *Dracula Sucks*, Frankenstein has been blessed with such burlesques as Mel Brooks's *Young Frankenstein* and the cultish *The Rocky Horror Picture Show*.

In *The Rocky Horror Picture Show*, both the individual fable and the myth-making process can be seen. To watch *Rocky Horror* on late Friday and Saturday nights, adolescents of both sexes come dressed up in the special outfits of their favorite character and literally "play out" the role in front of the theater screen. As in many initiation rituals, some of the audience's "liminoids" mimic established episodes in front of the group. Behind them the episodes appear projected on the screen. The rest of the audience prepares for the service by bringing water pistols, rice, toast, newspapers, and flashlights, also entering into what is essentially a recitative watching of the film. Just as *Punch and Judy* developed into a predictable miming of pre-established family roles, so too this audience mimes a deeper myth. The audience mocks certain characters, reinforces others, and safely celebrates what might otherwise be a violent saturnalia. While *RHPS* is the most popular of the "midnight movies," it is certainly not the most violent. Similar carnivalization of violence occurs safely distanced in the cult films of Cronenberg, Romero, Craven, De Palma, Hooper, Lynch, Raimi, and Waters. Films like *The Brood, Night of the Living Dead, The Hills Have Eyes, Sisters, Texas Chainsaw Massacre, Eraserhead, The Evil Dead,* and *Pink Flamingos* have been able to find their way to this enthusiastic and solvent adolescent audience.

What we have seen in the Dracula and Frankenstein myths is that once the tales make their way from print through stage melodrama to the moving pictures, two results are likely. Levels of violence are added which are progressively exaggerated as the stories turn into revenge dramas. This transformation happens as the consuming audience becomes younger and the medium of transmission more immediate and repetitive. The second result is not always the case, but both stories, when told repeatedly in the cinematic medium, will tend to play out some variation of reproductive anxiety. Older man interferes with adolescent male's reproductive patterns, either by stealing the virgin to "make her my queen" or by "making life" in the laboratory. Either choice co-opts the young man's sexual expectations, and social havoc results. On the screen at least, the monster violates social/sexual order and must be pursued to a violent and retributive death. The young males must band together and violently overthrow the evil patriarch. They then reassert their sexual demands and prepare to enter the breeding sweepstakes correctly.

The message of these violent stories is nowhere consciously explained. It is the inarticulated moral of repetitive tellings. Could it be that, like fairy tales, they carry a message about anxiety and violence that the audience wants and *needs* to hear? Within the various versions, one can almost see the process of audience interchange. When a motif "works," i.e., finds an eager audience, it is maintained in the sequel and becomes part of the "standard" version. Noteworthy in the renditions is not what is original and artistic but what is derivative and imitative.

While these two ceremonial texts of Dracula and Frankenstein, these fables of aggression, have now been subsumed into all mass media, other movies are carrying other fresh fables and legends to an eager audience. A glance at the movie advertisements in the local newspaper will show the sheer quantity of such scenarios of revenge. Although the observance may seem regressive, and probably is, adolescents still file into the dark cave to learn the secrets of life outside. The anthropologists and psychologists who mourn the passing of adolescent initiation rites should check the box office. What is striking—although predictable from a demographic standpoint—is that the levels of violence in these fantasies have been continually raised for the past century. The Hammer films now seem as tame to us as the Universal films seemed to the moviegoer of the 1960s. Obviously the twelve- to eighteen-year-old audiences, fresh from television, expect something in the theater that the tiny screen can't deliver. They want to see "special effects." They want to see versions of old scenarios with new characters which duplicate their own situations of anxiety. These young audiences want what their parents also desired: shocks, yes, but always within the circumscribed range of predictable myth. To their parents and critics, that "range" often seems excessive, as it has since the development of print media. While many of the violent movies produced from 1960 to the mid-1980s seem full of objectionable excess, they are worth a close study, if only because in rearticulating the past they predict the future.

If the generating filmic myths of the 1930s and 1940s were Dracula and Frankenstein, the modern shockers often find provenance in a third Victorian tale, that of Dr. Jekyll and Mr. Hyde.[8] As a literary text *The Strange Case of Dr. Jekyll and Mr. Hyde* hardly seems worthy of what it has become. In Stevenson's novella, we are given a chinabox of narratives which all deal with the mysterious comings and goings of the feral Mr. Hyde. The shock for our grandparents was that Jekyll should harbor Hyde, but for us this is a fact of modern personality. Of course we're all schizoid. Tell us something new. What we are interested in is what the repressed side of Jekyll does once out of Hyding. And what Hyde does is to elbow aside the relatively polite Dracula and the clumsy Frankenstein monster in order to play out the barely disguised misogyny of modern times.

There is none of this antiwoman violence in the book. Hyde confines himself to running over a little matchgirl, beating up an old man, messing up Jekyll's laboratory, and writing nasty obscenities in his better half's books. Even in the stage play, which predictably followed on the heels of the book, Hyde is passive. In fact, the stage play, commissioned by the famous actor Richard Mansfield, was from the outset more a vehicle to display virtuoso acting than a way to unfold a story. On the screen, however, Hyde has come alive with a vengeance. And what gives him pleasure is doing violence to specific women. The introduction of a female victim to the hitherto all-male story has proved to be one of the most stable additions to the myth. The Dracula and Frankenstein stories usually focus on a single isolated victim who is the object of the monster's attention, as well as of the attention of a young suitor and his friends. In Jekyll/Hyde, not only is the protagonist split; the victim is split as well. From Colonel William Selig's one-reeler, *The Modern Dr.*

Jekyll (1908), to the John Barrymore version of 1920, to the famous Fredric March 1931 film, and then to the Spencer Tracy extravaganza in 1941, the female roles have become more differentiated and more important. Hyde's violence is never directed against the object of Jekyll's (and the audience's) sexual anxiety—the fiancée—but toward a woman who is overtly sexual and seductive—a woman on whom he has no social claim.

The Jekyll/Hyde story, as now told, goes like this. Dr. Jekyll, like young "Dr." Frankenstein in the Universal films, is about to be married to a socially acceptable young woman. He has every reason to be happy. His fiancée is a pretty girl, proper, and eager to become his bride, that is, eager to become sexual. Her father, however, is a dolt who for some inane reason postpones the marriage (sex) and announces his intention of taking his daughter away. Dr. Jekyll is distraught but does not express his frustration. Rather, he repairs to the laboratory where he releases his tension—now clearly sexual—by drinking the nostrum. Out comes Hyde, and Hyde makes straightaway to female no. 2, a woman of the streets, a self-evidently sexual woman. Hyde seems to want sex (the sex Jekyll is being denied), but soon he wants violence. He starts to abuse this woman; abuse turns to torture. As he gets what he wants, and as what he wants becomes progressively more brutal, he wants to rid himself of Jekyll. Jekyll (*Je*/kill) cannot contain his id-infested self. In print Jekyll was able to kill himself and thus to rid the world of Hyde. But the movie demands chase, violence, and vengeance. So the police, who have proved to be impotent in all the other horror myths, must be called. They shoot the fleeing Jekyll. In the final scene—a scene which has ended the cinematic version since the Great Profile, John Barrymore—we see on the face of the dying Hyde the emerging visage of Jekyll. Jekyll has won; Hyde has lost. Repression has carried the day. The beast is back in the jungle. But it is a Pyrrhic victory. Both personalities are dead.

In each movie version, Hyde has become progressively more violent, more independent of Jekyll's repressive codes, and more willing to strike out on his own. Since Mansfield's original commissioning of the stage play in order to "showcase" his own talent, the story has remained a star vehicle. We even know the movie versions by the star's name: the Barrymore, the March, the Tracy, and recently, the Jack Palance or Oliver Reed Jekyll/Hyde. Clearly, the actors prefer to play Hyde; he is the center of excitement. Just as clearly, Hyde is the character the audience wants to see. Jekyll is, let's face it, a prig; after all, who is the more interesting, the Frankenstein monster or Victor, Dracula or Van Helsing?

Hyde's success in breaking loose from Jekyll is due to the decreasing age of the audience for this myth. He is now out on his own with no censorious Jekyll to remind him that he is making a terrible mess. Hyde has developed his own horror industry—that of the stalk-and-slash psychopath. Punch has gone *Grand Guignol.* Arguably, the most famous modern Hyde is Norman Bates in Hitchcock's *Psycho* (1960). As Dr. Loomis assures us in the final scenes, Norman is schizoid, but as R. D. Laing, Michel Foucault, and modern psychohistorians keep reminding us, these fancy terms are just a way of saying that we really don't know what has happened. Somehow someone else has torn loose from the host personality and is on the rampage. Regardless of the clinical diagnosis, Norman Bates has already lost whatever Jekyll he might have had and is now just waiting for the sexually active female to come along. Sexual activity is an interpretive key, because in the contemporary Hyde myth the molester rarely attacks indiscriminately. His victim is never a matron, a pregnant woman, a mother with children, or a spinster. His victim is the same female she was in earlier fables of aggression. She is the about-to-be-married or recently sexually active woman. The little matchgirl who is run over by the frantic Hyde in Stevenson's novella has grown up.[9]

While *Psycho* introduced a more violent generation of horror movies, it did something equally as important. *Psycho* made the picturing of turbulence, the virtuoso framing of violent scenes, a fit subject for cinematic consideration and critical acclaim. One could argue that such jarring of expectations was always part of the Jekyll/Hyde tradition. Observe Rouben Mamoulian's 1932 version of the stalker myth. Everything stuffed into those slack terms beloved by press agents, "state of the art" and "production values," is here: subjective camera, voice-over dialogue, 360-degree pans, split screen, dissolves, horizontal and diagonal wipes, contrast shots, montage, superimposition, arresting angles, jump cuts, and, best of all, the transformation scenes done with red filters. In many of the ways in which it forced us to see violence, Mamoulian's film presages *Psycho.* Just as Hitchcock forced us to become Norman Bates and peep through the knothole, so Mamoulian made us into Jekyll. Thanks to the famous opening shots, we merge, via the subjective camera, into Jekyll's consciousness. We hear his beating heart (actually Mamoulian's) on the soundtrack and look down to see his (our) hands on the keyboard pounding out a Bach fugue. We rise and travel down to the lecture room while the camera pans a complete arc, and we, for the first time, get outside and see who we have been. Similarly, in the forty-eight cuts of the *Psycho* shower scene, the knife is filmed as if it were in our hand. We look down into the tub to see what we have done. We are being willingly tricked into a far more intense connection with violent action than most of us would even have dreamed of. The director or, as the case may currently be, the special effects man has transformed the molester's point of view into our own and in so doing has done what films always have promised. We are forced to respond as if the action were real, as if the action were our own.

To be sure, special effects have always played an important part in Hollywood fantasy. They are the tropes of the visual language, the turns of imagistic phrase. The act of seeing filmic images is in itself a trick of consciousness, the "persistence of vision" phenomenon by which the brain holds one image until the next image supplants it, allowing us to think we are seeing reality. The manipulation of this special effect is what the movie industry sells. If the camera speed is increased to make more than twenty-four exposures per second, the result will be to slow the motion, as in the bloody scenes at the end of *Bonnie and Clyde*. If the camera is "undercranked," it will speed the action, as in the famous coach ride in *Nosferatu*. Either way is profoundly unsettling. Seeing is more than believing; it is experiencing. What gives film such power to portray action is that it does not wait for us to turn the page. Yet while film is perceived continuously, it is "shot" and processed in segments. All manner of illusions such as models or make-up can be inserted between frames. Our brain knows this; our viscera do not.

When we walk past the plexiglas box office and enter the semidarkness, we fully expect to see full-scale mechanical effects like the shark of *Jaws*, full-scale visual effects such as bridges or buildings exploding, or models miniaturizing such action. Since the 1930s, we have recognized rear projection as a contrived effect but easily give ourselves over to it in return for sensations of excitement. Almost from childhood, we now recognize stationary mattes, traveling mattes, stop-action photography, and superadded animation. All these innovations add to the excitement of action and we accept them almost unconsciously. We eagerly suspend disbelief. No wonder, however, that "primitive" tribes unaccustomed to such mimesis cannot bear to watch and so turn away sick with fear. Yet if you ask any Western teenage boy about breakaway glass, or ghoulish make-up, or any of the illusions of the past generation, he will readily explain them, and he will pay millions, nay, billions of dollars to experience them over and over and over.

To some extent what saved Hollywood from the television threat in the dark days of the late 1960s was a return to doing what the industry had done best since the 1920s: exaggerating motion. Directors start filming a scene by saying "Action" for a reason. If sufficient action cannot be generated in front of the camera, it can be edited into the film later. Putting action back into films made them more violent and also made them competitive with "free" television. But all the special effects that movies had been able to produce by the late 1960s were also possible on television. From filters, cuts, wipes, and dissolves to make-up, mattes, and stunts, the video camera could duplicate the movie camera. And in certain matters like animation, the product could be manufactured more cheaply for television with its low definition and small screen than for the movie house with its large screen.

However, what television could not do was to produce the startling effects of the optical printer and the computer-driven camera. The optical printer allowed individual frames to be manipulated while maintaining high picture quality. Contrast could be changed, colors balanced, screens split, frames skipped, reversed, zoomed, squeezed, and expanded for various lenses. Together with the Dykstraflex camera, which can be programmed to travel the same pattern over and over so that new imagery can be superadded to the same film, the illusion of heightened action cannot be found in any other medium. Special effects can now be added both inside and outside the camera, thus vastly increasing the impact of imagery. Computer-driven systems like the Multiplane System, Digital Scene Simulation, and Introvision have done more than demonstrate the application of high-tech to making movies. They have changed the visual field, literally. If you look at the top twenty films of any time in the last five years, you will see that more than half have depended on delivering some special effect not seen before. Usually the effects have been achieved inside the camera or during the printing process. Computer programmers who manipulate digital animation, analog image synthesis, and template interpolation have made technology's contribution to television, Chromakey, look like child's play. All that television can do with Chromakey is to make the weatherman look as if he is really pointing to the chart. Hollywood can make Indiana Jones look as if he is going to be run over by a huge boulder or about to fall off a sky-high cliff. The next generation of innovations promises still more verisimilitude. Film stock will increase from thirty-five to seventy millimeters, and film speed will more than double, giving a greater "realness" to the imagery. Because of the cost of refitting, these innovations—called Showscan and IMAX—are being seen only at theaters at the Smithsonian, the Boston Museum of Science, and, of course, at Disneyland and Disneyworld. Because the current audience is mature, the subject matter is toned down. But once these new systems make their way into the Cineplex and the adolescent audience shoves aside its elders, more violence will be seen.

No genre was more eager to cannibalize the developments of special effects than was horror, and no audience so eager as adolescents to patronize the results. Since horror depends on violating expectations, any innovation to interrupt the predictable is soon exploited. Also, since horror usually deals with an attack on a specific individual—the normal being disturbed by the abnormal—the special effects must be kept to human proportions. Hence make-up, the ways of disguising the human or monster form, has been the central effect since Lon Chaney. We need to see "it" if we are going to believe it. The first wave of modern Anglo-American horror at Universal depended on the artistry of individuals like Jack Pierce. His crowning achievement was the creation of the visage of the Frankenstein monster, complete with the overhanging forehead, bolts, stitches and all that we recognize so easily today. In the 1960s we were treated to the creatures from 20,000 leagues under the sea and the Black Lagoon and a lot of space bugs from beyond our galaxy, but nothing really startling. The English were characteristically reserved; their most prominent achievement was to fit Christopher Lee with red contact lenses so that his Dracula had a particularly iridescent glower.

Since the days of the "horror factory" at Universal and the rise of the House of Hammer, make-up effects have become more than methods of creating monstrosities; they have often become the story itself. Since the illusion of close proximity to action is crucial to generating audience excitement, we need to see the human physiognomy and lineaments to know how to react. Many adolescents go to the movies just to see such exaggerations as the head-bursting scenes in *Scanners*, the chest-popper in *Alien*, the head-spin in *The Exorcist*, the full-body transformations in *The Howling* and *An American Werewolf in London*, the ripped-open torsos in countless zombie films, most notably George Romero's *Day of the Dead* and *Dawn of the Dead*, the simian transformation in *Altered States*, and the bug and vegetable mutations in the remakes of *The Fly* and *Invasion of the Body Snatchers*. These and other sequences have literally transformed the imagery of violence and have provided the story lines. No longer do victims exit stage right to be brutalized; they perform full-face right at the end of our noses.

What started as a charcoal pencil, grease paint, and facial clips in the hands of one man like Jack Pierce has become the elaborate apparatus of teams headed by the likes of Dick Smith and his many pupils, such as Rob Bottin, Tom Savini, or Rich Baker. Using foam latex, pneumatic drives, plastic casts, and remote-controlled explosive caplets, they have made horror monsters simply terrifying.[10] To a considerable degree special effects have been responsible for the renewed interest in the Jekyll/Hyde myth and its current descendant, the psycho. The fragile and good man who changes into his robust and feral self has always been a favorite Western story, but since *Psycho* we have been playing the Hyde character independently of Jekyll. Norman Bates, now traveling with all the accouterments of up-close special effects, has been reincarnated in such maniacal forms as Freddie of the *Nightmares on Elm Street*, Michael of the *Halloweens*, Jason of the *Friday the 13ths*, Leatherface of the *Texas Chainsaw Massacres*, and countless has-beens who have played out their aggressive fables and are now best left unremembered.

Looking at these films, we see the lucrative but unpredictable economics of preposterous violence in the cinema. The producers who first developed their Hydes had no idea that their particular slashers would find an audience. For every *Halloween,* there are a hundred *He Knows You're Alone, Don't Go in the Attic, The House on Sorority Row, Hell Night, The Co-Ed Murders, Final Exam, Graduation Day, The Prowler, My Bloody Valentine, Slumber Party Massacre,* and others of their grisly ilk. The titles reveal both the age of the audience and the transience of individual entries. However, once an audience is found and safe money assured, the sequels are mindlessly manufactured until the audience gradually disappears. Like the story teller who waits for his audience to tell him which story to repeat, Hollywood waits for the receipts. In a folkloric sense, a successful story can as easily travel by imitation as by contrived sequel. So, for instance, the audience for *Texas Chainsaw Massacre* did not have to wait nearly ten years for *TCM 2,* but could consume the same general tale in *Mardi Gras Massacre, Drive-in Massacre, Hollywood Meatmarket Massacre, Slumber Party Massacre, Zombie Island Massacre,* or in *Slaughter in San Francisco.*

The ceaseless repetition of the never-say-die Hyde is matched only by the zombie-like parade of cloned films slowly stumbling around the country, eager to find a still-solvent audience. All the dross and dreck which made the old horror myths entertaining for a multilevel audience have been excised as films are now merchandised for a "target audience," the teenage male. Whatever "art" the myths once had has been replaced by "craft," and craft has been dominated by gory special effects. In a sense, the stories have been returned to where they came from—the fever dreams of youth. Dracula, on a personal level, evolved from Stoker's dream of a giant crab; Frankenstein from Mary Shelley's nightmare of her stillborn child; and Dr. Jekyll from Stevenson's "bogey" dream of a stranger at the window. Modern horror stories are the technicolor outlines of communal dreams. What we now see is what was there to begin with: big monster attacking little us; abnormal "it" threatening normal "us."

As we have seen in other media, preposterous violence tends to be a two-act drama. First the attack—violent and vicious—then the counterattack—more violent and more vicious. The gothic became a medium for shivers only after the relatively passive Romantic malfeasors such as Gil-Martin, Falkland, Schedoni, Ambrosio, and Melmouth were replaced by their Victorian counterparts like Dracula, Hyde, and Dr. Moreau, who were more than willing to initiate occasional violence. What has happened in the next generation, in modern violent film, is that the monsters have become so intense and concentrated that we find ourselves more interested in their careers than in their victims. After all, Norman Bates is more interesting than his victim and certainly more interesting than the detective and the psychiatrist.

To show the world from the point of view of the monster took an-

The Steadicam system (Universal Model III) (Lewis Communications)

other technical innovation—the Steadicam. The Steadicam is essentially a portable camera which moves with the body of the operator, making the photographed images seem to come from eye level. Thanks to miniaturization, and the way the unit is balanced and carried, the resulting footage seems to be "shot" from the point of view of a moving human. Indeed, point of view, whether in the novel or on film, has a most powerful effect on interpretation. We are by nature sympathetic with a first-person narrator. We see the experience through his eyes. Since the audience colludes with the camera, and since the Steadicam provides the visual field, the audience is perceptually in sync with the monster. Whether we consciously like it or not, we become Hyde.

Perhaps the best illustration of the anxiety this collusive point of view can engender is in Michael Powell's *Peeping Tom*. Although this film was made before the Steadicam—in fact, it was made in the same year as *Psycho*—its point of view is often literally inside the camera. The camera is used by Mark (played by Carl Boehm) who delights in memorializing on film what he has been "shooting." By day he is a "focus puller" for a movie studio; by night he is on his own, focusing his Kodak Super 8. He is so obsessed by movies that he can only see when he looks through the viewfinder. What he especially likes to look at are women under stress. Since much of what we see in *Peeping Tom* is the Peeping Tom's movies, we are forced to collude with this Norman Bates as he stands behind not the peephole but the camera lens. For a while it is titillating to see what he sees, but soon he is seeing things we do not want to see, let alone participate in. Soon he is stabbing women with the tripod tip to capture their reactions. Now we want out. Certainly the critics did too.[11]

Peeping Tom, however, carried the day or, rather, carried the last twenty years. Because of skillful editing, make-up, and the optical printer, as well as the Steadicam, we are no longer given much choice. Taking the part of the violent perpetrator, be he on the side of good or evil, is the current norm for action movies. As with other innovations, this shift in point of view, facilitated by technological developments, captured a young audience while raising the concern of their elders. The attack side of the attack/counterattack equation is gaining dominance. In fact, in many of the most popular modern horrors there is simply no counterattack at all. The monster has his way.

Let us examine *The Texas Chainsaw Massacre,* for example. In this movie, the archetypal first half of the modern fable of aggression exists independent of any resettling revenge. Victimage overwhelms vengeance. One morning a vanload of adolescents heads for the family homestead to check on the graves of two of their grandparents. There has been an outbreak of mysterious grave robbing, and the kids just want to be sure their family is at rest, even if only below ground. Along the way they stop to pick up a hitchhiker, an act which in this genre almost always signifies a vague collusion with the forces of destructive violence. The victim always unhasps the window for the vampire, or takes off the cross, or befriends the outcast, be he a vampire, a Frankenstein monster, or a wolfman. Monsters are rarely indiscriminate about victims, and victims almost always make themselves available. This hitchhiker is none other than a young Mr. Hyde traveling without Jekyll. When he starts to show his true colors by slicing his own hand with a razor and rolling his eyes in glee, the kids realize they would be better off without him. They dump him off at the roadside and continue heading for home.

In order to get home, they must leave the straight and narrow—literally, in this case, the two-lane blacktop. Here is yet another cliché of the horror genre. The victims voluntarily stop by Dracula's castle, or go up in the attic, or down in the cellar, even though they should know better. From Little Red Riding Hood onward, we are assured that the only way through the woods is by sticking to the path. In this contemporary case, once the teenagers have left the highway, crossed the field, and entered what they think is the deserted house, they have left the vernal wood of Wordsworth and have entered the jungle of Darwin.

Once back on the homestead, this is what happens: A man wearing a mask of human skin butchers all but one of the kids with a cleaver and a chainsaw. Leatherface, as he is known, looks rather like the Frankenstein monster in a hockey goalie's facemask. The last adolescent, Sally, is tied up and introduced to the rest of the "family." Leatherface has a grandfather upstairs who is barely able to sip blood, a dead grandmother who is still in her rocking chair, a father who is a milquetoast cannibal, and a brother who is none other than the already-encountered hitchhiker. There is, naturally, no mother. One of the rules to be deduced from rituals of gratuitous violence is that boys will not be turbulent when a mother is nearby. No monster ever attacks a mother and no mother allows her children to be attacked. This is an all-male family and it is ferocious. Sally has dinner with this entourage of Norman Bateses who have never read a word of Miss Manners. They are brutal and barbaric. Sally spends the day screaming. True to the preservation of the Aristotelian unities, once a full day has passed, Sally escapes at dawn back to the safety of the highway. She is rescued from the nipping end of Leatherface's whining chainsaw by a truck driver who is no agent of vengeance, no good woodsman, but just a passerby. *The Texas Chainsaw Massacre* ends when Sally, safely in the cab, is driven away from the monster who is left dancing a bizarre tattoo with the furious saw waving above his head.

There is an equal lack of vengeance in other contemporary cinematic horrors. George Romero's zombie trilogy, *Night of the Living Dead*, *Dawn of the Dead*, and *Day of the Dead*, John Carpenter's *Halloween* and its sequels, Wes Craven's *Nightmare on Elm Street* sequence, and Sean Cunningham's interminable *Friday the 13th*s are all more interested in following the attacker than in slowing him down. As tempting as it is to interpret this outpouring of films as a loss of will or as a reaction to the women's movement, it is more likely to be the result of the economics of sequelization. Why kill the goose that laid the golden box-office eggs even if the goose is a monster? Whereas a generation ago matinee audiences were eager to follow the adventures of Flash Gordon, Tarzan, or Hopalong Cassidy, they now follow the repeated adventures of Michael, Freddie, and Jason.

When revenge does come in this genre, it often comes at the hands of the primary victims. The intermediary males are disposed of, presumably for incompetence. The individual female victim takes it upon herself to do what the male hero used to do—battle the monster to its death. This victim turned victimizer has been played out from such out-and-out schlock as *Last House on the Left* (1973), in which an outraged mother bites the penis off her daughter's tormentor, to *I Spit on Your Grave* (1980), in which the young victim of a gang rape excises the genitalia of her attackers by using an electric knife and an outboard motor, to the more recent *Extremities*, *The Seduction*, *Mother's Day*,

Leatherface from Tobe Hooper's *Texas Chainsaw Massacre*
(New Line Cinema)

and *Eyes of a Stranger*, in which the female victim turns the tables on
the psycho-monster and lures him into a trap where he is brutalized.[12]
As she takes the law into her own hands, the female victim achieves a
level of violence every bit as concentrated as that which was visited on
her. The signifiers are reversed, but the interaction remains stable. First,
monster terrorizes victim, then victim is monstrous to monster; again
sex has become secondary to the violence.

Perhaps revenge violence can no longer be generated in the male-
oriented horror fantasies. Perhaps the audience has been worn away by
repetition. Or perhaps another ideological shift has occurred as a result
of a shift in audience composition. Increased numbers of women, especially young women, in the audience are paying to see an increased
number of self-sufficient women depicted on the screen. This does not
mean that we have done away with the revenge motive, but only that it
does not figure so prominently in mainline horror. In the current hybrid
of adventure/horror fables, we now have made the retaliator's role doubly explosive by making him the monster. In a sense, Van Helsing has
become Dracula. The old-style hero in traditional violent rituals, played
out in the 1950s by John Wayne and in later years by Clint Eastwood

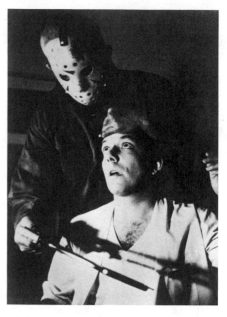

Michael Myers from *Halloween*
(Compass International Pictures)

Jason Vorhees from *Friday the 13th*
(Paramount Pictures)

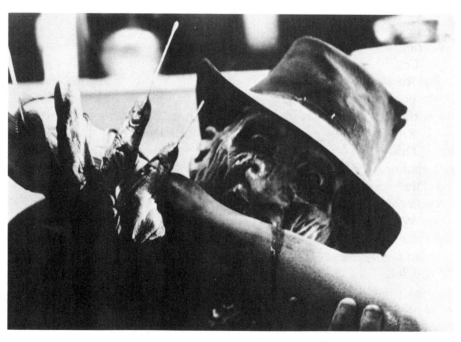

Freddie Krueger from *Nightmare on Elm Street* (New Line Cinema)

and Charles Bronson, has become progressively more violent as the theater audience has grown younger and younger.

One could argue that the transformation of the modern American action film was also partially the result of the Italian Westerns. Sergio Leone essentially removed everything from the Western—women, horses, scenery—in order to concentrate on the violence of men with guns. In *A Fistful of Dollars, A Few Dollars More*, and *The Good, the Bad and the Ugly*, Leone strips all moralizing convention away (the good man, the frontier, honor, protection of the women) and is left with only greed to motivate the violence. These movies found a worldwide audience for such pantomime. For the next decade, there were "Sauerkraut Westerns" (made in Germany), "Paella Westerns" (Spain), "Camembert Westerns" (France), and "Chop Suey Westerns" (Hong Kong). "Curry Westerns" are still being made in India. Carry this to a younger generation and one finds a cartoon rendition. As in *EC* comics, only the outline remains. In the hand-chopping, fist-flying, foot-kicking Kung Fu subculture of Chuck Norris, any similarity between real and fictive causality is only coincidental. The retaliative mode is dominant. This blond Bruce Lee whirs like a mixmaster while rescuing prisoners in *Missing in Action*, pummeling the daylights out of drug-pushing gangs in *Code of Silence*, and putting the kibosh on terrorists in *Delta Force* and *Invasion USA* (in which the deserving reprobates blow up shopping malls—the ultimate insult to this audience of mallgoers). One sees the same cartoon distortion when Arnold Schwarzenegger takes to the screen. Fresh from being Conan the Barbarian—the comic-book adaptation, not the character in Robert E. Howard novels—Mr. Schwarzenegger decimates most of the population of Southern California in *Commando* and does pretty much the same to Chicago in *Raw Deal*. The same exaggeration appears in the *Road Warrior* films with Mel Gibson, albeit with a bit more panache. The violence is so bizarre as to be parodic, but underneath the hyperbole lie the ancient rituals of induction through retribution.

Although these action films may have James Bond and/or the Road Runner as their spiritual forefathers, they are only tangentially related to the Westerns or patriotic melodramas of a generation ago. They have none of the steamy presence and complex motivation of the violent films included in the 1969 Museum of Modern Art show. Although they may seem political, in no way can they be compared to such early postwar films as *The Red Menace, I Was a Communist for the FBI*, or *My Son John*. In the modern action films, politics do not provide the motivation; they provide only a context in which the action/reaction motifs can be unwound. Naturally, this is not the way they are decoded by middle-aged critics. Messrs. Stallone, Eastwood, Norris, Bronson, and Nolte are lumped together with John Wayne as conservative, ultra-right vigilantes. But today's audience is not John Wayne's audience; it is too young to care much for philosophy or politics. It wants violence, and slouching within these vigilante films is another genre waiting to be acknowledged—the adolescent favorite: the violent horror film. If you look carefully, you will see that the villain in these films is none other than the last of the modern horror monsters—the psycho-killer, Mr. Hyde, or more precisely, a twisted Jekyll.

As the modern stalk-and-slash film has isolated the monster and made him an independent Hyde, so has the modern violent revenge drama isolated the avenger and made him an independent vigilante. Like their audience, these characters are marginal, on the threshold, neither inside nor outside of society. They are "liminal," literally on the edge. So Freddie, Jason, Michael, Leatherface, et al., from the slash-'em-ups violently circle around their victims, awkward and pathetically insecure although physically powerful. They delight in disorder and in the adolescent's need to be recognized even if it usually means, as it does, making a mess. They are, if you will, Frankenstein monsters—clumsy, ungainly, potent, confused, and most of all, unmothered.

To see their counterparts on the other side of the social norm, don't look for the avenger where he was a generation ago. The brittle Dr. Jekyll has now gone native, jumped the tracks, and is just as violent, just as outrageous as his monstrous alter ego. Nowhere is this transformation in better evidence than in the films of Sylvester Stallone. From *Rocky* to *Rambo*, Stallone plays out the same tale, a fable of the inarticulate, the big-bodied, small-brained, good-intentioned vindicator whose only motivation is somehow to make things right, to redress some imbalance. His motivation is the inverse of the stalk-and-slasher's, yet his actions are the same. He brutalizes people.

While it may seem that Rocky Balboa and John Rambo are ideologues (and to the mature audience, they are), politics are an afterthought, if a thought at all. Their appeal is deeper than current fashion; it is more visceral, more biological. In fact, when *Rambo* is shown in the Middle East, the subtitles tell an entirely different political tale. The time is World War II, the locale is transported to the Philippines, the enemy is not the North Vietnamese but the Japanese, and all references to the Russians are simply excised. The political plot is almost infinitely variable. The action and special effects carry the audience. The unsophisticated audience could not care less. Even in *Rocky IV*, Rocky Balboa fights the nasty Ivan Drago not for political reasons, not because Drago is a piece of steroid machinery made in the USSR, but because Rocky must avenge the death of his friend, Apollo Creed. As with all horror myths, particulars don't matter. Dracula only happens to live in Transylvania. What does matter is that you can't trust the cops; the government is corrupt. Only vigilante justice can set things right.

Stallone's telling of this fable of vigilante justice, this laterally displaced myth, has produced box-office receipts well in excess of one billion dollars. In fact, four of his films are among the twenty most popular of all time. His character is always the same—Rambo is simply Rocky as a POW. The sequences are identical and predictable. The mumbling nonspeech (in *Rambo First Blood, Part 2*, Stallone issues 163 lines in 93 minutes), the dependence on special effects, the music video choreography, the visual presence of an oiled-up Stallone reminiscent of Johnny Weissmuller's Tarzan or Steve Reeves's Hercules, and the utterly predictable plot show how close we are to folklore. What we watch is the barely disguised wish-fulfillment of adolescent boys—nonstop violence in the service of prescripted and prescribed vengeance.

When the vigilante meets the monster, the results can be instructive. In *Cobra* (1986), both modern eidolons collide and the result is, as Richard Schickel noted in *Time* magazine, "one of cinema's purest forms—a Road Runner cartoon." We need not understand plot, motivation, politics, or depth of character; all we see is Wile E. Coyote obsessed with capturing the pestiferous Road Runner. And we see it over and over. We need not sympathize with the bird, nor with the coyote—both are the same. We get an occasional "beep-beep," lots of smoke, screeching sound effects, but no plot development. The Road Runner, for all we care, could as easily be chasing the coyote. Violent action is what we see and this action is abstracted from any sense of truth, purpose, morality, or whatever—it just is. The "chase" is all.[13]

The supposed "heavies" in *Cobra* are the current psychos of the horror genre—hordes of homicidal maniacs. Here in one coven are Jason, Freddie, Michael, Leatherface, and all their hooded brethren, all descendants of Hyde via Norman Bates, all brandishing sparkling knives and rusty axes, which they wave over their heads like Leatherface's chainsaw and incessantly clank and sharpen. These sharp-bladed instruments are as lovingly photographed as sexual members in a porno short; the camera moves around them as if magnetized. While the psychos are loaded to the literal teeth with tools, they are noticeably lacking in motivation. They have no ostensible leader, no specified purpose, no raison d'être other than to do what they have been doing on the screen for the last twenty years. They rampage about mindlessly attacking almost everyone, but mindfully attacking young women.

As *Cobra* opens, we find ourselves looking down the barrel of a gun and hear the adenoidal voice of Mr. Stallone intoning the litany: "One burglary every 11 seconds in America, an armed robbery every 65 seconds, one violent crime every 25 seconds, a murder every 24 minutes and 250 rapes a day." After this comforting introduction, here briefly is what happens: Some psychos are messing up the local supermarket—at Christmastime, no less. They shove innocent shoppers down the aisles

Sylvester Stallone as Marion Cobretta in *Cobra,* 1986
(Warner Bros.)

and then open fire with shotguns. We close in on one of the psychos
who threatens a male shopper and makes him walk to an exit with the
promise that if he can get out the door alive he will be free. In superslow
motion the psycho shoots the man just as he gets to the door. The
innocent victim literally explodes.

The police, who have surrounded the store, soon realize how hopeless
things are. They have seen this kind of movie before. They say: "Call
the Cobra," and we cut to an old tank-like Hudson driven by Sylvester
Stallone. Stallone slithers out of the Hudson with a toothpick in his
teeth, reflective dark glasses, and skin-tight jeans. He looks as if he be-
longs with the psychos. We later learn that "Cobra" is short for Cobretta and that his first name is Marion. Personality established, motivation provided.

A psycho is holding several shoppers at gunpoint as Stallone enters, obviously wearing a pistol in his jeans for a penis, and stops by a large display of Coors beer. (Coors had to pay dearly for this association—upward of $25,000—as Pepsi will pay later when Stallone chugs the soft drink.) While the psycho is shooting up the place, Stallone drains a tall cool Coors and then saunters over to the store public address system to announce that this psycho is a "dirtbag" and that he will soon be "wasted." The psycho now claims to be carrying a bomb. He intends to blow everything up. "Go ahead," taunts Stallone in one of the film's best lines, "I don't shop here anyway."

While the psycho demands television time, Stallone utters the favorite *bon mot* of the genre since Clint Eastwood's Dirty Harry asked his nasty counterpart to "make my day." Stallone's update: "You criminals are the disease. I'm the cure." While the psycho attempts to refute this by emptying a few shells, Stallone throws his knife into the psycho's gut and then finishes the job by squeezing off a few rounds from his well-warmed handgun.

As Stallone leaves the store to the cheers of the crowd, an obnoxious reporter asks if such extreme force was necessary. Stallone retorts that shoppers have rights too. Not so for the unlucky Hispanic who has taken Stallone's parking space in front of his bungalow. After a hard day in the grocery store, Stallone deserves a place to park the tank. The sassy, jive-talking third-worlder has a cigarette ripped from his lip and his shirt stripped from his back. Back at the bungalow our hero commences the ritual cleansing of the weapons and flicks on the television. The news: A gang of nightstalkers is loose and is not just causing trouble for shoppers but is also murdering young women. They have just slashed another victim. They have become, the television reporter reports, "a plague."

Accompanied by strains of music video, we segue to slashers at work smashing out a car window with sledgehammers to get at yet another innocent female victim. They slash her to death. Enter Stallone, who mutters, "As long as we have to play by these bullshit rules and the killer doesn't, we're going to lose." Cut to yet another incident, this one witnessed by a foreign model played by Brigitte Nielsen, who just happens by. She sees the face of one of the slashers and he sees her. The face she sees looks just like Arnold Schwarzenegger's. This is one of a series of in-jokes which point to the parodic nature of the entire film: Arnold Schwarzenegger, Conan the Barbarian, and the Terminator vs. Sylvester Stallone, Rocky, Rambo, and Cobra. The slasher gang now starts after Brigitte, and the rest of the film hangs on this chase. Chasing the gang and protecting her, however, is our hero, Cobra.

Along the way we see the following: (1) Stallone punches out a man for withholding information. (2) The gang kills a man (played by the actor from TV's send-up of police violence, *Sledgehammer)*, as well as several people in Brigitte's parking garage, including a nightwatchman who is spattered against the bumper of a truck. (3) A traumatized Brigitte is taken to a hospital where the Schwarzenegger lookalike rampages the ward. Brigitte is trapped in the bathroom while the Schwarzenegger lookalike is chopping through with an ax à la the horror genre. (4) Stallone rescues Brigitte.

En route from the hospital the gang chases Stallone and Brigitte in the standard car chase, except that the Hudson runs on nitro and all but flies. Stallone, with the standard Uzi submachine gun in hand, spins the Hudson 180 degrees while firing at the carful of psychos.[14] Now he chases them, causing lots of explosions along the way until finally both parties tire of the excitement. The cutting is superb. We in the audience are also exhausted. The super-liberal police captain (played by Andrew Robinson who was the super-nasty psycho in *Dirty Harry*) arrives and, surveying the carnage, asks Stallone if he has to keep using "unnecessary force." Stallone is making a mess of the city. Stallone snarls. His car is ruined. Brigitte soon asks Stallone why so many bad guys are around and he mutters, "Talk to the judge. We put them away and they let them out." Point well taken; Brigitte is convinced. "It makes me sick," she says.

Stallone, Brigitte, and entourage (including a corrupt policewoman who has been informing the psychos) leave town and in time-honored fashion head for the hills. Once in the high country, they stay at a motel. Brigitte sleeps while her protector lovingly arranges his knives, hand grenades, machine gun, and pearl-handled revolver as if they were parts of his vampire-destruction kit. Brigitte asks Stallone for a kiss, and he grudgingly obliges. Romantic interest is not part of this toothpick-sucking Rambo in jeans. Violence first; sex about seventeenth.

Unbeknownst to our dour hero, hundreds of slashers are coming out of hiding and converging on his motel, presumably fresh from exploits in other slasher films. They surround the motel like whooping Indians around the wagon train, and so, of course, Stallone must shoot them off their motorcycle mounts. He does. He kills more than twenty of them with various of his prized and polished instruments. The Indians fly through the air like so many divebombing hedgehogs. The air is thick with them. Having used up most of his ordnance, Stallone escapes with Brigitte by stealing a conveniently parked pickup truck. She drives. He stands in the cargo bay, as Rambo had stood in the helicopter door, hipfiring the Uzi. He kills another twenty or so—who's counting?—allowing them to fly off their motorcycles and be crushed by oncoming traffic. The audience is now applauding each new dismount as they had earlier applauded the Road Runner's miraculous escapes and the coyote's pratfalls. The photography is stunning and the editing superb. If these scenes had about ten percent more exaggeration, the film would slip into animation.

Brigitte and Stallone escape into an orange grove and from there into a foundry. No one in the audience wonders how a foundry got into an orange grove. When you have a good set, you use it. In the foundry, a couple of slashers are machine-gunned and another doused with gasoline. Stallone lingers over the one who has been soaked and carefully reads the Miranda rights. Then he lights a match and casually tosses it on the bug-eyed slasher. It is now time to confront the Schwarzenegger lookalike. After a face-off of pectorals, they converse in lines shamelessly lifted almost verbatim from Charles Bronson's *10 to Midnight*:

> *Lookalike:* You pig, you Irish pig, you want to go to hell with me. We are the hunters. We kill the weak so that the strong survive. You can't stop the new world. We want you, pig. You won't shoot. Murder is against the law. You have to take me in. Even I have rights, don't I? Pig. They'll say I'm insane, won't they? The court is civilized.
> *Stallone* (after contemplation): But I'm not. This is where the law stops and I start. Sucker.

They now battle it out with knives and chains. Stallone finally impales the lookalike on a foundry hook, sending him, as in the horror movie, into the fiery blast furnace to be incinerated at least until the next sequel.

The L.A. city police arrive, complete with all the namby-pamby drones whom we have previously met. Stallone asks only for his car, the Hudson-tank, to be replaced, and when informed "that is not in the budget," he slugs the officious captain and mounts one of the motorcycles conveniently left by one of the late slashers. Brigitte, thoroughly disgusted with American jurisprudence, tucks herself in behind Stallone, and they ride off Western style into the sunset.

Needless to say, *Cobra* was excoriated in the press. Needless to say, *Cobra* was a box-office success. What does need to be said, however, is that *Cobra* represents the inexorable development of outrageous violence in the movies. It is a reduction of the medium to the level of cartoon. In fact, in Hollywood patois, this "new" kind of entertainment is called a "concept film." There is absolutely no social commitment or interchange here; there is only the most rudimentary call to the demands of attack, vengeance, chase, and retribution. *Cobra* is a primitive, amoral, almost lugubrious display of what much movie making has become or, to be more accurate, what the ripening audience wants to see when it goes into the theater. This film is urban folklore—a contemporary tall tale. Intellectually, it is dopey. Even *Dirty Harry* and the Charles Bronson revenge films provide the motivation for avenging the death of a loved one. But viscerally *Cobra* is superb. It is carnage opera.

While it may seem a melancholy reminder of the democratization of the media, *Cobra* is what the movies have been headed for since World War II. This too will pass but not because of an R rating, or critical scorn, or a shift in directorial sensitivity. Such hyperbolic violence will return to more realistic levels as the audience grows older. In the quaint analogy of demographers, the pig will have moved through the python. As the median age of the film audience works its way through the teens, different myths will be demanded. Already producers are welcoming back an older audience. Old for Hollywood means over twenty-five. And as different media compete to tell these myths, the movies may return to being an adult or a family experience. We are already seeing a spate of fables about divorce and single-parent childrearing. However, until that audience dominates and crowds out teenage films with their adult stories, the studios will continue to transmit fables of aggression to the eager and the curious.

Don't Touch That Dial:
Violence on the Video Altar

Depth and balance do not make for ratings in the way that sensationalism does. It seems to me that we, the viewers, must share the blame for these faults in our information sources because, ultimately, they give us what we ask for.

ALAN MAY,
Albuquerque, New Mexico

In his April 1985 letter to *TV Guide*, Mr. May makes an unpopular yet self-evident point about sensationalism. What he says is true not only on television but in all mass media: "You asked for it." The point is so unpopular, however, that its self-evidence is almost scornfully dismissed by most critics. We much prefer the notion that "they"—the culture industry, the press lords, the networks, the advertising agencies—are sending this vulgar stuff our way. "We" certainly never *asked* for it. Yet what we have seen in the history of mass entertainment is that when a particular audience, primarily adolescent male, gains access to a medium and can therefore influence the stories told, the stories will become progressively more sensational. Once technological or economic advances make a medium consumable in bulk by the teenage male, a kind of Gresham's law of myth sets in. Violent fables force out gentler ones. This is no recent phenomenon, although each generation thinks it is.

In ancient days, from the relatively small Flavian amphitheater to the massive *circus maximus,* the Roman audience was divided into wedges (*cunei*) whose shouts of approval or disapproval determined the course of entertainment. The shows were always more violent in the big coliseum since more than half its quarter-million spectators were young males. The wedges of enthusiastic young men literally drove out the old entertainments and replaced them with their own spectacles of violence. Also, mark the fate of the Commedia dell'Arte made into *Grand Guignol;* marionette farces made into hand-puppet Punch and Judy; the gothic novel made into penny dreadful; the illustrated story made into *EC* comics; and the *film noir* made into stalk-and-slash. The cartooning of action, the introduction of vivid and symbolic violence, not only generates its own violent stories but penetrates older stories with concussive hyperbole.

The history of all modern media has been similar. As the economies of mass production give greater access to previously exempted audiences—the young and the aggressive—the stories demanded and produced become progressively more violent. To those who originally patronized the medium, it will appear that the "golden age" is over. Intellectual distress, currently expressed as, "They're not making movies for *us* any longer," "You just can't read a good novel any more," or "The networks are only interested in producing junk," was first articulated in the early modern world by the eighteenth-century Augustans as a reaction against the wishes of the newly literate. What was Sir William Temple's plaint in the "Battle of the Books" but that the modern dreck obscures great ancient works. What is today's cry against the "Closing of the American Mind" and the necessity for "Cultural Literacy" but an attempt to reestablish a body of accepted knowledge? English professors now talk about "expanding the canon" as if this awareness were recent and radical. The democratization of myth has been occurring with gusto since the French Revolution. Theories blaming the "lowest common denominator," "cultural relativism," or "least objectionable programming" are criticisms advanced to explain what happens when one audience captures the stories of another.

Invariably the newest medium is the one undergoing the most intense audience shift and so the one most vehemently pilloried for present ills. The modern scapegoat is television, but the paperback book—especially the illustrated comic book—was far more censoriously treated only a generation ago. Who would now burn a television set? But then again, recall that Plato criticized the written language for despoiling the spoken, and that the printing press was not enthusiastically hailed by the monks whose illustrated manuscripts it rapidly rendered obsolete. Even the rise of literacy and the advent of publishing were hardly welcomed as advances. Many eminent Victorian critics considered them a disaster.

First, the novel was ruining literature; then the serial throwaway was ruining the novel; then the paperback was ruining the novel. Electronic media only accelerated the process. When the telephone was introduced in the 1870s, many people worried that telephone addicts would spend their lives inside talking on the phone. Public discourse would disappear. Radio was excoriated because it carried the mass-marketed fantasies of soap operas and detective and Western violence to a popular audience. And if cheap novels and radio drama were not enough to debase Western culture with sensationalism, just look at how Hollywood was ruining what was left. Lucky for the studios that the television networks came along to shoulder the blame. "Television is making a mess of things," we say as we turn on the set.

All mass media are audience reflectors and magnifiers. If they were not, they would cease to exist. When they stop reflecting and magnifying, they stop entertaining. Since they usually reflect the commonest of concerns, the most fundamental anxieties, the wish-fulfillment of the mass of people with (or with access to) disposable income, they are usually condemned by the elite as mindless or, even worse, as dangerous. The Marxists are certainly correct: What we watch/read/hear is an aspect of struggle. However, it is more a struggle of audiences than of economic classes. Fables promulgated by electronic mass media, consumed by the populace, and criticized by intellectuals are some of the most dependable registers of both social and species concern. Although the critical cant is that the media are manipulated by a few powerful business interests, the reverse is far more accurate. In no other industry are the promulgators manipulated so completely by the seeming whimsy of so many. For instance, we blame the television programmers and think nothing is amiss when in its perennial story on the "new season" *TV Guide* runs the headline, "SO THESE ARE THE PERPETRATORS!" and then goes on to profile Brandon Stoddard, Kim LeMasters, and Brandon Tartikoff as if they were the heirs of Rasputin, de Sade, and Goebbels. Contrary to such mythology, as bankruptcy filings in the entertainment business and the sixty-percent failure rate for prime-time television shows attest, there is nothing so difficult to exploit as popular taste. As Leslie Fiedler has often said, "predicting popular taste is the modern equivalent of riding a tiger." If it were not, we would still be driving Edsels, wearing Corfam shoes, and drinking the "new" Coke.

Everything network television is criticized for is, perversely, its strength. Mindless repetition, incessant cloning of the same genres and even the same shows, mediocre acting, short segments, fast action, endless commercial interruptions, abrupt cutting, and flashing imagery, overloud sound, predictable action, laugh tracks, reruns, mutilation of movies such as cutting and colorizing, superficiality—all these and more should alert us to this paradox. As terrible as the critics say it is, television is watched.

This Edsel is still driven. Perhaps we should forget *what* is broadcast and for the moment concentrate on *why* and *how* it is shown.

Network television is the almost perfect medium of popular culture. In the United States, and progressively elsewhere in the West, it is driven by audience desire. Programming decisions revolve around one question: "Who is watching?" If television broadcasts dreck, it is dreck well worth studying because we want to see it more than other dreck. "Don't touch that dial," we are told. But touch it we do. We spend most of our leisure hours turning that dial again and again. We watch what we want to, not what we are told to want. We choose the fables. Knowing this, why should academics endlessly analyze individual "works of art" by individual artists when with commercial television we are offered a window into mass consciousness itself? Realize that no show can exist without 12 million immediate viewers and you will realize that there is simply no comparison with other nonelectronic media. With a few notable exceptions, print artists create with an audience in mind; in the electronic media, it is impossible to create without an audience both in mind and specifically pinpointed. Call such entertainment escapism or demeaning, it is wish-fulfillment efficiently focused. Television, the "plug-in drug," "thief of time," "painkiller," "dreamkiller," "dream machine," "vast wasteland," "white noise," "idiot box," "toaster with pictures," is also a continually recording meter of desire.

Any study of television must begin with the recognition that in our culture most people watch it most of the time. After sleeping and working, watching video images is our favorite way to pass time. Well over ninety-five percent of American households have at least one television set, and the experience of watching has become the social and intellectual matrix which holds us together. Television *is* our culture. "Did you see . . .?" has replaced "Do you know . . .?," "Did you read . . .?," or "Have you heard . . .?" Television displays most of what we know and much of what we believe. It is such a reflective force that the only apt analogy from the past is not the movies, certainly not books, but rather the medieval church. And like the church, it is programmed not by the priests who claim the Word but by the parishioners who demand the Image.

What is the relationship between priest and parishioner, programmer and audience? How does the priest/programmer know which fables to tell? From the critics of the 1960s like a Newton Minow, a Fred Friendly, and a Nicholas Johnson to such current TV nay-sayers as a Neil Postman, a Jerry Mander, or a Thomas Radecki, one gets the impression that the television pulpit is consciously run by an executive class that knows what it is doing. At their most paranoid, such critics imply that these executive high priests intend not only to manipulate, which they clearly want to do, but also to debase. As George Gerbner, professor at the Annenberg School of Communication at the University of Pennsylvania and pioneer of nonjudgmental content analysis, has said: "If you can write a nation's stories, you needn't worry about who makes its laws. Today television tells most of the stories to most of the people most of the time" (as quoted by Waters). What Professor Gerbner does not say, and what most critics and commentators overlook, is that these stories, like the stories told to us in childhood, are the result of intense and ongoing collusion and collaboration. Naturally, to the print generation these stories, like much of folklore, seem raw and even decivilizing. As contrasted with print literature, these televised "texts" are never made in private by an artist, and they are never published and "done." The "interpretive community" for these "discourses" is a livingroom full of beercan-crunching "couch potatoes."

Television is created and consumed hour by hour, day by day in a never-ending, seamless flow. Its stories are fairy tales, not *belles-lettres.* The child says, "Daddy, tell me Little Red Riding Hood again," and the father, never reflecting on what the story "means" or where it comes from, tells it again. We tell children fables, yes, but they tell us which ones and how they want them told. Although the parent and the culture may try to alter parts—say, to tell the tale with a good but misunderstood wolf—the child knows better and asks that the story be told right. Folklore is essentially stories "told right." Television has made that process electronic.

The not-so-hidden agenda of fairy tales and television is social conditioning. "Behave this way" becomes "buy this product." The television network doesn't care which stories it broadcasts because its reward is not in the telling but in how many people it can persuade to listen and how long it can keep their attention. In a relatively free communications' market in which no government agency is telling the network what stories to tell, the programmers will attempt to tell whatever attracts the largest target audience. Audience share is the commodity that ABC, CBS, and NBC sell—not the shows. Or seen another way, production companies sell video sequences to the networks which broadcast them in order to sell the attention of the audience to advertisers. Robert Niles, vice-president of marketing for NBC, puts the matter like this: "We're in the business of selling audiences to advertisers. They [the sponsors] come to us asking for women 18 to 49 and adults 25 to 54 and we try to deliver" (quoted in Harmetz, "'Amazing Stories' Tries New Tactics"). Mr. Niles's predecessor, Sonny Fox, now an independent producer, made the point more politely at a lecture series sponsored by the Annenberg School at USC: "The salient fact is that commercial television is primarily a marketing medium and secondarily an entertainment medium." Or here is Arnold Becker, CBS's vice-president for research: "I'm not interested in culture. I'm not interested in pro-social values. I have only one interest. That's whether people watch the program. That's my definition of good, that's my definition of bad" (both quoted by Andrews, p. 64). No one but the critic ever pretends otherwise. Do parents telling the child the fairy tale concern themselves more with the story or with the child? Without the child's attention, there is no story. "What do you want to hear tonight?" the parent/priest/programmer asks, hoping to get in a "plug."

From the first narrow broadcast, television was an advertisers' medium. Once Hazel Bishop became, almost overnight, a million-dollar cosmetic company based solely on advertising, the direction of the medium was set. It was not happenstance that the image for the first test pattern was the dollar sign. In a free-enterprise culture, a sponsor says to the advertising agency: "Buy me a sequence of images which people who might want my product will watch. We will pay to broadcast that sequence providing we can insert certain images of our own in and around the story. If you can't get the right story we'll go somewhere else to find a story that will work." The agency goes to the network, which goes to the production company to find that story. The story is always secondary. The audience comes first. The network finds the audience for the story, and the advertiser pays for the broadcast. This *quid pro quo* is the dynamic which critics pass by en route to more interesting matters like plot, character, and social content. No one in television or advertising cares about such matters; they care about market share. Viewers are, in fact, even sold to advertisers in round lots of a thousand. If 12 million people wanted to watch goldfish racing, that is what would be broadcast. The only bad show is one not seen. The only bad story is an unpopular one.

Again, like the medieval Catholic Church, which layered itself onto the folklore and customs of each culture it encountered, television programmers cling to whatever is in demand, whatever is in fashion, whatever is watched. What is on the video altar is what the congregation will come out to view. The only threat both broadcasting institutions cannot withstand is the empty seat. Images of the crucified Christ were not displayed because of pastoral desire; in fact, many of the church fathers in the Renaissance were outraged by the corporality of the image. But the image was something the vast majority wanted to see, perhaps even needed to see. One may bridle at an analogy with the church, but recall that today the only network not supported by overt advertisers or private donations is the Christian Broadcasting Network. CBN, with all its hits and misses, essentially attempts to find the formula which elicits attention ("contributions") and then stays with that formula until more lucrative ones are found. There is nothing nefarious here—only the simple economics of the supply and demand of human attention. When a min-

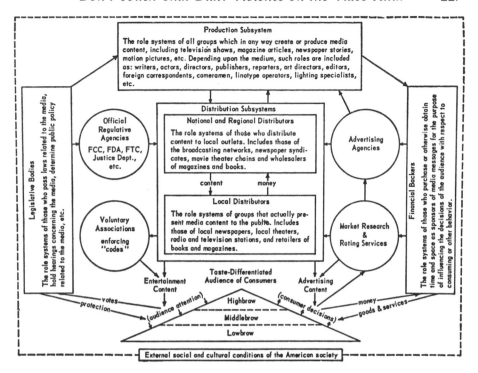

Schematic representation of the mass media as a social system (From *Theories of Mass Communication,* 4th edition, by Melvin L. DeFleur and Sandra Ball-Rokeach. Copyright © 1982 by Longmann, Inc.)

ute of broadcast time costs thousands of dollars, the preacher has to make sure he is telling the right fables, quoting the right scriptures.

The scheme above may help to describe the process of television broadcasting and explain why print critics are perpetually dissatisfied when watching it. The medium rests, literally and figuratively, on audience attention. Television is by no means free, by no means conspiratorial, and by no means exempt from criticism. The point to keep in mind, as Mr. May reminds us in his letter to *TV Guide,* is that we, the audience, are getting almost exactly what most of us want to see.

The majority audience will always have its stories told, first by patronizing its favorite story tellers and second by influencing the legislative bodies which "police" existing programming.[1] But how do we know which stories are most in demand? How are the network priests informed as to which myths are the ones to tell? Since the network cannot depend on copies sold, as with books or newspapers, or on gross receipts at the box office, the programmers have to guess as to how well they are doing. These guesses, misnamed "ratings," are generated by statistical probabilities.

It was in radio that these probabilities were first calculated. In the mid-1930s two professors at MIT developed an ingenious device called the "Audimeter," which measured where and when the dial on a radio was moved. Each time the dial was turned, a mark was made on a moving spool of paper, and a history of specific listening habits could be constructed. In 1936 A. C. Nielsen purchased the Audimeter, and the history of broadcasting stories was forever changed. Nielsen gathered and sold audience profiles. Since broadcasters are in the business of selling the attention of an audience to advertisers, these profiles provided a way to tell where the audience was and how long it would pay attention. Nielsen was soon able to determine precise audiences by using what still seems a ridiculously small sample.[2] Not only could he give a quantitative measure of audience, he could also tell who was listening to what. Hooking the Audimeter up to Junior's set, or to Grandmother's set, would give a different chart and would let a station know what percentage of its audience was working class, male or female, adolescent, retired, and so on.

The A. C. Nielsen Company always makes clear that it does not provide a "rating" but rather a "statistical estimate." Nielsen also makes clear that the process is not at all like polling, which requires prediction. The company has no interest in how an audience plans to act, or expects to act, or pretends to act; it wants only to calculate the act itself. To measure the television "acts," the company started using two systems. First, it installed a Storage Instantaneous Audimeter, a box the size of a cigar box, in 1,700 houses. Like the radio Audimeter, this device measures dial switching, not with a line on a moving sheet of paper but as an electrical impulse sent over telephone lines to a computer in Dunedin, Florida. This system, however, does not record *who* is watching, so a separate sample is made by asking a larger number of respondents, up to 2,600, to fill out a diary of their week's viewing. The group is chosen at random and one third is shifted each week.

This diary is a weak link. Having filled it in for a week myself, I can understand the industry's concern with it. Not only is entering data hard because of space considerations and the number of variables, but it is also susceptible to subterfuge. In most families one person is chosen to keep the diary. That one person is usually an adult female, and too often, say the ad agencies, she constructs a diary of what she would like to have seen or what she would like to keep on the air. This "halo effect" protected many family shows, most recently *The Cosby Show*. With the advent of cable and the complexity caused by the fact that almost half the nation's households are able to receive more than twenty channels, networks, ad agencies, and sponsors knew the system would have to change.

The English, who produced such dystopian masterpieces as *1984* and

Brave New World, provided a solution. In the early 1980s, a small corporation called Audits of Great Britain introduced the dreaded and ballyhooed "Peoplemeter." This device combines the functions of the Audimeter and the diary in yet another little cigar box which sits atop the set like a religious icon. The Peoplemeter is operated by a hand-held remote-control wand. The metering function acts as it did under the Nielsen system, but the diary function is activated by having each family member enter a number on the wand whenever he or she is watching the set. By the summer of 1988 Nielsen had co-opted the technology and the English were forced to retreat homeward. Nielsen's Peoplemeter is now in 4,000 households, demographically profiled in advance, and these 4,000 essentially control what stories the rest of us watch. To be sure, this system has quirks. It favors those who are not frightened by electronic gadgetry—the young and urban—and it can be neglected and abused. Junior may well enter Mom's number to preserve his professional wrestling, even though Mom may want to preserve reruns of *Family Ties.* So the R. D. Percy Company of Seattle is promoting yet another solution. Their "Voxbox" is a totally passive system which records the number of people in the room on the basis of body heat and body mass. All one does is turn on the television and the Voxbox records the rest. When someone leaves the room, a message on the screen asks who remains.[3]

Once we realize that the images we see on television are not the result of conspiratorial foreign forces, not the subterfuges of the networks, the worn-out schlock of Hollywood producers, the nefarious tricks of advertisers, or the brainwash of the captains of industry, we will begin to appreciate the profound and utter mindlessness of the medium. Certainly there is nothing unique about blaming the medium for the message—think only of how the publishing empires of Lloyd in the nineteenth century and of Murdock in our own century have been vilified, as have the Hollywood studios. Blaming television is so easy and so satisfying. It is just so omnipresent and so resolutely vulgar. Who but fools and toadies have ever risen to its support? But has criticism ever had less impact on a medium? Is television getting better? Most critics would say no—just the opposite. It is only getting better at what it does badly. There is precious little on commercial television to appeal to people who read books, let alone to those who write them, for a reason. Mass escapism is the nature of the televised medium, and most intellectuals prefer to escape elsewhere.[4]

So what is it that we see when we now watch television? Or, better yet, what is it that we watch when we see the television screen? Literally, we see images produced as a constantly moving field of winking dots in a transparent grid. The TV image is not a still shot, not *an* image. It is not a photo, or even a series of photos as are the "motion pictures." Rather, television is millions of pixels displayed in a see-through matrix of which the viewer's brain makes sense by focusing on only a small minority. The viewer unconsciously completes the image, fills in the blanks, connects the dots. In a sense, this is almost the reverse of reading, in which we follow nonwinking permanent little black marks in long straight parallel lines. Understanding the ontology of television doesn't necessarily lead to the McLuhanesque conclusions about the "temperature" of the medium (TV is "cool," the movies are "hot"), but only that the most successful television techniques are those which reassert its unique nature—short sequences, fast action, quick cuts, dissolves, facial close-ups. Television reverses the print reader's sense of line-by-line perception and replaces it with a much more fundamental visual experience. Television literally flashes. It blinks, just as we do.

The second phenomenon we notice when we see television is that just as there is flow through the screen, a flow of pixels, there is a flow between what we take to be discrete images. Rather than producing specific "texts," the event of watching begins and ends with a flick of the on/off knob and channel selector. Rarely do we sit down to watch a story from beginning to end. We know the story. We just turn the story on when we feel like it and turn it off when we want to move elsewhere. While apparent punctuation occurs at station breaks and commercial "interruptions," the images continue in a endless flicker. Television flows; it loops endlessly. If you watch people watching television you will see that receiving this flow requires a very low level of concentration. If we look at print and gaze at film, we glance at television. In fact, one *cannot* concentrate on television. It is too hard to see. Alfred Hitchcock, who used to doze off in front of the TV screen, contended that television was made for that purpose. He was not off by much. With children, both the effect and affect of watching can be observed: a slack jaw, a vacant stare, eyes barely deviating from blurred screen. When the Mackworth headcamera is worn by a television viewer, researchers even find that the viewer's eyes often move as if in *rem* sleep. The eyes are fixed with the movement on the screen, locked together.[5]

The closest analogy to television-watching is dreaming. In "Television as Dream," Peter Wood has even argued that dreams, which often move us through stages of sleep, may be one of the few counterparts to television, which moves us through stages of cultural awareness. And just as we seem to share dreams from a common unconsciousness, so we draw televised stories from a common myth pool. Also, television may perform some of the same functions as dream consciousness. As we mature, we dream different dreams; we change channels. It may not be happenstance that this machine often literally puts us to sleep; in fact, many of the newer sets even have a sleep control button which turns the set off after a specified time. Viewers pass from an external system of stimuli to an internal one. Still more curious is the research showing that those who watch a lot of television dream less than those who view in moderation. One active system of fantasy sublimation is being replaced by another far more subtle one.

Although one would be foolish to argue direct correlation, a number of interesting similarities exist. First, both television and dreams have a highly visual quality that mixes real and surreal as a norm. Second, this mix is conducted and decoded through symbols. We may be unconscious of the process, but once we realize that all the derogatory descriptions of television—endless repetition, frantic pacing, constant interruption, interpenetrating imageries, clichéd plot lines, exaggerated characterization, and an overwhelming disregard for "art"—are also descriptions of the dream process, we may at least entertain the possible parallel. Third, both television and dreams "entertain" by fulfilling wishes. They take us to a world of fantasy because only there can certain common desires find expression. Call it "escape," as critics often do, but whatever it is, the desire to experience these sensations is shared by most of the society. Finally, both television and dream content have shocking sequences, especially when generated for/by the human adolescent. Both are full of violent action that is accessible to analysis not by decoding what is seen but by exploring how we react to it. If we directly confront the "manifest content" of the dreams of our youth, we almost always recoil in fear. These dreams are seldom docile, comforting, or even understandable. They are full of conflict. They are often "nightmares."

The parallels between dreams and television aside, other explanations for the fantastic allure of television in terms of narratology, ideology, semiotics, and genre have not been totally satisfactory. No pundit has been able to explain why the average household watches more than seven hours a day or why that figure increased from more than six hours just eight years ago. In many households, the television is on more than any other appliance and is the object of more attention than any family member. When adolescents are asked if they would rather have the television or a parent temporarily removed from the house, they usually prefer to keep the television.

When we move beyond specific content and look at the type of program that succeeds in finding the largest audience, we learn that of the five categories Nielsen uses (sitcoms, movies, adventure stories, general drama, mystery/suspense), the most-watched are, first, adventure stories and, second, movies. As we have seen, movies have tended toward imaging action over character, and hence adventure, usually violent adventure, has prevailed. The very concept of adventure, of a hero going and doing something exciting, almost demands violence. If we can assume that the sponsors, networks, and advertisers have done their jobs in locating the largest target audiences, then what we will see at those times when the young male audience is in place (late afternoon, early evening and Saturday morning) will be the upper limit of socially acceptable action/adventure. And indeed, when adolescents watch their preferred version of action/adventure fables, the violence is almost four times greater than that consumed by the prime-time audience.

Surely something in the interaction between these humans, especially young males, and the television medium explains why so many watch so much that is violent. Could it be because the medium is approximating their dreams, possibly resolving their anxieties, offering and deleting alternatives? Freud used the terms "condensation," "displacement," and "inversion" to discuss how dreams dramatize conflict in a rebus-like symbolic language. He suggested that dream work was triggered by current anxieties, often by specific events which had occurred during the preceding day. In dreams we may work through what is repressed in the daytime. We might therefore approach the television medium as a collective dream. In Peter Wood's view,

> We ourselves are in some way responsible for television; we create it. More than any previous medium including drama and film, TV is a vivid projection of our collective subconscious. Obviously, in practical, individual terms, we are not "responsible" for TV in whole or in part. We lack the technical understanding, the financial capacities, and perhaps even the will and insight to "create" television programs. And yet, all logic and commentary notwithstanding, we can be discovered to shape television more than it shapes us. This is true not merely in the material sense that audiences build ratings which sell products which buy programs, but also in a larger and conscious way. Much as individuals purposefully and unconsciously create their own dream world and then react to it, I speculate that a TV society purposefully and unconsciously creates its own video world and reacts to it. (p. 525)

I would extend this speculation one step further by arguing that those in the audience with problems to resolve essentially elbow the others aside and insist that their stories, their dreams, be told. Those passing through particularly stressful times want to have certain myths retold, want to spend more time at the confessional, want to be both reassured and reminded. Unlike going to church, however, we can attend the television set daily to find out what is on the mind of others and how they have resolved their anxieties. The sense of resolving conflict, of hearing the stories of others, may be one of the socializing and beneficial influences of television. That such solutions are often violent may not be predictive or descriptive of actual behavior as much as simply wishful. After all, indulging repressed desire is the essential nature of dream life as well as of folklore and of religion.

Because television has been pilloried for broadcasting the images that we "should" repress, perhaps we should reexamine a medium which generates the same tension and with which television is closely associated: primitive story telling. Both of these seemingly disposable entertainments are desired by the child, told by the adult, and condemned by the culture-conscious critic. "Please tell me a story," we say as we turn on the set. "No, no, not that story, tell me a different one," we say as we change channels. In both primitive and televisied fables, the story teller has an ulterior motive, be it to inform the audience of social behavior or to instill the desire to purchase some product. In both cases, the production and consumption of these myths have inspired criticism and censorship, whether by well-meaning collectors and publishers in the eighteenth and nineteenth centuries who attempted to rewrite the folk stories or by reformers in the twentieth century who tried to excise certain visual sequences from television or the movies. All these critics acted from the commonsense suspicion that to see is to learn and to learn is to act out. In both TV and folk tales, what the audience often wants, and what the critics do not think should be communicated, are delineations of extreme violence.[6]

Although television and fairy tales are at opposite ends of the historical continuum of popular culture, they address many of the same audience concerns. Both deal with the most common anxieties of their dominant audience—the threat of violence—as well as with the most common resolution of problems—the initiation of revenge. Because we have displaced so much of our cultic violence onto the television screen, we might do well to recall just how much violence inheres in the stories of our youth. Remember stories like "Jack and Jill," "Humpty Dumpty," "Rock-a-Bye Baby," "Three Blind Mice," to name just a few. Indeed, the corpus of adolescent and preadolescent lore is loaded with physical trauma. In the 1950s Geoffrey Handley-Taylor undertook a content analysis of two hundred of the traditional Mother Goose nursery rhymes. Less than one-half showed the cheery side of life: a warm home and hot porridge. The rest showed something quite different. They showed something rather like what can be seen on Saturday morning television. Below is a list of some of the incidents which Handley-Taylor contended "may be accepted as a reasonably conservative estimate based on a general survey of this type of literature":

8 allusions to murder (unclassified)
2 cases of choking to death
1 case of death by devouring
1 case of cutting a human being in half
1 case of decapitation
1 case of death by squeezing

  1 case of death by shriveling
  1 case of death by starvation
  1 case of boiling to death
  1 case of death by drowning
  4 cases of killing domestic animals
  1 case of body-snatching
21 cases of death (unclassified)
  7 cases relating to the severing of limbs
  1 allusion to a bleeding heart
  1 case of devouring human flesh
  5 threats of death
  1 case of kidnapping
12 cases of torments and cruelty to human beings and animals
  8 cases of whipping and lashing
14 cases of stealing and general dishonesty
15 allusions to maimed human beings and animals
  1 allusion to undertakers
  2 allusions to graves
23 cases of physical violence (unclassified)
  1 case of lunacy
16 allusions to misery and sorrow
  1 case of drunkenness
  4 cases of cursing
  1 allusion to marriage as a form of death
  1 case of scorning the blind
  1 case of scorning prayer
  9 cases of children being lost or abandoned
  2 cases of house burning
  9 allusions to poverty and want
  5 allusions to quarreling
  2 cases of unlawful imprisonment
  2 cases of racial discrimination

Not only are Mother Goose rhymes rife with violence, their counterparts in fairy tales are worse, as Maria Tatar and Ruth Bottigheimer have recently shown. These tales are filled with graphic descriptions of murder, mutilation, infanticide, and cannibalism, almost always in the service of victimization, then revenge. We need think only of "Little Red Riding Hood," "Bluebeard," "Hansel and Gretel," "The Three Little Pigs" (pre-Disney), or "Jack and the Beanstalk" to realize that the demands made by the slightly older audience for these tales are still being made. Television, driven by the same audience forces, has become the repository of much of this folklore.[7]

One of the fundamental laws in the transmission of video images, and to a lesser degree of cinematic ones, is that action will ultimately displace stability. Conveying immediate movement is, after all, what distinguishes these media from painting or prose. Both television and films are appealing because they allow the audience to watch a magnification of a recognizable world unfolding in compressed time. This unfolding is most exciting when it involves conflict, and moving conflict is collision. We have craved violent spectacle whether it was carved on cave walls, engraved on Persian tablets, enacted in Roman coliseums, or imaged in pixels on illuminated screens. The action will be increased and distorted for younger and younger audiences who are both attracted to, and repelled by, any threat to well-being. When pubescent males, who centuries earlier had gone deep into the caves to throw their spears at the fearsome ocher images on the stone walls, start to patronize and then to commandeer the airwaves, the results are predictably extreme. The estimate that the average sixteen-year-old male in our culture has seen 18,000 murders on television is shocking, to be sure. But what of the fact that the sixteen-year-old male *wants* to see 18,000 imaginary murders? Once television started to be broadcast on weekend mornings, once advertisers found that this was a vast audience with access to disposable income, once the networks realized that the production expense of literal and figurative cartoon violence was little more than that of "Kukla, Fran and Ollie," the future of commercial television was cast. The Golden Age of television was only golden because Junior's chubby hand was not the first to flip the dial.

But let's see where that chubby hand has been since. In the rest of this chapter, I will examine two genres which have not only survived the influx of the adolescent and preadolescent viewers in the 1960s but have prevailed. In various transmutations, these "escapes," in a kind of media variation on the survival of the fittest, have pushed other stories aside. These genres are: (1) professional wrestling, a self-conscious parody of sport, which is no longer a once-a-week display for the beercan-crunching set but one of the major "profit centers" of cable, especially on the weekend; and (2) the action/adventure show, which has always clung to the airwaves but has now moved into the family hours of the early evening and lost whatever scant attention it once paid to plot and character. Action/adventure now means special effects. In the last chapter, I will examine a third genre: animated cartoons, of which the most violent have jumped from their Saturday morning perch to dominate after-school programming. I will also try to account for the still greater violence of television hybrids like the Music Television channel (MTV), video games, videocassettes of movies like the *Faces of Death* series, and interactive television toys.

Although animated cartoons, professional wrestling, and action/adventure programs are seemingly disparate genres, they are the central fables of our time. They are "texts" broadcast to the young and devoured by them—demanded by them—through multiple viewings. Adults may discern distinctions between specific types, but the adolescents and/or the unsophisticated do not. They view television as it is, as an endless flow of imagery which is not so much interrupted by commercials as punctuated by them. The stories are interchangeable variations of ancient fables of aggression that usher in audience after audience. The dramatization of danger, the laying down of the rules and the boundaries of hostilities, the simulation of crisis, the rehearsal of conflict, the alternate scenes of dominance and submission, the playing out of roles, the centrality of masquerade, the half-hearted resurgence of authority at the conclusion—all give the genres their incantatory and ritualistic power. Their power goes far below the surface, carrying us back to our primordial selves, as well as ahead to our socialized selves. The medium is indeed a "cultural forum" in which the audience essentially negotiates for its place around the campfire.

To link these various genres, I will concentrate on a figure as ludicrous as any in Roman braggadocio lore, yet central to the modern pantheon of heroes—the acronymic Mr. T. This is a modern humor character who ties together different violent myths. From the image alone, Mr. T is a fabulous hyperbole of contradicting racial stereotypes. He is a bizarre confection of Anglo anxieties, black wish-fulfillment, and biracial preadolescent problem resolution. This exaggeration is precisely what gives his persona a place in television fairy tales, for the small screen shows best those features that can be magnified and shown up close. Mr. T (for "trouble" or "tough") came and went in the overnight world of network television. Alas, he has been reabsorbed into the blotter of past events, now famous for clear-cutting more than a hundred oaks around his mansion in Lake Forest ("Tree City USA"), Illinois, to cure his allergies. But for several years, Mr. T was a personification of youthful violent fantasies as well as of adult apprehension. In tracing his career through *The A-Team* (in which Mr. T plays B. A. Baracus— "B. A." for "Bad Attitude" or, more clearly, "Bad Ass"), into professional wrestling (where he was Hulk Hogan's sidekick in *Wrestle-Mania*), and from there to his own Saturday morning cartoon show (where he plays Mr. T), we can see how television transmits certain fables of aggression and then merchandises them in every conceivable context.

As with many television humor characters like Dr. Ruth or Hulk Hogan, Mr. T has an extraordinary body type and presentation of self.

Mr. T and Nancy Reagan, Associated Press (Wide World Photos)

While miniaturized bodies are often the case with blacks on TV, e.g., Gary Coleman and Emanuel Lewis (which may be a comment on white desire to literally belittle), Mr. T is big and thick. He is also utterly implacable. He joins the fraternity of the Incredible Hulk and the Six Million Dollar Man in acting out the ritualized resolutions of those who a generation ago turned to Superman for wish-fulfillment. Whether or not he affects his snarl (David Steinberg said interviewing T was like talking to a shark), T's pugnacity is as much a part of his persona as his unique upside-down facial hair. Like the cartoon figure of the male face with bald head and flourishing goatee, which could be turned upside down to produce an equally recognizable image, so Mr. T's mohawk mane and close-cropped beard almost promise a visual palindrome. *If* he could be upended, he would still be a force to be reckoned with. From the neck down Mr. T is the modern image of a Venetian doge gone Hollywood. Below the bare midriff he wears skin-tight Levis; above is his *pièce de résistance*. Strewn about his bare chest is a veritable explo-

Mr. T working out (Titan Sports; photo: Steve Taylor)

sion of Zayres, K-Mart, and Rexall costume jewelry. Gold necklaces, crosses, chains, and medallions hang about his neck like a horse collar. In a provocative inversion of the semiotics of slavery, Mr. T is almost weighted down not with iron but with gold. His wrists are also brace-leted in gold; so too his ears are festooned with golden ornaments. In fact, dangling from his ear lobes are the feathers, rings, and baubles of a saloon dancer. Rings on his fingers? Of course, on every finger. Mr. T is a walking boutique or, as one commentator quipped, "a pawn shop on feet."

Visually, Mr. T joins the cartoon world of Punch, Varney the Vam-pire, Wyle E. Coyote, Dracula, Rambo, Mr. Hyde, He-Man, Clint East-wood of the spaghetti Western, G. I. Joe, the matador, Leatherface, and Freddie as an immediately recognizable stereotype of barely controllable male aggression. He is a bruiser, a pit bull with a pinky ring. Unlike his purely fictional counterparts, however, Mr. T has a real life in which he plays Mr. T—a public relation man's dream. Born Lawrence Tero (also Tureaud, Tureau), a minister's son with eleven siblings, Mr. T (always

"Mr.," he insists) is a self-created image of urban anxiety. Lawrence grew up on the South Side of Chicago, and according to his autobiography, *Mr. T: The Man with the Gold,* he was almost burned up, beaten up, and stomped on. Although he is understandably circumspect in his reminiscential prose, he implies that he had to threaten, maim, and even kill in order to stay alive. As a good Christian he is sorry, but such was the law of the urban jungle. Happily, he was able to escape the ghetto and to turn what he had learned about violence to his advantage. He became a bodyguard, and it was then that he adopted the Mr. T sobriquet, shaved his head with the characteristic median strip, and hung his first chain. He was not a media character yet, but already he knew television. Clearly conspicuous, T was really a bodyguard for people who wanted to have the image of someone who had a bodyguard. He was employed by actors, preachers, clothing designers, athletes, models, and most importantly, boxers—especially Leon Spinks.

When Spinks beat Muhammad Ali on January 15, 1978, Mr. T's picture and fame spread with the new champ's. And when Spinks proceeded to run into trouble because of his various bad habits, which usually included drug use and reckless driving, photographed by his side was the implacable Mr. T. As Spinks descended the ladder of fame, Mr. T climbed up. T was even able to garner some bad press of his own when he went AWOL too many times from National Guard drills. Soon the IRS became interested. And then there was the famous jaywalking incident in Chicago. In his autobiography, Mr. T explains the event in a way which foreshadows fiction. It is a scene his young audience also plays out over and over on the playground and in life:

> We started to cross the Outer Drive, but since we didn't see an opening in the crowd, we decided to walk down a little further on the median strip. One policeman said that it was okay to walk on the median strip until we saw an opening to cross at. But as we walked down the median, we were soon confronted by a very nasty, disrespectful Chicago policeman who began shouting at us to get off the median. I stopped and asked the police officer, "Why are you so rude and nasty?" He shouted back, "Are you trying to be smart with me?" I said, "No, I'm not trying to be smart, but I'm a man and there's no reason why you have to shout and disrespect us." Then he cut me off from talking and shouted again, "Do you want to get arrested for disorderly conduct? I told you to get off the median right here." He pointed with his finger. I tried to tell him that the other officer had said it was okay to walk on the median, but again he shouted, "What did I say?" I turned to my friend and said, "I don't believe this," and just at that split second the big, sloppy, unprofessional, ill-trained bully cop grabbed me from behind and started twisting my arm. (*Mr. T: The Man with the Gold*, p. 226)

Again, Mr. T's picture was in the paper. He was getting more than the fifteen minutes of notoriety promised by Andy Warhol; he was becoming a media figure, an image, a metaphor. T was now more than a Chicago figure; he was on the wire service. As with entertainment reviews, the only bad notice is no notice—Mr. T was a celebrity.

His transition to television was almost instantaneous. First, Mr. T was invited to compete on NBC's late night special, *America's Toughest Bouncer* (February 2, 1980). The competition consisted of jumping over a bar rail, running around some tables, leaping another rail, and bursting through a four-inch wooden door to ring a bell and stop the clock. The top two contestants then had to square off and punch it out in a boxing ring. Mr. T won. He became "America's Toughest Bouncer." T said it was just like life in the Projects. T had a presence. He was not just photogenic, he was informative. When you saw him you knew what he stood for. He was the image of barely repressed outrage.

Soon after becoming the toughest bouncer, T was called by a Hollywood casting agency which was looking for an unknown to play Clubber Lang in Sylvester Stallone's *Rocky III*. Mr. T *was* Clubber—snarly, rough, a loner, the "ebony death machine." A bass guitarist from Venice Beach, California, who had recently become a professional wrestler named Hulk Hogan, played the heavy with the unlikely name of "Thunderlips." The rest, as Mr. T himself says, is history. *Rocky III* was a success, Mr. T found his metier, added more gold chains, and was soon asked to appear as "just himself" at parties, parades, carnivals, and shopping-center openings. He was even asked to be the honorary chauffeur of one of the stretch limousines at the Larry Holmes/Gerry Cooney fight in June of 1982. Posing with his fulminating snarl at ringside, T was spotted by Brandon Tartikoff and cast in the NBC series, *The A-Team*.

The A-Team (1983–87) was one of the most popular television shows of the 1980s, reflecting the changing demographics of the prime-time audience and the increased demand for prime-time fables of aggression. From 8:00 to 9:00 every Tuesday evening, the show captured an enviable market share that it was able to retain for a few years. Conceived by Tartikoff after watching a videotape of *The Dirty Dozen*, *The A-Team* contained the predictability of *Mission Impossible* with the heroes-as-outcast mentality of *The Road Warrior*. Tartikoff told his idea to Stephen J. Cannell, the producer of *The Rockford Files*, *Riptide*, and *Hardcastle and McCormick*, who concocted the pilot as well as the finished product. There was to be no intellectual pretense; both agreed this show was to be to television what McDonald's was to food—quick delivery of easily digestible scenes. Almost from the outset on January 23, 1983, *The A-Team* satisfied a post-Vietnam hunger and remained in the national diet for the next four years.[8] The show was characterized by out-and-out pantomime violence. It was one of the most kinetic shows

The A-Team (Stephen J. Cannell Productions)

ever broadcast, averaging almost forty violent acts an hour. The violence was at a level never seen before on family hour television—pure *Road Runner.*

The show consisted of four proud American soldiers who, wrongly imprisoned in Vietnam for, of all the inconceivable crimes, robbing a bank, have escaped back to the U.S.A. where they must live as outcasts. As with *Rambo,* we are never to know exactly what happened; we only know they were set up and that their superiors were in the wrong. To make the scapegoat even more worthy, it is this same blundering Army that still dogs their tracks. They must—like another American, David Jansen in *The Fugitive,* who represents the post-Korean War anxiety— be perpetually hounded by the perverse forces of a failed Order. In the meantime, to make ends meet they do good deeds as soldiers of fortune in Los Angeles.

In the heroic picturebook introduction, an incantatory ritual of action/adventure television, we meet our plucky band of good-hearted "outlaws." First is a portly George Peppard who plays "Hannibal" Smith. He wears black gloves, smokes a cigar, is a master of disguises, and always has a "plan just like the one we used to nail the Vietcong" with which to frustrate the bad guys, whom he alternatively calls "dirt-" or "slimeballs." Peppard is forever winking at the camera as if to say "Hi" to the kids and to assure them the violent action they will be seeing is really all a big joke, which, of course, it is. In this update of *Bonanza*, Peppard plays Father Cartwright and his sons are straight from central casting. For yuppies-in-training there is Dirk Benedict, a George Hamilton lookalike who plays a California con-man named Templeton Peck. Dwight Schultz plays "Howling Mad" Murdock, which is the best role because it enables him to act unstrung most of the time by mugging at the camera. Between stress-induced, Nam-related nervous breakdowns, he pilots the requisite airplane, private jet, army transport, cropduster, helicopter, or biplane, which must be commandeered from the bad guys or, better yet, from the Army. He also does wonderful imitations of Kissinger, Brando, James Mason, and for the new generation of watchers of old shows, Mr. Ed. Then there is Mr. T himself, who as B. A. Baracus drives the entourage around in a conspicuous black van with a distinctive oval window and a broad running stripe along the side. While such a vehicle may make covert operations difficult, who cares? This is Southern California, and you are only as good as your most recent car. Lest we forget this, the last credit line reminds us that "The A-Team van was supplied by the General Motors Company."

The A-Team unfolds as a standard five-act television drama. In Act I we meet the victim. Usually this victim is a single young woman, and with the exception of a female reporter who was soon dropped from the show, she is the only female on the program. *The A-Team* is an action show, a boy's show, a violent show, and victimized women would just get in the way. Women can initiate action and stay around for the minor love interest, but otherwise they disappear to return only at the denouement, when they express gratitude. The victim usually comes into the city where she makes contact with our misunderstood commandos by first meeting the disguised Hannibal Smith. His disguises are usually outlandish (the best was Sally Fields's Flying Nun habit), and habitués of the show instantly know who he is because he winks at the camera. Come to find out that the young lady and her elderly father are being intimidated by the local gas companies, escaped convicts, Arab sheiks, mortgage bankers, North Vietnamese generals, lumber companies, or wildcat oil drillers who want to bamboozle the family out of their rightful holdings. Can the A-Team help? Well, yes.

After a commercial, the commandos load up in the van and are driven by the dour and snarly B. A. out to confront the nasties. One reason B. A. is so dour and snarly is that he would rather not have to leave his real job to fight the bad guys. He teaches toddlers at a daycare center. As Mr. T became more popular in the mid-1980s, a plot twist developed. In the later shows, B. A.'s only fear is the fear of flying, and to get him into a plane he must be knocked unconscious. The writers surely enjoyed suggesting the variations, all of which have to do with knocking Mr. T into the same condition he renders the "dirt/slimeballs." Since "Howling Mad" Murdock always flies the plane, a natural tension develops between the two commandos. This allows Mr. T to growl and say things like "Listen fool, yo' dead meat" or "I'll whup yo' up th' side of yo' head, sucker" when he finds he has been shanghaied onto the airplane. Even though he is so strong and so grown up, he still has fears. T delivers most of his lines like a leaf blower with no muffler, and everyone just steps back and waits until he is through. Soon we meet the bad guys and all our heroes seem to be doing very well indeed. They trade insults and then punches with some overgrown playground bullies who are pushing the little people around.

Act III, however, has our heroes trapped by the nasties, who plan torture. Heroes imprisoned do not quibble and complain; rather they patiently hear out the "Colonel" (as Hannibal now becomes known). He announces his plan—"just like the one in Vietnam"—and after a respite with yet another commercial, the plan leads us into Act IV. In this act, the mechanical-minded Mr. T finds some welding equipment, a laser, a Coke machine, a pair of pliers, a forklift, an old truck—anything!—and builds a weapon which usually throws some kind of projectile. In much the same manner as the *Transformers* or *Gobots* (both the television shows and the toys), some simple object, say, a station wagon, is turned and twisted into a halftrack. In *The A-Team*, turning the old jalopy into a tank is B. A.'s job and he does it with a vengeance: He welds some iron slabs around it, or fixes a milking machine on its roof and makes it a water cannon, or turns a chainsaw into a machine gun, or attaches an old stove to a lawn mower and turns it into a flamethrower.

After another commercial message, the fun and Act V begin. Our soldiers of fortune break loose and explode through the curtain of verisimilitude into a pure cartoon of stupendous violence. Just as the penny dreadful ended in a torrent of frantic action, just as the last *EC* comic frame almost burst across the page to release the violence, just as Stephen King concentrates on final explosions, and just as the camera is deliberately undercranked to magnify turbulence in, for instance, *Bonnie and Clyde*, so *The A-Team* is never content to show one Uzi burping bullets of fire or one Sherman tank slowly doing the airborne loop-the-loop. No, never. At the conclusion of an *A-Team* episode, the whole television picture is pulsing fire and smoke; all manner of ordnance flashes by; tanks, helicopters, and planes join the final free-for-all. This pure effervescence of convulsion is so vivid that often the viewer does not know what is happening, nor does he really care. He only knows he cannot stop watching. After the startling success of *Miami Vice*, these conclusions were often played out as music videos with the characters and their vehicles doing a slow-motion dance to the musical explosions.

Like *Batman*, which it so resembles without the "Pows!," *The A-Team's* last frenzied minutes always have a slightly mischievous sense, almost as if to say, "Well, you've waited through the standard plot, the same plot you could have seen on the other channels, now look at what we have in store for you. You want special effects? Well, here goes!" In fact, in one episode *The A-Team* spoofed the horror film, and the final special effects were just that—Hollywood special effects in the service of Hollywood special effects. Who cares? It's all pretend anyway. Recently, I had a chance to watch almost all *The A-Team* episodes for hours at a stretch, and I must say that while the campiness of these endings is tiresome, the enthusiasm is infectious. You cannot turn away. For *The A-Team* devotee, such violent pizzazz was sufficient to carry the show to the top of the Nielsen charts from 1983 to late 1985. *The A-Team* was almost always in the top ten shows of total U.S. households, in the top seven for males over 18, and in the top five for teens 12–17 and children 2–11. Needless to say, women over 18 had other interests. The major advertisers—beer, automobile, and shaving-product companies—didn't care. They had the audience they wanted, for a while anyway.

When, inexplicably, in late 1985 *The A-Team* went flat, the show's producers, sponsors, and network became desperate to regain lost audience share. When the "chemistry" is lost, everything is poured into the beaker. So in 1986, after extensive audience research in ten cities, two new characters were added. General Hunt Stockwell, played by Robert Vaughn, took to assigning the A-team on missions for which presidential pardons were supposedly promised. By casting Vaughn, the producers were counting on two attractions: (1) that older viewers would recognize this as the role in *Man from Uncle* in which Vaughn played Napoleon Solo; and (2) that, with Vietnam sentiment changing, our soldiers could be exonerated by putting the blame on politicians. The other new character was added for the younger Hispanic viewers. Frankie "Dishpan" Santana, played by Eddie Valdez, was supposedly a special effects coordinator in the movies before joining the team. He could blow anything up, anywhere. Alas, none of these new characters, nor cameos played by the likes of "Refrigerator" Perry, Boy George, and Isaac Hayes, nor plots involving the *Wheel of Fortune* television show, toxic waste, "USA for Africa," and women's liberation were sufficient to stave off the endless contract disputes (brought by Messrs. Peppard and T) and audience apathy. The show that almost single-handedly revived the moribund NBC in 1983 had become too stale and had slipped too low in the Nielsen ratings (#31 in 1986) to continue. Not with a bang but a whimper, *The A-Team* went into the syndication doldrums in 1987.[9]

When critics, reformers, ministers, psychologists, and the generally concerned public identified the program most reprehensible in portraying violence-gone-too-far, *The A-Team* was always at the top of the list. The National Coalition on Television Violence consistently reported *The A-Team* in the top five most objectionable shows. Stephen J. Cannell Productions defended its most popular show by claiming that in no *A-Team* episode did one person really get hurt, much less ever killed. In the grand finale, the only object that is even punctured is an automobile tire. However, there is no doubt that problem resolution à la *The A-Team* is invariably either to slug it out or blow it up. Either way the results are telegenic. That no one is ever injured may make the violence more entertaining, but to those who subscribe to associationist psychology, the violence is more reprehensible. Better to show the pain caused than to pretend nothing hurts. Such criticism misses the point, however. This audience is not interested in the real world; they want the resolution of the pretend.

As merchandisers of mass-market, mass-produced fantasies have known since the middle of this century, entertainment is only the bait by which you lure the consumer to your product. In the broadcast media, "show business" is essentially the "business" of making people pay (if only by watching commercials) in return for "showing" them some images in action. If the images are embedded in violence, the attractions seem to increase, regardless of the coherence of external context. Hence, until he fell from favor, Mr. T's visage could be seen on the cover of a breakfast cereal (simply called "Mr. T") right next to "Rainbow Brite," or as a doll on the toy shelf next to "Strawberry Shortcake." So it should come as no surprise that Lawrence Tero, who plays Mr. T, who in turn plays B. A. Baracus, should find himself being richly rewarded for playing the sidekick of Hulk Hogan (played by Terry Jean Bollea) in *WrestleMania*.

Hulk Hogan and Mr. T, *WrestleMania* (Titan Sports)

Hulk announcing the news, *WrestleMania* (Titan Sports)

As is characteristic of electronic media, the caricature is all; specific context is irrelevant; intertextuality is the norm. The audience knows what the critic forgets: it's all play-acting anyway.

On April Fools' Eve of 1985 Hulk Hogan, the "Hulkster" (6' 8" with 24" biceps, lovingly referred to as his "pythons"), joined T in a grudge match against "Rowdy" Roddy Piper and Paul "Mr. Wonderful" Orndorff in Madison Square Garden. This was the modern media event par excellence—a cornucopia of preposterous violence. "Hulkamania," a registered trademark of Marvel Comics Group, had run wild. Everything was a sham. On hand were Muhammad Ali (a real participator in real violence) as referee, Liberace (a send-up of male aggression) as time-keeper, and Billy Martin (an instigator of real sports violence of which professional wrestling is anti-image) as ring announcer. Andy Warhol had a ringside seat. Also on hand to view *WrestleMania*, as the spectacle was called, was a crowd so large that it sold out the Garden, and the overflow had to be packed into the adjoining Felt Forum to watch on a video monitor. More than one million fans watched the closed-circuit telecast around the world at more than two hundred locations. As befits such an extravaganza, the hype was far more interesting than the event. That the Hulk and Mr. T should cohost *Saturday Night Live* just twelve hours before their battle, that Mr. T should put the "sleeper hold" on a shill from the audience who booed the dynamic duo, that Mr. T should proclaim that he was teaching Hulk how to street fight "just the way they do in the Projects" only reinforced the self-conscious masquerade of violence. The masquerade, however, was the object of extraordinary public interest, for this charade was celebrating one of the most ancient and powerful of human interactions. *WrestleMania*, "the war to settle the score," was the carnival expiation of a "grudge."

This grudge, which only blood vengeance conducted in public could erase, had been carefully choreographed. To understand the attraction of such a public spectacle is to comprehend the nature of symbolic violence as well as the nature of broadcast show business. The names are unimportant; the ancient ritual is central. This electronically transmitted updating of the "copie," or reenactment of the cat massacre in the eighteenth-century Parisian print shop, was coproduced by David Wolf, a rock music producer, "Captain" Lou Albano, a one-time wrestler and now a wrestling manager, and Vince McMahon, impresario of the World Wrestling Federation and CEO of Titan Sports, Inc. And it was a culmination of a series of orchestrated events that began in January 1984.

At that time, Cyndi Lauper, a rock star who resembles a disheveled pixie from outerspace, had taken up managing a female wrestling star, Wendi Richter, who resembles Farrah Fawcett from Hollywood and Vine. Since the audiences for the two entertainments—"rock 'n 'rassling"— are the same, who cares about the illogic of the combination? To bridge the adolescent fables and to make a sin in one context punishable in the other was Lou Albano, who looks like a cross between a beer keg and a superannuated Hell's Angel. Mr. Albano wears rubber bands and safety pins in his cheeks and is as instantly recognizable as "Pigpen" in the *Peanuts* comic strip. In this boorish persona, he appeared as Lauper's repressive father in the rock video for "Girls Just Want to Have Fun," but he was better known as a manager of wrestling villains. In the hype of contrived conflict, Lauper and Albano supposedly had a falling-out over Ms. Richter's wrestling contract, and in February Ms. Lauper was introduced to the wrestling crowd at Madison Square Garden as Richter's manager. Although the crowd knew her as a singer, no one was upset that she was now the manager of a female wrestler. The crowd applauded. Mr. Albano's wrestlers, Paul "Mr. Wonderful" Orndorff, who in the role of psychopath can piledrive his opponents into the canvas mat, and "Rowdy" Roddy Piper, who is Peck's bad boy raised to the highest levels of bluster, rushed into the ring and threatened Ms. Lauper. Behind them Albano yelled one of the code clichés of wrestling, "Breach of contract!" As Mr. Orndorff was about to hit the defenseless pixie, who should come charging down the aisle to her rescue, throwing off his clothing en route? Mr. T. stripped down to what looked to be a spangled sweat suit from Rodeo Drive and pushed the villains back.

Wendi Richter and Cyndi Lauper, *WrestleMania* (Titan Sports)

He later explained, "I like to see good, clean wrestlin', no dirty stuff—when they hit a woman, that's too much for me." T was soon pummeled for his efforts. But wait! The gallant Hulk Hogan, who just happened to be in the neighborhood, came to T's aid and the villains fled.

This scenario, which was repeatedly broadcast *in toto* on MTV (Music Television), as well as in segments on the network news, and covered in print (even by the *New York Times* and the *Wall Street Journal*), not only established the interpenetration of texts, not just the "rock 'n 'ras-

Rowdy Roddy Piper and Paul "Mr. Wonderful" Orndorff,
WrestleMania (Titan Sports)

sling" connection, but promulgated the story line so that Mr. T could, with no dislocation of belief, be teamed with Hogan, the California Viking, to do violent battle again with Albano's two narcissistic thugs. After all, the allure of cartoon caricature demands that normal expectations always be partially overthrown, whether played out by Tom and Jerry, the Three Stooges, the Road Runner, or by overgrown wrestlers.

When *WrestleMania* finally took place, it had acquired still greater mythic proportions after the story line tied in sexual topics. Mr. Piper, who is Scottish and wears a kilt to prove it, claimed he also disliked the women's movement as typified by Ms. Lauper's hit recording "Girls Just Want to Have Fun." He considered himself a fan of splatter movies in which girls got tortured instead. Gloria Steinem claimed that Mr. Piper was a "disgrace to the skirt," and Geraldine Ferraro, then a candidate for the vice-presidency, told Piper to "shut up and fight like a man." Both women would regret these on-camera responses, as they soon became central motifs in the promotional advertising. However, on March 31, 1985, in a less than stellar performance of huge boys running and tumbling, Hulk and Mr. T did avenge the honor of rock 'n roll as well as of the women's movement. The battle ended when the swinish Mr. Piper mistakenly hit pretty-boy Mr. Orndorff and knocked him unconscious. Self-consummating victimage is one of wrestling's cherished mythologies. Black and white had struggled together and prevailed, thanks to the incompetence of evil. The hoodlums had been turned back. The *lex talonis* had been upheld.

Other hoodlums needed treatment, and so Hulk shifted media and twice appeared on *The A-Team* to repay the favor. Again, the viewing audience seemed oblivious to the shift in context and was as happy to entertain the Hulk on network television as it was to see him in music videos or as a best selling plastic doll. One of the keys to adolescent mythography is that, while adults need consistency of context and character, adolescents enjoy watching its subversion. The only audience which can staunch *Billy the Kid vs. Dracula* or *Beach Blanket Vampires* is an audience which wants the purposeful ironizing of stereotypes. So in an *A-Team* episode entitled "Body Slam," Mr. T appears at ringside to ask the Hulkster to help the team take care of some hoods who want to evict a young schoolmarm and her little charges from their day school. This episode ends with the heavies going into counseling and the World Wrestling Federation giving money to the nursery. In "Trouble with Harry," Hulk helps the A-Team protect a boxer who refuses to throw a fight. "Any man who takes a dive is no hero in my book," says Hulk, who has made a fortune doing just that.

Although critics of modern culture bemoan the loss of heroes, and although Mr. T and Hulk Hogan are hardly Beowulf and the Redcrosse Knight, they do represent an ancient yearning of a particular audience for larger-than-life figures with simple problem-solving techniques. In a sense, professional wrestling, one of the central cartoons of television, is a bizarre variation on the medieval tournament with its own pomp and circumstance. Television depends on easy-to-decode rituals, and none is easier than knights-at-joust. True, the knights have been democratized and unionized. They no longer play the parts of princes-in-training but are working men, braggarts, aspiring capitalists—all images drawn from the day-to-day world of the audience. In fact, in "real" life many professional wrestlers are one-time football players or body builders who like to act. If they can succeed, they are rewarded like royalty. Bob Temmey, a reporter for *The National Enquirer*, an authority on such matters, estimates that Hulk Hogan's annual income is well in excess of $2,000,000, "Rowdy" Roddy Piper's, $700,000, the Junkyard Dog's, $400,000, and Paul "Mr. Wonderful" Orndorff's, $350,000.

Unlike modern hybrid sports such as roller derby or kick boxing, professional wrestling has always pitted clearly recognizable good against equally recognizable evil. This is the kind of entertainment that can be profitably broadcast because it unfolds in easy-to-recognize pictures. The "fights" explode in short, photogenic scenes. Still, it was not until the advent of cable television that an adolescent audience could be assembled. The audience which attends the bouts is not at all the audience which watches at home. The standard joke among wrestlers used to be: "What has 14 teeth and an IQ of 50? Answer: The first 10 rows at a wrestling match." The home audience, however, is every advertising man's dream—predominately males between twelve and sixty years old. Little wonder that ESPN, the male network nonpareil, has taken to broadcasting its own brand of wrestling under the rubric of a sporting event. And little wonder that shaving-cream companies, chainsaw companies, motorcycle companies, and beer companies have lined up to sponsor it. On February 5, 1988, professional wrestling achieved the ultimate integration. *Main Event*, featuring Hulk Hogan and Andre the Giant, was broadcast live by NBC in the most prime of prime time, 8:00–9:00 Friday evening. Call it what you will, "that's entertainment."

That entertainment has depended almost entirely on non-network television to broadcast its fables. In the 1970s Vincent McMahon, who had inherited the World Wrestling Federation from his father, transformed a loose confederation of southern New England carnivals held in high-school gyms into an international multimillion-dollar enterprise. He did this by first contracting with the USA Cable Network and then with Ted Turner's WTBS until he had essentially created his own national network. With the kind of *quid pro quo* which characterizes entertainment ventures in a world of CPAs and tax schedules, McMahon provided the stations with carefully edited videotape footage of each week's matches. In return, the stations ran WWF promotional advertising. The stations made their profit (and it soon became a huge one) by selling the remaining commercial time. This relationship proved so successful that the WWF network soon "penetrated" almost ninety percent of American TV households. McMahon even developed a promotional talk show to promote his promotional video clips. Called *Wrestling TNT*, this surreal parody of *The Johnny Carson Show* consisted of McMahon interviewing his own circus acrobats. Making sure to include hostile guests, McMahon calmly sat back and watched in mock outrage while these behemoths proceeded first to squabble and then, on cue, to pummel each other and finally to destroy the set à la rock musicians. Just before the last commercial, Mr. McMahon would express outrage and promise to be back the next week. His viewers were there: *TNT* was the most popular program on USA cable and the number one cable show in sophisticated Manhattan.

Watching overgrown men heave each other about certainly has its attraction deep within male consciousness. Some of the first scenes painted on cave walls depicted men tussling; classical folklore is filled with Herculean characters blustering about. Even some of our earliest "art" literature depicts exaggerated combat. Consider the wrestling match between Ajax and Odysseus described in Chapter 23 of *The Iliad*. In ancient Rome, oiled and dusted men entered the Roman arena—even the word "arena," meaning "sandy floor," is still central to the ritual—for a no-holds-barred sport called *pankration*. Learned from the Greeks but exaggerated by the Romans, this combination of boxing and wrestling included pinching, eye-gouging, and above-the-belt mayhem. The bout was performed by professionals before an eager public, and instead of voice-over narration, a flute directed audience response. In the eighteenth century, the self-proclaimed second Age of Augustus, *pankration* was the stuff of "low Roman comedy" and just one of the reasons, contended Gibbon, for the fall of the empire. Had he waited two hundred years, he would have seen a pantomime of *pankration* revived.[10]

Wrestling did not become overtly professional, i.e., "fixed," until the vaudeville and saloon shows of the early nineteenth century. By 1908 the ring size had been fixed at the "squared circle" of eighteen feet, the parody of Greco-Roman holds had become standardized, and the establishment of regional organizations with high-sounding names like the National Wrestling Alliance organized the high-jinks and supplied the itinerant stuntmen. Under the influence of hustlers like P. T. Barnum, wrestling, an ancient heroic combat, became 'rassling, a modern contrived entertainment. With the advent of television, "professional wrestling" came into its own, found its audience, and evolved into a highly ritualized display of disorderly conduct. Television allowed the ritual to be seen in private, safe from censorious eyes. Newspapers and radio had always mocked the event, in part because they could not supply much commentary, in part because they knew it was sham. Professional wrestling is, after all, a charade—"a male soap opera with sweat." However, television lives on such charades, on "let's pretend," on make-believe.

In the last forty years, one can see an almost Darwinian struggle between boxing and wrestling on the television airwaves as pantomime violence has forced out real violence. (Real wrestling has never been a contender for attention since it is a test of balance, skill, and grace— hence boring.) Boxing is athletic, pugilistic, violent: working-class brutal. Professional wrestling is theatrical, histrionic, gesticulatory: blue-collar circus. In some states, such as New York, professional wrestling cannot even be called a "sporting event" but must be plainly labeled an "exhibition," while in other states like Texas professional wrestling is legally a "burlesque."[11] The audience doesn't split these hairs; let the lawyers and politicians call it what they will. That boxing, which was the first sport to be successfully broadcast on television, is now relegated to occasional showings on cable, while professional wrestling, which for a time was called "studio wrestling" and conducted on a sound stage in order to advertise upcoming events, has now become one of the most popular televised genres, is a testament to how kinetic ritual displaces "real" life when audiences change. And what an informing irony that boxing, which really is brutal, is criticized for violence, while professional wrestling, which is not violent at all, is condemned as fraudulent.

To understand why Mr. T could so easily jump from action/adventure format to passion play without anyone saying, "Stop! You don't belong in the ring—you belong in Los Angeles driving the A-Team van and blowing up bullies," we need to realize the Commedia dell'Arte illusion that television creates. Television is a masque with intermissions, a passion with pauses, an endless narrative with "newsbreaks." Since the commercial medium depends on maintaining the largest possible audience over the longest possible time, the one viewer conviction to break is the belief that programs are isolated and unrelated. The object of television is to generate sequences which can be repeatedly viewed. The object of *The A-Team* is to deliver the last fifteen-minute sequence of choreographic collisions. The object of professional wrestling is to deliver a burst of uncontrollable concussions in a few brief minutes. To get to the point of delivery, however, context must be provided even though it be a veritable replay of the previous show. In fact, the replay is preferable as it cuts down on any intellectual interpretation. With *The A-Team*, this formulaic introduction is accomplished in the first three acts in which the bad guys pick on the innocent female victim and invite, nay, demand, violent revenge. In so doing, *The A-Team* reiterates a thousand other shows which the viewer has seen. In professional wrestling, where female victims are rare, the need for vengeance must be accomplished primarily through the development of stereotypes. This less sophisticated audience does not need women to fight over; almost any pretext will do. The development of this pretext is dependent on many supporting players: ring announcer, television commentator, referee, and especially the villain. This villain must behave so badly that we can justifiably say, "Well, this sure is violent behavior, but he asked for it." To deliver the "just deserts" to this villain, an immediately recognized and ritualized drama must be constructed around him.

Like the bullfight, whose routines it dimly resembles, the wrestling "match" depends on a host of subsidiary characters and routines. Although there can be variations and ambiguities, the battle itself has a preestablished end: a pin, a disqualification, or the increasingly popular "outside interference." By no means will good always win. Evil often triumphs. But the playlet is constructed so that multiple contests are occurring. Since this is teletheater, a narrative voice preinterprets the action like a Greek chorus and explains these various contests. This announcer is always a rigid moralist, usually mildly anemic, who uses our habitual trust in the on-site observer (even though he himself is often watching a videotape replay and adding the voice-over), plus his power of naming ("a figure-four leg lock," "a back suplex," "a flying dropkick"), to establish the illusion of intense combat on a number of levels.

In the first act, the announcer articulates the order of events. He names the participants and in so doing outlines their identities: the "Junkyard Dog," a black who wears the chains of slavery around his neck as Mr. T wears the gold of emancipation; "Sergeant Slaughter," the tough but soft-hearted drill instructor; Andre the Giant, the affable and absurd behemoth; and characters like the Iron Sheik, Nikolai Volkoff, and Mr. Fugi whose names need no explanation since the crowd's xenophobia can fill in the motivation. Also, Swede Hansen, Pedro Morales, and Hillbilly Jim need no gloss. The names, however, are not enough. During brief periods of detente, even the Russians can reform.

In a self-conscious inversion of Christian salvation, good wrestlers often inexplicably turn bad and attack their one-time compatriots. Their fans are drop-jawed to witness such a transformation. All this backsliding is reversed at the eleventh hour when our hero "comes to his senses" and returns to his earlier role. While even the mighty may fall, wrestling preaches, it is never too late to be saved. Once upon a time Sgt. Slaughter was one of the "most hated," and now he is beloved. Kevin Sullivan was once a college boy from Boston, but then he fell under the influence of Satan and made a U-turn. Even Hulk Hogan used to be someone else, a villain named Terry Boulder. Although the character facade can be dropped, once it has been drawn, the actor must remember to keep it in place, especially in the pre- and/or postevent interview with the TV announcer. Nothing is so unsettling as to hear a Russian accent delivered in a deep Alabama drawl. Even more unsettling is when the pugilist forgets who he is supposed to be and starts uttering last month's lines.

To make sure that his "humor" is properly understood, the villain is often accompanied by a manager. The manager is usually a superannuated wrestler who, like Bobby (the Brain, the Weasel) Heenan, "Captain" Lou Albano, or "Classy" Freddie Blassie (who refers to the crowd as "pencil-necked geeks"), tricks the hero so the villain can win. Having a manager in tow clearly announces dependence on others and a willingness not to fight "the American way"—that is, alone. In addition, both contestants may wear operatic costumes over their spandex tights—the more outrageously narcissistic the outfit, the more villainous. Much is made of the undraping of the robes, be it the langourous uncaping of villains or the overeager shedding by the hero. Heroes are always enthusiastic about the bouts while villains are condescending. Hulk Hogan, who comes in a sling-shot tee shirt with "Hulkamania" writ large, is so eager to get to fighting that he literally tears his shirt off and throws it to an adoring crowd. The rock star throwing his sweaty bandanna, the matador tossing the trophy ear, or the knight-at-arms wearing the colors of his lady love are all exchanges of favors that announce a solidarity, a dedication to the ritual and to the audience. Villains exchange nothing but boos. To reinforce symbolism, as well as to show values shared with the crowd, wrestling heroes have taken to entering the arena accompanied by popular music. Since the hero usually is the second to enter the auditorium, he approaches the ring with a gladiatorial flourish. Mr. Hogan struts to the tune of "Eye of the Tiger," the Junkyard Dog to "Another One Bites the Dust," Jesse "The Body" Ventura to "My Body Rules." The concept of theme song is yet another reinforcement of the recognition code. Sgt. Slaughter leads the crowd in a rendition of "The Battle Hymn of the Republic," while Nikolai Volkoff drones what the announcer assures us is the Russian national anthem.

After the entry onto the fighting surface, which is as prescribed as Japanese Noh drama, the second act can begin. This is the "parade and pose," during which the combatants strut like roosters, snarl like tigers, howl like mad dogs, and often even climb the ring ropes like apes to show their personae. More than any wrestler, Gorgeous George in the 1950s set the tone for this act by having his valet come to disinfect the corner, set up a tea service, and prepare George's little throne. Since the demands of television are for immediate action, such elaborate ceremonies have been cut short. The referee checks the combatants' bodies for the infamous "foreign object," while the television announcer fills us in on what is at stake: the reputation of the Free World, the dignity of the family, the ancient unresolved grudges of races. We are always given a clear signal as to which side is personifying our hopes, and should we ever doubt, the villain will often announce his role by attempting a premature or an unsportsmanlike initiation of hostilities. He will not shake hands like a gentleman; he hits before the bell; he tries to throttle our hero while our hero is getting out of his costume. The announcer is outraged. "My goodness—it's just like Pearl Harbor up there." "This is most unsportsmanlike." "I'm shocked by this behavior." "Really, something should be done." "It looks like payback time coming up." "If this happens again we'll have to notify the Commissioner." The breach of conduct and the mandate for vengeance are established.

In Act III, the action begins in earnest, culminating in the villain's near victory and the hero's "reaching down deeper than ever before" to repel this attack and deliver his own. Often the villain is almost victorious by virtue of the referee, who always has his back turned when deceits are performed. In professional wrestling, Fate, the referee, is a stooge. Hair-pulling, having an arm or a leg outside the ring ropes, using the "foreign object," choking, and general misbehavior all occur while the crowd is imploring the referee to please look behind him and see what is happening! Our announcer will say something like, "I hate to say this, but really this disgusts me. Why won't he look? Something is going to have to be done." If the referee, perchance, does notice, he issues a warning that is recognized by all as thoroughly insincere. Only one person can reset the scales of justice.

This redress occurs as the hero, realizing now that he has been liberated from the laws of good sportsmanship, can become, *must* become, violent. The crowd has always known this. When violence is the only alternative, violence must out. Now is the time for villainy to suffer. "Give it to him," they yell, "make him suffer. Make him pay." "Yes indeed, it looks like payback time," says the television announcer as he launches into a litany of venerable clichés delivered like ancient kennings. The hero "unloads the heavy artillery," "administers punishment," "makes the challenger go to school," "powers out of submission holds," "has a ring savvy well beyond his age," and "drives the oxygen from the opponent body."

The final retribution is achieved through what is called a "hold" or a "move." All the movements of both wrestlers require collusion and often not-so-subtle illusion. The "forearm smash," for instance, requires foot-stamping to provide acoustic emphasis, as well as the backward hurl of the head to heighten the effect of impact. The "hold" is still more subtle. For instance, there are villains' holds like the "sleeper," in which the recipient nods off limply while the announcer says, "I hope [the villain] knows that he is legally responsible to revive his victim." Meanwhile, the victim's body is experiencing *rigor mortis*, jittering about in death throes. After the audience gasps, the villain wakes him and the victim behaves as if he has had a full night's sleep. He is often amazed

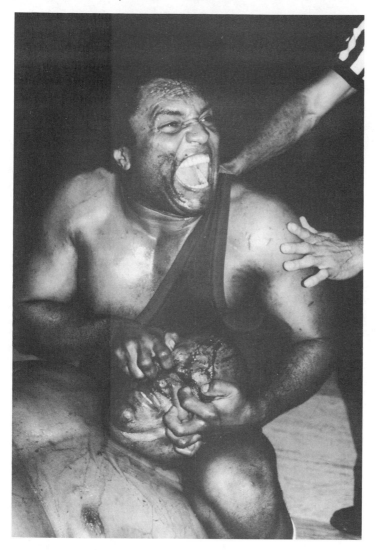

Carlos Colon and Abdulla the Butcher (George Napolitano)

to find he has lost the match. Other villainous favorites are the "pile-driver," in which the victim is jack-hammered head-first into the canvas, and the self-explanatory "heart-punch," "head-butt," and abdominal "claw." Of recent vintage is the "figure-four leglock," a submission hold in which the combatant's feet are pretzeled together and which can be applied by our hero only after it is first introduced by the heavy. The announcer opines, "This can do permanent damage. He will never walk normal again." Since the rise of gymnastics in the 1970s, the final *coup de grâce* often requires the victor to fly through the air, sometimes having leapt from the turnbuckle, and land, thud!, on his patiently waiting opponent.

Tully Blanchard and Robert Gibson (George Napolitano)

Until the 1980s blood was rarely, if ever, seen in a match. Now the "drawing of blood" has become a commonplace. This flash of red is evidence of authenticity, yet rarely is the blood from a legitimate wound. Usually it is from an incision which a combatant has inflicted on his own forehead with a small razor that he carries in his mouth or wristband or that he gets from his manager. He is exercised enough and his blood is pumping fast enough so that just a small prick will soon cover his face with what is called "juice" in the trade. Wrestlers' foreheads, especially those of the villains, are dotted with scar tissue. As Eddie Mansfield, a one-time heavy in the Southeast, told John Stossel on ABC's

20/20, "Blood runs green." By this, wrestlers mean that those who are willing to cut themselves are paid more. When a villain is bleeding, the crowd roars its excitement. When a hero is cut, the match comes to a stop. The villain backs off. The hero touches the blood with his hand and looks amazed, as if some threshold has now been crossed from which there can be no satisfaction short of utter brutality. The crowd is still. The tide turns. The villain must bleed.

Another recent development, again due to television, is in the actual field of battle. It is no longer the "squared circle" but has been extended to encompass the walkway around the ring. Wrestlers regularly hurl each other out of the ring into this perimeter and then continue pummeling, while the hapless referee proceeds to cajole, then warn, then count out the disqualifying "ten" count. Although the announcer assures us the combatants are being "thrown to the hard cement floor," here the wrestlers are especially careful. Many arenas spread gray gymnastic mats around the ring, just in case. Breakaway chairs from the first rows are conveniently empty so that they can be used, first by the villain and then by the hero.

Should the match end in a pinfall, the all-American will have his hand raised by the referee and then make a triumphal tour of the ring. Matadors have been accorded this passage for centuries, as were the knights and gladiators before them. Doubtless the ancient victors of the hunt paraded about the slain conquest with whoops of exhilaration. Violence is over, and no threat of revenge remains. If the match is for a championship—and on most wrestling cards, there is such a championship, even though it might be for the "Northeast Intercontinental Title of Georgia"—the victor will raise the trophy belt high above his head and bray. As with all other visual effects of this cartoon ritual, the belt is sparkling hyperbole. Twice the size of the belts won in boxing, these slabs of leather with their oversized medallions are continually referred to as the objects of intense desire. They are the holy grails of combat, the holy sepulchers—in a sense they are what is missing: displaced female attention. Wrestlers may even squabble in the ring like children on a playground over who is entitled to the belt. In regional matches and those televised in the studio, the victor will stop by the announcer's table after combat to express thanksgiving for having the belt, as well as to set up the context for the next battle for the belt.

The postmatch and especially the prematch interview have become, again because of television, a central part of the drama. The successful "'rassler" is not always the best stuntman but rather the best projector of his humor character. So figures like "Rowdy" Roddy Piper, who plays the part of *miles gloriosus;* Adrian Adonis, the underhanded sissy; Kevin Sullivan, the diabolical brat; Dusty Rhodes, the cornfed Texas plowboy; and George (Animal) Steele, the evolutionary throwback, are mediocre tumblers but coherent television personalities. They all have a particular presence and never violate the unity of their character. Their foil is the anemic announcer. His cravenness in the presence of their characters provides the internal norm. We see in the announcer's fawning affect how threatening their violence really is, and at the same time we imagine that we might be able to confront it.

While the five-act wrestling drama, like the five-act action/adventure drama, is rigorously prescribed in terms of beginning, middle, and end, it affords much internal variation. Whatever is visual, abrupt, and spectacular is soon absorbed. From the two-man match and the Australian tagteam (two men on a side who must "tag" each other in order to enter the ring; no one knows why "Australian"), variations abound and are cast through the evolutionary sieve of audience attention. So we now have the Steel Cage Match fought inside a barbed-, chicken-, or cyclone-wire cage from which the winner is the first one to escape. A variation is the Lights-Out Steel Cage Match, which is fought entirely in the dark, leaving little for the pugilists to do but grunt and groan and much for the audience to imagine. In the Canadian Lumberjack match, the ring is surrounded by other wrestlers so that the coward cannot escape. Although matches used to be the best two out of three falls, with television the limit is often stated as "television time remaining," which means the men must finish before the commercial. On ABC's *20/20* segment, we even see Vince McMahon telling one of his performers to "make it quick" since television time is almost up. The wrestler does. The match is all over in less than two minutes. The Texas Death Match, however, has the attraction of no such arbitrary limit. The end comes when one wrestler is unable to continue. Another Texan innovation is the Texas Bull Rope Match in which combatants are tied together with a cowbell in the middle of the rope. This is itself a variation of the Indian Death Match or the Chain Match in which a strap or a chain ties the fighters together. Such matches depend, of course, on having one of the actors play the part of the coward who wants to "cut and run." The hero pulls him back and makes him "fight like a man." When tempers are really flaring and a fight simply cannot be postponed, it is time for the free-for-all Bunkhouse Match or simply a Come-as-you-are Match. While the overtones of the Western frontier and the cowboy motifs are omnipresent in both the titles and the personae of these American innovations, in the ancient Battle Royal up to twenty wrestlers battle it down to the last king on the mountain or, in this case, canvas.

There are also women wrestlers—called "ladies" by the announcer in such sentences as "Now the ladies are really in a catfight." Midget wrestling exists as well. In both cases, the wrestlers imitate men and have no specifically distaff or dwarf routines other than more hair-pulling. The roles of bully, braggart, whiner, coward, narcissist, and other stereotypes are duplicated. Although there have been tag teams made up of midgets and giants, and all-female tag teams are popular, there seems little interest in mixed-sex teams. While men may taunt women, and women often have male managers who may become involved, hitting women is never countenanced, possibly because the code of vengeance would be too obvious to be invoked. This does not mean that from time to time men do not hit women; after all, it was just such a near act that roused Mr. T to take action and in so doing to inspire *WrestleMania*. With the rise of the women's movement, we may well see women wrestlers pummel some of the more cowardly men who will doubtlessly then be forced to respond.

Television programmers must respond not just to what can be broadcast to the small livingroom screen but also to what is compelling enough to attract and hold an audience. If they do their jobs successfully, they are themselves programmed by the audience in front of a small screen. They don't make viewing decisions so much as attempt to produce more of what can be consumed. Professional wrestling is the *The A-Team* of sports programming. It is the third most popular spectator "sport" in this nation. Such pantomime violence is the USA Cable Network's most popular show material, outdrawing even college football on Ted Turner's WTBS in Atlanta. Its allure is such that when *Saturday Night Live* was in the 1986–87 Nielsen doldrums, NBC aired *Main Event* as a once-a-month replacement. Professional wrestling's influence has even leaked into Saturday morning cartoon shows with CBS's *Rock 'n Wrestling*, which itself has spun off a family of wrestling toys. In addition, wrestling videos dedicated to individual wrestlers (*The Best of Hulk Hogan*, etc.) are popular rentals for those who wish to repeat the repetitious.

Clearly, these shows, toys, and promotions share much of the same young male audience. But why should these image sequences have proved so powerful that they dominate the airwaves? Why should such groundling entertainment make it through the web of programming, when so many of "us" can think of so many "better" attractions for "them"? Instead of either pretending such low and vulgar comedies don't exist or insisting that they should not exist, we might do well to see them in the context of what has endured through the ages. If Dr. Johnson was correct that "nothing can please many, and please long, but just representations of general nature," then what is the "general nature" of such theater? If these are the circuses which play out, and perhaps rearrange, our anxieties, what are those anxieties? Why haven't we grown out of them? And why, if they must be around, have we not developed a more tasteful way of expressing them? If such farce is the stuff of modern morality plays, what is the moral?

At the most obvious level, the action/adventure show and the televised all-male "sporting event" revolve around an easy-to-see-and-un-

derstand crisis. What television can do is to introduce not just fake violence but such preposterously fake violence that crucial parts of this crisis
are compressed and repeated *ad infinitum*. These rituals are outlined in
crayon. As the audience becomes younger, this outlined activity becomes more exaggerated and cartoonic. Women disappear. Objects like
belts replace them. Virtue and vice as expressed in characters come front
and center. The evil is foreign and unexpected, the good native and predictable. Enemies become distortions of adolescent anxiety; the heroes
become asexual titans. Once the synecdochic nature of conflict is established, the resolutions are treated as final. But, of course, they are not.
They will be repeated again and again until the audience switches channels. Such teletheater is, in Victor Turner's phrase, a liminal experience
played out between real and surreal, a masquerade of alternative behaviors, a map of possible routes of passage. The plots are endlessly played
out as exhibitions of attack, reversal, suffering, and salvation. The driving force remains the same. Violence, yes, but always in the safe confines of a prescribed resolution of hostilities.

Essentially the ur-adolescent myth is the monster story told over and
over. Something alien from out there comes in too close. It must be
pushed back far enough so that we are safe again. While it can't be
destroyed, it must be rendered incapable of revenge. It must be made
victim. It must be "counted out," disqualified, or rendered submissive.
With retelling, this tale becomes an allegory of life as perceived by an
audience fresh from the fairy tales and almost ready to be told the myths
of adulthood. As with fairy tales, these passion plays of adolescent
aggression are full of instructions: Stay together, fear the foreign, follow the leader, learn the boundaries, keep to the family, "know the
ropes," and most importantly, be prepared to fight. We may not always
like the messages such characters like Mr. T or Hulk Hogan offer as
resolutions to life's problems, but there is surely some need in the audience to hear them.

In these dreamlike worlds, one may dimly see the biosocial purpose
of violent display as part of the complex rite of passage. The audience
for such pantomimes willingly suspends disbelief and eagerly enters into
wishful thinking. Admittedly, some are confused some of the time, just
as we all were by fairy tales or by, say, Disney's *Snow White* or the
Three Stooges when the boundaries got blurred. We all go through a
period in which the wicked witch seems too real, and we wince when
Moe pokes Curley in the eye. This confusion is purposeful for these
entertainments are a variety of reality-testing through which we learn
to distinguish not truth from illusion but various degrees of truth
embedded in illusion. Ask almost any prepubescent viewer if *The A-
Team* violence is real and he will assure you that it is only "pretend."
Then ask if people are really shooting guns and flipping over cars, and

he will say yes, they are. Ask a wrestling fan if the action is real, and he will tell you essentially, "Of course not, it's fixed. But I hope my hero kills the SOB." Violence is not real, but the effects are, and during a period of adolescence many boys willingly give themselves over to certain of these effects. Successful rituals have it both ways: Violence is pretend, but it hurts. This is escapist fare to be sure, but the escape is temporary and ironically prepares the adolescent for the reentry into the predictable workaday world.

Although like *Punch and Judy* shows, stalk-and-slash movies, Stephen King novels, *EC* comics, penny dreadfuls, and dime novels, our contemporary televised displays of preposterous violence seem subversive, they are ultimately dramatizations of moral order. They seem bizarre, enacted as they are at the edge of social measurement, yet that is precisely their attraction. Such fables are dream work made visible, wishes fulfilled, fugues of breaking and reestablishing order. In them are the patterns of the culture, the articulations of the norms, the final establishmentarian doctrines of maturity. They pantomime what is too traumatic to learn by actual experience. These fictions prepare us for fact. Like fairy tales that prepare the child for the anxieties of separation, sequences of preposterous violence prepare the teenager for the anxieties of action. They are fantastic, ludicrous, crude, vulgar, and important distortions of real life situations, not in the service of repression or incitement (though they certainly have that temporary effect) but of socialization. These fantasies of aggression are neither for violence nor against it. What they abhor is unmediated and uncontrolled revenge. Such fables all reiterate the moral—get back in line—while at the same time they vouchsafe the vision of a life out of line, a life out of order.

7

Conclusion: Stay Tuned

Television is the first truly democratic culture—the first culture available to everybody and entirely governed by what the people want. The most terrifying thing is what the people do want.

CLIVE BARNES,
New York Times, 1969

It may seem willfully perverse to turn the critical language on its head, to consider judgments like mediocre, cultural wasteland, schlock, imitation, junk, spin-off, mindless, and even "terrifying" not as opprobrium but as accurate indicators of a centuries-old conflict over audience taste. As the English humorist Alan Coren has said, "Television is simply more interesting than people. If it were not, we should have people standing in the corners of our rooms." As much as we claim not to like the electronic interloper, we spend a considerable part of our day being entertained by it. No one asks us to buy a television receiver. No one makes us watch. Why blame the messenger when so many of us seem to want the message? Yet the concerns of many television critics today are the same as they were for the Victorian critics of popular print, to wit: The medium corrupts consciousness, the work ethic, natural desires, concentration, and culture itself. Somehow the dreck of the masses is changing the quality of an otherwise benign culture. The concerns of Matthew Arnold, Ortega y Gasset, T. S. Eliot, F. R. Leavis, and all protectors of the upper-class heritage still come through loud and clear: The Philistines are coming.[1] In the preceding chapters, I have argued that "Philistine" is often synonymous with "adolescent." Indeed, the words you will find in the vocabulary of television critics are reiterations of Victorian anxiety about what teenagers, mainly boys, were reading. So television dulls perception, flattens consciousness, manipulates desire, breeds decadence, fosters escapism, insulates the senses, rebarbarizes, infantilizes, is a narcotic, a plug-in drug, mediates experience, colonizes, pollutes, encourages commodity fetishism, leads to psychic privatization, makes us narcissistic and passive and superficial, and aggressive.

Television's triumphant sway over the electronic media or its impact on the adolescent audience cannot be denied. But does this "visitor in the corner" produce juvenile offenders, as contended by some of the more pessimistic social scientists, or merely more videots such as Chauncey Gardiner in Jerzy Kosinski's fable, *Being There?* Certainly, to most critics television provides a Hobson's choice: It either excites viewers to violent action or dulls their ability to act at all. Either our children are going to behave like Ronald Zamora, who overdosed on *Kojak*—or so his lawyer said—and murdered his next door neighbor, or worse yet, they will see too many sitcoms and go into politics like Ronald Reagan.

What the electronic media do is not as Panglossian as Marshall McLuhan promised, nor as apocalyptic as the Jeremiahs warn. At a fundamental level, television transmits stories that the masses of consuming viewers will stop to watch. As Paul Klein, in charge of programming at NBC in the early 1970s, theorized, since the size of audience is so crucial to how much income is generated, the networks attempt to broadcast the least objectionable programs. On both sides of the campfire, story teller and audience, there is a reward for a conservative folklore. Realizing this, how do we account for the increasing flood of violence on the airwaves? How do we account for the fact that, as Senator Paul Simon, a sponsor of one of the few bills to limit violence on TV, has written,

> Violence on television has risen more than 100 percent since 1980. From January to April (1986), prime-time television averaged 13.8 acts of violence per hour. The average child between the ages of 2 and 11 views television 27.3 hours each week. By the time a person is 16, he or she has watched over 20,000 hours of television, including 200,000 acts of violence, 50,000 of which are murders.

How do we account for the fact that mass-marketed fantasies are not only violent but becoming more so? How do we account for the fact that so many powerful critics, even governmental agencies, have so little influence? Once again, as with other mass media in the modern world, the explanation lies in the downward shift in audience age and the upward shift in that audience's disposable income. To see the impact of this audience, we will look at a few of the most recent and violent developments in the industry: toy-based cartoons, video games, music videos, and thanks to the videocassette recorder, the influx of movies which find their way to the youth market on videotape.

The explosion of violence in juvenile programming began innocently enough. In 1969, executives at the Mattel Company in Southern California had a brilliant idea. Instead of sponsoring entertainment with their advertising monies, why not create their own television show around their products and then get someone else to buy the advertising? Since the commercials on children's shows had always been more entertaining than the programs, and since the audience didn't know the difference, why not quit pretending? Make the entire show into a commercial. Mattel's show, based on their toy tricycle, was to be called *Hot Wheels*. But just as *Hot Wheels* was about to air, the Tonka Corporation, which had its own big wheels spinning, cried "foul" to the Federal Communications Commission. The rules of the television road were being violated. The FCC agreed with Tonka, decreeing that *Hot Wheels* "subordinated programming in the interest of the public to programming in the intent of salability." *Hot Wheels* was garaged.

The doors remained closed for the next decade. The FCC was worried about the intrusion of advertising into programming and especially cautious about the excesses of violence when the advertising and/or programming was directed toward children. But in 1981 Mark Fowler, a Reagan campaign stalwart whose fame rested primarily on his famous definition of television as "just another appliance—a toaster with pictures," was appointed to the chairmanship of the FCC. Within two years, the garage doors swung open and "hot wheels" spun out onto the tarmac of television. What followed were such violent shows as *He-Man*, *G.I. Joe*, *Thundarr the Barbarian*, *Blackstar*, *Mr. T*, and a host of other violent vigilantes who literally pounded good sense and manners into evil villains while all the time selling toys. The days of Bugs Bunny, Woody Woodpecker, Mighty Mouse, Popeye, and even the Road Runner were over. Gone also were such shows as *Captain Kangaroo*, *Kids Are People Too*, and children's specials. There was to be no protection from the ratings, and the ratings clearly showed that exaggerated aggression was what made the youngsters stop turning the dial and watch.

Once the advertising restrictions were lifted, the airwaves were overrun with preposterous violence. Not only did the cartoon ghetto of Saturday morning turn hyperactive, but weekday afternoon programming, the once-docile after-school time slot, was quickly co-opted by essentially violent cartoons advertising war toys. There are now almost thirty different shows. Before Fowler's FCC decision, there was only one. These shows are broadcast from one to five times a week in a never-ending loop of reruns. While violent cartoons consumed an hour and a half in 1982, they now account for more than forty-three hours of weekday programming. The National Coalition on Television Violence estimates that any American child between four and eight years of age will see 250 episodes of war cartoons and over 1,000 ads for war toys each year—the equivalent of twenty-two days of classroom instruction. While the most violent shows like *Inhumanoids, Centurions: Power Xtreme, G.I. Joe, Gobots,* and *Transformers* have between sixty to eighty violent acts per episode—far in excess of the nonanimated *A-Team*'s usual forty—the commercials are more violent still. Thanks again to the lenient FCC, the commercials of these show-length commercials have a bone-rattling six acts of violence per every thirty-second slot, more than triple the rate of the show itself. Whatever is attractive to the pubescent audience about the kinetic pacing of the episodes is still more attractive in the commercials.

The toys which sponsor the shows which sponsor the toys are not from Barbie and Ken's neighborhood. They are more likely to be from the thunder-and-lightning world of Zeus and Hercules. They include Hasbro, Inc.'s Transformers, which in turn include the evil Decepticons, like Shockwave. The inscription on the package informs us that Shockwave is "a military operations commando with a cold brutal scientific approach to war . . . using nuclear energy [and] can be manipulated from a laser gun to a robot." The old standby, G.I. Joe, also from Hasbro, comes with a cadre of thirty-four different good and bad troopers which can be purchased individually, as can their mines, mortars, laser rifles, AK-47 attack rifles, missiles, flying submarines (!), and whatever else is necessary "to protect democracy from the evil enemy." Needless to say, all "troopers" are male except Lady Jayne, a U.S. covert operations spy. The *G.I. Joe* cartoon, which shows the squad in heroic action, is seen five days a week in almost forty-five percent of the country, achieving, as Hasbro touts proudly, "penetration into ninety percent of the cabled nation." With a life-span of a little over two years, "concept toys" appear in easy-to-purchase "separates" which Junior can collect. Just as he is about to complete the collection, another new entourage appears to encourage him anew. There are many other such concept toys, like Manteck, Omni Force, Starriors, Super Powers, Beast Machines, Gobots, Thundercats, and RoboForce.

The progenitor of the modern bash-'em-up storm troopers is Prince Adam, a.k.a. He-Man, who, together with the Masters of the Universe, is continually at war. He-Man did for Mattel what Hot Wheels was unable to do. He opened up both the airwaves and the shopping aisles. In the early 1980s when Mr. Fowler and the FCC allowed commercially based commercials to leak into public view, He-Man existed as a minor league plastic figurine protecting his natal Castle Grayskull from the evil Skeletor. In a merchandising coup, "Filmation Associates," a subsidiary of Westinghouse, animated a fantasy around this 5½-inch plastic warrior and tried to sell it to the networks. *He-Man and the Masters of the*

Universe was a crude, poorly crafted cartoon, but it was full of screen-bursting violence. The networks, still cautious about the relationship between advertising and entertainment, were timid. However, hundreds of independent stations were desperate for "filler" shows to put on the air before the profitable prime time began at 8:00 p.m. The number of independents had tripled between 1972 and 1980, and most of them were unable to afford the prices of afternoon syndicated reruns which the majors ran primarily to cover these mid-afternoon doldrums. The independent stations bought *He-Man* and in so doing essentially allowed the toy companies to create their own temporary networks.

Filmation syndicated sixty-five half-hour shows to these independents through what is now called "barter syndication." Essentially the toy company or animator exchanges the video sequences advertising its toy in return for air time. The station then sells part or all of the commercial time and pockets the proceeds. Professional wrestling had also used this tax-free system to barter video footage for "promotional consideration," i.e., advertising of upcoming matches. Financial arrangements could become Byzantine as licensees joined the mêlée, selling rights to incorporate the toy's logo or image on everything from bubblegum to bedsheets. By the time *Thundercats* came to the market in the mid-1980s, Lorimar Telepictures cut a deal whereby they paid the station a percentage return based on how well the toys were selling in the broadcast area. In order to maximize its return, the television station saturated its audience with specific toy-driven cartoons. The more toys sold, the larger the station's cut.

Keeping up with the "kidvid" deals was enough to tax the endurance of Voltron CPAs and Gobot lawyers. Clearly, success was worth the effort. Since He-Man made his television debut in 1983, Mattel has sold almost 150 million Masters of the Universe figurines at $4.50 apiece. Lined up two by two, the 5½-inch figures would stretch from Los Angeles to New York and back. Little wonder that Cannon films and Mattel invested almost $20 million to have Dolph Lundgren, the evil boxer of *Rocky IV* fame, play He-Man in the movie version, or that there are several different He-Man magazines and books, or that Mattel has a Stanford University psychologist on the payroll (as well as on the credit run) to insert prosocial messages, or that He-Man now has a sister, Adora, a.k.a. She-Ra, Princess of Power, who rides a unicorn with a "groomable mane." We're not talking toy here, we're talking money pump.

The current threat to He-Man and the warriors of the airwaves is not from competing pectorals but from a new cross-over technology—this one created by combining arcade games with television. Such hybrids are usually compelling; after all, the He-Man craze was the result of televised myth and plasticine doll. The new threat is from "interactive

He-Man and Masters of the Universe (Mattel Toys)

toys,'' which respond to sound or light impulses sent over television. Once again Mattel is leading the market with *Captain Power and the Soldiers of the Future.* With the ''Power Jet'' in hand, the player shoots at moving objects on the screen, usually at Lord Dread, and the light signals emitted from the set record the score on the gun. Each half-hour show has only a few minutes of such ''interactive'' play, and even the videocassette version has about fifteen minutes' worth. Most of the time is spent in explaining instructions, or in exhorting viewers to pressure their parents for the expensive equipment. Nolan Bushnell, who pioneered video games at Atari, has his own variation called *TechForce and the Moto-Monsters.* In this system, sound frequencies activate motorized war toys. The child lines up the toys in front of the set before the show starts and then passively watches as they are guided into combat.

In the wash of technological innovations which has followed television, success has come to those hybrids which have been able not just to combine extant entertainments but to increase the level of preposterous violence. As each new cross-technology has entered the marketplace, it has met with adolescent enthusiasm and parental censure. Two of the most startling innovations of the late 1970s and early 1980s were video games, which combined pinball and television, and music videos, which combined rock songs with television. Although both amusements have exhausted their initial mass audiences and are now in declining periods, their rapid expansion and almost as rapid contraction show how quickly the dynamics of adolescent demand can draw forth scenarios of exagger-

Boys competing against *Captain Power and the Soldiers of the Future*
(Mattel Toys)

ated conflict. Put a roll of quarters, or a remote-control channel switcher,
into the hand of a teenage boy and he will find a way to "tune in"
turbulence and shock.

Video arcades, entertainment dens in the mall-caves of the modern
shopper, seem to be the descendants of the all-male clusters common in
many aboriginal societies. Although most adults enter these video haunts
only to hustle Junior out, the arcades are worth a leisurely tour. These
are the clubhouses of today's adolescents: tree houses in neon and cement. With names like "Aladdin's Castle," "Time Zone," "Dream Machine," "Funway Freeway," and "Barrel of Fun," these dimly lit grot-
toes are populated predominantly by males.[2] Like the shooting gallery
at the fair and the pinball machine down at the boys' club, the video
arcade has developed into a single-sex subculture with its own etiquette
and argot. For instance, to reserve a game, called "jamming," one places
a quarter in the appropriate place (different on each console); one never
touches or talks to someone who is playing, even to offer advice; one
maintains a territorial distance from a player so as not to interfere with
body motions; and players converse in a private language. In the jargon
of the arcade, "hyperspace" is the area of the screen into which one
maneuvers to escape attack, to "kill" is not only to destroy an attacker
but to master a game, a "wally" is a large flying saucer or meteor, a
"wraparound" refers to a shot which leaves the screen only to return

on the opposite side, and a "wave" is an assault with a distinct beginning and an end, as opposed to a "round" which may feature several waves. This is a private world, a world of pantomime violence and ritualized aggression.

The evolution of video games from Nolan Bushnell's *Pong*, which was little more than a white disk "bouncing" back and forth across a dark screen, to *SuperPong*, *QuadraPong*, *Pong Doubles*, *Breakout*, *Super-Breakout* . . . all the way to *Zaxxon*, *Berzerk*, and *Eliminator*, illustrates the compressed history of an amusement in the future-shock world of microchips.[3] Although the games look alike to the casual observer, there are at least six distinct types, almost all of which are unreservedly violent: (1) driving games in which you drive a race car until it crashes (*Turbo*, *Monaco GP*), (2) space-invader games in which you fire guns upward at enemies (*Centipede*, *Galaga*), (3) free-flight games in which you attempt to avoid obstacles while destroying attackers (*Asteroids*, *Star Castle*), (4) defender games in which you move in all directions while evading, repelling, and destroying attackers (*Scramble*, *Zaxxon*), (5) obstacle games in which you try to make your way from the bottom of the screen to the top (*Frogger*, *Donkey Kong*), and (6) maze games in which you do the same through walled passages, avoiding and/or pursuing others (*Pac-Man*, *Targ*). In addition, a new generation of game has appeared: *Battlezone* and *Q1X* either use three-dimensional graphics or else place the player in a cockpit which moves in sync with the screen. However, the essential nature of pursuit, escape, attack, and dominance is maintained. Like our prehistoric ancestors who went deep into the cave to throw spears at the images etched on the wall, this young generation does the same with buttons marked "fire" and "destroy."[4]

By their very nature, video games demand movement, and since this movement is visual, violence is almost mandated. When *TV Guide*, at the height of national interest in December 1982, reviewed eighteen games that could be played on home sets, they judged fourteen violent, two nonviolent, and two mixed (*Pitfall*—avoid being eaten by alligators—and *Frogger*—avoid being crushed by cars). Of Atari's *Berserk*, the *Guide* comments, "The game's main idea is to shoot it out against a gang of robots inside a maze—much like Wyatt Earp and the Clantons did at the OK Corral. It's a violent mess, of course, but nobody ever said it wasn't *very* exciting. Earlier this year, a young man in Indiana who was playing the coin-op *Berzerk* died of heart failure" (p. 54). Of the two nonviolent games, *E.T.* entailed moving back to the spaceship before "energy" ran out, and *Word Zapper*, a spelling game, let you shoot at letters. What could be more nonviolent than spelling? Again, the *Guide*:

> Distraught parents who worry that video games are the reason why Johnny can't read may settle for this game as a compromise. Call it

"Shoot 'n Spell." After a word is flashed briefly on the screen, the child is asked to spell it again from memory by shooting individual letters from a moving alphabet. Fortunately, the words are drawn from an alien language called "English." (Albin, p. 54)

If arcade games are the result of cross-breeding the pinball machine with the television screen, then the music video is the hybrid offspring of the 45 rpm record and the camera. In both entertainments, the cathode-ray tube sprays electrons across the visual fields of an adolescent audience for the profit of an industry barely extant a decade ago. While arcade games depend on quarters moving directly into a machine, in music videos the fantasy encourages the flow of quarters, or rather dollars, into the coffers of record companies. Call them art or junk, music "clips" are essentially advertisements. In fact, the genre has ancestors in filmstrips made in the late 1940s called "soundies," in which musicians and models posed and lip-synced lyrics to impress booking agents and Hollywood producers. In the early 1980s these "soundies" were revived by a moribund recording industry as promotional material for bands on tour. If a booking agent wanted to see how a group performed before engaging them, the musicians sent along a videotape. These performance tapes proved so popular that on August 1, 1981, MTV (Music Television Network) started to broadcast them in approximately four-minute segments twenty-four hours a day. The tapes were such a success that "concept videos," in which the song was acted out by performers other than the musicians, were soon added. In turn, these musical fables were so popular that the vignettes appeared on variety shows, news programs, and even on their own celebratory award show. In 1981 MTV reached 2.5 million homes; by the mid-1980s it entered fifteen times that number. The record industry's gamble had paid off: From 1982 to 1984 album sales of popular music increased by thirty-one percent.

Thus the impact of video was immediate, transforming not only the recording industry but popular music itself. Performers who could sing as well as project a slightly outrageous persona (called "great visuals"), such as Boy George, Prince, Cyndi Lauper, Billy Idol, Tina Turner, and especially Michael Jackson, became "recording artists." Mainline television programs like *Miami Vice* and *Hollywood Beat* were specially formatted to capitalize on the new imagery and pacing. Plots of such adventure shows soon included musical interludes lifted straight out of the MTV repertoire. Even news shows like *West 57th* were organized around musical scenarios. *Flashdance* and *Beverly Hills Cop* translated the stop-and-go modular techniques to film. For a while even the advertisers, who had helped introduce the music video, were the recipients of their own frantic styles. Coke, Levis, and Ford "spots" were almost interchangeable with what could be seen on MTV, except that the ads were in thirty-second segments. In fact, the advertisement and the music video occasionally interpenetrated. Michael Jackson promoted Pepsi in his videos and made Pepsi commercials that were "knock-offs" of these videos. What had started in 1969 with Mattel's *Hot Wheels* was complete: the entertainment was the advertisement and the advertisement was the show.

If the art of television is advertising, then MTV is an entire network dedicated to art. Quick cutting, slow dissolves, computer-generated images, animation, wild angles, multiple-image montages, hallucinatory special effects, Chromakey, magnified close-ups, masked screens—everything implied in that portmanteau term "state of the art" was involved. No wonder that Brian De Palma, Martin Scorsese, John Sayles, John Landis, and even Andy Warhol lined up to try the viewfinder. Here was a chance to make an *Andalusian Dog, Entr'acte,* or *Mecanique* and be paid for it. And little wonder as well that MTV suffered the modern reward of success—decreased audience share. Although MTV was to rule the weekday airwaves, the weekend audience was soon worn away by competition. Soon most videos were available to any station which promised to broadcast them. NBC had *Friday Night Videos,* WTBS had *Night Tracks,* but by the time ABC, the latecomer, tried *New York Hot Tracks* the audience had dispersed. MTV, which at the height of video mania in 1983–84 was the sole broadcaster of Michael Jackson's *Thriller,* capturing 1.2 percent of its potential audience, soon saw half of its audience go elsewhere.

The bloom is now off the video rose, yet its budding and fading show in almost time-lapse images what occurs in the entertainment garden of adolescents. While shifts in print content took generations, and shifts in filmic subjects took decades, shifts in television fashions happen in months. While no one was really looking but the kids, a strain of music video turned violent. Or, more appropriately, an audience clustered which demanded and rewarded a different level of visual activity. These aggressive videos, as the *New York Times* entertainment writer Jon Pareles has observed, were a continuation of male teenage maturation stories for the television generation: "The next step after Masters of the Universe is the likes of Billy Idol, Poison, Cinderella and other bands that look just threatening enough to get attention, but sound slick enough for radio play" ("Rock Video Refocuses on the Music"). To consolidate this next step, a new music was called for, a music which could provide the aural context for visual excitement, a music which had been lingering on hard-rock radio channels but had never been visually broadcast.

This new music was heavy metal, appropriately named for its reliance on the amplification of instruments which produce a harsh metallic sound. This distinctly urban sound resembled an amplified traffic jam. The accompanying imagery on video was rife with stilettos, chains, leathers, tortured women, monsters, dirty streets, male strutting, gang warfare, and all the trappings of urban male aggression.[5] Lyrics were all but obliterated. This was *West Side Story* not as high romance but as a punk mating call. No one ever argued that heavy metal was the music to sooth the savage breast—quite the opposite. This was the music of stage-diving, slam-dancing, and in the self-descriptive term of praise, head-banging. Groups of mediocre talent but with an arresting presentation of rage, such as Twisted Sister, Ozzy Osbourne, Judas Priest, AC/DC, Ronnie Dio, Mötley Crüe, Def Leppard, Ratt, KISS, Iron Maiden, Stray Cats, and Quiet Riot, as well as groups of almost no talent but even more pugnacious affect, like the Dead Kennedys, 3 Teens Kill 4, Sadistic Faction, Savage Republic, Pseudo Sadists, Alien Sex Fiend, and Rash of Stabbings, soon commandeered almost a third of MTV's clips. In time, they also attracted adult attention and predictable censure. In 1984 when the National Coalition on Television Violence surveyed more than nine hundred videos which had been shown on MTV and WTBS, they found that violence and sadism had extended into other videos as well. According to NCTV's press release (January 10, 1984), almost half of the video segments had become violent, averaging 17.9 violent acts per hour.[6]

While this overall percentage is less than prime-time action/adventure sequences, the acts portrayed in videos were especially violent. In fact, these offspring of Tom Nero were so preposterously violent that they demanded *not* to be taken seriously. Doctoral dissertations (of which there have been four) relating such viewing to increased anxiety and antisocial behavior notwithstanding, the videos so simple-mindedly personified pubescent male wish-fulfillment that they were self-consciously ridiculous. To wit: KISS's "All Hell's Breaking Loose" is an orgy of knives, fists, and swords directed primarily at critics of the band; Def Leppard's "Foolin' " has, among other outrages, skulls bursting into flame to the lyrics of "Does anybody care, anybody out there, do you really care?"; and Ronnie Dio's "The Last in Line" has critics of the band wired into helmets and electrocuted whenever the band plays certain noxious guitar chords. Presumably in the spirit of affirmative action, Mötley Crüe's "Looks that Kill" has a sexy laser-shooting woman who sets the band afire. He plays the unwilling/willing fly to her long-nailed, whip-toting spider. Twisted Sister's "We're Not Gonna Take It" has the father of an adolescent musician fall out of a window, dragged by the hair, and repeatedly slammed in the face by a door, all to the accompaniment of "We're not gonna take it any more . . . we'll fight, you'll see." When Dee Snider testified in 1985 before a Senate subcommittee investigating violence in popular music albums and videos, he explained that this video was merely a "cartoon with human actors playing variations on the Road Runner and Wile E. Coyote theme. Each stunt was

Alice Cooper (Jerry Olhinger)

selected from my personal collection of cartoons" (quoted by Zucchino, p. 66).

Record jackets reiterated the simple-minded aggression of the videos. The Plasmatics' *Metal Priestess* cover shows the female singer in spiked bra and leather boots glaring from the cover. Iron Maiden's *Piece of Mind* features a human mutant chained to a wall. Savage's *Loose & Lethal* has a Hell's Angel type cleaving the skull of a colleague whose blood and brains are spurting forth. The Scorpions' *Blackout* features forks stuck in the eyes of a strait-jacketed victim, while Quiet Riot's *Mental Health* pictures yet another poor unfortunate with a spiked mask chained over his head. Such images of aggression and violence also form a leitmotif in rock fan magazines—fanzines—which are a peculiar amalgam of album graphics and *EC* comics. In *Rock Video Magazine, Rock Fever Magazine, Rock Lives, Song Hits,* and others of indeterminate life-span, an endless pastiche of threatening fists, obscene gestures, transsexual make-up, feigned knife fights, torture, Nazi costuming, snarling androgyny, and all manner of self-conscious and not very convincing braggadocio passes in pubescent review. They are the same motifs seen in horror films, in professional wrestling, and in the panoply of cartoonic entertainment. In fact, there is not much image differentia-

Dee Snider (Mark Weiss)

tion between KISS, *Night of the Living Dead*, Dracula, the Road Warriors wrestling tag team, and *EC* comics. These sequences are the ten-
tative trying-out postures of budding male aggression, the "let's pretend,"
the "what ifs" of adolescent fantasy. What separates these sequences
from those of the past is not so much content as the speed of transmission and consumption.

While afternoon promotional cartoons like *He-Man* originated with
the toy manufacturers, and the music video was "packaged" by the record companies, a third hybrid on the television screen came from a one-
time competitor and then a major supplier of "product"—the film industry. Once again, a technological innovation—the videocassette recorder, or more appropriately, *player*—was responsible for expanding an
existing medium and including a still broader audience. The astonishing
growth of the VCR industry (VCRs are now in more than half of all

Mötley Crüe (Barry Levine)

The Road Warriors tag team (George Napolitano)

W.A.S.P. (Moshe Brakha)

American households) allowed the adolescent male back into yet another marketplace of myth. Parents and theater management might be able to exercise control over who could pass the box office, but no such control was possible at the neighborhood rental store. Rarely are ratings checked by store clerks, and when they are, an older adolescent can always rent the film and have his younger friends over to see it. Since most video outlets have memberships registered in a family name, there is really no control over who finally will be seeing the film.[7]

As the rental prices dropped and the supply of movies increased, the same audience which had patronized *Punch and Judy*, the bloody pulps, the Saturday matinee, and *EC* comics began to appear at the video store. In 1986 when the Junior League surveyed ten- to thirteen-year-old children in several areas of New York, they found that the average child watched four R-rated videos per month. The violent strain of the horror genre—*Halloween*, *Friday the 13th*, and *Nightmare on Elm Street*—made up twenty percent of their favorites. Typically, almost a third of the youngsters had seen *Nightmare on Elm Street* on videotape, and almost all of those reported they had seen it an average of four times (Junior League, p. 1). Even allowing for the bravado of the respondents, it is clear that all over the country adolescents are walking into one of the 27,000 video stores and walking out with cinematic myths they would not otherwise be able to consume.

While this proves once again how thorny the enforcement of adult censure of adolescent entertainment can become (many states are requiring the display of the Motion Picture Association of America rating and enforcement at the cash register), it also illustrates the depth of demand for certain violent fables. Content aside, video rentals show what occurs when various audiences enter the market and bid for their stories. There are some 1.5 billion transactions a year essentially answering the question: "What fable do I want to see tonight?" Not only do young males give greater currency to existing fables of aggression, but they also actually cause new variations to be introduced. Video films like *Bloodsucking Freaks, Ilsa, She-Wolf of the SS, Make Them Die Slowly, Alien Prey, Flesh Feast, 2,000 Maniacs,* and the trilogy from Troma Productions (*The Toxic Avenger, Class of Nuke 'Em High,* and *Surf Nazis Must Die*) were either specifically made for, or rereleased on cassettes expressly for, this audience. While a Hollywood movie usually needs to gross millions of dollars to be successful, the calculations for videotape rentals are usually made in the thousands. Their very cheapness becomes an asset reinforcing the aspect of forbidden viewing. As George Romero showed in his *Night of the Living Dead,* this audience does not value clarity of production as much as the promise that they are part of an underground, a cult, which has its own shared, yet private, stories.

The most famous of these "video nasties," as the genre is known in the trade, is a videotape of film clips that often show violent death and are entitled *Faces of Death.* As is typical of marginally contraband entertainment, the provenance of the images in this videotape was deliberately vague. The best explanation that *Variety,* the trade newspaper for the radio, television, movie, and now the video industries, could produce was that the original footage was assembled in Japan for theatrical release ("*Faces of Death:* Media Flap"). A production company called "FOD Enterprises" (controlled by William Burrud, Jr., whose father produced such wholesome entertainment as *Wild Kingdom*) purchased the rights, rewrote the script, and added an internal narrator who linked the segments. The tape was then distributed to retail stores by MPI, a large midwestern supplier of videotapes. Each party along the distribution chain had what in post-Watergate politics is called "instant deniability"—a lack, contrived or not, of knowledge about what the product is and where it came from.

What is clear, however, is where the product is going. Never originally shown in theaters, *Faces of Death* is one of the most popular rental docudramas—or in *Variety*'s shorthand, "deathumentaries"—for older teenagers. Although the video rental industry keeps no tabs on its own demographics other than by general listings like "adult comedy," "action/adventure," "children's," or "horror," the *New York Times* reports that *FOD* is "a cult favorite among high school and college students" (Nordheimer, p. 15). The film is, in fact, a kind of exit ceremony from adolescence, as illustrated by the fact that it is often shown to groups of dating couples. "Can you endure it?" is the criterion of judgment, just as "Can you ride it?" was the earlier challenge of the loop-the-loop. As compared to the horror film, however, the mutual agreement between audience and film is that this is not a "movie," as in "Oh, this is just a movie," but rather this is "real life."

As did its horror film cousins, the *Faces of Death* family expanded to meet increased audience demand. The first *FOD* was released in 1983 with no promotion or hype. Within a year it was selling a modest 10,000 copies. Although it is hard to estimate the number of viewers for films like this which are usually watched in groups, perhaps 100,000 people had seen the tape by 1984. As demand increased from rental outlets, Burrud assembled *Faces of Death Part 2* and then three years later *FOD Part 3*. Although word-of-mouth was the primary promotion, occasional critical outrage also spurred demand. When Gene Siskel and Roger Ebert damned the series in 1987 on *Sneak Previews* as a particularly reprehensible example of "mutilation and sadism," the mention boosted sales by 8,000 units ("*Faces of Death:* Homevid Pulls Series," *Variety*). Such popularity, however, also proved fatal. *FOD Part 4*, which MPI claimed was "in the production pipeline," was halted. The actual buyers of the cassettes were not the viewing public but the purchasing agents of video rental stores. The large chains like National Video, Blockbuster Video, and Video World did not want to be singled out for criticism. These tapes were only a small part of their inventory, and hence most stores were unwilling to defend them. Perhaps more to the point, the three cassettes already on the market were so similar that it was doubtful whether a fourth would increase market share.

Since the later *FOD*s were not just highly derivative but essentially copies of the first success, it might be worthwhile to catalog the major sequences of the original tape. In these clips we are shown a pastiche of "forbidden scenes." We are told the story of what happens at the end of human aggression, reminded that violence and death are a part of the natural process. Our informant is the avuncular Dr. Francis B. Gröss, the "renowned pathologist," whom we watch as he strips his surgical robes after a particularly grueling open-heart operation. Why a pathologist is involved in this operation is not clear, but the fact that the patient dies might be the reason. We know the patient dies because we watch the operation. We hear the heart monitor beep, see the blinking dot, and witness the blinks and beeps abruptly stop. We even see the pulsing heart muscle suddenly freeze as if the movie frame has stopped (indeed it has). We see death. We follow Dr. Gröss from the operating room into his hospital office where, to the strains of gentle organ music, we have a chance to chat about death. He is an affable man who has seen what we boys have not. He has seen death on a daily basis. In fact, Dr. Gröss has made a study of death. As the camera dollies in, he bows his head, pushes his half-glasses further down his nose, and addresses us in a professorial tone. Perhaps we might want to know a bit more about death. If so, we might stay to watch.

What follows is a veritable *Mondo Cane* of violent death, a "text" of fiction and fact interwoven by Dr. Gröss in such a skillful way that by the time we have figured out the fiction, we are watching the fact. In no way is Dr. Gröss ironic or mocking. He is always the scholar. If you ask a group of viewers, as I have, whether they believe Dr. Gröss is a real doctor, they assure you he is. Only when you slow down the credit run at the end of the film will you find that "Francis Gröss is portrayed by Michael Carr." Even then, young viewers have told me that this doesn't change a thing. Francis Gröss is real, and he really is a student of death. Telling them that "Gröss" (complete with umlaut) is not a German name but rather the way Americans think a German name should look, does little to convince them. The point is that, unlike viewers of horror films in which the violence is contrived, this audience wishes to believe what it now sees is true, almost as if to have done with it. No matter, Gröss seems to imply, the subject of violent death is important to contemplate in all its manifold forms. Quit worrying about whether it is real or not. We are old enough to study death as he has.

While we are thus lectured about death in general, we watch a burial. The casket is being lowered into the grave when, suddenly, the camera angle shifts, giving us the dead man's point of view. We watch helplessly as shovelfuls of dirt are tossed over him/us. For the audience which has seen hundreds of horror movies, this is a standard subjective camera "buried-alive" sequence and merits a few hoots of derision. From here on, however, the framing devices of fantasy are dropped, or seem to be, and the audience's hooting stops. So that we are disabused of our juvenile view of nature inherited from Romanticism, we now do what Aldous Huxley proposed for William Wordsworth: We take a trip up the Amazon. We see feeding piranha, snakes swallowing mice, bug-eating bugs, and blowgun-toting Indians shooting monkeys and shrinking human heads. We go to Africa where we watch the Masai slaughter water buffalo by cutting the jugular vein so that blood spurts as from a faucet. Animal death seems a proper way to introduce the "liminoids" to the subject of nature "red in tooth and claw." Dr. Gröss is showing us this footage from his "private collection" to help us understand. This is, we are repeatedly told, an "educational experience." Our instructor rarely expresses outrage until he comes closer to home. When we see pit bulls battle to a bloody death, even the good doctor admits to being repelled by man's "conditioning a species to declare war on its own kind." And when we next see a rooster beheaded by a "farmer's wife" (although she is wearing dark glasses), he suggests that vegetarianism almost seems an alternative. As he says this, we see the headless rooster flying about to an elevator-music rendition of "Old MacDonald Had a Farm." The music takes a particularly sardonic turn as beer-barrel polkas are softly played while we watch the graphically bloody slaughter of cows and sheep "in the kosher method." Vegetarianism does indeed seem an alternative.

The next segment is especially difficult for the audience to categorize. We are told of a ritual among gourmets which "students of death might find of interest." In what appears to be a Hong Kong restaurant, two Caucasian couples—they seem to be Americans—are ushered into a private room and seated at a dining table. The table has a hole in the middle. A squealing monkey is placed in this hole, his head fixed above the table in a neck vise. We see this operation from all angles including the point of view of the monkey. The men then take small hammers and appear to beat the monkey to death. The maître d' arrives, opens the cranium, and the couples eat what we are told is fresh, warm, monkey brains. This meal is, as Dr. Gröss explains, a celebration that even *he* cannot understand.

Neither can we, and it is almost a relief to return to the "legal" clubbing of seals on the Pribilof Islands and the "illegal" poaching of alligators in Florida. But eventually we break away from scenes of cruel man vs. innocent animal to what appear to be the "out-takes" of a television news show. A wildlife warden, after talking to a television news reporter about the menace of a stray alligator, rows into a thicket of sawgrass and attempts to lasso the rogue alligator. We watch as the warden seems to be yanked out of the boat and drawn under the water. This sequence is riveting because we watch the filming of the television crew filming the incident. We don't see what is happening as much as we see how the reporter responds. It does not occur to us that we are being gulled by our own predisposition to believe what we are seeing, because we are, after all, seeing what is being seen by another camera. This I-camera technique, which worked so well in *Peeping Tom* and in hundreds of horror films since, shows how dependent our visual sense is on point of view. That we don't see the alligator, that we cut to the turbid waters roiling with red "blood," that we don't even see the purported loss of the warden's leg doesn't overwhelm our credulity. Since so much of what we have seen so far is real, this must be too.

Again we segue back to uncontested reality. Again it is back to the morgue for us. We watch cadavers being cut open to the sounds of ripping paper and xylophone chords. We talk with the famous Thomas Noguchi, Los Angeles coroner and a favorite of the tabloids. We see bodies decomposing in fields and mutilated in automobile and airplane accidents. At last, we students of death are ready to be introduced to the purposeful taking of human life—the death penalty. Dr. Gröss doesn't know if what we will see is a deterrent at all; in fact, he is skeptical. But he is also a scientist. If the death penalty is a deterrent, how can it deter unless we watch it? So we do. Or, at least, we watch a reasonable facsimile thereof.[8] We watch a convicted killer poisoned with cyanide ("This graduate of the penal system is taking his last exam"), another electrocuted ("His time has come. It does for us all"), and a third beheaded ("We will have to go to the Middle East to see this display").

Perhaps chastened by now, we return to still another vignette, one supposedly filmed in San Francisco. We observe a coven of hippies as they smear themselves with the internal organs of a dead woman. Of all the minidocumentaries in the film, this one seems the most amateurish, complete with a bare-breasted female smearing herself with what Dr. G. assures us is human blood. Clearly, the sequence is a remnant of the infamous "snuff" films of the 1970s, which claimed to be the "real" killing and dismemberment rituals of "Brazilian thrill seekers." The doctor calmly opines that this is "just another of the many faces of death." As is the case in the other inserts, no time is wasted in entering or exiting from the fragment. So off to Appalachia we go to watch snake handlers, then to New Orleans for a suicide jump, then over to Arizona for cryogenic suspension, then out to California for washed-ashore bodies, and then to Wyoming for an outrageous bear attack in which the filming technique of the alligator attack is repeated. We watch the film of a tourist filming a tourist filming a bear in Yellowstone. Again we don't actually see the animal attack; instead we watch the camera-pointing tourist react with horror as the bear-filming tourist is clawed "beyond recognition."

After floods, tornadoes, fires, oozing magma, road kills, war footage, the requisite A-bomb explosion, self-immolating protesters (to the tune of "Why Jesus Doesn't Love Here Anymore"), urban rats, vampire bats, Biafran children, sharks in several feeding frenzies, skydivers with malfunctioning parachutes, and more auto and airplane accidents, we see another *cinema vérité* section. It seems that a Joseph Binder believes that the spirits of his dead wife and son have returned to earth. Professional ghostbusters are called in, and we have a chance to look over their shoulders at the "sensitive recording apparatus." These instruments show the parapsychologists that the house is indeed haunted. Nothing is particularly fake about this segment. Dr. Gröss makes no claim, but it does seem that he is running short of footage. The library of a lifetime of collecting is nearly empty. We return to his study to hear his final musings. "Death: is it the end of the beginning, or the beginning of the end? I'll leave that decision to you." Cut to a woman presumably giving birth. We see only her face as she pushes and pants and then . . . the cries of a newborn baby. Exhausted, she smiles. Roll credits.

The credit run is at least as interesting as the movie. Against the setting sun over a California surf à la Hallmark Cards, thanks are given to UPI, Independent TV News, the British Museum, various television stations, the National Archives, various public collections, and then, in print so small that one has to freeze the frame to read it, this appears: "Exiguous scenes within this motion picture have been reconstructed to document and further clarify their factual origin." While "exiguous" means "excessively scanty" to dictionary readers, to viewers of *FOD* it probably refers to the monkey-brain dining scene, the alligator-news-man tangle, the various executions, the omophagic hippies, and the "ghostbusting." In other words, it refers to about a third of the film.

Once these "exiguous" scenes are removed, what do viewers see? They see images remarkably close to what their great-great-grandparents would have seen in rural England or in frontier America. They see dogfighting, bull-baiting (bullfighting in the film), cockfighting, the slaughtering of farm animals. They see dead people in war and the unfortunate results of accidents. Admittedly, self-immolation, automobile collisions, skydiving with malfunctioning chutes, and airplane crashes were not seen generations ago, but by the same token, modern warfare and medicine have removed much of the lingering death and disease seen in earlier times. What Dr. Gröss has in his "personal library" is probably quite close in amount and degree to what teenage boys have wanted to see, have traveled to see, have paid to see for generations.

Ignoring for the moment the fact that these images are being exploited for profit, they do seem to have found an audience. Or, more appropriately, these images have never lost their audience; they have just found a new medium. That the sequences are now conveyed electronically rather than occurring at, say, a public hanging or in the barnyard might even argue for the refinement of the modern age. Still, these sequences of preposterous violence are distressing to us because they are so close at hand. We don't expect to see them on television.

Yet television is the major purveyor of myths, especially those for adolescents. The medium has insinuated itself into everything; in fact, most of us spend our lives within yards of a video screen of some sort. Like the blob of cinematic lore, television has not just arrived on the planet, it has oozed everywhere. Like all mass media, it has adjusted to us before most of us could adjust to it. We can flip it on with the touch of a finger and so can our children. Once it's on, we are never more than a few channels away from some sequence of violence.[9] What is "on" these screens is so transitory and yet so repetitive that sociologists use the terms "video grazing" and "video prospecting" to describe the process of adult watching. But "glued to the screen" more accurately describes the youthful experience. Children seem so close to it that they appear to be in a different transmission loop. To adults, their televised folklore is so frantic, so subversive, so threatening, so indulgent of unexamined passion that it should be tempered and contained. Professional wrestling, *The A-Team, He-Man,* heavy metal music, video games, music videos, stalk-and-slash movies, and even a video amalgam like *Faces of Death* are so visually available that they *seem* accepted and assimilated.

Without defending these cartoons of aggression, I have tried to show their provenance, transmission, and reception. I have tried to set our adult concerns about them in perspective and to show what happens when a mass-produced, profit-driven medium becomes accessible to an adolescent market. I have tried to show how that audience inspires exaggerated content and how fantasies of disorder are often formulaic rituals coded with precise social information which that adolescent audience needs. Like fairy tales that prepare the child for the anxieties of separation, these fables prepare the teenager for the anxieties of competition and then of reproduction. They are fantastic, ludicrous, crude, and important distortions of real-life situations, and often provided not in the service of repression or expression (although they may certainly have that temporary effect) but of instruction. "Extraordinary, how *potent* cheap music is," says Amanda in Noel Coward's *Private Lives,* and one might add, its potency, like that of fables of aggression, is that it cannot be rephrased or contained: It must be lived through and traveled past.

If the "road of excess leads to the palace of wisdom," as William Blake posits, then these fables are some of the roads. They are not clearly marked, in part because the travelers do not understand the destination, the risks, or even the purpose of the trip. They only know that for the first time in their lives, they are on the road alone. Like bewildered animals of all species, they are dangerous to be near. They can be violent. They may even want to be violent. Through the folklore of adolescence, they can observe and learn what no one wants to teach, namely, in Blake's words again, that "you never know what is enough unless you know more than enough." Boundaries are only known once crossed. Preposterous violence shows what is over the boundary.

Although we like to blame mass media for creating stress, for showing "too much," the folklore they broadcast translates rather than generates anxiety. As Gibbon argued two centuries ago, the events on the arena floor of the *circus maximus* reflect and even predict the wishes and resolutions of those in the coliseum stands. Perhaps television violence is showing us how the next generation plans to cope with stress. In fact, we may well find that just as the onset of menarche is occurring earlier in industrialized cultures, so too electronic media is introducing the anxieties of male aggression to a younger and younger audience. Adolescent males may be entering puberty earlier. Certainly it is self-evident that fairy tale violence has migrated from the stable canon of orally transmitted lore into the highly visual lore of television. If the function of make-believe violence is tied in some way to the rituals of separation from family, transition into adulthood, and reincorporation into a new family structure, we might be witnessing an evolutionary change in the patterns of socialization. A simpler explanation might be that as the bubble of adolescent males moves through the audience, we might soon find violent fables replaced by more peaceful family myths.

But the fables of adolescence, once sprung loose from prose, ink, celluloid, or pixels, are remarkably similar. They are all induction fables, all journeys over unfamiliar territory, all passages through what we fear most: uncontained violence. While we may want to pretend that such violence is not part of real life, or even of imaginary life, we know better. For a time in our lives, we eagerly pass from fable to fable to observe this metonymical mayhem. We watch the magical resolution of disorder. Wishes come true. Hulk Hogan piledrives the hapless Ayotollah. Mr. T bashes the nasty rent collector "upside da head." He-Man and the Masters of the Universe decimate Skeletor. A generation ago, cowboys humiliated Indians, detectives intimidated criminals, and in the comics, disenfranchised victims enacted an especially bitter revenge on deserving oppressors. Before that, in the gothic novel, young men redressed inequities on villains with more than necessary force. In nonprint fables, Punch regularly rampaged his family at the country fair, and Tom Nero, the first urban guerrilla, wreaked havoc on the innocent before he himself was consumed in retributive violence.

In retrospect, we can see how much popular culture has been dedicated to the construction and transportation of violent sequences. They support much, if not most, of what passes through mass media. For whatever we may have gained by moving out of the cave and into the high-rise apartment, we have not lost our desire to look at these vibrant images. We continue to pass before them in awe because there is something still resonant in the iconography of excessive violence, something not yet understood or categorized—something undeniably exciting. They have been with us for centuries. In the culture before repeatable print, the fables of aggression were carried in oral culture, as was the heroic combat of Ulysses, Beowulf, or King Arthur, in religious sequences such as the Passion of Christ and the saints' lives, or in the predictable routines of the blood-and-thunder revenge dramas and the projected imagery of the morality play. The ritualized killing of animals also reiterated this violent text—printed on rock by the cave dwellers, carved into basalt by the Assyrians, or actually played out in the flesh by later gen erations of males in celebrations of bull-running, bear-baiting, cock-scaling, or dogfighting.

Usually involved in these concussive fictions is the promise of submission, of surrender, be it the pleas of a vanquished wrestler, the lynching of Tom Nero, or the isolation of Leatherface. Usually involved is the "moral" of violence, namely its containment. As with fairy tales, both teller and audience want the "happily ever after" closure. Unlike the tales of early childhood, however, these myths of adolescence are ambiguous. Evil is not always defeated. The audience knows too much, knows that the good woodsman won't cut open the wolf's stomach and give Little Red Riding Hood a second chance. Violence works, but be careful. Mistakes get punished. The next best resolution must suffice. Retribution must be contained. This wolf has died. There are many other wolves in the forest. Stay alert. Stay tuned.

For however much we may wish to forget the folklore of adolescence, it gets told. Parents no longer tell it; industries of mass media do. Yet those stories we may want to forget may well tell us more than the valorized texts we claim we want to have told. Is there anyone who wants to preserve Twisted Sister, Asteroids, *Friday the 13th*, or the oeuvre of Stephen King? Ask an earlier generation how it felt about bloody pulps, *Punch and Judy*, bull-baiting, or the illustrated comic. Sooner ask the lads in the Paris print shop how they considered their enactments of the cat massacre. Yet in these ritualized entertainments, the most important caveats about desire, frustration, and resolution are encoded. Ultimately, although they seem to argue for action, they almost always propose caution; they paraphrase the final words of Frank N. Furter of *The Rocky Horror Picture Show:* "Don't do it, dream it."

Because these fantasies are so important, they need no artists to recreate them, no monks to protect them, no museums to hold them, and no scholars to explicate them. They are, and they have been, the commonplace dreams of adolescence. Their mythic forms are carried in our communal consciousness—the mass media is our shaman—drawn out by successive generations and given the most current context. Let an adolescent male audience near a bookseller, a movie theater, or a television set and soon these fables of aggression will appear. Once drawn out, such stories will always seem shocking to an older generation which had drawn its myths from a previous medium, but if one will listen closely, the same story will be endlessly told. The fantasies one generation considers as escapist and worthless—"trash"—the next generation lines up to see. What Tennyson said of Nature and individual species is also true of mass media and programming: "So careful of the type she seems/ So careless of the single life." While the individual tellings seem different and transitory, the genre confronts the same audience concern: What happens when force is applied, when the film between act and repression wears thin, when order breaks down and violence, albeit exaggerated violence, leaks out. These tales are the ritualized and formatted distortions of our worst fears. That many young males are drawn to these retellings, that the tellings are condemned yet form the major content of massive industries of transmission, and that no amount of censorship seems to contain them are all facts which point to the ironic conclusion that we will never understand the "nature of the beast" without first at least acknowledging the beast's presence and its centrality. Youth is rarely wasted on the young. While we would like to believe that maturation is artistically ordered like life on a Grecian urn, adolescence, at least for males, is more likely imaged by the vulgar Assyrians on stone. We may not want to acknowledge it, but these myths of preposterous violence are clearly still with us because so much of us is still unacknowledged in them.

Notes

Chapter I

1. Not all animal diversions were affected. Since deer, rabbit, and fox hunting were in the literal and figurative preserves of the wealthy and done in the name of crop control for the poor, they continue to this day.

2. Although anonymity is the norm in popular culture, it is noteworthy that when an author is present the author's name becomes the genus. Zane Grey, Margaret Mitchell, Edgar Rice Burroughs, Harriet Beecher Stowe, Arthur Conan Doyle, Robert Ludlum, or the "name" I will be discussing, that of Stephen King, have become "brand names" existing almost entirely outside the institution of literary studies. King's career has flourished in spite of often hostile criticism. I make this point now because my approach to King's "texts," be they literary or cinematic adaptations, will be from the opposite direction of literary analysis. I can't ask, "What is in this novel/film that should be appreciated?," but rather "Why should this sequence keep reappearing with such regularity elsewhere in popular entertainment?" What we may pass off as escape, as monotony, and as cliché may instead be far more telling of the human condition than what we isolate and commend as unique, as individual, and as artistic.

3. Freud unfortunately referred to preadolescence as the "latency period," a misnomer implying a sense of quietude, and he thought it primarily a time for the "dissolution of the Oedipus complex." (Freud used the phrase *Untergang des Ödipuskomplexes*, which even he realized was too passive, and so he occasionally substituted a stronger word, *Zertrümmerung* or demolition.) An apparent sense of quietude and peaceful composure may well have characterized the surface behavior of Viennese youngsters a century ago, but we now know how mistaken Freud was. Pubescence is anything but contained and latent; rather, everything about the adolescent teenager seems aroused and furious. All of a sudden there is hair emerging in strange places, mysterious bodily fluids secreted at unannounced times, breasts budding, voices cracking, and most important, those disturbing, exciting urges welling up inside. There is nothing more frightening than power without knowledge, unless it is knowledge without control.

4. It may be noteworthy that most of these panels are in the British Museum, stuck on the first floor in a nook around the corner from the Elgin Marbles. The Parthenon sculptures are a centerpiece of the Museum, have a room of their own, complete with booklets, postcards, and photographs, while the Assyrian murals are almost unexplained

and unattended. The panels in the Metropolitan Museum of Art are also hidden away on the first floor in two dark alcoves.

5. Helen Gardner, *Art Through The Ages*, thinks Assyrian art reflects a savage character and ruthless culture; R. C. Barnett, *Assyrian Palace Reliefs in the British Museum*, says Assyria was clearly a king-obsessed society; H. W. F. Saggs, *The Greatness That Was Babylon*, agrees that the obvious relish of brutality is shocking; Eva Strommengen, *Five Thousand Years of the Art of Mesopotamia*, calls it propaganda, not great art; André Parrot, *Nineveh and Babylon*, asks where the life force is in such hollow stereotypes, and Arlene D. Winter, in "Royal Rhetoric and the Development of Historical Narrative in Neo-Assyrian Reliefs," continues the tradition by saying that ideological art depends on just such lifeless forms as these. The only exception to the usual dismissal of Assyrian iconography is Leo Bersani and Ulysse Dutoit's provocative *The Forms of Violence: Narrative in Assyrian Art and Modern Culture*, which attempts a Freudian interpretation of violence in terms of deflected sexual desire.

6. While E. O. Wilson, *Sociobiology*, and Richard Dawkins, *The Selfish Gene*, have popularized the sociobiological strategies of violence, or the threat thereof, Garrett Hardin, "Is Violence Natural?," William D. Hamilton, "The Genetical Theory of Social Behavior," and R. L. Trivers, "Parent-Child Offspring Conflict," continue the discussion with specific details.

7. Far more frightening than any Brave New World, in which artificial violence is used to sublimate tension, is what happens when symbolic clusters and stylized displacements do not stick, when the "feelies" get unfelt, and voyeurism is replaced by action. One of the more shocking aspects of human behavior, as Robert Ardrey has conjectured in *The Hunting Hypothesis*, is what happens when we misconfigure certain rituals. The result is not that "pretend" violence becomes real, but that the "pretend" no longer dissipates the real. Repression eases and our worst fears become realized. The enigma of the Nazi death camps may be a function of what happens when symbolic codes are not invoked, when popular culture is commandeered by those who would cleanse it, when gratuitous violence has been excised from the mythlore. Nazi Germany was suffused with political propaganda but not with folklore. As historians of Weimar films like Sigfried Kracauer, *From Caligari to Hitler*, and Lotte Eisner, *The Haunted Screen*, have shown, folklore had become corrupted by propaganda. Certainly one of the most macabre aspects of the Holocaust is the emotionally sanitary method of "answering the Jewish question." Was this behavior without aggression, or behavior without enough aggression?

Certainly the Stanford experiments of Stanley Milgram show what happens when humans act without symbolic displacement, without the *Sprachregelugen* or "language rules" of behavior. By various elegant subterfuges, Milgram succeeded in having perfectly "normal" humans administer "electric shocks" to compatriots, all in the name of a fabricated "tough love." The shocks would do them good. Authority was respected, unquestioned. The lever-pullers who were giving people up to four hundred imaginary volts to their patients were not sadists, were not Nazis; they were simply following the instructions of scientists in white coats. Violence of this sort, as Hannah Arendt has written of Adolf Eichmann in *On Violence*, is banal for being so free of cultural context and hence of restraints. As we will see, although rituals of preposterous violence seem disruptive, they are uniformly conservative, even repressive. (See also note 5 of Chapter 6.)

8. Robin Fox argues in *The Red Lamp of Incest* that our social system has evolved into three parts: dominant males who monopolize the sexuality of females, females who have not yet entered the breeding system, and satellite males who must struggle by various means to be included. The willingness to avoid violence by all parties, not because of the stern prohibition on violence but because of the pragmatism of survival, is

one of many mechanisms holding this tripartite system together. The organization succeeds as all parties stabilize, not getting all they want but at least not running the risk of getting nothing. There is no doubt about which group is the first to be willing to risk violence, and no doubt which group will be the most dependent on restraint. The scenarios of preposterous violence may, albeit ironically, provide examples of restraint.

Chapter 2

1. We know this anecdote because it was written down by one of the participants, Nicolas Contat, who was in the unique position of knowing both written language and the life of the apprentice. His *Anecdotes typographiques où l'on voit la description des coutumes, moeurs et usages singuliers des compagnons imprimeurs* has been edited by Giles Barber who provides a historical background of printing and Contat's career. The complete incident appears on pp. 48–56 of the Barber edition.

2. Although cats are no longer used for such entertainment, we have "caterwauling" and the German "*Katzenmusik*" to remind us we have not always gotten along well with cats. Darnton, in *The Great Cat Massacre*, points to other cat diversions: burning cats at the stake, chasing cats on fire, dancing around a burning cat, tying a cat atop a Maypole, and placing a basket of cats above a fire to watch them jump from the basket into the fire (pp. 83–85).

3. For more on the subject of animal insults and taboos, see Mary Douglas, *Purity and Danger: An Analysis of Concepts of Pollution and Taboo*, and E. R. Leach, "Anthropological Aspects of Language: Animal Categories and Verbal Abuse."

4. We need to separate the violent scene created by the boys from its lookalike cousin—theatrical violence. Although theatrical violence springs from secular rituals (Sophocles's *Antigone*, for example, was even performed on the occasion of Dionysian rites in Athens), theatrical violence plays to a different audience for slightly different reasons. The medieval vice plays were probably the last rituals to play to both mature and adolescent audiences before the development of mass media. It is common in such drama to be startled by hearts brandished upon swords, severed human hands waved about under our noses, or a victim's brain seared by a burning crown. The sensational violence that one finds, say, in English Renaissance tragedy was already different in degree and category from the formulaic violence of adolescent ritual. This violence has also been called "gratuitous," "preposterous," and "indiscriminate," concerned only with making the audience shudder. What *is* different about these shivers is that they are in the service of plot, of drama, of performance. Much has been written on violence in Renaissance drama; see, for instance, Maurice Charney, "The Persuasiveness of Violence in Elizabethan Plays," Fredson Bowers, *Elizabethan Revenge Tragedy 1587–1642*, Huston Diehl, "The Iconography of Violence in English Renaissance Tragedy," and Richard T. Brucher, "Fantasies of Violence."

5. The pit bull still has an extraordinary reputation. It has become the "macho dog" of teenagers and drug dealers. Boys ranging between five and fourteen have been arrested for running dog fighting rings. There are between 2,300 and 3,000 pit bulls in the United States, ninety percent of them owned by juveniles. In other words, the fights are not only for betting and protection but for watching displays of animal violence.

6. In fact, in the 1830s one of the few "constructed" breeds was created to capitalize on this interest. The bull terrier was the result of interbreeding the white hunting terrier with a greyhound and then with a Dalmatian crossed with a pointer. The resulting bull terrier was such a fierce fighter that George S. Patton, Jr., kept his constantly by his side as a symbol to his fighting boys in World War II.

7. This transcription of the 1827 Piccini version of *Punch and Judy* was done by the

journalist John Payne Collier and published by Edward Prowett as *The Tragical Comedy or Comical Tragedy of Punch and Judy*. The later nineteenth-century transcriptions are notoriously censorious as the transcriber, the publisher, and the consuming audience were often at odds about what *should* be in the play. I am indebted to Robert Leach, *The Punch and Judy Show*, for much of the information and illustrations in this chapter.

8. Although I am interested primarily in fictive violence, the public hanging, and all its attendant ceremonies and illustrations, was one of the Augustan rituals of urban life. See R. M. Wiles, "Crowd-Pleasing Spectacles in Eighteenth-Century England."

Chapter 3

1. Changes in mass marketing became central to the transmission of myth in the modern world. Gothic romances were distributed like magazines—sold in drugstores and supermarkets. By the 1970s, they outsold all other categories of paperback fiction. Other producers had soon joined the market. Eight publishing houses distributed more than four hundred titles a year to an eager, seemingly inexhaustible audience. Changes occurred overnight. For instance, Avon introduced a subgenre, what is now called "the sweet savage romance" in the style of Rosemary Rogers, which exploited a level of barely repressed eroticism that had been lurking in the eighteenth-century gothic. Avon was able to market it so quickly that it controlled the market. Violent male fantasies are equally susceptible to changes in fashion.

2. All this activity in the marketing of words was not lost on American industry. The printed word had not been buried by the electronic image; instead both enlarged each others' audiences. Words created images, images attracted audiences, and audiences meant money. Words were "profit centers." And so, at last count, Knopf, which had been bought by Random House, was in turn bought by RCA, soon to be a subsidiary of GE, which sold it to Newhouse. CBS soon owned Holt, Rinehart & Winston, Praeger, Popular Library, and Fawcett. Doubleday had Dell; Hearst had William Morrow; Gulf + Western had its Simon & Schuster, Prentice Hall, and Pocket Books. The big German publisher, Dertlesmann, now owns Doubleday which owns Dell which owns Delacorte; Pearson P.L.C. owns Addison-Wesley; Time, Inc., owns both Scott, Foresman and Little, Brown; Rupert Murdock owns Harper & Row which owns Barnes & Noble. Macmillian is on the block. The only independent American publishers of note left are Farrar, Straus & Giroux (which owns Hill & Wang) and Harcourt Brace Jovanovich, and their days may be numbered.

3. It is a mark of Mr. King's extraordinary talent that he is held in such passionate disrespect by so many critics. In 1988, at a Brown University conference called "Unspeakable Practices: A Celebration of Iconoclastic Fiction," Leslie Fiedler concluded his remarks by saying, "None of us will be remembered as long or revered as deeply as our contemporary Stephen King" (quoted by Caryn James, p. 12). Many of the attendants were upset, so upset that they threatened to stay away from the evening dinner. Later in the day Mr. Fiedler was conciliatory. He said he had spoken with irony.

4. It is not happenstance that some of Stephen King's most perceptive prose is not in his reminiscential *Dance Macabre*, but in his introduction to the Signet Classic collection of *Dracula, Frankenstein and Dr. Jekyll and Mr. Hyde*. He understands what is in these scenarios, no longer art stories, which gather a paying audience, for it is the same audience he himself knows so well.

5. King himself describes his primary audience in *Danse Macabre:* "Kids are the perfect audience for horror. The paradox is this: Children, who are physically quite weak, lift the weight of unbelief with ease. They are the jugglers of the invisible world—

a perfectly understandable phenomenon when you consider the perspective they must view things from" (p. 105). King's talent is that he remembers just how to upset this world. This is a clearly profitable memory not only for him but also for many others, as demonstrated by the outpouring of books for adolescents which are directed toward generating fright.

6. It is appropriate that King started writing as a teenager by drafting novelizations of movies. In fact, he marks the beginning of his interest in creating shivers by recalling his attempt to put Roger Corman's adaptation of Poe's *Masque of the Red Death* into his own words. After that practice, he tried to write without consciously adapting, but as we will see, the scenic technique remained. After a few of his stories had been published by men's magazines like *Cavalier* and *Gent*, Doubleday published a few thousand copies of *Carrie*, an artless but effective retelling of Cinderella with flamethrower. The novel did not find many readers until the movie version, artfully directed by Brian De Palma, provided them. The movie made the book and the book made Stephen King into a household word. As was to become typical in the 1970s, this youthful reading audience saw the story first on the screen and then went to the printed text. The book version was clearly becoming the secondary experience, often interlarded with photographs from the movie to remind the audience of the perhaps more exciting experience.

7. For more on King in the movies, see Bill Warren, "The Movies and Mr. King," Jeff Connor, *Stephen King Goes to Hollywood*, and Jessie Horsting, *Stephen King at the Movies*. The best adapter of a King novel is someone like Brian De Palma who is interested in paying homage to the author, even literally using the printed text as shooting script, rather than an auteur like Stanley Kubrick who is trying to film an interpretation. After all, the King novel *is* a shooting script.

8. Along with a total lack of free will is an almost total lack of love-making. With the exception of the "Apt Pupil" section of *Different Seasons* (which is essentially King's attempt to write a Book of the Month Club novel), and a paragraph or two from *Cujo* and *It*, Stephen King characters hug each other for comfort only between violent episodes. When asked about this lack of sex, King explained:

> Actually, I probably am uncomfortable with it [sex], but that discomfort stems from a more general problem I have with creating believable romantic relationships. Without such strong relationships to build on, it's tough to create sexual scenes that have credibility and impact or advance the plot, and I'd just be dragging sex in arbitrarily and perfunctorily. ("Playboy Interview," p. 234)

The explanation may lie deeper. It lies in King's intuitive understanding of his audience. This audience doesn't want sex; sex is confusing. But while sex is not understood, feelings of excitement are. In "Meeting Stevie," Peter Straub, King's collaborator on *The Talisman*, provides insight when he says that King hasn't discovered sex yet. It may be more accurate to say that King's audience hasn't discovered sex—yet. When they do, they will move on into other genres like the private eye thriller where sex and violence mingle.

9. One might argue that King is again taking his cue from the movies, from the spate of child monsters who came alive after *The Bad Seed* and continued through *Rosemary's Baby*, *It's Alive*, and *The Omen*. The devil-child is like the vampire-zombie as portrayed in recent films. The monster has taken over the body of some innocent and is using it as a husk. Therefore, the killing of the body expunges the demon and releases the innocent spirit. Hence the smiling face as the sweet character is returned to life just before "dying." This interest in child monsters is a modern twist, for instead of having the parents (usually the father) turn on the child, it is now the child who turns on the

parents. This new scapegoat may well presage a trend in preposterous violence, as over-population and intense competition for scarce resources transform one-time angels into miniature villains.

Chapter 4

1. The *Reader's Guide to Periodical Literature* shows two outbursts of articles on juvenile delinquency: one from 1943 to 1945 and another from 1953 to 1958. Mass-circulation journals like the *Saturday Evening Post, Life,* and the *Reader's Digest* had found a mother lode of anxiety and mined it with the enthusiasm of the '49ers. Holly-wood was not far behind. In the 1950s there were more than sixty films of kids-gone-amok. Some, like *The Wild One, Rebel Without a Cause,* and *Blackboard Jungle,* broke loose from their moorings at movie theaters and became national concerns.

2. The center of gravity in American culture was shifting. Working-class entertain-ments were commandeering more cultural space, and adolescents were clamoring to be included. As James Gilbert has recently written in *A Cycle of Outrage: America's Re-action to the Juvenile Delinquent in the 1950s,* the Eisenhower years are a textbook illustration of a populace under internal stress. This was partly the result of new media which were competing for audience attention or, more appropriately, new and younger audiences which were competing for media attention. After sifting the statistical data, Gilbert concludes:

> The great fear of delinquency in the 1950s rests on at least three impor-tant factors. The first is an unmeasurable but probable increase in the inci-dence of juvenile crime, attention paid to crime, or both. The second is a probable shift in the behavior of law enforcement agencies, prodded by gov-ernment and private pressure groups and public opinion to assert authority over the behavior of young people. The third includes changes in the be-havior of youth that were susceptible to interpretation as criminal. These, in turn, were embedded in both long- and short-term changes in youth culture that became especially apparent after World War II. (p. 71)

3. The Senate committee tacitly endorsed what Rowland Howard had already con-cluded in 1944 about radio dramas in the *Educational Research Bulletin:*

> By and large, radio crime dramas offer no realistic portrayal of the influ-ences which produce criminals. There is some evidence that children from delinquent areas listen to crime programs proportionately more than chil-dren from nondelinquent areas. This does not mean, however, that listening to crime programs necessarily is a cause of delinquency. Instead, it is more probably that the same economic and cultural factors which produce delin-quency also produce a greater number of young people who enjoy crime drama more than other types of programs. ("Radio Crime Drama," p. 213)

4. It may be worth noting that soon after Robert Louis Stevenson's *Dr. Jekyll and Mr. Hyde* was performed on the London stage in 1888, Jack the Ripper made his first appearance. The Ripper was the first serial killer popularized in the tabloid press, and Mr. Hyde was one of the first transformation monsters on stage. This appearance of fiction and fact marks the first time in the modern world that popular culture was blamed specifically for the outbreak of aberrant social behavior. So obvious was the causality that the stage production was immediately canceled. Serial murders, however, contin-ued. What had changed was the terminology.

5. Not only had Wertham seen the horrible future at first hand, he had been born in Germany and so could explain it to us, like the founder of psychoanalysis, in a distinct accent. To make his case even stronger, Wertham had even visited the Vienna office of Freud, albeit on a matter unrelated to psychoanalysis. He emigrated to America in 1922 and continued his studies to become chief psychiatric resident at Johns Hopkins. Ten years later, he was appointed senior psychiatrist at Bellevue and then director of the Psychiatric Clinic of Queens Hospital. Wertham had continually agitated for the delivery of low-cost psychiatric help for the poor. Had it not been for his crusade against the comic, he would still be remembered for providing the central testimony in one of the cases later consolidated by the Supreme Court into *Brown v. The Board of Education.* What Wertham had found in his contacts with those who are now called the "disadvantaged" or the "disenfranchised" is that self-esteem is a function of social context. You act as you are treated. As long as different races share the same social culture, he argued, there can be no institution which is separate *and* equal. With reference to delinquency, Wertham was able to point to what was then becoming a cant of the social sciences: "experience in the field." First, as organizer of what he called the "hooky club" for troubled teens, and later as director of the LaFargue Clinic in Harlem, which provided low-cost care to the needy, Wertham staked out a unique territory. If Harlem was presaging a new transformation in youth culture, why not ask the man who has been there?

6. The first time this argument had been put forth in the modern world was at the end of the eighteenth century, at the end of the Age of Reason. When crop failures put many marginal farmers out onto the street to beg, some well-meaning reformers sounded the alarm. Shouldn't we remove the beggars from sight, lest *hoi polloi* assume that the life of a panhandler was a legitimate alternative to hard work? If you don't see beggars, you won't think begging exists, and all will be well. However, as logical as it seems, the cure was worse than the disease, as compassionate commentators from Samuel Johnson (reviewing Soame Jenyn's "Essay into Nature and Origin of Evil") to William Wordsworth ("The Old Cumberland Beggar") knew. Street poverty was a fact of modern life and not to admit it was at least wishful thinking, at worst willful denial.

Still, the argument of "out of sight, out of mind" is so commonsensical that it has surfaced many times. By the nineteenth century, it was applied to mass media, particularly to print. The French criminologist, L. J. G. Proal, argued in his massive *Le crime et le suicide passionnel* that, based on his comprehensive study of criminals, he had found one common attribute. They all had read novels. Not just trashy novels, but works by the great realists like Dostoevsky and Flaubert. Furthermore, he opined that other writers who had lingered over violent scenes, writers he even named—Ovid, Shakespeare, Goethe—were directly responsible for murders and suicides. Proal was not happy to suggest the remedy, but he certainly recognized violent literary scenes as a possible influence. There were plenty of *belles-lettres* to go around; why not selectively remove the more disquieting ones?

7. Wertham even invokes the concept of infection as his headnote to *The Seduction.* He quotes from Sir Thomas Elyot: "And I verily do suppose that in the braines and hertes of children, whiche be membres spiritulall, whiles they be tender, and the little slippes of reason begynne in them to bud, ther may happe by evil custome some pestiferous dewe of vice to perse the sayde membres, and infecte and corrupt the softe and tender buddes."

8. "Pests" and "weeds" do not exist in nature. They are part of man's labeling system. When we humans wish to uproot a plant, we first label it a "weed"; when we wish to kill some animal, we call it a "pest"; when the animal is large and we want it destroyed, we call it a "predator"; when we wish to destroy a fellow human being, we call him "Commie," "Jap," "Kraut," or "Gook." Such dysphemisms exist for the efficiencies of deletion, destruction, and excision.

9. In the generation before *Playboy* and *Penthouse*, comics often performed the same imagistic role of mass-marketed "soft porn." What was euphemistically called "good girl art," by which was meant erotic images of full-breasted, active young women, as in the *Dragon Lady* or *Wonder Woman* comics, served the purpose of arousing young males. Wertham, however, neglects (or represses) this kind of titillation of adolescents for more sophisticated arguments about the encouragement of homosexuality.

10. Here is Wertham on *Howdy Doody* comic books: "Take one that looks even more harmless, *Howdy Doody*. I discussed this with a group of white and colored children. Their reaction was partly giggling, partly inhibited. The book depicts colored natives as stereotyped caricatures, violent, cowardly, cannibalistic and so superstitious that they get scared by seltzer tablets and popping corn and lie down in abject surrender on their faces before two white boys" (*The Seduction*, p. 309).

11. Wertham includes, but does not gloss, some of the responses of intellectuals (*The Seduction*, p. 269). He reports that to Marya Mannes "comic books kill dreams"; for John Mason Brown they are "not only trash about the lowest, most despicable and most harmful and unethical form of trash"; for Heywood Broun they are scruffy "proletarian novels"; John Houseman finds them "horribly savage," and Father Ong warns that they might well instill a communal "persecution complex of the neurotic."

12. In *The Great Comic Book Heroes*, Jules Feiffer argues that "swiping," as it is known among modern cartoonists, is still a hallmark of the trade. If one artist finds a technique or image which is popular, his colleagues will quickly copy it. While this might annoy the innovator, it assures the audience of an efficient market for what it wants and assures the critic that "art" and individual innovation are secondary.

13. In fact, in a monograph on Milton Caniff by a John Paul Adam, we learn that Rembrandt, Raphael, DaVinci, and Michaelangelo were the predecessors of the likes of Al Capp and Milton Caniff. After all, argues Mr. Adam, unaware of the painterly term, they were "cartoonists," weren't they? The English especially enjoy the joke of the American looking at a Raphael "cartoon" saying, "The drawing's good, but I don't get the joke."

14. Spain and Poland also had a scanty history of popular iconography. It may be that without a strong lower middle class this illustrated form could not find an audience. In the twentieth century, the audience for comics is worldwide, especially in marginally literate societies, as in much of Latin America, or else among adolescents in affluent societies. Hence teenagers read comic books in North America, while adults are the major consumers in South America. Not so in Western Europe which has had a long tradition of sophisticated comics which continues to this day.

15. In this discussion of the comic, I am indebted to David Kunzle, *The Early Comic Strip*, for background, illustrations, and translation information.

16. In the modern morality play two parties appear on stage—Satan and the avenging angel, victim and executioner. Long before illustration had made it one of the most common subjects, hanging had become a popular public spectacle. Although the victim has no prescribed role—he can appear terrified, vindictive, unrepentant, morose—his interaction with the crowd, as well as with the executioner, is central to the drama. The executioner must allow the victim full freedom to say whatever he pleases; in fact, the dying speech, especially in the eighteenth century, was almost sacred and often legally binding. In an extension of the church service, the crowd is never idle but acts the recitative depending on the minister/victim. Many an executioner feared for his safety should the crowd become too sympathetic with the victim; yet the show must go on. Violent spectacle can only exist if momentary chaos is quickly resolved by a prepared structure. The victim's role continued well past death with his body becoming a source of good luck charms. His blood was supposed to cure epilepsy, teeth and finger nails were signs of good luck, and even his finger joints were so magical that they were often auctioned off.

17. The revival of Roman law in the twelfth century made torture a standard judicial practice from Italy to France to Germany and the Netherlands. Spain was never without torture. This iconography makes its way across the English Channel with Romanticism and its attendant tendency to picture the sensational, however bizarre. First, Edmund Burke sanctified the "sublime," and then de Sade almost made a religion out of algolagnia. In Romanticism the consumption of such imagery was not just acceptable but educational. How could the man of feeling know feeling unless he had felt? Little wonder then that Thomas Mackenzie should send young Harley in *The Man of Feeling* to Bedlam for a dollop of violence. Once being shocked became a positive aesthetic response, there was no reason to pretend that we had not always experienced these feelings. This honesty was, as Goethe pointed out, the great achievement of Romanticism.

18. To see how juvenile delinquency was linked to culture in the nineteenth century, see Margaret May, "Innocence and Experience: The Evolution of the Concept of Juvenile Delinquency in the Mid-Nineteenth Century," and John Gillis, *Youth and History*, as well as his "The Evolution of Juvenile Delinquency in England: 1890–1914."

19. However, in *Boys Will Be Boys*, a critical survey of Victorian stories for young men that was written in 1948 and revised in the 1970s, E. S. Turner contends that, "It is difficult to defend the extreme examples, but even the worst compare favorably with the 'horror comics' which were to cause an outcry in the nineteen-fifties" (p. 59).

20. The English role in the development of the violent, or more euphemistically, the "adventure," comic, is actually more one of importation than of innovation. For the illustrated broadside, the sequential pictograph, which was brilliantly conceived and marketed by Hogarth in such works as *The Rake's Progress*, *Marriage à la Mode*, and *Industry and Idleness*, never really found a sustained audience. The father of the modern comic, the originator of modern action sequence, is the Swiss Rodolphe Töpffer. Töpffer's relatively simple line doodles showed the possibility of creating the illusion of real action in two dimensions. Töpffer was prescient about the future of his craft. He wrote in the early nineteenth century that

> the picture story to which the criticism of art pays no attention and which rarely worries the learned, has always exercised a great appeal. More, indeed, than literature itself, for besides the fact that there are more people who look than can read, it appeals particularly to children and the masses, the sections of the public that are particularly easily perverted and which it would be particularly desirable to raise. With its dual advantage of greater conciseness and greater relative clarity, the picture story, all things being equal, should squeeze out the other because it would address itself with greater liveliness to a greater number of minds, and also because in any contest he who uses such a direct method will have the advantage over those who talk in chapters. (Quoted by George Perry and Alan Aldridge in *The Penguin Book of Comics*, p. 13)

The frozen scene, which had to be examined to be understood, was soon replaced by the frantic scene where just a glance told you all you wanted to know. The master of such scenes of preposterous violence in cartoon form was the master illustrator of the nineteenth century, Gustave Doré. His *L'Histoire de la Sainte Russie*, a whimsical and thoroughly sardonic interpretation of Russian events, slowed down violent action to concentrate on every act of capricious outrage. Forgetting for the moment his nationalistic ax-grinding, (the book was a singular success in Germany during the first World War), these illustrations show an exuberance in detailing violence at a frantic pitch. Doré foretold much of what was to become the modern comic lingua: speed lines, long and short shots, collapsing perspective, frames frozen in mid-act, counterpoint silhouettes, and most importantly, a concentration on scenes of concussion rather than of exposition.

21. Violence has characterized American comics since Krazy Kat threw his first brick. Because of the intense competition between Joseph Pulitzer's *New York World* and William Randolph Hearst's *Morning Journal,* the newspaper strip standardized the serial adventure by directing the focus to a few central characters. More importantly, the adventure comic underwent a sea change caused by the publication of the daily strip in color for the Sunday supplement. The countrywide battles between the great American newspaper empires proved that it was not the front page or the editorial page that sold papers. What mattered was tucked away in the Funnies. Syndicators of strips could make or break a daily newspaper, and they still can. Once the audience for the daily strip, as well as the Sunday cartoon insert, was located, the separate comic "book" became inevitable. The lessons of Harmsworth had been learned: Never sell once what you can sell twice. Color the daily, reprint it as a pamphlet, and sell it.

22. In fact, *Gang Busters* was one of the most popular radio shows of the late 1930s, complete with screaming police sirens, burping Tommy guns, and screeching tires. These radio shows had pulp magazines like *Master Detective, True Detective,* and *Official Detective* behind them and the crime comics ahead. Ahead of that, of course, the first of the violent television programs appeared—*The Untouchables.* Again, what the crime comic initially did was to adapt another medium—in this case Philip H. Lord's radio show—by decreasing text and increasing illustration.

23. The Batman was not alone in being "updated" and made "more vulnerable." The industry calls this process "adultification." In Marvel's most recent Superman series, the Man of Steel visibly winces while holding back a Boeing 707; Clark Kent has a Nautilus machine in his apartment, is more "open about his feelings," is a feature writer at the *Daily Planet* (no longer a reporter), and most importantly, is involved with Lois Lane in a Bruce Willis/Cybil Shepherd *Moonlighting* way. However anemic they may now seem, the comics are still alive, if not totally healthy. They now cost more than two dollars a copy, are sold in bookstores (Waldenbooks has special seventy-two-pocket racks for comics in front of many of its stores), are often known as "graphic novels," and are published by conglomerates. At last report, New World Pictures controls Marvel, and Kinney Corp. owns *DC* together with airport parking lots. While these new owners were initially interested in franchising and licensing business and are more concerned with "tying in" with toy producers than in creating original stories of astonishment, they have been startled to find there is a sizable older audience for comics. In December 1985 *Publishers Weekly* surveyed the health of the industry in a ten-page section, "Comic Books Regain Their Readership and Outlets," but even it was forced to conclude that nothing could now bring back the splendor of the late 1940s and early 1950s. How could illustrated paper compete with electrons? Still, "graphic novels" now command over ten percent of the book market in Europe and Japan, and the startling success in this country of *Maus,* a fable in which the Nazis are cats and the Jews are mice, may portend yet another development in the genre. After all, *Maus* has sold over 100,000 copies and was nominated for the National Book Critics Circle Award, and the University of California Press, no less, is already on its third printing of a 313—page comic, *Japan, Inc.*

Chapter 5

1. Every year the Opinion Research Corporation of Princeton conducts a study for the Motion Picture Association of America. These results are from the 1980 survey, as reported in Cobbett Steinberg, *Reel Facts,* p. 45.

2. Movie producers have not been slow to exploit, or in the polite jargon of the

industry, to channel this demand. As the audience has moved downward in age, it has also expanded laterally, consuming the product far from the theater. The average movie barely breaks even on theatrical release but must depend on videotape and television audiences, the "home movie" audience. In 1950 average Americans "consumed" one movie per week; in 1986 they watched more than twelve hours of movies, both at home on the television and down at the Cinema 16. Some of the top rentals of 1985 are, for instance: *Rambo* (#2), *Rocky IV* (#3), *The Goonies* (#4), *Police Academy* (#8), *National Lampoon's European Vacation* (#9), *A View to a Kill* (James Bond), (#10), *Fletch* (#11), *Spies Like Us* (#12), and *Jewel of the Nile* (#14). To be sure, the movies which find their way to the major television networks are not, by and large, the most violent ones. However, when you look at what is seen on the cable channels like HBO, Showtime, and Cinemax, the story changes. The National Coalition on Television Violence contends that these pay channels have more than three hundred percent more violence than the regular channels, primarily because they show uncut and R-rated films.

3. In a sense, demographics and technology have returned us to the nickelodeon. The nickelodeon, which followed the cabinet-sized peep shows, or Kinetoscopes, was approximately twenty feet wide and eighty feet deep, divided by a single aisle. Although the size exploded in the 1920s and 1930s into such "cathedrals of motion pictures" as the Roxy (1927) and Radio City Music Hall (1932) in New York, Grauman's Chinese (1927) in Los Angeles, the Majestic (1922) in Houston, and the Riviera and Rivoli (1920s) in Chicago, which could seat about 5,000 viewers, the opposite trend since the 1960s has been just as swift. Once the studios were forced to divest their production and distribution interests in the late 1940s, and once television had captured a huge share of the studios' audience in the 1950s, big theaters were not being built—they were being razed. In 1948 there were 18,000 theaters, in 1958 only 12,000. Add to this the impact of the drive-ins, which grew from 800 to 4,000 in the 1950s, and even then the promise of darkness and privacy was delivered better elsewhere. One could make the case that the contemporary theater, and hence contemporary movie fare, was the invention of entrepreneur Stanley Durwood. In 1963 Durwood had the cost accountant's happy inspiration that since costs of projection were fixed ("house costs" are about fifty percent of total expenditures—24.5 cents for rent, mortgage, etc., 26.5 cents to staff), why not show two movies at the same time? Durwood opened a "twin" theater in Kansas City. The twin grew, and soon, like Godzilla, multiplexes gobbled up the market. Although these "twins" are only ten percent of all indoor theaters, they command more than fifty percent of the screens.

4. Because recouping costs is so important and artistic judgment so poor at predicting audience taste, most studios use preview audiences. No one in the industry thought it strange that Paramount spent $1,300,000 to shoot a new ending to *Fatal Attraction*. In the original version, Glenn Close slit her throat with a knife that had Michael Douglas's fingerprints on it. The preview audience didn't like it. Adrian Lyne, the director, explains his willingness to change endings: "I adored this ending. It was totally horrifying. She's got him from the grave! But audiences in this country would have thrown rocks at the screen. If you really don't care what an audience thinks, make a home movie and show it on your wall" (quoted by Harmetz, "*Fatal Attraction* Director Exults Over His Film").

5. Nowhere is the R rating better spelled out, or the hypocrisy more obvious, than in the industry guidelines for "trailers" or advertising previews:

> It should be clearly understood that Restricted trailers cannot carry the same scenes of sex, violence and language that may be approved in the R rated feature. The advertising must necessarily eliminate all strong sex or excessive violence in theater trailers. Again the impact of those scenes is height-

ened when compacted in a short trailer. Some of the scenes unacceptable in R trailers are: excessive sex or violence; dismemberment; genitals; pubic hair; use of sexually connotative words; humping, lesbianism, fondling or masturbation.

We suggest you use the following procedure: let us look at your rough cut before going to a composite. And even before we see it, you should eliminate excessive violence—close-up shootings, stabbings, hacking with axes, etc. Show the weapon, not the meeting against the flesh. Eliminate all blood in general audience trailers and as much as possible in a R trailer, do not use close-up shots where the bullet hits body, but cut to body on the ground or just before body hits the ground. (*Rules and Regulations of the Classification and Rating Administration,* as quoted in Cobbett Steinberg, *Reel Facts,* p. 423)

6. In *The Vampyre,* the gentleman vampire becomes Lord Ruthven, a clear reference to the fact that his erstwhile employer, Lord Byron, had been so named in Lady Caroline Lamb's *roman à clef, Glenarvon.* In fact, Polidori's piece is a wry send-up of the society cad as leech, with Byron himself playing the role of crass seducer. What better illustration of the temporizing powers of prose than that one bit of urbane folklore—Byron as fatal lover—could subsume the raw lore—Nosferatu as social carnivore? Byron's fragment, proffered more to counter Polidori's claim that Byron had had a hand in composing *The Vampyre* than as a work of literature, casts the vampire as Augustus Darvel, a mysterious man-of-the-world. This Darvel is an aesthete whose designs on his male victim are more psychic than sanguine. "Vampire" is a mess, a hurry-up outline of Byron's project, resulting from the June 1816 pact between Percy Shelley, his wife-to-be, Mary Godwin, her stepsister, and John Polidori to write a scary story.

7. Lee found his match in the newly empowered Van Helsing played by Peter Cushing. Just as Universal found that Bela Lugosi could play the Dracula as well as the Frankenstein monster roles, or the gypsy in the Wolfman sagas, without causing the audience to say "No, he's supposed to be Dracula," so Hammer found that Cushing could play both Van Helsing and Dr. Frankenstein. Horror actors can migrate between similar roles and the audience is not distracted because they know the parts are interchangeable anyway. This is a ritual, not a stable text. Even more curious is the fact that adolescents really don't seem to care if the myth is blatantly confused with reality. Hence a 1949 *Abbott and Costello Meet the Killer, Boris Karloff* was followed in 1953 by *Abbott and Costello Meet Dr. Jekyll and Mr. Hyde,* in which Karloff was first a bogeyman, and then both Jekyll and Hyde. However, the audience knew full well that he was really the Frankenstein monster. Critics in the 1940s often complained about Universal's "monster mash" movies like *House of Frankenstein* or *House of Dracula,* saying that the monsters should be kept separate, but such a comment only shows a misplaced concept of categories—a concept that respects genres and the unities, not image clusters and sequences. The inappropriateness of *Billy the Kid vs. Dracula* or *Jesse James Meets Frankenstein's Daughter* never bothered their audiences' sensibilities; it more probably bored them.

8. S. S. Prawer perceptively claimed in *Caligari's Children: The Film as a Tale of Terror* that Jekyll/Hyde was an adventure almost made to order for film; that there was an almost perspicacious relationship between print and celluloid renditions already embedded in the text. He reminds us that the "cinematic image existed well before the cinema" by citing this revealing passage from the novella:

Six o'clock struck on the bells of the church that was so conveniently near to Mr. Utterson's dwelling, and still he was digging at the problem. Hitherto it had touched him on the intellectual side alone; but now his imagination also was engaged, or rather enslaved; and as he lay and tossed in the gross darkness of the night and the curtained room, Mr. Enfield's tale went by before his mind *in a scroll of lighted pictures* [Prawer's italics]. He would be aware of the great field of lamps of a nocturnal city; then of the figure of a man walking swiftly; then of a child running from the doctor's; and then these met, and that human Juggernaut trod the child down and passed on regardless of her screams. Or else he would see a room in a rich house, where his friend lay asleep, dreaming and smiling at his dreams; and then the door of that room would be opened, the curtains of the bed plucked apart, the sleeper recalled, and lo! there would stand by his side a figure to whom power was given, and even at that dead hour, he must rise and do its bidding. And still the figure had no face by which he might know it; even in his dreams, it had no face, or one that baffled him and melted before his eyes; and thus it was that there sprang up and grew apace in the lawyer's mind a singularly strong, almost an inordinate, curiosity to behold the features of the real Mr. Hyde." (pp. 13–14)

9. We may recall that, as *Psycho* opens, we see Janet Leigh rising from the adulterous bed. Does she now "deserve" Norman Bates? In the contemporary version, the female victim no longer needs such an elaborate transgression to get the story under way. In the days of women's liberation and its backlash, innocent sexual activity alone will trigger the onslaught of Hyde. While in the novella and the early films, Hyde's barely displaced sexual weapon was his walking stick, Norman now comes complete with the modern phallic knife, which may be a chainsaw, power drill, straight razor, hypodermic needle, ice pick, hammer, pitchfork, red-hot poker, or ax.

10. By no means have their talents been confined to horror movies. Think only of such riveting scenes as the throat-cutting in *Marathon Man*, the knife-through-the-hand in *Taxi Driver*, the bullets-entering-the-body scenes in countless shoot-'em-ups most especially *Bonnie and Clyde* and the two *Godfathers*, as well as the choreographed brutalities in *Straw Dogs*, *Clockwork Orange*, or *Midnight Express.*

11. British-made *Peeping Tom* was eviscerated in the press: "The only really satisfactory way to dispose of *Peeping Tom* would be to shovel it up and flush it swiftly down the nearest sewer. Even then the stench would remain . . ." (Derek Hill in the *Tribune*); "*Peeping Tom* stinks more than anything else in British films since *The Stranglers of Bombay*. . . . What worries me is that anyone could entertain this muck and give it commercial shape . . ." (William Whitebait in *The Newstatesman*); "It is only surprising that while the Marquis' books are still forbidden here after practically two centuries it is possible within the commercial industry, to produce films like *Peeping Tom*. De Sade at least veiled his enjoyment under the pretense of being a moralist" (David Robinson in the *Monthly Film Bulletin*); and "I was shocked to the core to find a director of his standing befouling the screen with such perverted nonsense. It wallows in the discarded urges of a homicidal pervert. It uses phony cinema artifice and heavy orchestral music to whip up a debased atmosphere. From its lumbering, mildly salacious beginning to its appallingly masochistic and depraved climax it is wholly evil" (Nina Hibbins in *The Daily Worker*).

12. The most important of the female retaliation films is *Alien* (1979) and its sequel, *Aliens* (1986). In the first film the shape-shifting phallic slug wreaked havoc in the space freighter, *Nostromo*, popping in and out of various bodies unannounced until being finally shown the door by our heroine, Ripley. In *Aliens*, Ripley returns to the incubating lair of the pod monsters and there rescues an orphaned child from the tentacles of the mother Alien. In a custody/maternity battle which makes any action that Dracula, the Frankenstein monster, or Hyde could inspire seem like child's play, these two mothers have at it like gangsters.

13. I am indebted to the National Coalition on Television Violence for alerting me to the content of *Cobra*. Ironically, while *Cobra* clearly revels in violence and deserves its R rating, *Indiana Jones and the Temple of Doom* gets a PG. Mr. Jones is almost as violent as Mr. Cobretta; in fact, the film has 215 acts of violence, or 108 per hour. These include 39 attempted murders, 33 of which were by the evil villains. Indiana kills 14 villains and a boy hero and group of children kill five more. The villains kill only one good guy, who makes a brief appearance at the beginning to set the revenge motive in action. As in *Raiders of the Lost Ark*, there is plenty of sadism and gore, an intense romanticizing of violence, nonstop combat and murder. The major difference between *Cobra* and *Indiana Jones* is that Mr. Jones has a ten-year-old boy as his sidekick, much as in the violent comics. Mr. Cobretta commits his violence alone.

14. Just as the car has replaced the horse in the chase rituals, so the submachine gun has replaced the six-shooter. Whereas the original movie codes forbade the Tommy gun, now no violent film would be without one. And the gun of choice is the Uzi. In movies like *Rambo, Missing in Action,* and *Commando,* as well as in television shows like *The A-Team, Miami Vice,* and *The Equalizer,* the weapon acts like the sidekick character in the Western. If the modern hero in the violent rituals is to act the part of a one-man army, he needs the firepower of hundreds. Again, as with so many of the innovations in these rituals, film technology has played a crucial role. As Joseph Zito, director of some of the Chuck Norris films, claims, the look of the automatic blaze is as important as the body count: "You have all kinds of different patterns of flash. We sometimes choose our weapons based on the lighting of a scene. Sometimes we choose rounds based on the size of the flare you'll see. The sound of an automatic is very contemporary. The blaze and the sound of casings hitting the ground provide an important punctuation to the action" ("Sons of Rambo," *Newsweek*).

Chapter 6

1. The current view of the Federal Communications Commission is that television is a business, not a charitable enterprise, or an extension of education. Thanks to Mark Fowler's five-year reign at the FCC, the high-sounding, but unrealistic, mandate of the Communications Act of 1934 that broadcasters serve the public "interest, convenience and necessity" has been replaced by laissez-faire economics. The public interest, Chairman Fowler has said, should be determined by the "public's interest." To be sure, this view has created all manner of what Fred Friendly has called "an electronic midway": barter syndication by which stations trade air time for commercials, the buying and selling of stations as if they were newspapers, the creation of home shopping networks, and most interesting for the study of preposterous violence, the program-length commercials—shows that essentially promote what is usually a war toy. Under the old FCC, commercials were only a part of the program, but now toy companies manufacture the toy and then produce the television show to promote the toy. Also notice the desultory attempts to establish objective standards in such matters as political advertising, or attempts to regulate public service programming, or better yet, the proscribing of levels of violence during the "family hours."

2. Here is the Nielsen rationale. Imagine 100,000 beads in a washtub; 30,000 are red and 70,000 are white. Mix them thoroughly, then scoop out a sample of 1,000. Even before counting, you expect that not all beads in the sample will be red. Nor would you expect the sample to divide exactly at 300 red and 700 white. The mathematical odds are about 20 to 1 that the count for red beads will be between 270 and 330—27 percent to 33 percent of the sample. This is called a "rating" of 30, plus or minus 3 with a 20

to 1 assurance of statistical reliability. These basic sampling laws wouldn't change even if you drew your sample of 1,000 from 80 million beads instead of 100,000—assuming that the 80 million beads had the same ratio of red to white. In many ways measuring a television audience is counting beads. With advances in computer technology, sampling became an overnight inquisition. "Is the set turned on or not? If on, is it turned to channel A . . . or B . . . or C?" These questions are just as simple as asking if the bead is red or white. The answer in each case is a simple yes or no. Producers can now know almost within an hour how large their audience was.

3. Ironically, after more than thirty-five years of cooperation between the networks and the advertisers in the use of the Nielsen system, it was the networks which balked at the Peoplemeter. No wonder—one of the most glaring facts the Peoplemeter showed was just how much market share the networks have lost to the independents. ABC threatened to drop the Peoplemeter altogether, as did a half hearted CBS. Why should they pay millions of dollars a year to be told that their campfire was not being attended? CBS was especially concerned because it uses a system of "make-goods" which guarantees advertisers free time on other programs if the contracted market share is not delivered. To make matters still worse, women aged twenty-five to fifty-four, an audience CBS prided itself on entertaining, was wandering away to other campfires. The advertisers didn't care about the networks' problems. With thirty-second spots costing from $80,000 to $400,000, who could be concerned about the digestive problems of network executives? The real alliance is no longer between network and sponsor, as it used to be in the days of the *Firestone Hour* or the *Kraft Theater*, but between sponsor and advertising agency. It is certainly a sign of the shift that not only do agencies prebuy television time and then resell it but that the Peoplemeter was introduced over network objections by the largest worldwide advertising agencies.

4. It is worth recalling that the only noncommercial networks in the United States are PBS, which has minicommercials and major begathons, and CBN, which is an extended commercial for a generally accepted, and often violent, mythology. When CBN is not broadcasting religious programs, its audience prefers to be entertained with violence. On Saturdays from 9 a.m. to 9 p.m. and on Sundays from 1 p.m. to 6 p.m., violent Western programming takes over. Although Pat Robertson has claimed that CBN programming is typified by *Leave it to Beaver*, the National Coalition on Television Violence found that thirty-four of the forty-three hours set aside for action/drama were of the *Rifleman, Branded* or *Guns of Will Sonnett* ilk. When queried, CBN executives said that the audience for such shows helps to fund the ministry and "brings more people to Christ" (Radecki, *NCTV News* vol. 7, nos. 7–8). Equally interesting is what is happening at PBS. As *TV Guide* has recently reported, public broadcasting is looking increasingly like network television. WTTW in Chicago, "the nation's most-watched PTV station," no longer refers to itself on the air or on its stationery as a public television station. Why should it? WTTW is doing what more than 71 of the 319 public stations are doing: broadcasting syndicated programs like *I Spy*. When *Lassie* outdraws Bill Moyers and when supposedly the best shows PBS has to offer, like *The Jewel in the Crown*, trail even the worst shows the networks have to offer, the dilemma is clear. Does PBS run *American Playhouse* during its pledge weeks, or does it rerun "musical toasts" to Bing Crosby, the Beatles, and Elvis Presley? Although PBS was established to "address itself to the idea of excellence not the idea of acceptability," if you want audience you have to show it what it wants to see. Still, PBS and CBN together account for less than four percent of the total audience. Critics used to say that if there were only more networks, we would be seeing better shows. Once we had pay TV, shows would get even better. After the demise of almost five arts and entertainment channels and the dominance of HBO and Showtime, we now know better. Having twenty-five channels means only, in George Gerbner's analogy, that you can be told possibly two different

stories but see them at different stages. The National Coalition on Television Violence estimates that, instead of being less violent, pay TV broadcasts approximately twenty percent more violence, largely because of uncut movies (Radecki, *NCTV News,* vol. 7, nos. 3–4).

5. Because children *seem* to respond to television differently—more tightly locked into the experience—there is a temptation to conclude that it affects them differently. It does. Millions of dollars and thousands of research hours have been dedicated to proving that what is seen on television then leaks into behavior. As with the eruption of concern over pulp novels in the last century, and with comics and movies in our own time, this causality has been a favorite explanation of complex antisocial adolescent behavior. Given this premise, it is understandable that most of the scientific study of television has been to prove a direct and necessary causality.

Although I have tried to steer clear of the relationship between fictional preposterous violence and human behavior, when considering television the relationship must be addressed, if only in passing. The relationship between viewing violence and violent behavior is widely discussed: in reports of the Surgeon General, in every introductory social psychology textbook, and in numerous scholarly and popular books, monographs, and articles. There appears to be such widespread agreement on the connection between watching violence and the increase in aggressive behavior that one might wonder why one should even question the causality. Yet recently those people who have examined the scientific studies have questioned both methodology and conclusion. Here is the gist of the methodologies.

First are field studies in which one control group is assigned to watch either violent or nonviolent programs and is then judged by some index of aggression. Correlational studies, on the other hand, attempt to measure the viewing of violence with a scale of aggressive behavior. Finally, cumulative-effect studies attempt to correlate viewing over time with increased aggressive behavior.

In a thoroughgoing review of all the studies published (literally thousands, although only a few hundred core studies are continually replenished by graduate students looking for dissertation material and by assistant professors looking for tenure), Jonathan L. Freedman, a statistician and psychologist at the University of Ontario, concluded that, "First, there is a consistent, small positive correlation between viewing television violence and aggressiveness; second, there is little convincing evidence that in natural settings viewing television violence causes people to be more aggressive" ("Effect of Television Violence on Aggressiveness," p. 227). For every study which announces a causality, there is one which rearranges the information and concludes the opposite. For instance, Paul Hirsh, a sociologist at the University of Chicago, has even argued in "The Scary World of the Nonviewer" and "On Not Learning from One's Mistakes," that the really anxious and disturbed part of the population are not those who watch television but those who spurn the medium. Nonviewers are more alienated and fearful than heavy viewers. As one wag has commented, this brouhaha is not only the longest running soap opera in the social sciences, and the only firm conclusion that can be drawn is that television can indeed foster violence—among social scientists.

Still, the nexus between watching and acting is so commonsensical that the academic consensus seems justified. Of course, academics have incorrectly argued common-sense conclusions before, as Stephen Jay Gould repeatedly shows in *The Mismeasure of Man.* (See also note 6 of Chapter 4.) What makes the correlation between TV violence and aggressiveness so compelling is that so much other information, like rising crime rates or even declining SAT scores, seems to reiterate the connection. But some rethinking may be in order. Crime rates have decreased as the demographic bulge has passed, like a rabbit swallowed by a python, and SAT scores are being reinterpreted in terms of the influx of ethnic and lower-income test takers who previously were not in school and were not applying to college. The baby boom and the TV boom were simultaneous occurrences. Jib Fowles concludes his article "The 'Craniology' of the 20th Century" in *TV Quarterly:* "The remarkable thing about the [television] medium is not that it has so much negative influence, but that it has so little. Given the vastness of the audience and the enormity of the programming (something over five million hours of broadcasting annually), it is interesting that there is so little traceable impact upon the nation. Even the number of reported untoward incidents—when an impressionable viewer imitates something seen on a show with damaging results—cannot be more than a few dozen a year" (p. 477).

6. Although we often blame the Europeans for censorship of nursery rhymes, "trimming" has a rich Anglo-American history as well. In the seventeenth century, George Wither warned of the dangers of nursery rhymes, and by the nineteenth century reformers like Sarah Trimmer and Samuel Goodrich predicted even more dire consequences. The most recent reviser is Marjorie Ainsborough Decker. In her *Christian Mother Goose Treasury,* the three mice are "kind" and the crooked man who walked a crooked mile is cured by faith. Another revision: "Tom Tom, the Piper's son/ Stole a pig and away did run,/ The Lord said,/ 'Tom, take it back right away,/ Or you'll never be happy,/ Day after day.' "

7. In the only rigorous comparison made between folkloric and televised violence, Catherine Kirkland found that television violence pales in comparison with orally transmitted lore. In "Fairy Tales in the Age of Television: A Comparative Content Analysis," Kirkland uses George Gerbner's "Cultural Indicators" to compare his data from a tenyear study of 750 prime-time and 544 weekend/daytime shows ("The Mainstreaming of America: Violence Profile No. 11") with her sample of the ninety-two stories from *The Complete Grimms Fairy Tales.* Her conclusion:

> Both [television and fairy tales] exhibit social and gender bias, and the theme of violence appears frequently and is emphasized in both worlds, but these tendencies are differently manifested. One might not expect fairy tales to exhibit an emphasis on violence similar to that of TV. In fact, examples from the Grimm collection are even more explicitly gory, and evil characters quite frequently earn bizarre comeuppances—e.g., Snow White's stepmother is forced to dance herself to death wearing red-hot iron shoes; a traitorous serving maid is put into a nail-studded barrel and rolled down an incline; and a malevolent wizard who keeps the dismembered bodies of his former wives in a blood-filled basin is burned alive by the ladies' irate relatives. . . . (p. 125)

The audience has no time to contemplate such violence in either medium, not just because the jittery audience prefers movement, but also because oral story telling has always depended on focusing audience attention on current action.

8. In the history of post-Vietnam reconciliation, *The A-Team* will doubtless be seen to play a pivotal role. In the first generation of the mass-media attempts to picture national distress and still retain an audience, the vet was a lunatic (*Coming Home, Taxi Driver*), then bizarre and misunderstood (*First Blood, Missing in Action*), then well adjusted but in a maladjusted world (*Magnum P.I., The A-Team*), and finally victorious—the later *Rambo* movies. It could be argued that *The A-Team* lost its audience not from repetition as much as from anachronism.

9. How *The A-Team* will fare in the afternoon is not yet clear. Although no definitive study has been done on reruns, it seems that violence does not wear well. *Starsky and Hutch, Baretta, Kojak,* and other police shows are rerun mainly to fill up time. The only historical exception is *The Untouchables,* which was first shown by ABC in 1959 and is

still in syndication. Violence, perhaps because of its dependence on special effects, always seems dated, while *The Odd Couple, Get Smart, M*A*S*H, Taxi, The Mary Tyler Moore Show*, and other sitcoms which reiterate human situations continue to find an audience. The obvious argument that the afternoon audience is not interested in violence is self-evidently untrue as shown by the spate of hyperviolent after-school cartoons like *G.I. Joe, He-Man and the Masters of the Universe, Thundercats, She-Ra*, as well as the standard *Tom and Jerry*, and *The Road Runner*.

10. In fact, while Gibbon was bemoaning the fate of Rome, crude burlesques of gladiatorial battle were being enjoyed and reported on by Samuel Pepys. In his *Diary*, Pepys notes all manner of contrived violence—"ludic license," he called it—in carnival displays. Meanwhile, more violent still, on the American frontier "collar and elbow" wrestling, as well as eye-gouging and catch-as-catch-can, were often part of a young man's entertainment. The level of pretense depended on the level of audience sophistication. The folklore of the American West, which details the heroic combat of Mike Fink and Davy Crockett, is part of this mythic tradition of carefully regulated chaos. See Elliott J. Gorn, "'Gouge and Bite, Pull Hair and Scratch': The Social Significance of Fighting in the Southern Backcountry," for a sampling of nineteenth-century exaggerated wrestling.

11. In *Mythologies*, the French critic Roland Barthes unfolds the semiotic distinction between events:

> The audience knows very well the distinction between [professional] wrestling and boxing; it knows that boxing is a Jansenist sport, based on a demonstration of excellence. One can bet on the outcome of a boxing-match: with wrestling, it would make no sense. A boxing-match is a story which is constructed before the eyes of the spectator; in wrestling, on the contrary, it is each moment which is intelligible, not the passage of time. The spectator is not interested in the rise and fall of fortunes; he expects the transient image of certain passions. Wrestling therefore demands an immediate reading of the juxtaposed meanings, so that there is no need to connect them. The logical conclusion of the contest does not interest the wrestling-fan, while on the contrary a boxing-match always implies a science of the future. In other words, wrestling is a sum of spectacles, of which no single one is a function: each moment imposes the total knowledge of a passion which raised erect and alone, without ever extending to the crowning moment of a result. (pp. 15–16)

Chapter 7

1. Read Daniel Boorstin, Stanley Aronowitz, Milton Shulman, John M. Phelan, Marie Winn, Jerry Mander, Richard Sennett, Christopher Lasch, or Neil Postman and you will find few good words for the medium. Two exceptions, however, should be mentioned. First was *Understanding Media* by Marshall McLuhan, an English professor whose primary interest was in applying a form of macroanalysis to the extracorporeal nervous system. Content was purposefully beside the point because, in McLuhan's all too fluent catch phrase, "the medium is the message." The other academic interpretation came from the Marxists, notably from the Frankfurt theorists (Horkheimer, Adorno, Marcuse) who traveled to this country after the war, settled at the New School for Social Research in New York City, and accounted for their traumatic pasts in terms of our cultural decadence. This view still has much academic respectability; witness the rise of the Uni-

versity of Birmingham Centre for Contemporary Cultural Studies (CCCS) as well as the influence of *Screen* theory. Such critics as Stuart Hall, Raymond Williams, Colin MacCabe, and John Fiske have continued and updated the work of Louis Althusser and Antonio Gramsci to make fashionable such concepts as the "ideological state apparatuses" (ISAs), the audience as "cultural dupe," "culture as deception," and the like. As one might imagine, their analysis centers around economic exploitation ("hegemony") by which the culture industry transforms ("reifies") desire into commodity-driven anxiety. The ruling class attempts to make "common sense" into what they believe. We are dulled and gulled by propaganda not into McLuhan's global village but into Aldous Huxley's *Brave New World.* Neither view, however, attempts to situate television in the context of audience-driven folklore.

2. For more, see Sidney Kaplan, "The Image of Amusement Arcades and Differences in Male and Female Video Game Playing," Sidney and Shirley Kaplan, "Video Games, Sex and Sex Differences," and Gillian Skirrow, "Hellivision: An Analysis of Video Games." The few females who do wander in to play arcade games are supplied with the least aggressive game—*Ms Pac-Man*—a simpler version of *Pac-Man* with a perplexing name.

3. Although obstacle and maze games were developed first, raster graphics, or fields of colored dots, have been superseded by screens of light outlines, called vector graphics or Quadrascan. Vector graphics not only allow for more complicated programming but also produce a far more realistic screen. Just as hand-puppets displaced marionettes in *Punch and Judy*, in the economic struggle for a quarter the vector graphic games, the more explosive and violent games, now dominate the business.

4. As an extinct species often points to the direction of an evolutionary turn, so games removed from the market indicate the pressures on the producers of adolescent entertainment. While all video games use violence to some degree (shooting, eating, trapping, killing), some games were "voluntarily" removed by manufacturers or distributors. In *Mugger* the player walked through an urban setting, earning points by shooting, literally splattering, muggers before they attacked. Points were lost if the player hit the "innocent bystander" or the "old lady." *Death Race* was a driving game like *Turbo* except that the player piloted a little car around to hit pedestrians. A tombstone appeared and a dirge was played after every successful encounter. In response to numerous complaints, the manufacturer contended that the victims were not to be known as "pedestrians" but as "gremlins." Too late, this morbid game ("So many pedestrians, so little time") was removed. In the wake of the movie *Jaws, Shark Attack* let the player be a shark that swam along and gobbled divers. By pushing a "thrust" or "munch" button, the player dined on divers who screamed when "munched." For an older audience wanting to combine violence and sex, rape games like *Custer's Revenge* or *Bachelor Party* were developed. They were test-marketed in bars. Patrons liked them; women's groups did not. They were removed often by local ordinances prohibiting pornography.

5. Preposterous violence is not unique to contemporary heavy metal music; it is just more celebrated. After all, Wayne Cochrane in the 1950s and Peter Townshend of The Who in the 1960s were breaking furniture and smashing guitars. But music violence now has become so stylized that one can distinguish the "punk" routines of a Sid Viscous, a Johnny Rotten, or the Sex Pistols from the cosmic storm-trooper show of KISS and the bash-'em-up show of Twisted Sister. What remains constant is the overwhelming maleness of such entertainment. Almost without exception, these are all-male groups, in an almost all-male industry, playing to an almost all-adolescent male audience. As one would expect given such components, the behavior is aggressive because the real anxiety is focused on what is missing, namely, women.

6. In the wash of awareness that followed the criticism of music videos, media attention focused on the least important factor of rock music, the lyrics. In September 1985, down the corridor from where the Kefauver committees had heard testimony on the

comic-book menace thirty years earlier, a committee of the Senate again was reminded of the need to control adolescent entertainment before irrevocable damage was done. In place of Fredric Wertham brandishing reams of lurid comics were two wives of politicians and a born-again Christian.

The Parents' Music Resource Center (PMRC) was represented by its cofounders, Mary Elizabeth "Tipper" Gore, wife of committee member and presidential aspirant, Senator Albert Gore, and Susan Baker, wife of James A. Baker, secretary of the treasury. Their expert in the field of media studies was Jeff Ling, a twenty-eight-year-old minister and "youth counselor" whose "relationship with Jesus Christ" motivated him to speak out against "rock porn." At first, Senator Ernest Hollings proclaimed that "the only redeeming social value of such music is that the words are inaudible," but members of the PMRC showed this to be an overstatement. This music, as they proved by distributing mimeographed transcriptions, was rife with allusions to incest, masturbation, suicide, sex change, sexual intercourse, and most of all, violent antisocial behavior. Not only were these subjects improper topics of musical discussion, they were certainly not being discussed properly in music. Although none of the PMRC members wanted to take the feminist position that the lyrics revealed rampant misogyny, the fact remained that the lyrics' hostility toward women was virulent. Here, for instance, are lyrics from the irredeemably vulgar "Golden Showers" by the Mentors on their *You Axed for It* LP:"Listen little slut/ Do as you are told/ Come with daddy for me to pour the gold./ All through my excrements you shall roam/ Bend up and smell my anal vapor/ Your face is my toilet paper/ On your face I leave a shit tower." Or this lyric from Mötley Crüe's *Shout at the Devil* LP: "Touch my gun but don't pull the trigger/ Shine my pistol some more./ Here I cum/ Reach down real low/ Slide it in real slow/ You feel so good./ Do you want some more?/ I got one more shot/ My gun's still warm."

After a surfeit of such lyrics, Senator Paula Hawkins, who was neither a committee member nor a member of the PMRC but was campaigning for reelection in Florida, showed segments from two rock videos. She introduced Van Halen's "Hot for Teacher" and Twisted Sister's "We're Not Gonna to Take It," stopping the latter just as the "father" is about to be blasted through a wall by his guitar-playing son. "We've seen enough," she said. Senator Hawkins also distributed copies of other lyrics, asking the senators "not to let them go beyond your possession lest they fall into the wrong hands" (quoted by Zucchino, p. 65). Jeff Ling then showed his slide collection of various record covers while reading especially foul lyrics. He first exhorted the C-SPAN audience to remove any children from the room or risk their injury.

The case had been made. Senator Hollings was convinced and promised to "get the best Constitutional minds around" on the case to see if the "outrageous filth" could be outlawed. What the PMRC wanted was "just a rating system so that the eight percent of objectionable lyrics could be identified." To some extent they succeeded. The Recording Industry Association of America encouraged its members to place "Parental Guidance—Explicit Lyrics" stickers on albums, but that was not enough. The PMRC wanted all albums rated. The problem was, as the industry spokesmen were quick to point out, that there were about 325 movies released each year, compared to about 25,000 songs. In the tradition of such media events, after a burst of attention on *CBS Morning News, The Phil Donahue Show*, in full pages in *Time* and *Newsweek*, as well as in supportive columns by Ellen Goodman ("Help, Buyer Beware of Porn Rock"), William Raspberry ("Filth on the Air"), and George Will ("No One Blushes Anymore"), the concern evaporated. One conclusion was clear as the senators disbanded after taking no action: The recording industry had a lot more money and a lot better lawyers than the comic-book industry ever had.

7. In addition, once the adolescent audience was located, films appeared on the rental market that had no theatrical release and therefore carried no rating whatsoever. In a

bizarre variation of free-market censorship, if the Motion Picture Association of America decides a film merits an X, a producer can elect to release that film with no rating—NR. In the video stores, NR films are rented as if they are PGs. There have even been instances, as in *Scarface* and *Crimes of Passion*, when scenes cut for a movie rating were reinserted into the film before it was put out on videocassette.

8. Although I have not checked with all the state statutes which govern the role of the media at executions, I have been assured by the associate warden at the Florida Department of Corrections that other states follow a uniform procedure. In the "Rules of the Department of Corrections," that procedure is announced: "No electronic or mechanical devices including but not limited to still, moving picture or video-tape cameras, tape recorders or similar devices, or artistic paraphernalia, will be permitted in the execution observation room" (Chap. 33–15.02b). Recently, however, a reporter in Texas did photograph and print an image of an executed man and claimed the protection of the First Amendment. This case is currently being adjudicated.

9. The condition is worldwide. In fact, there are high levels of televised violence in every country that has independent programming. The Fuji and Asahi commercial networks in Japan, the Fifth Channel in France, the English ITV, the Canadian CTV, and the New Zealand TV1 and TV2 are examples of what happens when advertiser-(i.e., audience-) supported broadcasting competes with the state channels. As the recent BBC-underwritten report, "The Portrayal of Violence on British Television," makes clear, state-supported television has had to become more violent to win back audience share from the independents. Only in countries like West Germany, which has no independent stations, is there anything like violence-free television in the "free" world. To be sure, most (up to sixty-five percent) of the violent programs on Canadian, English, Australian, and New Zealand television are imported from the U.S., but this high proportion is a function of taste as well as economics. Because of a scarcity of American violent programming, independent German, French, Italian, and Spanish are combining to market their own Eurocop series.

Works Cited

Although in the last twenty years, there has been voluminous scholarship in the social sciences on the effects of violence in mass media, most of it reiterates about a dozen core studies. The best general overview is the seven-volume Report by The Royal Commission on Violence in the Communication Industry (Toronto: Publications Centre, 1967), commissioned by the Province of Ontario to examine the flood of violence coming into Canadian media primarily from the south. The Canadian scholars who conducted the study made few recommendations, but they produced a compendious overview of Anglo-American violence in movies, television, books, and music. Aside from occasional polemics from Parents' Music Resource Center, the American Academy of Pediatrics, and Junior Leagues, the most useful current newsletter is Thomas Radecki's crusading *NCTV News*, especially vol. 4, no. 3 (1983), which is a bibliography of TV/film violence from 1933–83, published by the National Coalition on Television Violence.

Adam, John Paul. *Milton Caniff, Rembrandt of the Comic Strip.* New York: David McKay, 1946.

Agee, James. *Agee On Film.* Edited by Paul Ashdown. Knoxville: University of Tennessee Press, 1985.

Albin, Len. "The Best Video Games of 1982." *TV Guide* (December 4, 1982): 50–54.

Allen, Robert C., ed. *Channels of Discourse: Television and Contemporary Discourse.* Chapel Hill: University of North Carolina Press, 1987.

Alloway, Lawrence. *Violent America: The Movies 1946–1964.* Descriptive Catalog, Museum of Modern Art Show from April 24 to June 6, 1969. Greenwich, Conn.: Graphic Society, 1971.

Altick, Richard Daniel. *The English Common Reader: A Social History of the Mass Reading Public 1800–1900.* Chicago: University of Chicago Press, 1957.

Andrews, Peter. "Peddling Prime Time." *Saturday Review* (June 7, 1980): 64–65.

Anglo, Michael. *Penny Dreadfuls and Other Victorian Horrors.* London: Jupiter, 1987.

Ardrey, Robert. *The Hunting Hypothesis: A Personal Conclusion.* New York: Atheneum, 1976.

Arendt, Hannah. *On Violence.* New York: Harcourt Brace & World, 1970.

Aronowitz, Stanley. *False Promises: The Shaping of American Working Class Consciousness.* New York: McGraw-Hill, 1973.

Augustine, St. *Confessions.* Translated by R. S. Pine-Coffin. Baltimore, Md.: Penguin, 1961.

Axelrod, Robert. *The Evolution of Cooperation.* New York: Basic Books, 1984.

Barnett, R. C. *Assyrian Palace Reliefs in the British Museum.* Translated by Christina Haglund. London: British Museum, 1960.

Barrie, J. M. *Sentimental Tommy.* 1896; rpt. New York: Scribner's Sons, 1924.

Barthes, Roland. *Mythologies.* Translated by Annette Lavers. New York: Hill & Wang, 1972.

Beckford, William. *The Journal of William Beckford in Portugal and Spain.* Edited by Boyd Alexander. New York: J. Day Co., 1955.

Bersani, Leo, and Ulysse Dutoit. *The Forms of Violence: Narrative in Assyrian Art and Modern Culture.* New York: Schocken, 1985.

Bettelheim, Bruno. *The Uses of Enchantment: The Meaning and Importance of Fairy Tales.* New York: Alfred A. Knopf, 1975.

———. "Violence: A Neglected Mode of Behavior." In *Surviving and Other Essays.* New York: Alfred A. Knopf, 1979.

Biro, Yvette. *Profane Mythology: The Savage Mind of the Cinema.* Translated by Imre Goldstein. Bloomington, Ind.: University of Indiana Press, 1982.

Bischoff, Dan. "The Wrestling Sensation Rocks the Nation." *Village Voice* (March 19, 1985): 8.

Bocock, Robert. *Ritual in Industrial Society: A Sociological Analysis of Ritualism in Modern England.* London: George Allen & Unwin, 1974.

Bogart, Leo. "Comic Strips and Their Adult Readers." In *Mass Culture: The Popular Arts in America.* Edited by Bernard Rosenberg and David Manning White. New York: Macmillan, 1957.

Boorstin, Daniel J. *The Image: A Guide to Pseudo Events in America.* New York: Atheneum, 1961.

———. As quoted by Christopher Lehmann-Haupt, reviewing James Lardner, *Fast Forward. New York Times* (May 11, 1987): 15.

Bottigheimer, Ruth. *Grimms' Bad Girls and Bold Boys.* New Haven, Conn.: Yale University Press, 1987.

Bowers, Fredson. *Elizabethan Revenge Tragedy 1587–1642.* Princeton, N.J.: Princeton University Press, 1940.

Brantlinger, Patrick. *Bread and Circuses: Theories of Mass Decay as Social Culture.* Ithaca, N.Y.: Cornell University Press, 1983.

Browne, Ray B., ed. *Popular Culture and the Expanding Consciousness.* New York: John Wiley, 1973.

Brucher, Richard T. "Fantasies of Violence: *Hamlet* and *The Revenger's Tragedy.*" *Studies in English Literature* 21 (1981): 38–49.

Bryant, Jennings, and Dolf Zillman. "Sports Violence and the Media." In *Sports Violence*. Edited by Jeffrey H. Goldstein. New York: Springer, 1983.

Burgess, Anthony. *Clockwork Orange*. New York: Norton, 1963.

Burkert, Walter, René Girard, and Jonathan Z. Smith. *Violent Origins: On Ritual Killing and Cultural Formation*. Stanford, Calif.: Stanford University Press, 1986.

Byron, Lord (George Gordon). "The Vampire (a fragment)." In *Three Gothic Novels*. Edited E. F. Bleiler. New York: Dover, 1966.

Canby, Vincent. "Are the Ratings Just Alphabet Soup?" *New York Times* (April 20, 1986): 19.

———. "Pretty Soon, All You'll See Are Big Hits in Tiny Theaters." *New York Times* (January 25, 1987): 17.

Chambers, Sir Thomas. "Comments on Popular Reading." *Boy's Own Paper* (September 5, 1885): 783.

Charney, Maurice. "The Persuasiveness of Violence in Elizabethan Plays." *Renaissance Drama* 2 (1969): 34–51.

Children's Bureau, *Facts about Juvenile Delinquency*. No. 215. Washington, D.C.: Government Printing Office, 1953.

Cohen, Yehudi. *The Transition from Childhood to Adolescence: Cross-Cultural Studies of Initiation Ceremonies, Legal Systems, and Incest Taboos*. Chicago: Aldine, 1964.

Collier, John Payne. *The Tragical Comedy or Comical Tragedy of Punch and Judy*. London: Prowett, 1828.

"Comic Books and Juvenile Delinquency." Interim Report. 84th Congress. Hearings before the Subcommittee to Investigate Juvenile Delinquency. 84th. Congress, Report 62, April 21, 22, and June 4, 1954.

"Comic Books Regain Their Readership and Outlets." *Publishers Weekly* (December 6, 1985): 34–40.

Comstock, George, Steven Chaffee, Natan Katzman, et al. *Television and Human Behavior*. New York: Columbia University Press, 1978.

Connor, Jeff. *Stephen King Goes to Hollywood*. New York: New American Library, 1987.

Contat, Nicolas. *Anecdotes typographiques où l'on voit la description des coutumes, moeurs et usages singuliers des compagnons imprimeurs*. Edited by Giles Barber. New York: Oxford University Press, 1980.

Corry, John. "As Violence Thrives, the Debate Goes On." *New York Times* (April 6, 1986): section 2, p. 1.

———. "Time for Public TV To Go Private?" *New York Times* (November 1, 1987): 35.

Culhane, John. *Special Effects in the Movies: How They Do It*. New York: Ballantine, 1981.

Dalziel, Margaret. *Popular Fiction 100 Years Ago: An Unexplored Tract of Literary History*. London: Cohen & West, 1957.

Daniels, Les. *Comix: A History of Comic Books in America*. New York: Bonanza Books, 1971.

Darnton, Robert. *The Great Cat Massacre and Other Episodes in French Cultural History*. New York: Basic Books, 1984.

Davis, David Brion. *From Homicide to Slavery: Studies in American Culture.* New York: Oxford University Press, 1986.

———. *Homicide in American Fiction 1798–1860: A Study in Social Values.* Ithaca, N.Y.: Cornell University Press, 1957.

Dawkins, Richard. *The Selfish Gene.* New York: Oxford University Press, 1976.

Deane, Hamilton, and John Balderston. *Dracula: The Vampire Play in Three Acts.* New York: Samuel French, Inc., 1960.

Decker, Marjorie Ainsborough. *Christian Mother Goose Treasury.* Iowa Falls: World Bible Publishers, 1978.

De Fleur, Melvin, and Sandra Ball-Rokeach, *Theories of Mass Communication.* New York: David McKay, 1966.

De Levie, Dagobert. *The Modern Idea of the Prevention of Cruelty to Animals and its Reflection in English Poetry.* New York: S. F. Vanni, 1947.

Didion, Joan. *Essays and Conversations.* Edited by Ellen Friedman. Princeton, N.J.: Ontario Review Press, 1984.

Diehl, Huston. "The Iconography of Violence in English Renaissance Tragedy." *Renaissance Drama* 11 (1980): 27–44.

Doré, Gustave. *L'Histoire de la Saint Russie.* Paris: Imprimerie Lacour, 1857.

Douglas, Mary. *Purity and Danger: An Analysis of Concepts of Pollution and Taboo.* London: Routledge & Kegan Paul, 1966.

Dryden, John. "The Tenth Satyr of Juvenal, Translated into English Verse." In *Poems.* Vol. 2. Edited by James Kinsley. Oxford: Clarendon Press, 1958.

Dunae, Patrick A. "Penny Dreadfuls: Late Nineteenth-Century Boys' Literature and Crime." *Victorian Studies* 22, no. 2 (1979): 133–50.

"Editorial on Popular Literature." *Punch* (February 20, 1886): 96.

Eisner, Lotte H. *The Haunted Screen: Expressionism in the German Cinema.* Berkeley, Calif.: University of California Press, 1973.

Elias, Norbert, and Eric Dunning. *Quest for Excitement: Sport and Leisure in the Civilizing Process.* New York: Basil Blackwell, 1986.

Engelhardt, Tom. "The Shortcake Strategy." In *Watching Television: A Pantheon Guide to Popular Culture.* Edited by Tod Gitlin. New York: Pantheon, 1986.

Evans, Walter. "Monster Movies and Rites of Initiation." *Journal of Popular Culture* 4 (1975): 124–42.

———. "Monster Movies: A Sexual Theory." *Journal of Popular Culture* 11 (1973): 353–65.

Eysenck, H. J., and D. K. B. Nias. *Sex, Violence and the Media.* New York: St. Martin's Press, 1979.

"*Faces of Death:* Homevid Pulls Series." *Variety* (July 22, 1987): 1.

"*Faces of Death:* Media Flap." *Variety* (September, 25, 1985): 29.

Farber, Stephen. "Vigilante Themes in TV Films Arrive, but with Qualifiers." *New York Times* (January 11, 1986): 12.

Feiffer, Jules. *The Great Comic Book Heroes.* New York: Dial, 1965.

Feshbach, Seymour. "Mixing Sex With Violence—A Dangerous Alchemy." *New York Times* (August 3, 1980): 29.

Fiedler, Leslie. "Giving The Devil His Due." *Journal of Popular Culture* 12, no. 2 (1979): 197–207.

————. *What Was Literature: Class Culture and Mass Society.* New York: Simon and Schuster, 1982.

Fiske, John. *Television Culture.* New York: Methuen, 1987.

Fleisher, Michael. *Batman: The Encyclopedia.* New York: Macmillan, 1976.

Foltz, Kim and Penelope Wang. "The Unstoppable Thriller King." *Newsweek* (June 10, 1985): 62.

Fowles, Jib. "The 'Craniology' of the 20th Century: Research on Television Effects." *TV Quarterly* 20, no. 4 (1984): 474–77.

————. *Television Viewers vs. Media Snobs: What TV Does for People.* New York: Stein and Day, 1982.

Fox, Robin. "The Inherent Rules of Violence." In *Social Rules and Social Behavior.* Edited by Peter Collett. Totowa, N.J.: Rowman and Littlefield, 1977.

————. *The Red Lamp of Incest.* New York: Dutton, 1980.

Frank, Josette. "What's in the Comics." *Journal of Educational Sociology* 18, no. 4 (1949): 214–22.

Fraser, John. *Violence in the Arts.* Cambridge, Eng.: Cambridge University Press, 1974.

Freedman, Jonathan L. "Effect of Television Violence on Aggressiveness." *Psychological Bulletin* 96, no. 2 (1984): 227–46.

Freeman, Daniel. *Human Sociobiology.* New York: The Free Press, 1979.

Freeman, Edward Augustus. *The Morality of Field Sports.* 1869; rpt. London: Animal's Friends Society, 1920.

French, Philip. "Violence in the Cinema." *The Twentieth Century* 17 (1964–65): 115–130.

Freud, Sigmund. *Moses and Monotheism.* Translated by James Strachey. New York: W. W. Norton and Co., 1952.

————. *Totem and Taboo.* Translated by James Strachey. New York: W. W. Norton and Co., 1950.

Frohock, W. M. *The Novel of Violence in America.* Dallas, Tex.: Southern Methodist University Press, 1946.

Gans, Herbert J. *Popular Culture and High Culture: An Analysis and Evaluation of Taste.* New York: Basic Books, 1974.

Gardner, Helen. *Art Through The Ages.* 5th ed. New York: Harcourt Brace & World, 1970.

Geertz, Clifford. "Feathers, Blood, Crowds, and Money: Notes on the Balinese Cockfight." In *The Interpretation of Culture.* New York: Basic Books, 1973.

Gerbner, George. "Science or Ritual Dance: A Revisionist View of Television Violence Effects Research." *Journal of Communications* 34, no. 3 (1984): 164–75.

————, and Larry Gross. "Living with Television: The Violence Profile." In *Television: The Critical View.* Edited by Horace Newcomb. New York: Oxford University Press, 1979.

————, Larry Gross, et al. "The Mainstreaming of America: Violence Profile No. 11." *Journal of Communication* 30, no. 3 (1980): 10–29.

Gilbert, James. *A Cycle of Outrage: America's Reaction to the Juvenile Delinquent in the 1950s.* New York: Oxford University Press, 1986.

Gillis, John. "The Evolution of Juvenile Delinquency in England: 1890–1914." *Past and Present* 67 (1975): 96–126.

———. *Youth and History.* New York: Academic Press, 1974.

Girard, René. *The Scapegoat.* Translated by Yvonne Freccero. Baltimore, Md.: The Johns Hopkins University Press, 1986.

———. *Violence and the Sacred.* Translated by Patrick Gregory. Baltimore, Md.: Johns Hopkins University Press, 1977.

Gitlin, Tod. *Inside Prime Time.* New York: Pantheon, 1985.

———, ed. *Watching Television: A Pantheon Guide to Popular Culture.* New York: Pantheon, 1986.

Gluckman, Mary, and Max Gluckman. "Of Drama, and Games, and Athletic Contests." In *Secular Ritual.* Edited by Sally F. Moore and Barbara G. Myerhoff. Amsterdam: Van Gorcum, Assen, 1977.

Goethals, Gregor T. *The TV Ritual: Worship at the Video Altar.* Boston: Beacon Press, 1981.

Golding, William. *Lord of the Flies.* New York: Coward-McCann, 1962.

Goldstein, Alan. "Cable TV's Shame: 'Gore-nography.'" *New York Times* (July 3, 1984): A15.

Gorn, Elliott J. " 'Gouge and Bite, Pull Hair and Scratch': The Social Significance of Fighting in the Southern Backcountry." *American Historical Review* 90, no. 1 (1985): 18–45.

Goulart, Ron. *Great History of Comic Books.* Chicago: Contemporary Books, 1986.

Gould, Stephen Jay. *The Mismeasure of Man.* New York: Norton, 1981.

Graalfs, Marilyn. "Violence in Comic Books." In *Violence and the Mass Media.* Edited by Otto N. Larsen. New York: Harper & Row, 1968.

Gray, Paul. "Stephen King: Master of Postliterate Prose." *Time* (August 30, 1982): 87.

Green, John Paul. *"Homo Furiosus": Violence in Some Modern Fiction.* Unpublished Dissertation. Washington State University, 1981.

Greenway, John L. "Ritual and Narrative in the Sport Spectacular." *Journal of Popular Culture* 19, no. 3 (1985): 55–63.

Grossman, Gary H. *Saturday Morning TV.* New York: Dell, 1981.

Gunter, Barrie. *Dimensions of Television Violence.* New York: St. Martin's Press, 1985.

Guttman, Allen. "Roman Sports Violence." In *Sports Violence.* Edited by Jeffrey H. Goldstein. New York: Springer, 1983.

———. *Sports Spectators.* New York: Columbia University Press, 1986.

Hamilton, William D. "The Genetical Theory of Social Behavior: I and II." *Journal of Theoretical Biology* 7 (1964): 1–52.

Handel, Leo A. *Hollywood Looks at Its Audience: A Report of Film Audience Research.* Urbana: University of Illinois Press, 1950.

Handley-Taylor, Geoffrey. *Nursery Rhyme Reform.* Manchester, Eng.: True Aim Press, 1957.

Hanhardt, John C., ed. *Video Culture: A Critical Investigation.* Rochester, N.Y.: Visual Studies Press, 1986.

Hardin, Garrett. "Is Violence Natural?" *Zygon* 18, no. 4 (1983): 405–13.

Harmetz, Aljean. "'Amazing Stories' Tries New Tactics." *New York Times* (June 2, 1981): 21.

———. "*Fatal Attraction* Director Exults Over His Film." *New York Times* (October 5, 1987): 20.

———. "New Movies are Battling for Space in Theaters." *New York Times* (October 14, 1987): 22.

———. "Now Playing: The New Hollywood." *New York Times* (January 10, 1988): section 2, p. 1.

———. "Where Movie Ticket Income Goes." *New York Times* (January 18, 1987): 20.

Harris, Jay, ed. *TV Guide: The First 25 Years.* New York: New American Library, 1980.

Harwood, Dix. *Love for Animals and How It Developed in Britain.* Unpublished Dissertation. Columbia University, 1928.

Henderson, Joseph. *Thresholds of Initiation.* Middletown, Conn.: Wesleyan University Press, 1967.

Henricks, Thomas. "Professional Wrestling as Moral Order." *Sociological Inquiry* 44, no. 3 (1974): 177–88.

Hirsh, Paul. "The Scary World of the Nonviewer and Other Anomalies: A Reanalysis of Gerbner et al.'s Findings on Cultivation Analysis, Part 1." *Communication Research* 7, no. 4 (1980): 403–56.

———. "On Not Learning from One's Mistakes: A Reanalysis of Gerbner et. al.'s Findings on Cultivation Analysis, Part 2." *Communication Research* 8, no. 1 (1981): 3–37.

Hitchman, Francis. "The Penny Press." *Macmillan's Magazine,* 43 (1881): 152–55.

Hoffman, Professor. *Drawing Room Amusements and Evening Party Entertainments.* London: Routledge, 1879.

Hogarth, William, *Public Advertiser,* February 13, 1751. Excerpted in Ronald Paulson, *Hogarth's Graphic Works.* Vol 1. New Haven, Conn.: Yale University Press, 1970.

Hoover, J. Edgar. "To All Law Enforcement Officials, May 1, 1958." In Harry J. Skornia, *Television and Society: An Inquest and Agenda for Improvement.* New York: McGraw-Hill, 1965.

Horsting, Jessie. *Stephen King at the Movies.* New York: Starlog, 1986.

Howard, Rowland. "Radio Crime Drama." *Educational Research Bulletin* (November 15, 1944): 210–14.

Hughes, Winifred. *The Maniac in the Cellar: Sensation Novels of the 1860s.* Princeton, N.J.: Princeton University Press, 1980.

Huizinga, Johann. *Homo Ludens.* London: Routledge & Kegan Paul, 1949.

Hutchinson, Bruce "Comic Strip Violence, 1911–1966." *Journalism Quarterly* 46, no. 2 (1969): 358–64.

Jacob, W. W. "The Monkey's Paw." In *Wolf's Complete Book of Terror.* Edited by Leonard Wolf. New York: Clarkson N. Potter, 1979.

Jacobs, Will, and Gerard Jones. *The Comic Book Heroes from the Silver Age to the Present*. New York: Crown, 1985.

James, Caryn. "Aging Avant-Garde Has a Family Gathering." *New York Times* (April 9, 1988): 11.

James, Louis. *Fiction for the Working Man*. London: Oxford University Press, 1963.

Jameson, Fredric. "Reification and Utopia in Mass Culture." *Social Text* 1 (1979): 130–48.

Janeczko, Paul. "An Interview with Stephen King." *English Journal* 69, no. 2 (1980): 10–11.

Johnson, Samuel. *Selected Poetry and Prose*. Edited by Mona Wilson. Cambridge, Mass.: Harvard University Press, 1957.

Junior League of Bronxville, New York. "Report on Movie Accessibility and Viewing Habits of Children in New York State." Mimeographed. 1987.

Kaminsky, Stewart. *American Film Genres: Approaches to a Critical Theory of Popular Film*. New York: Dell, 1977.

Kaplan, Sidney J. "The Image of Amusement Arcades and Differences in Male and Female Video Game Playing." *Journal of Popular Culture* 17, no. 1 (1983): 93–99.

———, and Shirley Kaplan. "Video Games, Sex and Sex Differences." *Journal of Popular Culture* 17, no. 2 (1983): 361–66.

Kawin, Bruce F., *Telling It Again and Again: Repetition in Literature and Film*. Ithaca, N.Y.: Cornell University Press, 1972.

Kearns, Katherine Sue. *Some Versions of Violence in Three Contemporary American Novels:* John Irving's *The World According to Garp*, Tim O'Brien's *Going After Cacciato*, and Alice Walker's *The Color Purple*. Unpublished Dissertation. Chapel Hill: University of North Carolina, 1982.

Kidd, William J. *Village Wakes; Their Origin, Design and Abuse. A Sermon Preached in the Parochial Chapel of Didsbury, on Sunday Afternoon, August 1, 1841*. Manchester: J. Pratt, 1841.

King, Stephen. *Carrie*. New York: New American Library, 1975.

———. *Christine*. New York: New American Library, 1984.

———. *Creepshow*. New York: New American Library, 1982.

———. *Cujo*. New York: New American Library, 1982.

———. *Danse Macabre*. New York: Everest House, 1981.

———. *The Dead Zone*. New York: New American Library, 1980.

———. *Different Seasons*. New York: New American Library, 1983.

———. *Firestarter*. New York: New American Library, 1981.

———. "Introduction." In *Dracula, Frankenstein and Dr. Jekyll and Mr. Hyde*. New York, New American Library, 1978.

———. *It*. New York: New American Library, 1986.

———. *Misery*. New York: Viking, 1987.

———. *Pet Sematary*. New York: New American Library, 1984.

———. "Playboy Interview." *Playboy* (June 1983): 65ff.

———. *'Salem's Lot*. New York: New American Library, 1976.

———. *The Shining*. New York: New American Library, 1978.

————. *The Stand*. New York: New American Library, 1979.

————, and Peter Straub. *The Talisman*. New York, Viking, 1984.

Kirkland, Catherine. "Fairy Tales in the Age of Television: A Comparative Content Analysis." In *Studies in Communication*. Vol. 1. Edited by Sari Thomas. Norwood, N.J.: Ablex Publishing, 1984.

Klancher, Jon P. *The Making of English Reading Audiences, 1790–1832*. Madison: University of Wisconsin Press, 1987.

Klein, Paul. "Why You Watch, What You Watch, When You Watch." In *TV Guide: The First 25 Years*. Edited by Jay Harris. New York: New American Library, 1980.

Kosinski, Jerzy. *Being There*. New York: Harcourt Brace, 1971.

Kracauer, Sigfried. *From Caligari to Hitler: A Psychological History of German Film*. 1947; rpt. Princeton, N.J.: Princeton University Press, 1971.

Kunzle, David. *The Early Comic Strip: Narrative Strips and Picture Stories in the European Broadsheet from c. 1450 to 1825*. Berkeley: University of California Press, 1973.

La Fontaine, J. S. *Initiation: Ritual Drama and Secret Knowledge Across the World*. Manchester, Eng.: Manchester University Press, 1986.

Lange, David, Robert K. Baker, and Sandra J. Ball. *Mass Media and Violence*. "A Report to the National Commission on the Causes and Prevention of Violence." Vol. 11. Washington D.C.: U. S. Government Printing Office, 1969.

Larsen, Otto N., ed. *Violence and the Mass Media*. New York: Harper & Row, 1968.

Lasch, Christopher. *The Culture of Narcissism: American Life in the Age of Diminishing Returns*. New York: Norton, 1978.

Leach, E. R. "Anthropological Aspects of Language: Animal Categories and Verbal Abuse." In *New Directions in the Study of Language*. Edited by E. H. Lenneberg. Cambridge, Mass.: Harvard University Press, 1964.

Leach, Robert. *The Punch and Judy Show: History, Tradition and Meaning*. Athens, Ga.: University of Georgia Press, 1985.

Legman, Gershorn. *Love & Death: A Study in Censorship*. 1949; rpt. New York: Hacker, 1963.

Levinson, Daniel. *The Seasons of a Man's Life*. New York: Knopf, 1978.

Lewis, Gregg. *Telegarbage: What You Can Do About Sex and Violence on TV*. Nashville, Tenn.: Thomas Nelson, 1977.

Linz, Daniel, Edward Donnerstein, and Stephen Penrod. "The Effects of Multiple Exposures to Filmed Violence Against Women." *Journal of Communication* 34, no. 3 (1984): 130–47.

MacCabe, Colin, ed. *High Theory/Low Culture: Analyzing Popular Television and Film*. New York: St. Martin's Press, 1986.

Macdonald, Dwight. "A Theory of Mass Culture." In *Mass Culture: The Popular Arts in America*. Edited by Bernard Rosenberg and David Manning White. New York: Macmillan, 1957.

Malcolmson, Robert W. *Popular Recreations in English Society 1700–1850*. Cambridge, Eng.: Cambridge University Press, 1973.

Mander, Jerry. *Four Arguments for the Elimination of Television.* New York: Morrow, 1978.

Mankiewicz, Frank, and Joel Swerdlow. *Remote Control: Television and the Manipulation of American Life.* New York: Ballantine Books, 1978.

Marc, David. *Demographic Vistas: Television in American Culture.* Philadelphia: University of Pennsylvania Press, 1984.

Marsh, Peter E. *Aggro: The Illusion of Violence.* London: J. Dent, 1979.

Maslin, Janet. "Movie Bloodlines Lead to Rambo's Children." *New York Times* (March 1, 1987): 21.

May, Alan. "Letter to the Editor." *TV Guide* (April 28, 1985): A-4.

May, Margaret. "Innocence and Experience: The Evolution of the Concept of Juvenile Delinquency in the Mid-Nineteenth Century." *Victorian Studies,* 17 (1973): 7–30.

McCarty, John. *Splatter Movies: Breaking the Last Taboo of the Screen.* New York: St. Martin's Press, 1984.

McLuhan, Marshall. *Understanding Media: The Extensions of Man.* New York: McGraw-Hill, 1964.

Mead, Margaret. "Ritual and Social Crisis." In *The Roots of Ritual.* Edited by James D. Shaughnessy. Grand Rapids, Mich.: William B. Eerdman's Publishing, 1973.

Meredith, George. *An Essay on Comedy.* 1877; rpt. New York: Charles Scribner's Sons, 1897.

Misson, Henri. *Memoirs and Observations in His Travels over England with Some Account of Scotland and Ireland.* Edited by John Ozell. London: D. Browne, 1719.

Modleski, Tania. *Loving with a Vengeance: Mass Produced Fantasies for Women.* New York: Methuen, 1982.

———, ed. *Studies in Entertainment: Critical Approaches to Mass Culture.* Bloomington: Indiana University Press, 1986.

Monaco, James. *Media Culture.* New York: Dell, 1978.

Moore, Sally F., and Barbara G. Myerhoff, eds. *Secular Ritual.* Amsterdam: Van Gorcum, Assen, 1977.

Morgan, Roberta. *Main Event: The World of Professional Wrestling.* New York: Dial, 1979.

Morton, Gerald W., and George M. O'Brien. *Wrestling to Rasslin': Ancient Sport to American Spectacle.* Bowling Green, Ohio: Bowling Green University Popular Press, 1985.

Murphey, A. D. "Audience Demographics, Film Future." *Variety* (August 1975): 3.

Nagourney, Peter. "Elite, Popular and Mass Literature: What People Really Read." *Journal of Popular Culture.* 16, no. 1 (1982): 99–107.

Newcomb, Horace, and Paul Hirsh. "Television as Cultural Forum: Implications for Research." *Quarterly Review of Film Studies* 8, no. 3 (1983): 45–55.

Newcomb, Horace, ed. *Television: The Critical View.* New York: Oxford University Press, 1979.

Nordheimer, Jon. "New Issue as VCRs Expand: Violent Films and the Young." *New York Times* (May 18, 1987): 1.

North, Sterling. "Editorial." *Chicago Daily News* (May 8, 1940): 21.

"Not So Funny." *Time* (October 4, 1948): 46.

Pareles, Jon. "Out of Tune with the Times?" *New York Times* (April 24, 1988): 28.

———. "Rock Video Refocuses on the Music." *New York Times* (August 23, 1987): 20.

———. "Should Rock Lyrics Be Sanitized?" *New York Times* (October 13, 1985): section 2, p. 1.

Parrot, André. *Nineveh and Babylon: The Arts of Mankind.* New York: Golden Press, 1961.

Paulson, Ronald. "The English Dog." In *Popular and Elite Art in the Age of Hogarth and Fielding.* Notre Dame, Ind.: University of Notre Dame Press, 1979.

Peake, Richard B. *Presumption, Or the Fate of Frankenstein, A Romantic Drama in Two Acts.* London: J. Duncombe, 1824.

Penny Dreadfuls and Comics: English Periodicals for Children from Victorian Times to the Present Day. Catalog of Exhibition at the Bethnal Green Museum of Childhood, 1983. London: Victoria and Albert Museum, 1983.

Pepys, Samuel. *Diary.* Edited by Robert Latham and William Matthews. Berkeley: University of California Press, 1970.

Perry, George, and Alan Aldridge. *The Penguin Book of Comics.* Baltimore, Md.: Penguin Books, 1967.

Phelan, John M. *Disenchantment: Meaning and Morality in the Media.* New York: Hastings House, 1980.

Plumb, J. H. "Can Society Banish Cruelty?" *Horizon* 18, no. 3 (1976): 84–85.

Polidori, John. *The Vampyre.* In *Three Gothic Novels.* Edited by E. F. Bleiler. New York: Dover, 1966.

Postman, Neil. *Amusing Ourselves to Death: Public Discourse in the Age of Show Business.* New York: Viking, 1985.

Prawer, S. S. *Caligari's Children: The Film as a Tale of Terror.* New York: Oxford University Press, 1980.

Prest, Thomas Pecket. *Varney the Vampyre: or, the Feast of Blood.* 1860; rpt. New York: Dover, 1970.

Proal, L. J. G. *Le crime et le suicide passionnel.* Paris: Alcan, 1980.

"Punch and Judy, Reviewed." *Harper's Weekly* (January 6, 1872): 5.

Punter, David. *The Literature of Terror: A History of Gothic Fictions from 1765 to the Present Day.* New York: Longman, 1980.

Radecki, Thomas, ed., *NCTV News.* 9 vols. Champaign, Ill.: National Coalition on Television Violence, 1983–88.

Radway, Janice A. *Reading the Romance: Women, Patriarchy, and Popular Literature.* Chapel Hill: University of North Carolina Press, 1984.

Ranly, Ernest W. "Defining Violence." *Thought* 47 (1972): 415–27.

Reade, Julian. *Assyrian Sculpture.* London: British Museum Publication, 1983.

Richardson, Samuel. *Pamela, or Virtue Rewarded.* New York: Century, 1905.

Riches, David, ed. *The Anthropology of Violence.* New York: Basil Blackwell, 1986.

Rios, Charlotte Rose. *Violence in Contemporary Drama: Antonin Artaud's Theater of Cruelty and Selected Drama of Genet, Williams, Albee, Bond, and Pinter.* Unpublished dissertation. University of Notre Dame, 1981.

Ritvo, Harriet. *The Animal Estate: The English and Other Creatures in the Victorian Age.* Cambridge, Mass.: Harvard University Press, 1987.

Rosenberg, Bernard, and David Manning White, eds. *Mass Culture: The Popular Arts in America.* New York: Macmillan, 1957.

Rovin, Jeff. *Special Effects.* New York: A. S. Barnes, 1977.

Royal Commission on Violence in the Communication Industry. *Report.* 7 vols. Toronto, Canada: Publications Centre, 1976.

Saggs, H. W. F. *The Greatness That Was Babylon.* 1962; rpt. New York: New American Library, 1968.

Salmon, Edward G. "What Boys Read." *Fortnightly Review,* 45 (February 1, 1886): 255–56.

Salvianus. *On the Government of God.* Translated by Eva M. Sanford. New York: Columbia University Press, 1930.

Schechner, Richard, and Mady Schuman, *Ritual, Play, and Performance.* New York: Seabury Press, 1976.

Schickel, Richard. "Cobra: A Man of Few Grunts and No Beeps." *Time* (June 2, 1986): 80.

Schwartz, Tony. "Do the Networks Need Violence?" *New York Times* (May 23, 1982): 23.

Searle, John. "Sociobiology and the Explanation of Human Behavior." In *Sociobiology and Human Nature.* Edited by Michael Gregory. San Francisco: Jossey Bass Press, 1978.

Sennett, Richard. *The Fall of Public Man.* New York: Knopf, 1977.

Shanks, Bob. *The Cool Fire: How to Make It in Television.* New York: Norton, 1976.

Sheehy, Gail. *Passages.* New York: Dutton, 1976.

Shelley, Mary. *Frankenstein.* 1831; rpt. New York: New American Library, 1973.

Shulman, Milton. *The Ravenous Eye: The Impact of the Fifth Factor.* London: Cassell, 1973.

Simon, Paul. As quoted in "Washington Notes, Required Reading." *New York Times* (July, 22, 1986): 18.

Skirrow, Gillian. "Hellivision: An Analysis of Video Games." In *Watching Television: A Pantheon Guide to Popular Culture.* Edited by Tod Gitlin. New York: Pantheon, 1986.

Slade, Joseph W. "Violence in the Hard-Core Pornographic Film: A Historical Survey." *Journal of Communication* 34, no. 3 (1984): 149–63.

Slotkin, Richard. *The Fatal Environment: The Myth of the Frontier in the Age of Industrialization, 1800–1890.* New York: Atheneum, 1985.

———. *Regeneration through Violence: The Mythology of the American Frontier.* Wesleyan, Conn.: Wesleyan University Press, 1973.

Smith, Sally Bendell. "Why TV Won't Let Up on Violence." *New York Times* (January 13, 1985): section 2, p. 1.

Solie, Gordon. *Master of the Ring.* Croton-on-Hudson, N.Y.: North River Press, 1984.

"Sons of Rambo." *Newsweek* (October 14, 1985): 50.

Spershott, James. *The Memoirs of James Spershott.* Edited by Francis W. Steer. Chichester Papers, no. 30, 1962.

Stark, Steven D. "10 Years Into the Stallone Era: What It, Uh, Means." *New York Times* (January 22, 1987): 19.

Stein, Eliot. "A Very Tender Film, a Very Nice One': Michael Powell's *Peeping Tom*," *Film Comment* 15, no. 5 (1979): 57–59.

Steinberg, Cobbett. *Reel Facts: The Movie Book of Records.* New York: Random House, 1982.

Steinberg, Leo. *The Sexuality of Christ in Renaissance Art and in Modern Oblivion.* New York: Pantheon, 1983.

Stevenson, Robert Louis. *The Strange Case of Dr. Jekyll and Mr. Hyde.* 1886; rpt. New York: Bantam Books, 1967.

Stoker, Bram. *Dracula.* 1897; rpt. New York: Signet, 1965.

Stone, Gregory P. "Wrestling: The Great American Passion Play." In *Sport: Readings from a Sociological Perspective.* Edited by Eric Dunning. Toronto: University of Toronto Press, 1972.

Storr, Anthony. *Human Aggression.* New York: Atheneum, 1968.

Straub, Peter. "Meeting Stevie." In *Fear Itself: The Horror Fiction of Stephen King.* Edited by Tim Underwood and Chuck Miller. New York: New American Library, 1982.

Strommengen, Eva. *Five Thousand Years of the Art of Mesopotamia.* New York: Abrams, 1964.

Summers, Montague. *The Vampire: His Kith and Kin.* 1928; rpt. New Hyde Park, N.Y.: University Books, 1960.

T., Mr. *Mr. T: The Man with the Gold.* New York: St. Martin's Press, 1984.

Tar, Zoltan. *The Frankfurt School: The Critical Theories of Max Horkheimer and Theodor W. Adorno.* New York: John Wiley, 1977.

Tatar, Maria. *The Hard Facts of the Grimms' Fairy Tales.* Princeton, N.J.: Princeton University Press, 1987.

Taylor, J. T. *Early Opposition to the English Novel: The Popular Reaction from 1760–1830.* New York: King's Crown Press, 1943.

Temmey, Bob. "Wow! Top Pro Wrestlers' Wages Will Throw You For A Loop." *National Enquirer* (September 2, 1986): 38.

Temple, Sir William. *Battle of the Books.* Oxford: Clarendon Press, 1909.

Tertullian. *Apology and De Spectaculis.* Translated by T. R. Glover. New York: Loeb Classical Library, 1931.

Thomas, Keith. *Man and the Natural World: A History of the Modern Sensibility.* New York: Pantheon, 1983.

Tompkins, Joyce H. S. *The Popular Novel in England 1770–1800.* Lincoln: University of Nebraska Press, 1961.

Tracy, Ann B. *The Gothic Novel 1790–1830.* Lexington: University of Kentucky Press, 1981.

Trivers, R. L. "Parent-Child Offspring Conflict." In *Readings in Sociobiology.* Edited by T. H. Clutton-Brock and Paul H. Harvey. San Francisco, Calif.: W. H. Freeman, 1978.

Turner, E. S. *Boys Will Be Boys.* 1948; rpt. London: Michael Joseph, 1975.

Turner, Victor. *The Ritual Process: Structure and Anti-Structure.* Chicago: Aldine Publishing Co., 1969.

———. "Variations on the Theme of Liminality." In *Secular Ritual.* Edited by Sally F. Moore and Barbara G. Myerhoff. Amsterdam: Van Gorcum, Assen, 1977.

Twitchell, James B. *Dreadful Pleasures: An Anatomy of Modern Horror.* New York: Oxford University Press, 1985.

———. *Forbidden Partners: The Incest Taboo in Modern Culture.* New York: Columbia University Press, 1987.

Uffenbach, Zacharias Conrad von. *London in 1710, From the Travels of Zacharias Conrad von Uffenbach.* Edited and translated by W. H. Quarrell and Margaret Mare. London: Faber & Faber, 1934.

Underwood, Tim, and Chuck Miller, eds. *Fear Itself: The Horror Fiction of Stephen King.* New York: New American Library, 1982.

Van Gennep, Arnold. *The Rites of Passage.* 1909; rpt. Chicago: University of Chicago Press, 1960.

Walpole, Horace. *Castle of Otranto.* London: Lownds, 1795.

Warren, Bill. "The Movies and Mr. King." In *Fear Itself: The Horror Fiction of Stephen King.* Edited by Tim Underwood and Chuck Miller. New York: New American Library, 1982.

Warshow, Robert. "Paul, the Horror Comics, and Dr. Wertham." In *Mass Culture: The Popular Arts in America.* Edited by Bernard Rosenberg and David Manning White. New York: Macmillan, 1957.

Waters, Harry F. "Life According to TV." *Newsweek* (December 6, 1982): 136.

Wertham, Fredric. "The Comics . . . Very Funny." *Saturday Review* (May 29, 1948): 6.

———. *The Seduction of the Innocent.* New York: Holt, Rinehart and Winston, 1953.

———. *A Sign for Cain: An Exploration of Human Violence.* New York: Macmillan, 1966.

Wiles, R. M. "Crowd-Pleasing Spectacles in Eighteenth-Century England." *Journal of Popular Culture* 1 (1967): 90–105.

Williamson, Judith. *Consuming Passions: The Dynamics of Popular Culture.* New York: Marion Boyars, 1986.

Wilson, Edward O. *Sociobiology.* Cambridge, Mass.: Harvard University Press, 1980.

Wilson, James Q., and Richard J. Herrnstein. *Crime and Human Nature.* New York: Simon & Schuster, 1985.

Wilson, William. "Riding the Crest of Horror (Stephen King)." *New York Times Magazine* (May 11, 1980): 42ff.

Winn, Marie. *The Plug-in Drug.* New York: Viking Press, 1977.

Winter, Arlene D. "Royal Rhetoric and the Development of Historical Narrative in Neo-Assyrian Reliefs." *Studies in Visual Communication* 7, no. 10 (1981): 26–39.

Winter, Douglas E. "Interview with Stephen King, May 4, 1982." In *Stephen King: The Art of Darkness.* New York: New American Library, 1984.

Wood, Peter H. "Television as Dream." In *Television: The Critical View.* Edited by Horace Newcomb. New York: Oxford University Press, 1979.

Wordsworth, William. *Poetical Works.* Edited by Ernest De Selincourt. New York: Oxford University Press. 1969.

Zagorski, Edward J. *Teacher's Manual: The Novels of Stephen King.* New York: New American Library, 1981.

Zucchino, David. "Big Brother Meets Twisted Sister." *Rolling Stone* (November 7, 1985): 9ff.

Index

Abbott and Costello Meet Frankenstein, 194
Abdulla the Butcher, *256*
Abel, 41
AC comics, 173
Ace Books, 94
Adams, Richard, 122
Adonis, Adrian, 258
Adrenalin, 40
Agee, James, 181
Aggression, 32–47, 49–55, 277; dangers of, 32; and incest taboo, 32; as male trait, 32; reward for, 32; and ritual, 33, 37, 53; and sex hormones, 33; taboo on, 33; and violence 33, 37; and gangs, 34. *See also* Aggro
Aggression, fables of, 10, 31, 34, 37, 43–45, 91–95, 101, 163, 173, 200, 206, 220, 223, 236, 240, 262, 278, 285–86; and mass media, 38, 44; and real violence, 38; and desire, 44; and revenge motif, 44; *Punch and Judy* as, 81; and the gothic, 100; and comics, 133, 136; and adolescent audience, 284; in fairy tales, 284; on television, 284
Aggro, 39–40; and fables, 39; and heavy metal music, 39; during latency, 39; in punk style, 39; and sexuality, 39
Ajax, 41, 251
Albano, "Captain" Lou, 247, 249, 254
Aldine Press, 136
Ali, Muhammad, 239, 246
Alien, 206, 301*n*12
Alien Prey (video movie), 278
Aliens, 103, 301*n*12
All-Famous Crimes, 174
Allingham, John W., 168
Alloway, Lawrence, 178–79
Altered States, 206
Alypius, 5
Amalgamated Press, 136, 170
Ambrosio (gothic villain), 95, 207
American Action Movie 1946–64, The, (Museum of Modern Art show), 10, 186–88; entries in, 188. See also *Violent America: The Movies 1946–64*
American Broadcasting Company (ABC), 32, 184, 225, 272
American International Pictures, 72
American Werewolf in London, An, 206
Analog image synthesis, 205

Andalusian Dog, 272
Andre the Giant, 250, 253
Anelay, Henry: *Varney the Vampire, 191*
Angelico, Fra: *Christ on the Cross with the Virgin and St. John, 26*
Aragon: *The Flagellation, 30*
Arcade games. *See* Video games
Archer, Lew, 10
Ardrey, Robert, 290*n*7
"Are You A Red Dupe?" (*EC* comic editorial), 145–46, *146*
Arendt, Hannah, 290*n*7
Argosy, 93
Arnold, Matthew, 263
Ashurbanipal, King, 16–20; killing lions, *17, 18, 19*; at war, *17*
Assyrian lion hunt (stone reliefs), 4, 16–20, 31, 157, 235, 285, 287; like a movie, 16; role of king, 16; as cartoon, 17; role of victims, 19; audience for, 20; criticism of, 20, 290*n*5; and ritual, 20; current location of, 289*n*4. *See also* Ashurbanipal, King
Asteroids (video game), 286
Atari, 268, 270
A-Team, The, 7, 13, 20, 39, 46, 61, 83, 138, 236–45, 249, 266, 284, 302*n*14; conception of, 240; and post-Vietnam America, 240, 305*n*8; characters in, *241, 242*; and ritual, 241; violence in, 241, 242; adolescent audience for, 242, 244; as drama, 242; plot of, 242–45; villains in, 242; and women, 242; as cartoon, 243; conclusions to, 243; and machinery, 243; and music video, 243; weaponry in, 243; advertisers for, 244; criticism of, 244–45; demise of, 244; and horror film, 244; and Nielsen ratings, 244; special effects in, 244; NCTV concern with, 245; and Hulk Hogan, 249–50; in syndication, 305*n*9. *See also* T, Mr.
Audimeter, 228
Audits of Great Britain, 229
Augustine, St., 5, 11, 155; on gladiatorial games, 5
Authentic Police Cases, 174
Axelrod, Robert, 38

Bachman, Richard, 106. *See also* King, Stephen
Bacon, Francis, 167

Badger-baiting, 57. *See also* Violence to animals
Baker, Rich, 206
Balderston, John, 192
Baracus, B. A. *See* T, Mr.
Barnes, Clive, 263
Barnum, P. T., 251
Barrie, J. M., 88
Barrymore, John, 202
Barthelme, Donald, 104
Bartholomew Fair, 76
Basket Case, 188
Bates, Norman, 203, 207, 215
Batman, 152–53, 156, 174–80, 244; and Superman, 174–77; history of, 175–78; and Robin, the Boy Wonder, 175–78; villains in, 175; illustrated in 1939, *176*; revived, 177; sexual ambivalence in, 177; on television, 177–78; interpreted by Wertham, 177; illustrated in the 1950s, *178*; in pop art, 178–80; updated, 298n23
"Battle of the Books, The," 222
Battleship Potemkin (Odessa Steps), 186, *187*
Bayeux tapestry: violence depicted on, 157
B. Dalton (bookseller), 94, 183
Beach Blanket Vampires, 249
Bear-baiting, 56–57. *See also* Violence to animals
Becker, Arnold, 225–26
Beckford, William, 54, 55
Beham, Hans Sebald, *Peasant Dance*, 163
Belline, Giovanni: *The Blood of the Redeemer*, 27
Bender, Laurelta, 157
Benedict, Dirk, 242
Bennett, James, 135
Bertie, Lord Albermarle, 74–75
Bettelheim, Bruno, 23, 37
Beverly Hills Cop, 271
Bilderstreifen, 158
Billy the Kid vs. Dracula, 193, 249, 300n7
Binder, Joseph, 282
Blackstar, 265
Blake, William, 63, 167, 284
Blanchard, Tully, *257*
Blassie, Freddie, 254
Blockbuster Video, 279
Blood Feast, 188
Bloodsucking Freaks (video movie), 278
Bloody pulps, 95, 103, 286. *See also* Penny dreadful
Bloom, Allan, 7
Blousons noirs, 399
"Bluebacks" (nineteenth-century novels), 96, 97
"Bluebeard," 234
Bocock, Robert, 53
Boehm, Carl, 208
Bollea, Terry Jean. *See* Hogan, Hulk
Bond, James, 3, 10, 122, 213
Bonnie and Clyde, 177, 188, 204, 243
Bosch, Hieronymus, 157, 167
Boswell, James, 98

Bottingheimer, Ruth, 234
Bottin, Rob, 206
Boulder, Terry (Hulk Hogan), 253
Boy George, 244, 271
"Boy Reading *Menace*," *137*
Boys' Own Paper, The, 169, 170
Boys' Standard, 168
Boys' World, 168
Brain from Planet Arous, The, 105
Brave New World, 229
Bread and circuses ("panem et circenses"), 7, 12, 86
Brett, Edwin J., 136, 168
Breughel, Pieter, 157, 167
Bronco Billy, 186
Bronson, Charles, 213, 219, 228
Brood, The, 200
Brooks, Mel, 199
Brothers Grimm, 156
Brown, Charles Perry, 168
Browning, Tod, 192
Bugs Bunny, 265
Bull-baiting, 55–57, *56*, 286; contemporary description of, 55–56. *See also* Violence to animals
Bulldog (English), 57–58; symbolism of, 57
Bullfight, 54
Bull-running, 9, 57–59, 286; as scapegoat, 57; and "brigging," 59. *See also* Violence to animals
Bunker, Archie, 79, 89
Burgess, Anthony, 39
Burke, Edmund, 118, 279n17
Burkert, Walter, 44
Burroughs, Edgar Rice, 179, 289n2
Burrud, William Jr., 278
Busch, Wilhelm, 171–72
Bushnell, Noland, 268, 270
Byron, George Gordon, Lord, 190, 195, 300n6

Cain, 41
Campbell, Lord, 96
Cannell, Stephen J., 138, 240
Canning, Elizabeth, 166
Cannon Pictures, 32, 184, 267
Capital Cities Broadcasting, 184
Capp, Al, 135
Captain Kangaroo, 135, 265
Captain Marvel, 174–75
Captain Power and the Soldiers of the Future, 11, 268–69, *269*
Carpenter, John, 210
Carr, Michael, 280
Carreras, Sir James, 181
Carrie (movie), 108
Carrie (novel), 107–10, 166, 293n6; violence in 107–9; and wish-fulfillment, 110
Cartoons, 7, 46, 103, 235. *See also* Comic books, Strip cartoon, Toy-based cartoons
Cassidy, Hopalong, 210
Catholic Church. *See* Christ, Passion of
Catholic Legion of Decency, 185

Cat Massacre, The Great, 48–52, 65, 286; and cats, 291*n*2. *See also* Violence to animals

Catnach, James, 96

Cave paintings (Lascaux), 4, *8*, 19, 35, 157, 235, 285

Centurions: Power Xtreme, 266

Chambers, Sir Thomas, 169

Chandler, Philip, 10

Chaney, Lon, Jr., 103

Chaney, Lon, Sr., 192, 206

Changeling, The, 54

Chaplin, Charles, 172, 182

Charles II (English), 75

Children's Bureau, The, 134

Christ, Passion of, 23–32, *25, 26, 27, 29, 30, 31, 159*, 285; and audience, 24–25; and ithyphalic imagery, 24; as preposterous violence, 24; in Renaissance painting, 24; as ritual, 25, 28; and blood, 28; imagery fixed, 28; and Roman soldier, 28; as spectacle of violence, 28; flagellation painted, 29–32; and Romantic view of animals, 63–64; in strip cartoon, 158–60

Christian Broadcasting System (CBN), 226

Christianity, 65. *See also* Christ, Passion of

Christine, 107, 122, 125–26; and adolescence, 125; and two-part violence, 125–26

Chromakey, 205

Circus maximus, 222, 284

Clare, John, 63

Clark, Samuel Dacre, 168

Class of Nuke 'Em High (video movie), 278

Clendenen, Richard, 135

Clockwork Orange (movie), 186, 188

Clockwork Orange (novel), 301*n*10

Cobra, 215–20; as fable, 215; female victims in, 215; plot of, 215–19; psychos in, 215, 217, 218–19; and *The Road Runner*, 215, and chase motif, 217–19; and parody, 217; as ritual, 217; as cartoon, 218–19; and sex, 218; and audience, 219–20; at box office, 219; as "concept film," 219–20; as folklore, 219–20; as horror movie, 219; and reviews, 219–20; as Western, 219; and ratings, 220, 302*n*13; violence in, 302*n*13

Cockfighting, 59–61, 73–75; and audience, 60; and betting, 60; nineteenth-century description of, 60

Cock-scaling, 59–60, 286; nineteenth-century description of, 59. *See also* "Throwing at cocks"

Code of Silence, 213

Co-Ed Murders, The, 207

Coleman, Gary, 237

Coleman, Samuel: *The Delivery of Israel out of Egypt*, 119

Coleridge, Samuel Taylor, 63

Coles, Robert, 23

Collier, John Payne, 83, 292*n*7

Collins, Jackie, 90

Colon, Charles, 256

Colonel Blood, 166

Columbia Broadcasting System (CBS), 225

Columbia Pictures, 184

Comic books, 4, 11, 12, 20, 31, 38, 52, 102, 129–57, 170–80, 286, 304*n*5; Senate investigation, 11, 133–48; history of, 93, 298*n*21; criticism of, 133–57, 296*n*11; and communism, 134, and juvenile delinquency, 134–57; defense of, 135, 147, 156–57; and advertising, 136; description of 136; distribution of, 136; printing of, 136; and profits, 136; merchandising of, 137; recycling of, 137; like television, 137, 174; and audience demand, 138; plot summaries, 138–40; recalled by Stephen King, 139–40; and movies, 140, 173, 213; and preposterous violence, 140–42; criticism begins, 154–55; as aid to learning, 156–57; and fairy tales, 156; influence of print media, 157, 298*n*22; early examples of 157; audience for, 173; and crime stories, 173–74; and pulp novels, 173, 297*n*19; and radio shows, 173–74, 298*n*22; as ritual, 173; and soldiers, 173; and FBI, 174; masked avengers in, 174; sidekicks in, 174; and villains, 174; as art, 178–80; new directions in, 179–80, 298*n*23; and soft porn, 296*n*9; worldwide audience, 296*n*14; and "graphic novels," 298*n*23. *See also* Batman, Cartoons, Strip cartoon, Wertham, Fredric

"Comic Books and Juvenile Delinquency," 139, 140, 144

Commando, 213

Commedia dell'Arte, 80, 222; and professional wrestling, 252. See also *Punch and Judy*

Comstock, Anthony, 96

Conan the Barbarian, 179, 213, 217

"Concept video," 271

"Concupisentia oculorum," 6

Contat, Nicolas, 51, 291*n*1

Cooney, Gerry, 240

Cooper, Alice, *274*

"Copie," 52, 65. *See also* Cat Massacre

Coren, Alan, 263

Corman, Roger, 293*n*6

Corticotropin, 40

Cosby Show, The, 228

Council of Chalcedon, 28

Count Choculas, 194

Court of Common Council, 76

Cousins, Norman, 146

Coward, Noel, 284

Crane, Stephen, 76, 107

Craven, Wes, 200, 210

Creepshow, 129–33, *131;* stories in, 130

Crime and Justice, 174

Crime-Fighting Detective, 174

Crime Must Pay the Penalty, 174

Cromwell, Oliver, 62

Cronenberg, David, 200

Crucifixion, 4, 8. *See also* Christ, Passion of

"Cruelty to Animals Act," 64

Cruikshank, George, 79, 83; *Punch's Final Triumph*, 83

Crypt Keeper, The, 130, 162

Cudgeling, 61
Cujo, 122–25, 293n8; and movies, 122–23, 125; characters in, 123; and Romanticism, 123; as television movie, 123; violence in, 123–25
Cunningham, Sean, 210
Curse of the Undead, 193
Cushing, Peter, 198, 300n7

Dale, Jimmy, 173
Dallas, 138
Darnton, Robert, 49, 50, 52
Darwin, Charles, 36, 42, 76, 209
Davis, David Brion, 37
Davis, Jack: "Foul Play," 141
Dawkins, Richard, 290n6
Dawn of the Dead, 111, 129, 188, 206, 210
Day of the Dead, 111, 129, 206, 210
DC comics, 83, 173
Deane, Hamilton, 192
Defiant Ones, The, 189
Def Leppard, 273
DeFleur, Melvin: "Schematic Representation of the Mass Media as a Social System," 227
Defoe, Daniel, 166
DeLevie, Dagobert, 64
Delta Force, 213
DeMaurier, Daphne, 94
DePalma, Brian, 186, 272, 293n6, 293n7
DerGoes, Van, 28
Derrida, Jacques, 22
Detective Comics. See DC comics
Detective novel, 10
Dick Tracy, 173, 175
Dickens, Charles, 67, 98, 103
Dickey Dare, 172
Dickinson, Emily, 7
Didion, Joan, 181
Digital animation, 105
Digital Scene Simulation, 205
Diller, Phyllis, 90
Dime novels, 170, 184, 262
Dio, Ronnie, 273
Diocletian, Emperor, 158–59
Dirty Dozen, The, 240
Dirty Harry, 217, 218, 220
Disney, Walt, 65, 66, 156, 184, 261
Dog-fighting, 57–58, 291n5, 291n6. See also Violence to animals
Don't Go in the Attic, 102, 207
Don't Go in the House, 68
"Don'ts and be Carefuls," 185
Doré, Gustave, 297n20
Doyle, Arthur Conan, 10, 289n2
Dozier, William, 177
Dracula (movies), 100–103, 192–95, 193; role of Van Helsing, 192; and audience, 193–94; as fairy tale, 194; Hammer versions, 194; and parody, 194; and sex, 194; story in, 194; and two-part structure, 194
Dracula (myth), 9, 85, 98–99, 100–103, 179, 194–95, 200, 209, 211, 214, 238, 275. See also Vampire, Van Helsing, Abraham

Dracula (novel), 110–11, 191–92
Dracula A.D. 1972, 102
Dracula Sucks, 199
Dreiser, Theodore, 107
Drive-in Massacre, 207
Dr. Jekyll and Mr. Hyde (movie), 201–3; conclusion to, 202; and misogyny, 202; role of victim, 202; sexual anxiety in, 202; Mamoulian version, 203
Dr. Jekyll and Mr. Hyde (myth), 9, 46, 98–99, 100–103, 179, 201–4, 206, 214, 300n8; emergence of Hyde, 201–204; role of victims, 201, 301n9; and modern psycho, 203; stalk-and-slash genre, 203. See also Hyde, Mr.
Dr. Jekyll and Mr. Hyde (novel), 99, 201
Dr. Jekyll and Mr. Hyde (stage play), 201, 294n4
Dryden, John, 80, 86
Duccio: The Flagellation, 29
Dueling, 37, 38, 41–42; and mass media, 41; as ritual, 41; role of seconds, 41
Dunae, Patrick A., 168
Dürer, Albrecht, 167
Duval, Claude, 96, 166, 168
Dykstraflex (camera), 205

Eastwood, Clint, 211, 213, 217, 238
Ebert, Roger, 279
EC comics, 4, 11, 13, 32, 103, 106, 107, 129–36, 139, 162, 191, 213, 222, 243, 262, 274, 277; history of, 132; "Foul Play," 141; editorial against Wertham, 145–46, 146
Eclipse Comics, 180
Education Act of 1870, 92
Educational Sociology, The Journal of, 147, 156
Edward II (English), 54
Eisenhower, Dwight D., 133
Eisenstein, Sergei, 186; Battleship Potemkin (Odessa Steps), 187
Eliot, George, 98
Eliot, T. S., 7, 22, 263
Emmett, George, 168
Emmett, William, 168
Empire Strikes Back, The, 182
Enclosure Acts, 62
Entertainment and Sports Programming Network (ESPN), 250
Entr'acte, 272
Eraserhead, 200
Erasmus, Saint, 158–60, 160
Esau, 41
E.T. The ExtraTerrestrial, 182
Evil Dead, The, 200
Execution of Mary Queen of Scots, The, 186
Exorcist, The, 182, 206
Extremities, 210
Eyes of a Stranger, 211

Faces of Death (video movie), 11, 236, 278–80; provenance of, 278; as ritual, 278–79; content of, 279–80; criticism of, 279; history of release, 279; and horror film, 279; and sequels, 279; and adolescent audience, 280; plot of, 280–83; and Romanticism, 280–81; and subjective camera, 281; credit run, 283

Facts About Juvenile Delinquency, 134

Fairy tales, 286; and horror, 200–201; and censorship, 305n6; and television violence, 305n7

Family Ties, 229

Famous Funnies, 173

Federal Communication Commission (FCC), 265, 266; and television violence, 302n1

Feiffer, Jules: on comics, 296n12

Ferraro, Geraldine, 249

Few Dollars More, A, 213

Fiedler, Leslie, 22, 91, 223, 292n3

Fielding, Henry, 81

Fields, Sally, 242

Filmation Associates, 266–67

Final Exam, 207

Firestarter (novel), 107, 116, 117, 118–22; explosions in, 120–22

Fistful of Dollars, A, 213

Flashdance, 271

Flash Gordon, 156, 172, 210

Fleming, Ian, 10

Flesh Feast (video movie), 278

Fly, The, 103, 106

Ford, Garrett, 192

Forster's Education Act. *See* Education Act of 1870

Foucault, Michel, 203

Four Stages of Cruelty, The, 67–74, *68, 69, 71, 73*; like *EC* comics, 67–68; role of Tom Nero, 67–73; and cinematic technique, 69, 72; and crucifixion, 70; gothic elements in, 70, 72; and law, 70

Fowler, Mark, 265, 266, 302n1

Fowles, Jib, 304n5

Fox, Charles, 168

Fox, Robin, 4, 37, 290n8

Fox, Sonny, 225

Fox hunting, 64

Frank, Josette, 157

Frankenstein (monster), 195–200, *197, 198*; and vampire, 195–96; and scientist, 197

Frankenstein (movie), 100–103, 195–200, *195*; and motivation, 196–97; new characters in, 197–98; at Hammer Studios, 197–99; and audience, 198; changing heroes in, 198; creation myth in, 198; conclusion to, 199; and moral in, 199; sequels to, 199; victims in, 199. *See also Rocky Horror Picture Show*

Frankenstein (myth), 9, 46, 54, 98–103, 179, 200, 209, 214; and science, 198–99; and Dracula, 199; in popular culture, 199; as ritual, 199

Frankenstein (novel), 195–96; and Golem, 195; revenge in, 195–96; and doubling, 196

Freddie. *See* Krueger, Freddie

Freedman, Jonathan, 304n5

Freeman, E. A., 64

Freud, Sigmund, 7, 36, 42, 43, 232, 289n2,

289n3; *Totem and Taboo*, 42–44; and latency period, 289n3

Freund, Karl, 192

Friday Night Videos, 272

Friday the 13th, 7, 68, 102, 210, 277, 286

Friendly, Fred, 224, 302n1

Fugi, Mr., 253

Fugitive, The, 241

Funny Wonder, 171

Fuseli, Henry, 167

Gaines, William, 144–47; and Kefauver, 144–47

Gallup, George, 134

Gans, Herbert J., 15

Geertz, Clifford, 48, 50, 60

Gentleman's Magazine, 96

Gerbner, George, 224–25, 303n4, 305n7

Gibbon, Edward, 251, 284

Gibson, Mel, 213

Gibson, Robert, 257

G.I. Joe (television show and toy), 83, 180, 238, 265, 266, 305n9

Gilbert, James, 294n2

Gillray, James, 167

Giotto di Bondone, 157

Girard, René, 41–46

"Girls Just Want to Have Fun," 249

Gladiatorial games, 37, 235

Gleason, Jackie, 89

Gobots (television show and toys), 243, 266

Godfather, The, 182, 188, 301n10

Goethe, Johann Wolfgang von, 190

"Golden Age of Comics, The," 174

Golding, William, 39

Golem, the, 195, 197

Gone With The Wind, 182

Good, the Bad, and the Ugly, The, 213

Gorgeous George, 254

Gothic novel, 8, 9, 10, 12, 29, 94–104, 168, 285; central story of, 92; in nineteenth century, 95; and sex, 95, 100, 102; and censorship, 96; criticism of, 96–97; violence in, 96; and doubling motif, 100; and victims, 100; and detective genre, 101; and romance in, 101; and mass media, 102; family romance in, 102; incest in, 102; and movies, 102. *See also* Horror movies, Monsters

Goya, Francisco, 67, 167

Graduation Day, 207

Grand Guignol, 9, 46, 80, 85, 222

Grease, 182

Great Train Robbery, The, 186

Gremlins, 182

Grien, Hans Baldung: *Holy Family*, 25

Griffith, D. W., 186

Groshin, Frank, 177

Gröss, Francis B., 279–83

Gross, Gerald, 94

Grosz, George, 167

Gruenewald, Matthias: *The Dead Christ*, 26

Gulf + Western Corporation, 184

Gumby Show, The, 135
Guy Fawkes Day, 62

Halbstarke, 39
Halloween, 103, 207, 210, 277
Hammer, Mike, 10
Hammer studios, 102, 129, 194, 197–99, 206, 300n7
Hammett, Dashiell, 10
Handley-Taylor, Geoffrey, 233
"Hansel and Gretel," 234
Hansen, Sweede, 253
Hardcastle and McCormick, 240
Hardy, Oliver, 172
Hardy, Thomas, 107
Harkaway House, 136
Harlequin Romances, 92, 94
Harmsworth, Alfred, 170, 298n21
Harper's Weekly, 86
Harwood, Dix, 64
Hasbro Inc., 266
Haunt of Fear, The, 133
Hays, Issac, 244
Hays Office, 10, 135, 185
Heavy metal music, 11, 20, 52, 272–77, 284; and aggro, 39; defined, 272–73; and adolescent audience, 273; lyrics to, 273, 307n6; and performers, 273; Senate investigation of, 273, 307n6; violence in, 273, 307n5; and wish-fulfillment, 273; and braggadocio, 274; as cartoon, 274–75; fanzines for, 274; and horror films, 274; and professional wrestling, 274–75; record jackets of, 274; and adolescent masculinity, 307n5; rating system for, 308n6. *See also* Music videos
Heenan, Bobby, 254
Heisey, Lawrence W., 94
He Knows You're Alone, 68, 102, 207
Hell Night, 207
He-Man and the Masters of the Universe (television program and toys), 83, 172; 238, 265, 266–69, *268,* 284, 285, 305n9; in syndication, 267; violence in, 267
Hercules, 215
Herrnstein, Richard, 33
Hill, Walter, 186
Hillbilly Jim, 253
Hills Have Eyes, The, 200
Hirsh, E. D., 7
Hirsh, Paul, 304n5
Hitchcock, Alfred, 140, 203, 230
Hitchman, Francis, 169
Hoffman, Professor, 88
Hogan, Hulk, 4, 236, 240, 245, 253, 285; and Mr. T, *245;* as modern hero, 249–50
Hogarth, William, 4, 8, 9, 12, 39, 65–78, 99, 158, 166–67, 297n20; and pit bulldog, 57–58; *The Bruiser, 58,* and engraving, 66; *Gin Lane,* 66–67, *67,* 70; *Rake's Progress,* 66; *Southwark Fair,* 66, 76–78, *77, 78; The Cockpit,* 73–75, *74;* and satire, 75. *See also Four Stages of Cruelty*

"Hogarth Act," 66
Hogarth House, 136
Holbein, Hans, 167
Holloway prison, 169
Hollywood, 7, 9, 185, 204, 223, 229, 294n1
Hollywood Beat, 271
Hollywood Meatmarket Massacre, 207
Holmes, Larry, 240
Home Box Office (HBO), 184
Hooper, Tobe, 200
Hoover, J. Edgar, 134
Horrible Deed Committed by the Jews, A, 161
Horror comics, 184. *See also* EC comics
Horror movies, 10, 29, 35, 129, 189–220; monsters in, 189–214; and adolescent audience, 201; increasing violence in, 201; and special effects, 201; and make-up, 206; and victims, 206; and Steadicam, 208–9, *208;* and heavy metal music, 274–75; actors in, 300n7. *See also* Monsters, Stalk-and-slash film, *Texas Chainsaw Massacre*
Horror myths, 36, 200–201; and adolescent audience, 200–201; as fairy tales, 200; evolution of, 200; as initiation rites, 200; as ritual, 200
Horror of Dracula, 102, 194
Horse racing, 64
Hot Wheels (television program and toy), 265, 266
House of Dracula, 97, 193, 300n7
House of Frankenstein, 193, 300n7
House on Sorority Row, The, 207
Howard, Robert E., 179, 213
Howling, The, 206
Hugo, Victor, 76
"Humpty Dumpty," 233
Hunter, Evan, 10
Huxley, Aldous, 280, 306n1
Hyde, Mr., 85, 207, 209, 215, 238. *See also* Dr. Jekyll and Mr. Hyde, Stalk-and-slash film

Idol, Billy, 271
Iliad, The, 251
Ilsa, She-Wolf of the SS (video movie), 278
IMAX, 205
Incest taboo, 42–44
Incredible Hulk, the, 237
Indiana, Robert, 179
Inhumanoids (television program), 266
Inside Crime, 174
Intaglio engraving, 65, 167
Interactive toys, 236, 267–70
Interstate Circuit v. Dallas, 185
Introvision, 205
Invasion of the Body Snatchers, The, 206
Invasion USA, 213
Iron Maiden, 274
Iron Sheik, the, 253
Isenmann, Gaspard: *Christ at the Column,* 31
I Spit on Your Grave, 210
I Was a Communist for the FBI, 213

"Jack and Jill," 233
"Jack and the Beanstalk," 234
Jackson, Michael, 271, 272
Jackson, Shirley, 114
Jacob, 41
Jacobs, W. W., 126
James, Henry, 7
Jansen, David, 241
Jason. *See* Vorhees, Jason
Jaws, 182
Jesus. *See* Christ, Passion of
Jimmy Dean Show, The, 135
"Joberie," 52, 65
"Johnny! Where IS That Boy?" (advertisement
  for comics), *148*
Johns, Jasper, 179
Johnson, Nicholas, 224
Johnson, Samuel, 13, 80, 98, 260, 295n6
Jolly Bits, 171
Junior League of New York, The, 277
Junkyard Dog, 250, 253, 254
Juvenal, 7, 86
Juvenile delinquency: caused by movies,
  294n1; eruption of, 294n1; and radio drama,
  294n3; in nineteenth century, 297n18

Kamen, Jack, 130
Karloff, Boris, 102, 103, 196, *197*, 300n7
"Katrharma," 46
Keane, Walter, 123
Kefauver, Estes, 133–57
Kemp, Tom, 87
Kerkorian, Kirk, 184
Ketch, Jack, 82
Kick boxing, 250
Kids Are People Too, 265
King, Billy Jean, 40
King, Stephen, 4, 7, 12, 14, 72, 90–128, 243,
  262, 286, 289n2; genius of , 94; reputation
  of, 94; *Misery*, 95; achievement of, 103–4;
  and monsters, 103; and New American Library, 103; and mass culture, 104, 128; and
  Maximum Overdrive, 104, 125; and movies,
  104–5, 114, 116, 120, 123, 125, 293n6;
  293n9; preposterous violence in, 104, 113;
  reading as initiation, 104; and students, 104;
  and audience, 105, 107, 113, 292n5, 293n8;
  and filmic technique, 105; and narrative
  voice, 105, 122; as popular culture entertainer, 105; and vulgarity, 105; ways to
  read, 105; and wealth, 105; and Bachman
  books, 106; on bestseller list, 106; and counterphobia, 106; in newsmagazines, 106; and
  publishing industry, 106; and repetitive consumption, 106; *Skeleton Crew*, 106; and *The
  Talisman*, 106, 293n8; *The Dead Zone*, 107;
  and fairy tales, 107, 122, 125; and initiation
  rites, 107; and *It*, 107, 293n8; and motivation, 107; role of children in, 107–28,
  293n9; and supernatural, 107; and plots,
  113, 114; and specific details, 113, 115; and
  gothic tradition, 114; explosions in, 117–22;
  and nineteenth-century paintings, 118; fails

in *The Dead*, 122; and comics, 125; and music, 125; and television, 125; and evil children, 126; and *Dance Macabre*, 128, 133,
  292n4, 292n5; on his technique, 128; on *EC*
  comics, 132–33, 139–40; on public executions, 166; criticism of, 292n3; as editor,
  292n4; and horror, 292n5; publishing his-
  tory of, 293n6; and absence of sex, 293n8;
  in *Different Seasons*, 293n8; and scapegoats,
  293n9. *See also Carrie, Christine, Creep-
  show, Cujo, Firestarter, Pet Sematary, 'Sal-
  em's Lot, Shining, The, Stand, The*
King Arthur, 285
King Lear, 54
KISS, 273, 275, 307n5
Klein, Paul, 264
Koren: *Alllll Riiight!*, 21
Kosinski, Jerzy, 264
Kramden, Ralph, 79
Krueger, Freddie, 206, 210, *212*, 214, 215, 238
Kubin, Alfred, 167
Kubrick, Stanley, 115, 116, 293n7
Kukla, Fran and Ollie, 235
Kung-Fu (movies), 180, 213
Kunzle, David, 164

La Fontaine, J. S., 53
Laing, R. D., 203
Lamentation over the Body of Christ, 159
Lande dessinée, 158. *See also* Strip cartoon
Landis, John, 272
Langella, Frank, 102
Larks, 171
Lascaux, 35. *See also* Cave paintings
Last House on the Left, 68, 210
Lauper, Cyndi, 247–49, *248*, 271
Laurel, Stan, 172
Leatherface, 206, 210, *211*, 214, 215, 238, 286
Leavis, F. R., 263
Lee, Bruce, 213
Lee, Christopher, 102, 194, 198, 206, 300n7
Legal Procedure against the Criminal, 165–66,
  165
Legman, G., 145, 155
Le Masters, Kim, 223
Leonard Elmore, 10
Leone, Sergio, 213
Levinson, Daniel, 15
Lévi-Strauss, Claude, 51
Lewis, Emanuel, 237
Lewis, Hershell Gordon, 189
Lex talonis, 249
Liberace, 246
Lichtenstein, Roy, 179; *Whaam!*, 179
"Little Red Riding Hood," 23, 209, 225, 234,
  286
Lloyd, Edward, 97
Lloyd, House of, 190, 229
Lloyd Harold, 172
London Illustrated News, 170
Lorenz, Konrad, 37
Lorimar Telepictures, 138, 184, 267
Love at First Bite, 199

Lucas, George, 98
Lugosi, Bela, 102, 103, 192, *193*, 300*n*7
Lundgren, Dolf, 267
Lynch, David, 200

Macaulay, Thomas Babington, 62
McCarthy, Joe, 133
Macdonald, Dwight, 14
Mackworth headcamera, 230
McLuhan, Marshall, 230, 264, 306*n*1
McMahon, Vince, 247, 250, 259
Mad (magazine), 133
Magnum P.I., 36
Main Event, 250, 260
Make Them Die Slowly (video movie), 278
Malcomson, Robert, 61, 64
Mamoulian, Ruben, 203
Mander, Jerry, 224, 306*n*1
Mannix, Joe, 10
Mansfield, Eddie, 257
Mansfield, Richard, 201, 202
Man with the Golden Arm, The, 189
March, Fredric, 202
Mardi Gras Massacre, 207
Marlowe, Philip, 10
Marsh, Peter, 37, 39
Martin, Billy, 246
Martin, John, 118–21; *The Deluge, 120; The Fall of Babylon*, 121
Marvel comics, 246, 298*n*23
Marx, Karl, 7
Marx Brothers, 89
Mass culture: criticism of, 14, 41, 263–64; and fairy tales, 23; and television, 23; and adolescent audience for, 90–94, 98, 168–74; opposed to art, 90–91; as escapist, 91; and violence in, 91–98, 144, 222, 245; effect of printing, 92–95; and repeat consumption, 94–98; and Stephen King, 104; and illustrations, 157; and boys' literature, 167–70; at the movies, 183, 245; and fables of aggression, 285–86. *See also* Popular culture
Mass media, 4, 14, 53–54; and criticism, 5, 306*n*1; and works of art, 12–13; and repetition, 14; and anxiety, 15; and audience, 15; and ritual, 15; and sex, 15; and "taste cultures," 15–16; and judicial system, 44; and religion, 44; and juvenile delinquency, 134–57; and communism, 135; programming in, 135; economies of, 170; sensationalism in, 221; Marxist interpretations of, 223; as social system, *227*; and Mr. T, 239; and corporate control, 292*n*2
Mattel Corporation, 266–67
May Day, 62
Mead, Margaret, 53
Mecanique, 272
Medea, 41
Mercury Publishing Co., 93
Meredith, Burgess, 177
Meredith, George, 86
Merry and Bright, 171
Methodism, 62, 63

Metro-Goldwyn-Mayer (MGM), 184
Metropolitan Police Act of 1839, 84
Meyer, Russ, 189
Miami Vice, 243, 271, 302*n*14
Michael. *See* Myers, Michael
Midnight Cowboy, 186
Mighty Mouse, 265
Miller, George: *The End of the World, 119*
Minerva Press, 96
Minow, Newton, 7, 224
Missing In Action, 213, 302*n*14
Mission Impossible, 240
Misson, Henri, 55–56
Mondo Cane, 280
Monsters, 103; in print, 98–104; psychology of, 99; and revenge, 99–100; as scapegoats, 99–102; in preposterous violence, 261; as children, 293*n*9. *See also* Dracula, Dr. Jekyll and Mr Hyde, Frankenstein, Gothic novel
Moore, Hannah, 96, 97, 155
Morales, Louis, 28
Morales, Pedro, 253
Moreau, Dr. (from *Island of Dr. Moreau*), 85, 207
Mother Goose, 156, 233, 234
Mothers' Day, 210
Motion Picture Production Code, 186
Motion pictures, 4, 65, 181–200; and juvenile delinquency, 135; and audience for, 181–82, 184, 185, 188, 189, 205, 214, 215, 298*n*2; history of, 181; innovation in, 181; and criticism of, 182; and economics of, 182, 184; opposed to art, 182, recent examples of, 182–83; scholarship of, 182; and television, 182, 188, 189, 204, 205, 223, 229–30, 298*n*2; and theaters, 182, 299*n*3; and mass culture, 183; as ritual, 183, 185; as business, 184–88; as ideology, 184–85; Marxist interpretation of, 184; the chase in, 185; and motion, 185; and rating systems, 185, 186, 299*n*5; regulation of, 185; violence in, 186–89; and genres, 188; increasing violence, 188–89; and victims in, 188; in the 1950s, 188; in the 1960s, 188; in the 1970s, 188; and carnival, 200; exaggerated motion in, 204; and make-up, 204; computer innovations in, 205; special effects in 205; action genre, 212–220; and cartoons, 213; and comic books, 213; Italian westerns, 213; as parody of action, 213; politics of action movies, 213–14; new avengers in, 214; and folklore, 215; box-office control, 298*n*2; and demographics, 299*n*3; and preview audiences, 299*n*4; and weapons in, 302*n*14. *See also Cobra*, Horror movies, Special effects
Mötley Crüe, 273, *276*, 307*n*6
Movie Channel, The, 184
Mr. T (cartoon), 265
MTV (Music Television), 235–36, 271–73; and *WrestleMania*, 248–49; and audience, 271; influence of, 271–72; and recording industry, 271; and advertising, 272; and techniques, 272. *See also* Music videos

Multiplane System, 205
Munch, Edvard, 167
Munsters, The, 199
Murdock, Rupert, 184, 229
Music videos, 4, 11, 12, 20, 271–75, 284; history of, 271; and technique, 272. *See also* Heavy metal music, MTV
Mutual Film Corporation v. Ohio, 182
Muybridge, Eadweard, 185
My Bloody Valentine, 207
Myers, Michael, 206, 210, *212*, 214, 215
My Son John, 213

Napier-and-Hoe press, 93
National Association for Better Radio and Television, 135
National Broadcasting System (NBC), 225, 250
National Coalition on Television Violence, 11, 115, 265–66, 273, 302n13, 303n4; on *The A-Team*, 245
National Comics Publications Inc., 147
National Video, 279
National Wrestling Alliance (NWA), 251
Nero, Tom, 159, 273, 285, 286. *See also Four Stages of Cruelty*
"Newgate Calendar," 168
Newgate novel, 96, 97
Newgate prison, 169
"New historians," 50–52
Newmar, Julie, 177
Newsagents Publishing Co., 136, 169–70
New World Pictures, 184
New York Hot Tracks, 272
New York Society for the Supression of Vice, 96
Niaux, 35
Nicholson, Jack, 115
Nielsen, Brigitte, 217–19
Nielsen ratings, 23, 82, 228, 231, 244, 302n2; defined, 302n2
Nietzsche, Friedrich, 7
Nightmare on Elm Street, 188, 206, 210, 277
Night of the Living Dead, 111, 129, 200, 210, 275, 278
Night Tracks, 272
Niles, Robert, 225
Nimrud, 20
1984 (novel), 228
Nineveh, 20
Noguchi, Thomas, 281–82
Nolte, Nick, 213
Norris, Chuck, 213, 302n14
Norris, Frank, 107
North, Sterling, 154–55
Northcliffe, Lord, 170
Nosferatu, 99, 189, 204. *See also* Vampire

Obscene Publication Act (Lord Campbell's), 96, 170
Odysseus, 251
Oedipus, 44
Oldenburg, Claes, 179
On the Waterfront, 189

Optical printer, 205
Orion (studio), 184
Orndorff, Paul "Mr. Wonderful," 246–50, *248*
Ortega y Gasset, José, 7, 263
Otway, Thomas, 80
Our Boys' Paper, 168

Palance, Jack, 202
Pankration, 251
Paramount Studios, 184
Pareles, Jon, 272
Parents Music Resource Center (PMRC), 307n6
Parthenon friezes: violence depicted in, 157
Patriarchy, 42
Paulson, Ronald, 57
Payne Educational Sociology Foundation, 156
Peake, R. B., 196
Peckinpah, Sam, 186
Peeping Tom, 208–9, 281; criticism of, 301n11
Pee-Wee's Big Adventure, 182
Penny dreadful, 95–97, 102, 103, 136, 166–71, 184, 186, 190, 222, 243, 262; and literacy, 167–68; criticism of, 168–70
"Penny healthfuls," 170
Peoplemeter, 229, 302n2
People's Police Gazette, 97
Peppard, George, 241–42
Pepys, Samuel, 80, 306n10
Percy, R. D., 229
Perfect Crime, The, 174
Perrault, Charles, 156
Perry, "Refrigerator," 244
Peasant Dance, 162–63, *163*
Pet Sematary, 106, 107, 126–28; evil child motif, 126–27; and life after death, 126; role of Gage, 127, 128
Pharmakon, 45, 46
Picture Stories from the Bible, 144
Pierce, Jack, 206
Pink Flamingos, 200
Piper, "Rowdy" Roddy, 246–50, *248*, 258
Plan 9 from Outer Space, 105
Plasmatics, 274
Plato, 223
Plough Monday, 62
Pocket Books, 93
Poe, Edgar Allan, 10, 114, 115, 293n6
Polidori, John, 99, 190, 192, 195, 300n6
Popular culture, 44; and art, 13, 22; and audience, 13; and criticism of, 22; and folklore, 22; and modernism, 22; and repetition, 22. *See also* Fairy tales, Mass culture, Mass media
Postman, Neil, 7, 224, 306n1
Powell, Michael, 208–9
Precious, good, hallowed Recipe for Men who have Shrewish Wives A, 162–65, *164*
Prest, Thomas Pecket, 99
Primal Horde, 42–44, 194. *See also* Freud, Sigmund
Prince (singer), 271

Printing, 64–67; illustrations important, 65; and mass production, 66; and television, 95–96, 222–23; and illustrated broadside, 168; serialization in, 168–71; and violent illustrations in Europe, 297n17

Proal, L. J. G., 295n5

Proclamation Society for the Suppression of Vice, The, 96

Production Code of 1908, 185–86

Protectorate Ordinance of 1654, 62

Prowler, The, 207

Psycho, 203–4, 206, 208, 301n9

Puck, 171

Pulcinella shows, 9

Pulp novels, 4, 11, 31, 80, 94–98, 304n5

Punch (magazine), 170, 238, 285

Punch and Judy, 4, 9, 13, 39, 46, 75–89, *79, 83, 84, 85, 86, 87, 88*, 184–85, 222, 262, 277, 286, 291n7; *The Tragical Comedy or Comical Tragedy of Punch and Judy*, 75; criticism of, 76, 85–89; in Wordsworth's *Prelude*, 76–77; in Hogarth's *Southwark Fair*, 78–79; as cartoon, 79; as Commedia dell'Arte, 80; as *Grand Guignol*, 80, 85; Punch as hand-puppet, 80; recalled by famous, 80–81; as ritual, 80, 89; role of Punchman, 80, 83–85, 89; sources of, 80; violence in, 80–83; role of Judy, 81; role of minor characters, 81–82, 84; role of Scaramouch, 81; role of Toby, 81; sexual innuendo in, 81; adolescent audience of, 82–89; and devil, 82, 84–85; and revenge, 82; and aggression, 83–88; as morality play, 83; as carnival, 84; like television, 84–87; current status, 87; rewriting of, 88–89; and print media, 89; Punch as archetype, 89; symbolism in, 89

Pure Literature Society, 169

Pynchon, Thomas, 104

Quiet Riot, 274

Radeki, Thomas, 11, 155, 224

Radio drama: and violence, 11, 13

Raggare, 39

Rambler's, 96

Rambo (movie and character), 7, 19, 20, 83, 155, 180, 182, 214, 215, 238, 241, 302n14, 305n7

Ramos, Mel, 179; and *Photo Ring, 180*

Rangers' Magazine, 96

Raw Deal, 213

Rawling, Nan, 75

Reagan, Nancy: with Mr. T, *237*

Rebel Without a Cause, 189

Red Menace, The, 213

Reed, Oliver, 202

Reeves, Steve, 215

Religious Tract Society, 169, 170

Return of the Jedi, The, 182

Reynolds, G. W. M., 97

Rhodes, Dusty, 258

Richter, Wendi, 247–48, *248*

Riddle, Nelson, 177

Riggs, Bobby, 40

Riptide, 240

Rites of passage, 33–35, 44. *See also* Ritual

Ritual, 13, 14, 20, 29, 34–47, 51–55, 70, 75, 163, 211; and revenge, 34; and anxiety, 35; and pornography, 36; and reproduction, 36; and women, 39; as a map, 53–55; and scapegoats, 54; of bull-baiting, 55–57; of dogfighting, 57, and industrialization, 61–62; and adolescence, 65; and printing, 65–66; and comic books, 173; and Frankenstein myth, 197; on television, 236; and *The A-Team*, 241–42; and professional wrestling, 252; aggression and, 275; and violence, 285–87. *See also* Motion pictures, *Punch and Judy*, Television

Ritvo, Harriet, 64

Road Runner, The (cartoon and character), 79, 89, 172, 213, 215, 218–19, 241, 249, 265, 273, 306n9; role of Wyle E. Coyote, 338

Road Warrior, 213

Road Warriors, The, 240, 275–76, *276*

Robinson, Andrew, 218

Robocop, 13

"Rock-a-Bye Baby," 233

Rockford Files, The, 240

Rock 'n roll, 7, 12. *See also* Music videos

Rock 'n Wrestling, 260

Rocky, 214

Rocky IV, 214, 267

Rocky Horror Picture Show, The, 183, 199–200, 286; as parody, 199; as ritual, 199–200; and *Punch and Judy*, 200

Roller Derby, 61, 250

Romance (genre), 91–95, 292n1; central story of, 92

Romanticism, 63, 118–20; and sublime, 297n17

Romero, Cesar, 177

Romero, George, 111, 129, 130, 200, 206, 210, 278. See also *Night of the Living Dead*

Rowlandson, Thomas, 167

Royal cockpit, 75

Royal Society for the Protection of Animals, 64

Rymer, G.: *The Hanging Scene of Punch and Judy*, 84

Saints' lives: violence in, 8, 285

'Salem's Lot, 107, 110–13, 116, 133; like *Dracula*, 110–12; as vampire story, 110–11; and sex, 111; staking of Susan, 112

Salisbury Square novels, 97

Salmon, Edward, 168–69

Salvianus, 5

Satanic Rites of Dracula, 194

Saturday Night Live, 246, 260

Savage (recording group), 274

Savage, Doc, 173

Savini, Tom, 129, 130–31, 206

Sayles, John, 272

Scanners, 206

Schedoni (gothic villain), 95, 207
Schickel, Richard, 215
Schultz, Dwight, 242
Schwarzenegger, Arnold, 213, 217–19
Scorsese, Martin, 28, 186, 272
Seduction, The, 210
Seduction of the Innocent (comic), 180
Seduction of the Innocent, The, 147; indict-
    ment of comics, 148; analysis with organic
    metaphors, 149–50; comics blunt taste, 150–
    51; encourage homosexuality, 151–52; sex
    and violence in comics, 151–52; and Bat-
    man, 152–53; and Superman, 153–54
Segal, George, 179
Seldes, Gilbert, 135
Selig, Colonel William, 201–2
Seminole Massacre, 186
Sendak, Maurice, 103
Sesame Street, 194
Shadow, The, 173
Shadwell, Thomas, 80
Shaftsbury, Seventh Earl of, 169
Shakespeare, William, 140
Shalit, Gene, 185
Shaw, George Bernard, 38
Sheehy, Gail, 15
Shelley, Mary, 99, 195–96, 198, 207, 300n6.
    See also *Frankenstein* (novel)
Shelley, Percy B., 63, 65, 350n6
Sheppard, Jack, 96, 166, 168
Sherak, Tom, 183–84
Shining, The, 107, 114–17, *116*; lady in room
    217, 114–15; movie of, 115–16; Overlook
    explosion, 117
Showscan, 205
Showtime Channel, 184
Silent Scream, 68
Simon, Senator Paul, 264
Siskel, Gene, 279
Sisters, 200
Six Million Dollar Man, The, 237
Slaughter, Sergeant, 253–54
Slaughter in San Francisco, 207
Slotkin, Richard, 37
Slumber Party, 207
Slumber Party Massacre, 207
Smith, Dick, 206
Smith, Jonathan, 44
Sneak Previews, 279
Snider, Dee, 273, *275*
Snow White, 261
Society for the Prevention of Vice, 170
Sophocles, 140
Southey, Robert, 54, 63
Southwark Fair, 76–78. See also Hogarth, Wil-
    liam
Spade, Sam, 10
Spanish Tragedy, The, 54
Spenser (creation of Robert Parker), 10
Spershott, James, 59, 60
Spielberg, Stephen, 90
Spillane, Mickey, 10
Spinks, Leon, 239

Stalk-and-slash film, 12, 20, 31, 52, 61, 68,
    102, 214–20, 205–14, 222, 262, 284; and ad-
    olescent audience, 207; and dreams, 207;
    monsters in, 207; and sequels, 207; special
    effects in, 207; and female avengers, 210;
    and victims, 301n9
Stallone, Sylvester, 213, 214, *216*, 217–20,
    240. See also *Cobra*
Stamp Act of 1712, 93
Stand, The, 117–18; role of Elbert, 117–18
Star Wars, 106, 182–83
Steele, George, 258
Steele, Richard, 80
Steinberg, David, 237
Steinberg, Leo, 24
Steinem, Gloria, 249
Stevens, M.: *The All Collision Channel*, 5
Stevenson, Robert Louis, 9, 99, 201–202, 207.
    See also *Dr. Jekyll and Mr. Hyde* (novel)
Stoddard, Brandon, 223
Stoker, Bram, 99, 110–11, 191, 207. See also
    Dracula (novel)
Stooges, The Three, 89, 249, 261
Storr, Anthony, 40
Stossel, John, 257
Straub, Peter, 105, 293n8
"Strawberry Shortcake," 245
Straw Dogs, 188, 301n10
Strickfaden, Kenneth, 102
Strip cartoon, 156–68; and crucifixion, 158–
    60; etymology of, 158; and saints' lives,
    158–60; subjects of, 158–66; and Jews, 160–
    62; and women, 162–65; and capital punish-
    ment illustrated, 163–68; and law, 163–67;
    and torture, 164–67; in England, 166–72,
    297n20; as comic strip, 170–74; and artistic
    techniques, 171–72; and action strip, 172–
    73; American influence, 172–73; and mov-
    ies, 172; and television, 172
Student Bodies, 186
Sublime (aesthetic category), 118–20, 297n17
Subotsky, Milton, 129
Sullivan, Kevin, 253, 258
Summers, Montague, 189
Superman (character and comic), 153–54, 156,
    174, 175, 182, 298n23
Surf Nazis Must Die (video movie), 278
Swabian, *The Tortures of St. Erasmus*, 160
Swift, Jonathan, 80, 103

T, Mr., 19, 35, 236–53, *237*, *238*, 285; image
    of, 236; as cartoon, 237; and gold, 237; and
    ritual, 237; and supermen, 237; in personal
    life, 238–40; as bodyguard, 239; and mass
    media, 239; *Mr. T: The Man with the Gold*
    (autobiography), 238–41; as "America's
    Toughest Bouncer," 240; as celebrity, 240;
    in *Rocky III*, 240; merchandised, 245–46; as
    hero, 249–50. See also *A-Team*, *Wrestle-
    Mania*
Tales from the Crypt, 133
Tarar, Maria, 234

Tartikoff, Brandon, 90, 223, 240
Tarzan (character and novels), 172, 179, 215
Taxi Driver, 188, 301*n*10, 305*n*8
"Teaching the Young Idea," *171*
TechForce and the Moto-Monsters, 268
Television, 4, 8, 31, 36, 38, 52, 65, 102, 221–62; and crime, 11; and SAT scores, 11; and violence, 11, 231, 235, 264, 283–84, 302*n*1, 303*n*4, 304*n*5; and popular music, 12; and sports, 12; and technology, 12; as business, 23; and carnival, 76; programming on, 95–96, 223, 227, 260, 265–69; and audience, 221–30, 232, 235, 264; and sensationalism, 221; and printing, 222–23; as scapegoat, 222–23; criticism of, 223–24, 233, 229, 304*n*5, 306*n*1; as "junk," 223, 263–64, 303*n*4; and movies, 223, 229–30, 235, 298*n*2; as wish-fulfillment, 223, 224, 231, 232; and art, 224; and audience share, 224; like church, 224, 226–27, 232; and desire, 224; and networks, 224, 225, 231–32; as reflector, 224; and advertising, 225–26, 231–32, 302*n*2; and fairy tales, 225, 233–35, 305*n*7; and ratings, 226–29; and escapism, 229; imagery on, 229; and dreaming, 230, 232; and flow, 230; transmission of, 230; attraction of, 231; genres of, 231, 235; and nightmares, 231; and sponsors, 231–32; and sublimation, 231; and nursery rhymes, 233–35; on Saturday morning, 233–34; golden age of, 235; prime time on, 235; as ritual, 251–52; and cross technologies, 266–80; and "kidvid," 267–68; and myth, 283–84; penetration into culture, 283–84; weaponry on, 302*n*14; and Frankfurt critics, 306*n*1; in other countries, 308*n*9. See also *A-Team*, Cartoons, Interactive toys, MTV, Music videos, Video games
Temmey, Bob, 250
Temple, Sir William, 222
Tennyson, Alfred Lord, 286
10 to Midnight, 219
Tero, Lawrence. *See* T, Mr.
"Terry and the Pirates," 172
Tertullian, 5
Texas Chainsaw Massacre, The, 200, 207; as fable of aggression, 209–11; plot of, 209–11; victims in, 209; and lack of revenge, 210; role of absent mother, 210
Thackeray, William M., 98
Thomas, Keith, 64
Thompson, Jean, 157
"Three Blind Mice," 233
"Three Little Pigs, The," 234
Thriller (video), 272
"Throwing at cocks," 9, 64. *See also* Cockscaling
Thundarr the Barbarian, 265
Thundercats, 267, 305*n*9
Tiptop Comics, 173
'Tis Pity She's a Whore, 54
Titan Sports Inc., 247
"Tit-for-tat," 38, 41

Titus Andronicus, 5
Todd, Sweeney, 168
"Tom and Jerry," 249, 306*n*9
Tompkins, J. H. S., 97
Töpffer, Rodolphe, 172, 297*n*20
Tortures of St. Erasmus, The, 160
Townshead, George, 167
Toxic Avenger, The (video), 278
Toy-based cartoons, 4, 265–69; history of, 265; and ratings, 265; and "concept toys," 266; violence in, 266. See also *He-Man and the Masters of the Universe*
Tracy, Ann, 95
Tracy, Spencer, 202
Trajan's Column: depicting violence, 157
Transformers, 243, 266
Trollope, Anthony, 98
Troma Productions, 278
True Confessions, 93
Turner, Ted, 250, 260, 271
Turner, Victor, 33–36, 261
Turpin, Ben, 172
Turpin, Dick, 68, 96
TV Guide, 70–71, 221, 223, 227, 303*n*4
Twain, Mark, 103
Twentieth-Century-Fox, 184
20/20 (television show), 258
Twisted Sister, 273, 286, 307*n*5, 307*n*6
2,000 Maniacs (video movie), 278

Uffenbach, Zacharias 60
Ulysses, 5, 6, 285
Uniform Crime Statistics, 134
United Artists, 184
Universal Studios, 103, 172, 180, 184, 192, 194, 196, 199, 206, 300*n*7
USA Cable Network, 12, 250, 260

Valdez, Eddie, 244
Vampire, the, 13, 46, 54, 189–95, 209; and Catholic Church, 189–90; in prose fiction, 190–91; and scapegoat, 190; on stage, 190; and vengeance, 190; and victim, 190; and audience, 191; in nineteenth-century fiction, 191–92; history of in prose, 300*n*6. See also *Dracula*
Vampyre, The (by Polidori), 99
Van Gennep, Arnold, 33, 52
Van Heemskerck, Maerten: *Man of Sorrows*, 24
Van Helsing, Abraham, 99, 110–11, 211
Varney the Vampire, 99, 168, 190–91, 238
Vaughn, Robert, 244
"Vault Keeper, The," 130, 162
Vault of Horror, 133
Ventura, Jesse, 254
Viacom Corporation, 184
Videocassette recorder (VCR), 265, 275, 277–80; and adolescent audience, 276–78; and horror films, 277–78; films not rated for, 278, 308*n*7; movies made especially for, 278. See also *Faces of Death*

Video games, 4, 11, 20, 80, 236, 268–71; and adolescent audience, 269; in arcades, 269–70; evaluated, 270–71; examples of, 270; violence in, 270–71, 307n4; criticism of, 307n2; innovations in, 307n3

Video World, 279

Violence, 3, 44, 39–47; etymology of, 3; as retaliation, 33, 42–45; in trench warfare, 37. *See also* Violence, preposterous

Violence, preposterous. criticism of, 1, 4, 5, 6, 7, 11, 15, 133, 135, 146–57, 167–68, 222, 286; as cartoon, 3; definition of, 3; etymology of, 3; audience for, 4, 6, 7, 11, 14, 16, 30, 31, 32, 37, 41, 46, 48, 49, 52, 54, 92, 97, 103, 128, 157, 167–68, 211, 221–29, 286, 287; and fantasy life, 4, 43; as "junk," 4, 7, 12, 286; on stage, 4; transmission of, 4; types of, 4; and aggression, 7, 8, 20, 42, 70, 275; and the barbaric, 7; and carnival, 7, 11, 50, 61, 75–79, 163, 306n10; as entertainment, 7; and professional sports, 7; and rock 'n roll, 7; in various media, 7; as wish-fulfillment, 7, 81, 207–8; in gladiatorial games, 8, 222; in print, 8, 9, 49, 51–54, 65–66, 75, 91–128, 159–60, 166–80; in revenge tragedies, 8, 14, 54, 166, 285, 291n4; in saints' lives, 8; directed toward animals, 9, 54, 63; directed at family, 9, 95; and monsters, 9, 189–220; and pornography, 9, 36; and Puritanism, 9; and Romanticism, 9, 63–64; scapegoats in, 9, 29, 45, 49; and victims, 9, 19, 29–30, 66–67, 70, 100, 158–67, 210, 203, 285; censorship of, 10; and juvenile delinquency, 10; in motion pictures, 10, 130, 181–220; causing *frisson,* 11, 29, 37, 73, 114, 118; and radio drama, 11; on television, 11, 16, 231; escapism, 13; and Greek drama, 13; and folklore, 14; in mass media, 14, 23, 30, 65–66; relation to art, 14, 16, 287; and religion, 14, 44; repetition of scenarios, 14, 16, 51, 53; and stereotypes in, 15; meaning of, 16; and spectacle, 16, 53; and Christ as victim of, 26–32; in historical context, 31–32; sociobiological explanation of, 32–43; as rite of passage, 33–36, 53; and revenge, 34, 40, 41, 44, 82, 120, 163–68, 211, 234–35, 252–53; and mass culture, 36, 157–58; and real violence, 36, 38, 40, 41, 45, 55, 140–41, 155–56, 169, 285, 290n7, 291n8, 292n8, 295n5; as ritual, 36, 44, 46, 47, 49, 51, 52, 285, 286, 291n4; and voyeurism, 36, 74, 128; as fables of aggression, 38, 43, 233–35, 284–86; and feminism, 39–41; and patriarchy, 39–40, 42; women in, 39–40, 162–64; as counterphobia, 40; cultural changes in, 40; two-part scenario, 41, 102–3, 110–11, 125–26, 133, 173–74, 194 207; and incest taboo, 42; and primal horde, 42–44, 194; as reproductive strategy, 42; and retribution, 43; and judicial system, 44, 164–67, 170; as catharsis, 46; as "pharmakopic," 46; taboo on, 46; as education, 47, 285–86; and cats, 48–75; and economics, 48–52; and sexual anxiety, 48–52, 70, 110, 186, 211, 285; in eighteenth century, 49–75; and apprentices, 52; in Catholic cultures, 54–55; in Protestant cultures, 54; in Christianity, 62–63, 74–75; in urban life, 66–67; psychology of, 70; as visual, 70; and aristocracy, 74–75; in nineteenth-century popular culture, 75–89; in eighteenth-century popular culture, 80–81; at the end of nineteenth century, 85; and the novel, 91–128; and formulae, 92; as commodity, 93, 179; distribution of, 93; and gothic, 95; in illustrations, 97; in serialization, 97–98; and adolescent anxiety, 106–7; and special effects, 106, 117, 129, 131, 204, 207, 215, 301n10, 305n9; as painted in nineteenth century, 118–20; role of John Martin, 118; and sublime, 118–20; illustrated, 129–180; and distortion, 132; anti-Semitism in, 160–62; and rape, 162–63; and torture, 164–67; English history of, 166–68; in toys, 172; point of view, 208–9; personified by the Road Runner, 215; new directions in, 219–20; in Mother Goose, 234; and post-Vietnam anxiety, 240–41; and professional wrestling, 252–53; displays compared, 262; in excess, 284; heroes in, 285; genres of, 286; moral to, 286; surrender motifs in, 286; associationist psychology of, 295n5; and public executions, 296n16, 309n8. *See also* Aggression, fables of, Assyrian lion hunt, *A-Team, Cat Massacre,* Cave paintings, Christ, Passion of, *Cobra,* Comic books, *EC comics, Faces of Death, Four Stages of Cruelty,* Gothic novel, Heavy metal music, Horror movies, King, Stephen, Mass culture, Mass media, Monsters, Motion pictures, Music videos, Popular culture, Printing, *Punch and Judy,* Ritual, Stalk-and-slash film, Strip cartoon, Television, T, Mr., Toy-based cartoons, Videocassette recorder, Video games, Violence to animals, Wrestling, professional

Violence to animals, 9, 12, 48–65; in eighteenth century, 53–61; and class structure, 59–64; in decline, 61–65; in Protestant cultures, 61; and Puritans, 62–63; and laws prohibiting, 64; to cats, 48–52, 68

Violent America: The Movies 1946–64 (catalog to the Museum of Modern Art show), 187–88. See also *American Action Movie 1946–64*

Volkoff, Nickolai, 253, 254

Voltaire, 103

Vonnegut, Kurt, 41

Vorhees, Jason, 206, 210, *212,* 214, 215

"Voxbox," 229

Waldenbooks, 94, 183, 298n23

Warhol, Andy, 65, 179, 246, 272

Warner Brothers, 184, 192

W.A.S.P., 277

Waters, John, 200

Wayne, John, 211, 213, 214

Webling, Peggy, 196
Weissmuller, Johnny, 215
Wells, H. G., 9
Werewolf, 54
Wertham, Fredric, 11, 46, 135, 142–57, *143,* 174, 180, 307*n*6; and Senate testimony, 142–47; articles on comic books, 145–47; and professional life, 295*n*5; analogies of disease, 295*n*7, 295*n*8; on Howdy Doody, 296*n*10. See also *Seduction of the Innocent*
Wesley, John, 62
West 57th, 271
Westminster pit (dogfighting), 56
Wheel of Fortune, 244
When a Stranger Calls, 68
Whitman, Walt, 13
Wild, Jonathan, 166
Wild Boys (books), 169–70
Wild Bunch, The, 117, 188
Wilde, Oscar, 9
Wilson, E. O., 290*n*6
Wilson, James Q., 33
Windt, Christopher, *The Horrible Murder committed in famous Halle, Saxony,* 166
Winn, Marie, 306*n*1
"Witch, The Old," 130
Wolf, David, 247
Wolfenbach (gothic villain), 95
Wolfman, the, 180
Wood, Peter, 230–31
Woody Woodpecker, 265
Wordsworth, William, 78, 167–68, 209, 280, 295*n*6; and *Hart-leap Well,* 63–64; criticism of fair, 76–77
World Wrestling Federation (WWF), 32, 247, 250–51
WrestleMania, 20, 245–49; merchandising of, 246–47; as sellout, 246; Mr. T's role in, 247–50; and MTV, 248–49; and publicity, 248–49; as cartoon, 249
Wrestling, professional, 4, 12, 30, 39, 46, 61, 235, 284; as carnival, 247; as fable, 247; and grudge, 247; as ritual, 247, 250, 254, 258,

261–62; and rock 'n roll, 247, 251, 254; and audience, 249, 252, 261; and interpenetration of texts, 249; and cable television, 250; as cartoon, 250, 261; relationship with television, 250, 253–54, 258–59; sponsors of, 250; wrestlers' incomes, 250; and cave paintings, 251; history of, 251; and the A-Team, 252; and boxing, 252; and Commedia dell'Arte, 252; and villains, 252–55; like bullfight, 253; and Christianity, 253; and "holds," 253, 255–56; and stereotypes, 253, 254, 259–60; costumes for, 254; role of manager, 254; roles played in, 254–55; announcer in, 255, 258; and hero, 255; referee in, 255; and gymnastics, 256; and blood, 257–58; and ring, 258; and trophy belt, 258; as drama, 259; types of matches, 259; women wrestlers, 259; attraction of, 260; and feminism, 260; merchandising of, 260; as morality play, 260–61; role of women, 260; evil in, 261; and fairy tale, 261; and monster story, 261; and revenge, 261; as rite of passage, 261; moral of, 262; like other adolescent displays, 262; and barter syndication, 267; and heavy metal music, 274–76; interpreted by Roland Barthes, 306*n*11. See also World Wrestling Federation
Wrestling TNT, 254
Wrightson, Berni: *Father's Day, 131*
WTBS, 12, 250, 260, 273
Wycherly, William, 80

X-Men, the, 179
Xylography, 65

"Yellowbacks" (nineteenth-century novels), 97
Young Frankenstein, 199

Zamora, Ronald, 264
Zombie Island Massacre, 207
Zorbaugh, Harvey, 157
Zorro, 173